Contents

To the memory of my Father,
who put the first books in my hand,
and to my Mother for teaching me
perseverance among so many other gifts.

To my daughter, Juliana,
for whom this book is a drop in her ocean of desire to learn.

Preface

Why is there so much fighting in politics today?

I spent five years writing *The Divided Era* in response to that simple and direct question from a friend of mine—although the study of history and politics has been a passion of mine for decades. Laura Cox is a mother of two, an owner of a small business, and a community volunteer. She is not a partisan and, in her busy world, follows politics only sparingly. She wanted to know, as many others do, why there is so much fighting in American politics today. It certainly was not the first time I had heard the question, but I thought it was time for me to answer it in detail. *The Divided Era* is the result.

We can start by recognizing that partisanship and political fighting are not new to our time or place. They are at least as old as government itself. At their core is human nature. We are and have been acquisitive, territorial, and competitive since our origins. We are associative as well, and, over time, we come together as a family, a group, a clan, a town, a city, a state, and a nation. Along the way we come to grips with governing ourselves, and governing necessarily implies choices.

Among the first governing choices is determining who will be in charge. At the beginning of most civilizations, that choice is often made by force. Later on, if the right conditions develop, choices are made by the more cooperative but complex rubric of the ballot—and so it has been for America.

In the hands of a monarch or a despot, the choices made by government tend to be limited and concentrated among a few. Dissent or partisanship among the governed, under such circumstances, carries with it the risk of imprisonment or worse. Nevertheless, if it emerges to a sufficient degree, it can be rebellious—as in the case of the founding of our country.

Democracies, by contrast, feature a more populated governing class. At first, relatively few officials are elected under a comparatively simple charter. Over time, the number of elected grows, the governments become increasingly bureaucratic, and their charters become more complex. In the process, they tend toward a proliferation of choices.

Whenever and wherever the freedom of political choice exists, competitions naturally develop. They are competitions not just among those making the basic choice (i.e., voters) but also among those who want to exercise power (i.e., parties and politicians). As governments grow, those competitions intensify and increase. A different type of competition also arises—a competition among those seeking the favors and spoils of government. That is where we are today, and that is *the* central focus of this book.

To understand our current divisions, *The Divided Era* considers the three most divisive periods in our history: the time from just before our Revolution through the adoption of our Constitution; the period after Lincoln's election, known as the *Secession Crisis*, in conjunction with *Reconstruction*—the period that followed our Civil War; and finally, the *Gilded Age*—the name given to the closing decades of the 1880s. We can then contrast those periods with our two most unifying periods: George Washington's success as President, which we can call *Washington's Unifying Moment*, and the *Era of Good Feelings*, when James Monroe ran unopposed for president. I also include lessons from Ronald Reagan and John F. Kennedy about rising above partisan troubles.

In writing *The Divided Era*, my goal is to place our current divisions in historical context—to understand our current thoughts and actions in light of our past thoughts and actions. I will ask you to consider the facts we know from a different perspective, to make comparisons and see the political competition of the *Gilded Age* as the most like our own and the *Era of Good Feelings* as the least.

In the end, I hope the new perspective we gain from examining the past will not only help us understand our problems today but also shed light on the way forward. Only in understanding the real cause of partisanship and division can we hope to avoid the worst of its effects, including the fraying of our social fabric (as represented by the frayed American flag on the cover of this book), and to start down a better path and away from the *Divided Era*.

Finally, a note to the reader about methodology is in order. First, the book is written chronologically rather than addressing the periods of division and then the periods of unity. I chose to write it that way so that all of those periods would be kept in the historical context of the unfolding American story. Second, the book references such periods as the *Era of Good Feelings* and the *Gilded Age*. Those are recognized periods in our history and throughout the book they shall be italicized to set them apart. As part of my analysis, I will also italicize certain periods of time upon which we will be focused so they too can be recognized. For instance, I will make reference to *Our Revolutionary Thoughts*. That is the period of time just before the Revolution wherein rebel colonists began thinking about breaking with England. Another example is my use of the term *Our Gilded Age of Division*. Although we will focus on the details of the *Gilded Age*, as we consider it in a new light, we might well refer to it as *Our Gilded Age of Division*. Overall, each time I use those italics, it is meant to help us recognize a specific period or dynamic.

The Divided Era

Men by their constitutions are naturally divided . . .
—Thomas Jefferson

We live in the *Divided Era* of American politics. It is a period characterized as much by lasting political differences as by shared cultural values—a period with equal numbers on opposing sides of most political issues. Partisanship, sometimes bitter and often reflexive, is on the rise, and many ask why it has to be so.

This era of broad societal division is neither accidental nor temporary. Its root cause is simple but not easily remedied. America today is no longer a place of a largely singular cultural vision as it was for most of its history. It is now the home of widening and competing cultural views that play out in the massive size and scope of the federal, state, and local governments that we have created—and those differences and high-stakes competitions are driving us apart. Now making up a third of our economy, our governments are doling out trillions in government spoils. As they do, they are fostering the now central and growing cause of our *Divided Era*—competitions for those spoils, a dependence on them, the division over the taxes needed to pay for them, and for the power to dispense those spoils. Our much larger governments are also making decisions on an unprecedented number of issues, large and small, in our lives. That fosters a slightly different, but still divisive, competition among Americans—a competition to obtain favorable government treatment. Each time we enlarge government, however incrementally, we increase those competitions, the number of partisan political battles, our philosophical divisions, and the importance of our elections. If we do not correct our current course, we are setting the stage for irreconcilable divisions for decades to come, not only over the broad, philosophical issue as to the proper role of government but also over those spoils of government and how to pay for them.

Those competitive dynamics are relatively new. For most of our history, our limited governments allowed us to pursue our happiness nearly unfettered. There was far greater unanimity about the size and scope of our governments when they were smaller and, as a result, the breadth of our differences was smaller. Although we fought over what comparatively little our governments did, there were literally fewer reasons to fight. Just as importantly, if not more so, we taxed each other less and therefore fought each other less over taxes.

Over the last forty years, however, governments have moved to the center of our lives. Spending, from the local level to the federal level, now exceeds $6 trillion per year and with such resources there is almost no aspect of our lives that goes unregulated or untaxed. The nature of our governments has changed dramatically and, in a very real sense, our governments choose winners and losers for those $6 trillion, in addition to those who are forced to bear the tax burden for that spending—not to mention those that must bear the nearly $2 trillion in annual federal regulatory costs.

At one end of the spectrum, city councils decide the scope of our property rights, including the size of our homes—or what used to be our inviolate castles. At the other end of the spectrum, the federal government restricts and regulates the mattresses on which we sleep, the food we eat, the cars we buy, the fuel we use to get to work, the rules that apply at our work, the TV we watch after work, and the lights we turn off at night—not to mention the manner in which our children are taught. In between, are state governments rushing to fill the vacuum of virtually every freedom we leave unattended. Each such regulation or tax is to someone's detriment and another's profit. We take that competition to new heights in our tax code, which long ago abandoned its principal purpose—to raise money—in favor of political favoritism.

With so much at stake each day, it has become nearly impossible for Americans and their businesses to sit on the sidelines while others decide their fate. As a result, our coliseums, once known for sports, have become our chambers of government, pitting citizen against citizen, business against business, taxpayer against tax user, and endless combinations of the same. Among Americans, genuine and deep disagreements over difficult issues such as immigration are certainly prevalent. However, the core dynamic that elevates our otherwise situational partisanship over issues into persistent societal division in the *Divided Era* is this boundless competition among innumerable participants for the favors and funding by our now unlimited governments.

Those many fights and the growing competition to control our growing governments are the hallmark of the *Divided Era* and the very reason you so often hear that each ensuing election is the most important election yet. That competition has also resulted in an intense increase in a slightly different type of partisanship—one based more on self-interest than simple party affiliations. We can call this partisanship "my part of the pie partisanship," and it is helping to create a nation of special interests. As we shall discover, those competitions stand in stark contrast to George Washington's efforts to unify our country behind a common goal at a time when separate interests were tearing it apart.

★   ★   ★

Of course, there are those who would blame our current differences on partisan "extremists" on either side of the aisle. According to this narrative, partisans of the Far Right or the Far Left have captured the two major parties—partisans who create the divide and then refuse to cross it for the good of the country. That analysis only scratches the surface and blames the symptom (i.e., partisanship) rather than the cause. A greater understanding of history demonstrates that there have been partisans in every age—especially when government is deciding significant issues. Under such circumstances, it is human nature for people to cling to their beliefs and to fight for them. We shall find that in the hands of great leaders like Lincoln, a refusal to compromise can forge great and beneficial change. We shall also come to understand that, overall, it is rarely the citizen who creates partisanship for sport but, instead, government actions that cause opposite and not always equal reactions.

As we consider these actions and reactions throughout this book, keep the following example in mind. Imagine the federal government appearing at your door tomorrow and telling you that you must take down the fence that surrounds your yard. Most people would be distraught, if not angered, at that governmental intrusion. Many would join the newly founded Fence Party or start supporting the party that championed "fence rights." Government, we can fairly say, in that example, would have catalyzed them to act, if not to become "partisan," along with the parties they support. Today, of course, government regularly dictates what we can and can't do with our property, our businesses, and our health-care choices. A key dynamic of the *Divided Era* is the geometric rate of increase in those intrusions and our reactions to them. We shall find that the severity of our reactions varies with the severity of the imposition—say, in the difference between our hypothetical fence and the government's regulatory War on Coal, which threatens an entire industry and the way of life of many people. Should we really expect people to sit quietly while they are taxed, while they are mandated to buy health insurance, or when their entire industry, if not way of life, is threatened? Or while their competitor gains an advantage with the help of elected officials? Such cheerful compliance is actually rather unknown to *History*—italicized here to mean the muse of time that has greater understanding of human events, not just the recitation of our follies and perhaps less frequent accomplishments.

In fact, throughout history people have fought for their beliefs and/or rights—and at times virulently so—whenever government has attempted to take them away or abridge them. In large part, that is the story of the American Revolution. Our Revolution changed the world for the better by unleashing an American form of *Liberty*—a breadth and scope of freedom hitherto unknown to *History*. Keep in mind throughout this book that the early proponents of American *Liberty* likely would have been frowned upon by the same set that decries partisanship today.

The key to understanding the *Divided Era* is that by allowing government to decide more and more issues, we are inviting more and more partisan fights and ultimately broader and more persistent division. Simply put, a government that decides one hundred thousand issues will find exponentially more partisans than a government that decides just one hundred. Today, we literally set up and promote competition for government benefits and fights over taxation each time we enlarge the sphere of government. We cannot be so shallow as to think that it is the fault of those affected by the government action. They are merely acting as countless others have in the past—in their perceived self-interest to protect their cherished fences or jobs—and unless we legislate away human nature, they will continue to do so in the future. We must come to understand the source of their motivations rather than blame them for having them.

Most importantly, under the divisive dynamics we now promote, the fabric of our nation—to the extent that it has not already—will eventually be torn apart in this competition to gain such advantages and tax each other. Taxation is of particular concern in the years ahead and is the troubling basis for our division today. The explosive growth in government, as it always has in history, has meant an explosive growth in taxation. As with prior societies that faced burgeoning social welfare programs, our current tax system, which imposes income taxes on roughly half of Americans, is tending toward ideological ends instead of economic means. It pits Americans against each other in the historically destructive competition of class warfare. Further, the increasingly progressive federal income tax is reducing America's economic activity (and therefore tax revenues) at the worst possible time—the very time our country's population is aging and our welfare state growing. Together, the punitive tax code and growing welfare state will result in an economy that stagnates for long periods of time; and, historically, any time an economy stagnates, political division increases, as voters and politicians emphasize redistribution over production, and civilizations fray.

The United States is far from alone on the historical path described above. Even so, the social engineers of our time, like many before them, clothed with the power of government, are wont to ignore Michael Crichton's warning that "it is the conceit of every generation that it has pushed aside the weight of history to be living in a present time so unprecedented that the past no longer matters." The question for Americans is whether they can recognize that conceit and avoid the errors of the past before it is too late.

★   ★   ★

If we have a wide enough understanding, we recognize that political division is familiar to all of history, including our own. It is quite natural, and, throughout all of history, the larger the political stakes, the more partisan and eventually divided a people become. In our own history, there have been three major divisive periods prior to today's. The first started in the 1760s. It led up to and included our Revolution and continued to the adoption of our Constitution. The second period occurred during the Civil War and *Reconstruction* periods. The third such divisive period was at the end of the 1800s, in what is known as the *Gilded Age*.

During each of those periods, Americans were in pitched battles, often rhetorical and sometimes real, over fundamental issues that determined the course of our history. The participants resorted to government and all of its force and sometimes harsh finality to decide the great issues of the day—and we shall find that anywhere government is the forum to decide such large issues, understandable and intense partisanship can be found on both sides, along with those in the middle attempting to reach compromise.

For instance, during the founding of the United States, the protagonists, known as the Federalists, and their opponents, who would become known as Anti-Federalists, shaped the very nature of how we would be governed. They fought over what freedoms we would hold and the initial parameters of government. In the end, our Constitution emerged, but not before the Articles of Confederation were adopted and scrapped and states' rights advocates fought bitterly with those seeking "a more perfect union" in the form of a more centralized federal government. The partisanship of the time featured invective that makes our current discourse seem tame by comparison. Those high-stake political battles, in the wake of bloodstained memories, could not help but be divisive.

Of course, our partisan heights and divisions were reached during the Civil War, when our differences were decided with guns—not ballots. Again, government and its blunt force decided the very nature by which we would exist—either as two nations or one—and whether this experiment with freedom would extend to those previously denied their freedom by slavery. *Reconstruction*, the period following the Civil War, featured an aggressive use of government power to decide the nature of Southern governments and determine who should be able to vote. During those times, people were extremely partisan. Often the very lives of the participants depended on which side of the issues they took.

As the nineteenth century wound down, government once again was deciding the fate of many. We fought each other over the use of tariffs not only to raise money but also to support chosen and well-connected industries. We also fought over the nature of our currency and over what eventually became known as the Southern Question: the fight to ensure the rights of freed slaves, remnants of which lasted deep into the twentieth century and strains of which were still seen in 2014. All were part of a larger discussion of just how active our government should be when it came to the people's welfare. In each case, the victorious holders of government powers were picking winners and losers. In the case of the currency and tariff wars, farmers were pitted against industrialists, as were the North and East against the South and West. Meanwhile, the right of Blacks to effectively exercise their right to vote saw the North do battle with the South as part of the Southern Question. Amidst such high stakes, division was rampant and partisanship in the *Gilded Age* featured intense party affiliation, third parties, and some of the highest average voting rates in our history at nearly 80 percent—if only among men.

As we know from our history, the questions that vexed each of those periods were decided, and division gave way because each of those issues was capable of a largely closed-end decision (although, as I pointed out earlier, considerable remnants of the Southern Question would endure). For instance, the Constitution was adopted. We may now fight over its meaning, as Hamilton and Jefferson did at the very outset, but whether to have a constitution or amend the Articles of Confederation is no longer an issue. Similarly, the Civil War is over and we are one nation. The nature of our currency—gold, silver, or paper—was decided as well.

The dynamic that gives rise to the *Divided Era*, however, is likely not susceptible to an "up or down" resolution. To the contrary, the added dynamic that is widening our philosophical divisions—our growing fight over the spoils of omnipresent, bureaucratic, and active governments—cannot simply be voted away or unwound. That source and the cause of our persistent divisions, which define our age, along with their historical implications, is the subject of this book.

Of course, we were not always divided. *The Divided Era* includes a chapter named Washington's Unifying Moment—a moment in time we will need to recognize as well. As I hinted above, that *Moment* refers to the time during which consensus coalesced around Washington's leadership. It also refers to Washington's ability to unify the once-bitter protagonists, for however brief a period, around a common goal, known as the founding of the United States, so that this experiment in freedom could take hold. From there, *The Divided Era* will explore the dynamic that resulted in a similarly unified country during the *Era of Good Feelings*. Our early lack of government-centric competition left our castles nearly unassailed and allowed our fifth president, James Monroe, to run for reelection unopposed. An unopposed school board race is rare today. An unopposed presidential election is unimaginable.

The Divided Era will also plumb the depths of our current divisions, which take many forms. Today we not only have the usual fights between our parties, we also have Red States fighting Blue States and states suing the federal government. We have income-tax payers at odds with those not paying income tax and public employee unions fighting the public they were meant to serve over benefits and even over the scope of their authority. We also have the federal government imposing unprecedented laws such as Obamacare, and the daily threatening of such cherished rights as the Second Amendment. Sometimes caught in the middle and at other times the catalyst of those battles are everyday Democrats and Republicans of near equal numbers—along with discontent movements such as the Tea Party and Occupy. *The Divided Era* also will draw a contrast between the issues of our prior and largely resolved periods of divisiveness, and the intractable and likely irresolvable nature of our divisions today.

If we come to understand all of those dynamics in our reading, we can then ask the basic questions: Can we end the *Divided Era*? and if so, how? In answering those questions, we will do well to appreciate how the magnitude of state and federal government spending, along with tens of trillions of dollars in debt, complicates not only our financial state but also any hope to end the division we are experiencing. It will demonstrate that because so many are reliant on some aspect of government, they are much less ideological in their concerns and are likely beyond the reach of simple partisan or philosophical appeals. They are voters who might otherwise be responsive to an issue such as the

national debt, but because they are too tied to government as a beneficiary of a particular program or business issue, in ever-greater numbers,
they are voting that interest above the national interest.

At the end of our journey through the past, we will come to understand that unless we change our existing political dynamics, division will
plague us for decades to come. In order to avoid that, I offer four suggestions for a future president to help America rise above the *Divided
Era*, and

With that, *let our story begin . . .*

CHAPTER 1

A Glimpse at
Our Divided Present

*One of the most curious things about American politics
is that without historical exception a partisan is
invariably a member of the other party.*
—Anonymous

Just before the 2012 presidential election, pollster Scott Rasmussen published the results of a poll as to whom voters preferred: sitting Vice President Joe Biden, or his challenger, Congressman Paul Ryan. The two men could hardly be more different. Biden is a long-time Washington fixture, having served three decades in the Senate before being elected to the Vice Presidency in 2008. Biden has been an Eastern liberal from the start of his political career when he ran for New Castle County Council in Delaware and is a bombastic sort—prone to a gaffe or two.

By contrast, Midwesterner Paul Ryan was born the year Joe Biden first won elective office. Ryan is quiet by comparison, careful, if not uninspiring, in his speech, and known for his unafraid, budget-crunching policy prowess in a town that often raises style over substance. In 2012, the youthful conservative cut a virile contrast to the older, white-haired Biden.

The result of the poll between those two completely different men was a tie of 44 percent of Americans favoring Biden and 44 percent favoring Ryan—and that is a good place to begin considering our partisan present.

Few people think that the differences between Joe Biden and Paul Ryan decided the 2012 election. The fact that Americans were equally divided between those men despite their rather significant contrasts, however, does shed significant light on the *Divided Era* of American politics.

Broadly speaking, there are three different but closely related aspects to our heightened divisions today. First, there are significant disagreements over numerous large issues such as immigration, war, and health care that are prevalent in the *Divided Era*. Issues that large would result in significant partisan competition in any era. In the chapters ahead, we will see just that. However, in the *Divided Era*, in addition to those large issues, there are simply many more issues over which we are fighting than in any previous era (because our governments are doing so much more)—even if no one issue rises to the divisive level of some issues in prior eras, like the Civil War.

Second, over the last forty years an active competition has developed among our citizens, businesses, unions, foundations, charities, and even among our governments for preferences, regulations, funding, and control. Closely tied to that is the equally if not more heated fight over whose ox to gore (i.e., who to tax in order to pay for such things) and the problems caused by the imbalance of our progressive income tax system and the growing welfare state.

Finally, there is the ever-present philosophical divide among Americans over what the nature and scope of our government should be. The growing magnitude of the first two aspects, especially the competition for government spoils and taxes, is a central feature of our broad, growing, and persistent divisions today. For now, let us briefly consider each of those three aspects.

The Divided Era

The Economy. Immigration. Taxes. Obamacare. Medicare. Jobs. Welfare. Energy. Deficits. Regulations. Voter fraud. Voter ID. The Middle East. Global warming. Common Core. Public pensions. Property rights. Gay rights. Pro-choice versus Pro-life. Regulations. Government contracts. The Second Amendment. Race. Gender. Class warfare: the 1 percent versus the 99 percent. Church versus State. Big business versus Labor. NeoCons, Hawks, and Doves. Red States versus Blue States. Rural Americans versus urban dwellers. Taxpayers versus tax users. Government unions versus taxpayers. States versus the federal government. The Executive branch versus Congress. The EPA and Justice Department versus free enterprise. The IRS versus conservatives. The NSA versus Americans. Government pensioners versus government operations.

Those are just a few of the issues our governments decide some aspect of every year, if not every day. Hundreds of thousands of decisions are made as part of that process. Beyond those issues, we cannot forget the wars we have fought in the last twenty years. Obviously, with our governments making so many decisions each year at the local, state, and federal level, the opportunities for disagreement and, therefore, partisanship among Americans are equally numbered. In the pages ahead, we shall see that our prior eras simply did not have the sheer number of divisive issues that we have now for one simple reason: our governments did much less and, therefore, decided much less.

Beyond those fights over policy, the IRS scandal that began in 2013 exposed the heavy hand of government in ways rarely seen in our history. Instead of simply administering the law, the IRS scandal laid bare the dynamic of government officials acting against groups who publicly express disapproval about the direction government is taking. Of course, the nature and complexity of our tax code requires government officials to make innumerable judgment calls about the actions people have taken and want to take. However, amidst those many decisions lies an equal number of opportunities for bias, opportunities that a simplified code could not mathematically perpetuate—which once again demonstrates that a larger government has a greater potential to divide its people. Further, the growing abilities and desire of the federal government to conduct surveillance of Americans have not only awakened many Americans on both the political Left and Right to the dangers big government poses to their freedoms but also placed them at distinct odds with their government.

Going forward, perhaps the greatest source of division will be the fight over taxation and the closely related issue of class warfare. There have been thousands of tax revolts in history. Our country was born of a tax revolt. After the Revolution, despite huge public debt, our Founding Fathers were so sensitive to the issue of taxing people that they never even considered instituting an income tax. Back then, government collected nearly all tax revenues from commerce, including tariffs on imported goods. During the discussion of the *Gilded Age*, we shall find that the fight over tariffs was a huge flash point for partisanship and a central issue in each congressional and presidential campaign. Before that time, scholars will tell you, some in the South harbored thoughts of secession from the Union on that issue alone, because the South had to pay the lion's share of those taxes.

Yesterday's fights over tariffs have been replaced today with fights over income taxes. It is now fairly well known in the body politic that nearly half of Americans pay no federal income tax at all. Given that more than 41 percent of all federal revenue is derived from income taxes or nearly two-thirds of all revenue, if you exclude Social Security taxes, the division between taxpayers and those who obtain government services without paying federal income taxes is a growing emotional, political Grand Canyon. Also, given that $18 trillion in federal debt is carried on the books and more than $80 trillion in federal obligations is not on the books, we must come to understand that this is only the beginning of an extremely divisive fight. Moreover, paying for that debt is not simply an issue of raising revenues. At the same time that many Americans are not paying taxes, a huge percentage of them are out of work and receiving government benefits. Cries of income inequality have arisen, and in the harsh tones of class warfare, many have demanded that one sector of Americans pay more for the benefit of the others. Combined, they are fueling a division growing in intensity—a dynamic that has proven very corrosive throughout all of history.

Competition for Government Spoils

The second aspect and most critical of our current political divide—the competition for government spoils—is unique to our time in size, but not nature. From the outset of our history, Americans have competed for government preferences and spoils—though the competition was for far, far fewer spoils.

Prior to adopting our Constitution, the state governments decided the major issues of the day. In doing so, they picked the winners and losers in the competition for government benefits. Perhaps the greatest issues of their day were the magnitude of private and public debt, and—you guessed it—taxation. It was an irony of the times that Americans' tax burden was significantly higher after the Revolution than it was before the revolt. The plight of American farmers was particularly difficult. Those partisan farmers beseeched their governments to ease their debt and tax burdens. In response and to varying degrees, with the help of sympathetic politicians, state governments passed laws that dramatically impacted those issues, including, among other things, the printing of their own paper money (state by state), which generally devalued a state's currency, and in turn generally helped debtors (the political winners) at the expense of creditors (the political losers).

That period, which will be considered in greater length in chapter 3, was a highly partisan time given what was at stake. It included dramatic moments such as Shays' Rebellion—part of an armed insurrection movement that shut down courts and blocked the imposition of judgments against debtors. As dramatic as those actions were, and as significant as the actions taken by governments were during that time, the sheer number of issues decided by government today dwarf any other period in American and world history.

Today our combined local, state, and federal governments spend more than $6 trillion per year. More than half of Americans are either employed by our governments, are dependent directly or indirectly on a government contract, or receive government assistance (i.e., welfare, Social Security, etc.). Today, in an era of tight budgets, Americans compete directly against each other for program funding. Further, nearly every aspect of our lives is either regulated or taxed, or threatened to be so. Each year our governments pass tens of thousands of laws and promulgate an immeasurable number of regulations. Our Code of Federal Regulations is approaching two hundred thousand pages, and the simple task of cutting a tree in your own backyard may well require a permit. On January 1, 2014, alone, forty thousand new laws and resolutions came into force. To support countless government programs, those same governments pass and enforce a countless number of ever more innovative tax measures.

Keep in mind that no funds are appropriated, no laws passed, and no regulations instituted in a vacuum. Instead, they come into being in the greatest competition of our age—the election of and then lobbying of our elected officials. Individuals and entities of all sizes together spend well over $3 billion a year, just at the federal level, on lobbyists to ensure their interests are heard if not protected, subsidized, or at least not hurt in the process. Often those expenditures are made just to counter the expenditures of a direct adversary. The expenditures for lobbying are but a small part of the money spent in the competition of modern-day American politics. Spending on the 2012 presidential and congressional elections reached nearly $6 billion, with the Obama campaign spending nearly $1 billion itself. Again, in the fight to control spending of nearly $4 trillion in federal funds, a good deal of which are political spoils—not to mention how a president can affect the economy at large or specific industries—even $6 billion may not be that much.

Our discussion, however, cannot end there. Our modern divide over government spoils is not limited purely to funding, electioneering, or lobbying. Today some of the most visible peaks of our divisions are the fights between the government, its public employee unions and the rest of America. In these difficult times, the government sector continues to grow and has now reached 16 percent of the workforce. When private-sector unemployment officially averaged more than 8 percent at the start of the decade, and by broader unemployment measures, more than 14 percent, public-sector unemployment was less than 4 percent. In California, studies suggest that government workers' pay significantly exceeds private-sector pay. Nevertheless, when he was the California Treasurer, Bill Lockyer said that the deficit would not be closed "on the backs of our employees" (i.e., state workers). He wanted taxpayers to endure the pain—thereby completely subverting the meaning of public service. Notwithstanding their good fortune on the rest of America's tab, the public sector continues to demand more, which places them at odds with taxpayers who must pay for their benefits.

That division reached spectacular heights in Wisconsin starting in 2011. Governor Scott Walker and his sympathetic voters staged pitched battles with public-employee unions, and their Democrat supporters over union rights, dues, and benefits. The partisan fight became a national sensation when union forces sought to recall Republican Scott Walker. That partisanship continued into 2014 with what some believe is a partisan state investigation of alleged coordination between Governor Walker's campaign and conservative groups—which is part of a dynamic that veteran political observer George Will characterizes as the "criminalization of politics." Texas Governor Rick Perry was subjected to a similar fate in 2014 when he was indicted for what many consider to have been policy differences—an indictment that was criticized by Republicans and Democrats alike.

Across the country, similar fights are on the front burner of politics, including a $100 million fight in California over Prop 32 in November of 2012 that would have banned the compulsory collection of union dues. In addition to those divisions, a fight is brewing between those concerned with the funding of current government operations in an age of diminished state treasuries, and those who want to fund the retirement of an ever-growing number of government workers. That fight is in addition to the normal fight between those who compete for government funding as part of the operations of governments, much like the guns and butter competition (domestic spending versus military spending) that started in the 1960s. Given our growing deficits, we can only expect more such divisions in the future.

Our Divide Over the Proper Role of Government

The proper role of government is a question as old as government itself. Certainly our Founders struggled with that issue, Federalists and Anti-Federalists alike. As each of the thirteen nation-states that comprised our Confederation wrote their constitutions, they dealt with that same question, with active and partisan parties strenuously advocating their side of the issue. According to the legendary Chief Justice John Marshall in his five-volume work, *The Life of George Washington*, first published in 1804, "At length, two great parties were formed in every state, which were distinctly marked, and which pursued distinct objects, with systematic arrangement."

Marshall describes them as follows:

> The one struggled with unabated zeal for the exact observance of public and private engagements.... The distresses of individuals were, they thought, to be alleviated

only by industry and frugality, not by a relaxation of the laws, or by a sacrifice of the rights of others. . . . The other party marked out for themselves a more indulgent course. . . . Viewing with extreme tenderness the case of the debtor, their efforts were unceasingly directed to his relief. To exact a faithful compliance with contracts was, in their opinion, a harsh measure which the people would not bear.

By writing those words, Marshall, who at the time was serving as our fourth Chief Justice and laying the foundation of our constitutional law, spoke to the very nature of the philosophical divide at the time of our Founding and even today: Just how active should our government be in the case of the general welfare? Today, much of our division in the *Divided Era* is centered on that very question. Keep in mind that life in America was not originally so subsidized, regulated, or taxed. According to Harlow Giles Unger in his book *Lion of Liberty: Patrick Henry and the Call to a New Nation*,

> Settlers isolated in the hamlets and woods of New England had lived free of almost all government authority for more than 150 years. They had cleared the land, felled great forests, built homes and churches, planted their fields, hunted, fished and fought off Indian marauders on their own, cooperating with each other, collectively governing themselves, electing their militia commanders and church pastors and turning to assemblies of elders to mediate occasional disputes. . . . Like Patrick Henry, they had lived in freedom, without government intrusion in their lives and saw little need for it.[1]

At the time Marshall set the stage, the spending of our governments had grown to approximately 3 percent of our national economy—still a very small amount. There were no regulations, and presidential cabinets totaled five members. Today, by stark contrast, their spending equates to more than 36 percent of the economy, they make well over $1 trillion social welfare transfers a year (excluding Social Security and Medicare), and they are slated to spend much higher amounts in the years to come. As intense as the debate was during Marshall's life and times, the current gulf between Americans on that question is magnified because our governments today are so much larger than John Marshall ever could have imagined.

★   ★   ★

Evidence of our current divide over the proper scope of government manifests itself in numerous and very significant ways. Most people think of that difference in terms of party affiliation. If you consider the last twenty-five years, polling has shown that those who call or have called themselves Democrats, and who generally prefer a more active government by comparison, have been within single digits of those who call or have called themselves Republicans, and who generally support a less active government. Our national voter registration has tracked closely during that same period of time. Our division in the *Divided Era*, however, is hardly limited to a discussion of the number of Democrats and Republicans.

Perhaps the more significant indicator of the growing philosophical divide over the growth in our governments is the emergence of movements, initiated by groups resembling third parties, that focus on the proper scope of government. In our discussion ahead, we shall find that throughout our history third parties have emerged during divisive times. They usually get started because a significant minority of Americans does not feel the major parties of the time are resolving a specific issue in their favor. For instance, in the 1800s, the Greenback Party had significant success. It was primarily focused on the very divisive currency issue (i.e., whether we should have only gold as a currency, or gold, silver, and what they favored—paper money). Paper money was considered easy money that would help farmers and westerners pay off their debts. Eastern bankers, the holders of much of their debt, opposed paper money. The Republican Party was divided over the issue, as were the Democrats; and their positions on the issue evolved over time. In the absence of decisive major party action, the fortunes of the Greenback Party rose. The decline of the Greenback Party occurred at roughly the same time as the major parties took up the issue in earnest and the issue started to move toward resolution.

Today we have third party–like movements that are focused principally on the proper role of government. The movement started to some degree with Ross Perot and the Reform Party of the 1990s, which focused on runaway government spending and deficits. For that and other reasons such as the Republican takeover of the House of Representatives in 1994, it is fair to say that the *Divided Era* began in the 1990s. Today, the Tea Party Movement and the Liberty Movement, both of which are vitally concerned with the proper role of government, while not technically separate third parties, have had a substantial impact not only on elections but also on the question of the proper role of government. In their view, both major parties support too much government.

Those movements took a leap forward in 2009. It was that year that President Obama and congressional Democrats significantly increased the nature and scope of our government through a series of laws, beginning with the so-called Stimulus Bill (a near-trillion-dollar spending initiative) and including the large health-care legislation known as Obamacare. Both of those initiatives comprised dramatic expansions of the nature of our government. Yes, there had been government spending before to boost the economy. A single bill of nearly $1 trillion, by contrast, was new and significant. Similarly, our governments have sought to regulate markets and industries in the past. Obamacare, on the other hand, created an unprecedented increase in government activity, which includes a power to "mandate." That mandate required a Supreme Court ruling to uphold, much like Roosevelt's expansion of government power under the New Deal legislation of the 1940s.

As the Democrats' 2009 legislative agenda coalesced, it brought forward the Tea Party Movement in America—as we shall see, that represents a sure historical sign that Obama's expansion of government was significant. The Tea Party Movement membership initially was comprised of up to 40 percent self-identified Democrats and Independent voters. By and large, they were of the mind that both major parties are too supportive of a large, active government and that those parties were practicing poor, if not reckless, fiscal management, as the nation racked up trillions in national debt. The Tea Party Movement's concerns were matched by supporters of the former Texas congressman and three-time presidential candidate Ron Paul, including one presidential run as the nominee of the Libertarian Party. Prior to his retirement, Congressman Paul long decried the expansive scope of modern American governments, including not only social welfare spending, but defense expenditures and our overseas posture as well. Paul also spawned the Liberty Movement, the more libertarian but still close cousin of the Tea Party Movement. That third party–like activity and concern has meant that both major parties, but especially Republicans, face electoral challenges over their policies from the Tea Party Movement and Ron Paul supporters, as well as conservative groups not aligned with either major party.

The combined force of those movements weighed on the national parties, strongly influenced the 2010 election, and made it fashionable again to raise the question of whether a particular government action or program was within the proper role of government. Fashionable or not, the emergence of this third party–like movement highlights the increased divide among Americans. Given that government continues to grow, it is likely the Tea Party and Liberty movements are here to stay in some form. Indeed, it is the premise of this book that ever-growing government will increase the American divide. Overall, a significant part of the 44/44 split between Americans on Joe Biden and Paul Ryan was actually based on the divide among Americans regarding the proper scope of government.

Other Markers of the Divided Era

As we will see throughout the book, disagreements over significant issues are often accompanied by increasing political activity. That is certainly true in America today. The major parties are raising and spending unprecedented amounts of money, recruiting huge numbers of volunteers, and engaging in ever more sophisticated get-out-the-vote operations. Meanwhile, the Tea Party Movement and the Liberty Movement, along with Ron Paul and, now, son Rand Paul, are involving huge numbers of previously sidelined voters and activists in the political process. In addition to those rising partisan activities, the rise in the number of special interests groups, political action committees (PACs), and even super PACs is another indicator of the heightened levels of our partisanship, divisions, and competition for power.

Our divisions in the *Divided Era* also can be measured in ways beyond simple party affiliation, third party movements, and difficult issues. Exceedingly close presidential elections is another way to measure the nature of our divisions. It is no coincidence that during the *Divided Era*, for the first time in 120 years, we had a president, George W. Bush, lose the popular vote but win the electoral vote, and therefore, the presidency. The last time we had such an outcome was in 1888 during our highly partisan *Gilded Age*, which is discussed in chapter 7. That year, Republican Benjamin Harrison defeated Democrat Grover Cleveland decisively in the Electoral College 233 to 168 but lost the popular vote to Cleveland by ninety thousand votes. Beyond the 2000 Bush/Gore presidential election, in 2012 President Obama won reelection by the slimmest margin of any reelected president in the last 120 years—again highlighting our closely partisan age. In addition to close presidential elections, we have seen control of the House of Representatives flip three times since 1994. That is a marked contrast to the forty years of one-party dominance in that chamber, which the Democrats held between the 1950s and 1995. The *Gilded Age* also featured similar changes in control of the Congress.

The split between party affiliation and the resultant seesaw election results, however, still does not tell the full story of our philosophical divide. Two more examples will suffice for now. The first is the dramatic fight between the states and the federal government. In response to the passage of Obamacare, nearly half the states have sued the federal government to stop the imposition of that law upon them—and a slightly lesser number of states has sued over President Obama's Executive Order on immigration in 2014. In our history, we have had many fights between the states and the federal government over the imposition of policy. No less than Thomas Jefferson authored the Kentucky Resolutions, which proclaim that states have the right to ignore, or nullify, federal laws that go beyond the bounds of federal power. According to Jefferson, whether the federal government overstepped its bounds was for the states to decide. Sure enough, some states did just that, including South Carolina and Georgia, with the latter going so far as to pass a law inclusive of the death penalty for any federal enforcement of the disputed federal court order. Of course, the ultimate collective state nullification of federal law was the South's secession prior to the Civil War. While today's laws and lawsuits to nullify Obamacare and executive orders are far less dramatic, they represent the most significant, concerted state action against the federal government in more than a century and are a visible and troubling marker in the *Divided Era*.

Perhaps the most visual evidence of the *Divided Era* is that of the contrasting red-state versus blue-state map, which dominates American politics today. During the Civil War and *Reconstruction Era*, our nation was starkly divided between the North and South along the Mason-Dixon Line. Many results of a state's presidential electoral preference could be predicted with reference to whether that particular state lay above or below that line. Indeed, Lincoln did not win a single electoral vote from the South. Today, with a good deal of regularity, we find similar results in the red-state/blue-state divide. If we dig deeper into the issue, even within the fifty states we find a similar divide between the cities and the rural areas—so much so that a vote just between the cities and rural America would result in a nearly equal divide between Democrats (who dominate urban voting) and Republicans (who find most of their votes in rural counties). As we shall see, that red-state/blue-state divide has become so prominent that migration patterns within the United States have taken hold. Citizens are voting with their feet by moving to live in states more compatible with their philosophical leanings and thereby deepening the red-state/blue-state divide and sentiment in the *Divided Era*.

★　　★　　★

That is a glimpse of our divisions within the *Divided Era*. They are, in part, driven by broad and deep philosophical beliefs, just as they were at our nation's Founding. There are also real fights over specific issues, not unlike what occurred in other divisive eras in our history—some of which may resolve. Unlike at our Founding and our subsequent divisive period, however, as a nation we are engaged in an unprecedented and heated competition for countless government benefits and preferences, along with a pitched battle on how to pay for it—all of which result in divisions, which may not resolve.

Before we delve any further into our current divisions, let us understand the first major divisive period in our past—the period leading up to a unique moment in time when we were of one purpose and there were no national parties. That unifying period was authored by none other than George Washington, and it was preceded, as we shall see in chapter 2, with the periods we can now call the *Storm Before the Calm* and *Our Constitutional Divide*.

CHAPTER 2

The Storm Before the Calm

No people will tamely surrender their Liberties,
nor can any be easily subdued.
—**Samuel Adams**

More than anyone else, George Washington deserves credit for "uniting" our United States. That is the assessment of George Washington's contemporaries and of historians alike. Perhaps unlike any other figure in history, there has been remarkably little revision of the overall assessment of this leader who stands among history's greatest.

As we consider the *Divided Era*, including the role political parties play, we know that much has been made of Washington's dislike of factions, or what we know as parties. But such a simple assessment does not tell the whole story and only relates it in the negative. George Washington's life and his *Unifying Moment* as president were not based on him being *against* something but, instead, being *for* something. Before, during, and after his presidency, Washington had a vision for an American future. He was single-mindedly for a new *idea* of a single nation, comprised of colonies and beyond, that would be an example of *Liberty* to the world. Washington frowned on factions and personal agendas because they did not serve his goal of establishing something unknown to *History*: a freely unified set of states—a United States.

What makes Washington's achievements even greater is that he accomplished them amidst intense division, uncertainty, and difficulty. In the years before Washington's presidency, America endured division and partisanship in deciding to rebel and in fighting and winning the Revolution. The division of the time did not end there. In post-Revolutionary America, there would be more rebellion, bitter fights over the Articles of Confederation and the proposed constitution, states nearly at war with each other, and other divisive dynamics. It was our first major divided period, and it started with what we can refer to as the *Storm before Washington's Calm.*

A Unified Assessment of George Washington

Before we consider that first major divided period in depth, let us consider history's view of Washington. According to his famous and early biographer, Supreme Court Chief Justice John Marshall, Washington's actions "probably saved his country." He devoted "himself to the duties of his station, . . . pursuing no object distinct from the public good." Marshall believed that "no man has ever appeared upon the theatre of public action, whose integrity was more incorruptible, or whose principles were more perfectly free from the contamination of those selfish and unworthy passions, which find their nourishment in the conflicts of party." So great were Washington's achievements, that Chief Justice Marshall concluded: "It is impossible to contemplate the great events which occurred in the United States under the auspices of Washington, without ascribing them, in some measure, to him."[2]

Writing more than two hundred years later, biographer and historian Ron Chernow wrote of a battle in terms that could be a metaphor for Washington's career: "The American panic was stemmed by Washington himself."[3] Chernow believes that Washington "helped to mold the very character of the country."[4] "By the time of his death," according to Chernow, "Washington had poured his last ounce of passion into the creation of his Country."[5] In addition to Washington's "honesty and absolute moral fearlessness,"[6] biographer Richard Brookhiser writes of the president that the "greatest of the Virginians was the greatest man in America, George Washington."[7] David McCullough once said that

Washington "above all was a leader" with a "commanding presence"[8] and the "symbol of unity." He believes that Washington was "much more important than most Americans have any idea."

That is not to say that Washington never had any detractors. Henry Cabot Lodge, in his two-volume biography called *George Washington*, dispensed with them, including claims that Washington had no opinions of his own, that he was a figurehead and not "an American in anything but the technical sense."[9] Lodge, the historian and one-time holder of the position we now think of as US Senate Leader, wrote in the late 1880s that those criticisms "were of no real moment except as illustrations of the existence and meaning of party divisions," or, in Jefferson's case, "Jefferson disliked him because he blocked his path."[10] Even Jefferson, however, in response to a serious illness of Washington's, would write, "You cannot conceive the public alarm on this occasion. It proves how much depends on his life."[11] Jefferson also said of Washington that "he united the confidence of all America, and was the only person who did so."[12]

Lodge believed Washington's "devotion" was to the "good of the country." He posited that "Washington's personal influence was very great, something we of this generation, with a vast territory and seventy millions of people, cannot readily understand."[13] More than one hundred years after Lodge wrote those words and with a population now 250 million people larger, Americans and historians alike remain remarkably unified in that view of Washington.

Our Revolutionary Thoughts

If we can agree with Jefferson in believing that Washington "united the confidence of all America"—and we should—it's worth our time to understand the difficult years between *Our Revolutionary Thoughts* (the period leading up to the Revolution, during which the ideas of revolution and liberty took hold) and *Washington's Unifying Moment* (the period wherein Washington unified a divided nation). Those years in between were filled with seminal actions taken by government and against government, many of which threatened to dramatically disrupt the lives of the colonists. Those actions had far-ranging economic and political implications. Amidst such consequential and uncertain times, divisions naturally arose, opinions varied, and colonists all but had to take sides. Their choices were usually consistent with their immediate self-interests—economic, and even religious—that were being jeopardized. One side acted, the other reacted, and partisanship escalated. It is a pattern we shall see again and again in our history, and it helps shed significant light on the *Divided Era*.

The years just before the American Revolution mark the start of our first major divided period. We need to keep in mind what Harlow Giles Unger wrote and I referenced before—parts of America had lived "free of almost all government authority for more than 150 years."[14] In the years leading up to the Revolution, the English Crown and the colonial government simply were not ubiquitous or onerous by prior revolutionary standards in history. Moreover, the colonies were fairly stable politically and economically. The notion of seriously disrupting that stability resided among very few. By no means was there unity or excitement toward breaking with England via an armed conflict. Instead, it would start slowly and gain momentum in response to each escalating British *action* and Patriot *reaction*.

As for the catalyst of the Revolution, according to historian Gordon S. Wood,

> There was none of the legendary tyranny that had so often driven desperate peoples into revolution. The Americans were not oppressed people; they had no crushing imperial shackles to throw off. In fact, the Americans knew they were probably freer and less burdened with cumbersome feudal and monarchial restraints than any part

of mankind in the eighteenth century. To its victims, the Tories, the revolution was truly incomprehensible. Never in history, said David Leonard, had there been so much rebellion with so "little real cause."[15]

Even so, Americans did revolt. As with many of history's maturing commercial classes or colonies, the American colonists of the 1760s were beginning to itch for a political freedom and self-determination commensurate with their growing economic power and maturity. Somewhere along the line of such development, there is often some spark that turns those simmering thoughts into heated desire. The spark that many suggest lit the lasting flame of America's revolutionary fervor was the Stamp Act, which the British Parliament passed in 1765. The law required a stamp to be affixed to certain legal documents and it also applied to certain services. Along with that stamp, of course, the Stamp Act imposed a tax.

A similar stamp tax had been imposed on the English for decades.[16] The proceeds from the American version would be used to offset about 20 percent of the costs to station British troops in America "to protect American colonists against Indian attacks."[17] Remarkably, the American revenue stamps would "often [be] worth less than a penny."[18] However, as Harlow Giles Unger points out in his book *American Tempest*, the timing of the tax proved quite bad for the English. Americans were in tough economic times due to a loss of hard currency, bad crop yields, and more. Worse yet, the new tax, however slight, would be the first direct tax (i.e., paid at the time of the transaction by the consumer), and therefore, highly visible tax levied by the English in America. Prior to the Stamp Act, governments in America collected indirect taxes, revenues raised by taxing goods as they came into the country (i.e., levying tariffs at our ports). Hence the characterization of "indirect taxes"— consumers would not feel the tax levied at the port when they purchased the product in a store.

From our present-day vantage point, the demand to pay 20 percent of the troops' costs does not appear to be an exorbitant request. The attacks of the Indians were a real and present danger, and the French and Indian War was a recent memory. Moreover, the British Parliament, facing near bankruptcy, first tried to pay 100 percent of the costs of the troops by raising taxes in England.[19] Those increased taxes levied in England, however, "plunged 40,000 Englishmen into debtor's prison and provoked widespread anti-tax riots."[20] After those riots, some of the taxes were repealed and Americans were asked to pay, dare we say, their fair share of the costs of the troops.

Whether the tax was reasonable or not, it was an unprecedented exercise of government power by the British. In response to that small but potentially far-reaching tax, Patrick Henry took *History*'s center stage and chose to raise the stakes even further. Not only did he denounce the Stamp Act, he introduced five revolutionary resolutions for passage in the Virginia House of Burgess in 1765. One of his resolutions stated what never had been said before—namely, that only the Virginia General Assembly had the right to lay taxes against Virginians—*not* Mother England. During the debate of that resolution, the speaker of the Assembly and other burgesses accused Patrick Henry of treason for making such an assertion and others like it, to which Henry famously replied: "If this be treason, make the most of it."

★   ★   ★

The interplay between Patrick Henry and the British encapsulates the very historical premise this book highlights. Government action, especially action that alters or takes away the rights of its people, can cause intense reactions—what some today would consider extreme partisanship. But for the imposition of the Stamp Tax, Patrick Henry would not have been so partisan at that moment in time. Left relatively free of the agitation of government action, he would have had no reason to be so. It was government action that spurred his historic partisanship—his treason.

The importance of the sequence of that dynamic, which we can call the *Partisan Catalyst Dynamic*, is lost on most of us today. Indeed, the order of cause and effect is exactly the opposite of what is often said of present-day partisans. Many, especially in the media, blame partisans for generating political conflicts—blaming them for their supposed refusal to get along or to compromise with the opposition. They fail to understand, however, that there is a catalyst to most partisan activity and it is not an innate desire to disagree with others. Instead, it is a natural reaction to government impositions or decisions—the taking of a fence, restrictions placed on earning income, or granting favors to a competitor. The loss or restriction of a right is viewed by the partisan as a taking by government—not something to be cheerfully compromised.

The degree of resultant partisanship correlates closely to the extent partisans perceive they will be harmed or how interested they are in a pending outcome. Like Patrick Henry, many today would not be motivated to rise up if government did not affect them so much—if the fence between them and their government was not jeopardized in so many ways. That order of cause and effect will be evident throughout our review of the Revolution, the adoption of the Constitution, the period of time before the Civil War, and beyond. It is key to understanding today's conflict. Indeed, the *Divided Era* in which we live is the result of government affecting more people in more ways than ever before—and they are reacting by getting involved and demanding that others do so.

★　★　★

The Stamp Act is considered by many as the first major spark to the fire of the American Revolution. However, Americans at that moment, Patrick Henry's eloquence notwithstanding, were anything but unified on the notion that they should rebel against Mother England. Even Henry, a critical figure in the run-up to the Revolution, while he was saying those treasonous words, was not asking for America to be set free. After all, his fourth resolution acknowledged that Americans had the same rights as the people of Great Britain, and nowhere did he suggest, at that time, that we should declare our independence.

Nor did anyone else, at that time, go so far as to advocate independence—including the New England firebrands James Otis and Samuel Adams. Otis and Adams, early and important figures in the revolutionary process, would be considered extremists in today's media. Both used considerable hyperbole to fan the early flames of opposition to the Crown's new colonial policies.[21] Like Patrick Henry, they strongly believed that the British had gone too far and wanted others to join them. Yet they were realists. Just before Henry's resolutions were introduced, Otis, the author of *The Rights of the British Colonies Asserted and Proved*, readily acknowledged that "nine hundred and ninety-nine in a thousand of the colonists will never once entertain a thought but submission to our sovereign and the authority of parliament."[22]

James Otis's assessment about the colonists was correct because most colonists had yet to conclude—either through lack of knowledge, genuine belief, or fear of the implications—that the British had irretrievably breached their fences. The start of the Revolutionary War, in April of 1775, was still a decade away. In between Patrick Henry's openly treasonous words and the start of the war, the movement toward revolution occurred in uneven partisan fits and starts, riding on the waves of action and reaction. The Stamp Act, the Townsend Acts, and other British acts fostered ever-escalating responses and made partisans of previously sanguine colonists.

We shall see, in our look at the Civil War and the *Reconstruction Era*, a similar dynamic of escalating government action and political reaction. We can call that the *Escalating Partisanship Dynamic*. It represents a second historical dynamic important for us to recognize in our consideration of the *Divided Era*. It is a predictable and natural dynamic with interested parties on both sides—more often than not inclusive of partisans interested not in mending fences but, instead, in philosophical or political victory. As we watch that unfold, we would do well to note that even our greatest leaders—Washington, Franklin, and Lincoln to name a few—got caught up in that dynamic of rising political tensions. If even they could be part of it, if not fuel it, perhaps we should be far more philosophical about our battles today and more understanding of their cause.

Returning to the Stamp Act, we should note that it fueled the colonists' protests, which already were brewing in New England, to become more organized. Indeed, it resulted in the assemblage of the Stamp Act Congress. That congress passed the Declaration of Rights and Grievances. The colonists then imposed a nonimportation embargo against English goods. That embargo hurt British traders, further dividing England, and eventually led to the repeal of the Stamp Act. Along with the repeal, however, the English Parliament passed the Declaratory Act, which warned Americans that the British Parliament had the right to pass the Stamp Act even as they were repealing it. Still strapped for money, however, the next year the British Parliament passed new taxes under the Townsend Acts. Once again, Americans lodged their protests, and once again, they imposed a nonimportation embargo.

By 1768 Samuel Adams and James Otis were calling for a more unified resistance of the colonies against "taxation without representation." The Royal Governor of Massachusetts dissolved the Massachusetts legislature and British troops began their uneasy stay in Boston. In 1769, the Virginia legislature came to the fore again, and in response passed resolutions condemning the British actions against Massachusetts. Their reward was the dissolution of their own legislature by English authorities. The year 1770 saw a momentary step back from the brink with the repeal of the Townsend Acts, which was due, in part, to discontent in England over the embargoes. The colonies responded in kind by calling off their nonimportation boycott. However, that comity would not last.

The highlight of 1770 was the Boston Massacre, in which Americans confronted British troops in Boston, resulting in deaths of colonists. That event reignited the flame of the American Revolution and set the stage for the Boston Tea Party, "the most notable protest undertaken by the American radicals."[23]

The year was 1773 and the British troops' presence in Boston had been keeping the embers of discontent burning among Bostonians— embers that Sam Adams and James Otis continued to fan along with the Sons of Liberty, a group of discontented Bostonians that often acted like a mob. That year the British Parliament passed the Tea Act, which reduced the tax on British tea, clearly slanting the commercial field in their favor. On December 16, the famous Boston Tea Party took place and the pace of the events leading to the Revolution picked up yet again.

The next year, the British Parliament passed the Coercive Acts. Included in those acts, and meant to punish the colonists for the Boston Tea Party, was a bill to close the port of Boston. One act, the Massachusetts Governing Act, took away election rights for the colony in favor of Crown control. Another act, the Quartering Act, allowed the British government to station troops in private homes. That act inspired part of the Third Amendment to our Constitution barring the "quartering" of troops in our homes.

As the tension thickened amidst action and reaction, the First Continental Congress met in September of 1774. The state at the vanguard of the fight for the *Liberty* to come, Massachusetts, created its own rebel "government" in the form of the Provincial Congress and a Committee of Safety. Then, in what perhaps would be the last straw, the British government imposed the New England Restraining Act, which restricted the trade of the New England colonies with England. Not long after, in April of 1775, "the shot heard round the world" took place at Lexington and Concord. Revolution was in the American air as sure as the bullets shot by the American Patriots.

★   ★   ★

In such condensed form, it could appear that the run-up to our Revolution followed a straight-line course of events—that perhaps the Revolution was destined to occur, spurred on by a series of partisan actions and reactions.But as John Ferling wrote in his book *Independence: The Struggle to Set America Free*, "History is more complicated than that."[24] In fact, there was no certain outcome and at this juncture we must recognize a third core historical dynamic. As high stakes unfold and uncertainty abounds, in the same train you are likely to find lasting and intense political division. This dynamic features an actual inability for a clear and broad consensus to form. It can't or doesn't form because some disagreements are beyond philosophical or practical resolution between opposing camps. The partisans, at those points, may agree to disagree. Those disagreements, however, quite often are not on friendly terms and the higher the stakes, the more likely it is that that dynamic will emerge. Let us call this third dynamic the *Persistent Division Dynamic*.

It was that dynamic at play that, despite the demonstrative actions toward independence taken by powerful and persuasive leaders, kept the colonists hopelessly divided on the issue of breaking with England. That remained true even after the war started. According to Ferling, "It seems certain that most Americans did not favor independence when what we know as the War of Independence broke out in April of 1775. Even after the war had raged for several months, many Americans—again probably most—still did not want American independence."[25]

Another historian surmised that "hundreds of thousands in the thirteen colonies sympathized more with Britain than with Congress."[26] Strikingly, Ferling notes that "at the beginning of 1776, a majority of those who served in the Continental Congress preferred reconciliation with the mother country to American independence. Had the Continental Congress voted on independence in January or February of 1776, no more than five of thirteen colonies would likely have favored a final break with Great Britain."[27] In short, there was no unity among the colonists on the notion of revolution.

We were divided politically, economically, and even religiously. Starting with an economic perspective, during the run-up to the war, division took the form of sectors of America's merchant trading class being "uncooperative" when it came to the nonimportation embargoes.[28] The reduction in international trade hurt them economically and favored locally produced articles.[29] The first embargo was "a one year ban on . . . products imported from Britain except ten essentials, including salt, coals, fish-hooks and lines, hemp, duck and shot."[30] Beyond that, the "degree of enforcement [of the embargo] varied" across the country.[31] When it was enforced, violators could be placed under surveillance "or have their names published as 'enemies of the country.'"[32] Obviously, the application of Revolutionary politics resulted in certain winners and losers—separate from those chosen by the marketplace. Facing real economic losses, if not public shame, it is easy to understand why certain merchants, depending on their wares, may have been less supportive of rebellion than others. It was in those fallows that revolutionary division was sown and partisanship grew.

Our divisions at the time were uneven, often demonstrating regional differences. As between the colonies, to "the shock of Boston's patriots . . . Revere's ride produced little unity or sympathy for Boston's plight. While most New Yorkers and Philadelphians shrugged their shoulders in disinterest, Virginians debated the wording of a resolution to support the innocent people of Boston without condoning the Boston Tea Party or provoking Parliament into closing Virginia's ports."[33] In other words, we must add regional dynamics to the division in America over the idea of breaking with England in an armed revolution. Certainly, in the beginning, the intensity for rebellion was greatest in the Northeast and around the major ports in America. Those were the areas most affected by the actions of the Crown and the Patriot embargoes. It was less so inland and in the South, other than Virginia.[34]

To those divisions we can add "religious and ethnic factionalism" as well.[35] At the time, Anglicans were generally thought to espouse "passive disobedience," and therefore were considered more deferential to the Crown and less supportive of revolution. The idea of it apparently stirred old passions and divisions between Anglicans across the colonies and their occasional foes, the Congregationalists and Presbyterians, who were considered less deferential[36] and supported the Revolution in greater numbers. Meanwhile, "many of the Quakers, Peace Germans, and Dutch, in particular, distrusted the rebellion-minded Yankees, Scotch-Irish, and Virginians."[37] Old loyalties, in other words, found new reasons to be partisan.

Those are but a few of many possible representative examples of how the idea and the practice of breaking with England caused economic, political, and religious division among Americans. Those divisions and partisan activities would not have occurred but for the dramatic government action and the revolutionary reactions. Obviously, those actions affected the colonists in different ways and to different degrees, thereby causing different degrees of reaction or partisanship. Many reacted in their self-interest. Can we really blame them? After all, if we consider again our fence analogy, not only were the British and the colonists curtailing the rights of some to have fences but they were also telling others they could no longer sell fences. Those actions caused serious economic repercussions, and therefore, added to the emerging *Persistent Division Dynamic* of the day.

Returning to our timeline of events, those divisions lasted to one degree or another all the way up to our Declaration of Independence in 1776, and beyond. That meant Americans and their representatives in their rebel Congress remained divided over the very idea of a revolution well after the war started in April of 1775. That division, if not ambivalence, is best highlighted by noting that even after the war started, and even after Washington took charge of the Continental Army and the Battle of Bunker Hill took place, our Continental

Congress sent the Olive Branch Petition to King George. The petition was written by a committee appointed by Congress. It expressed "loyalty to the Crown"—even going so far as to ask King George to "find a way to reconciliation."[38] In other words, it was an attempt by some to reach a compromise.

★ ★ ★

The Olive Branch Petition is representative of a fourth important historical dynamic for us to keep in mind throughout our consideration of the *Divided Era*. As we now understand, with significant government action such as taxation, people take sides—some intensely so—depending on their level of interest or the degree to which they are affected. We now must also recognize that as sides are drawn on any one issue, there are those drawn to the prospect of compromise. Some do it for political gain, others out of a genuine interest in seeking resolution—sometimes both. History remembers, and the media often describes, if not heralds, such participants as moderates or middle-of-the-road politicians. They are often portrayed as having a wider, more reasonable perspective than partisans. In the process, sometimes compromise is achieved. However, other times it is not. Throughout history, many have pounced on the latter occurrence, deemed it a failure of the participants, and blamed the actions of partisans. We see this nearly every day in the *Divided Era* and will refer to the dynamic of emerging centrists and the attention they are given as the *Olive Branch Dynamic*.

Despite what the media declares in any given age, however, many times history demonstrates that being a moderate, defined here as one who wants to compromise so tensions can lessen, is not always of value—either at the time or in retrospect. That shall be our fifth historical dynamic to watch, and we shall name it the *Refusal to Compromise Dynamic*.

For instance, in chapter 6, quite literally we shall find that politicians seeking compromise between the North and South asked Lincoln to moderate his views against the spread of slavery. Should Lincoln have followed his predecessors and compromised? If he did so, we might have had slavery in the South for decades longer than we did, and America would be a very different place today. Returning to Washington, should he have asserted his leadership and sought to reduce the amount of the Stamp Act tax in the spirit of compromise? Would America be the same if that compromise had occurred? As some have suggested, could we then have gone without a revolution? Would we have evolved into a country like England with no Constitution and no Bill of Rights—two of the most inspiring and important documents in history? Obviously Washington and Lincoln chose differently. They didn't moderate their views when faced with difficult political and military challenges—and *History* is grateful to them. Their examples demonstrate that, at times, only what has sometimes been described as extreme partisanship can achieve certain results. So it may well be today.

★   ★   ★

In any case, by the time of the Olive Branch Petition, the opportunity for moderation was over. King George rejected the petition and with that, the pace of the Revolution picked up once again—but even then, not without continuing angst and division. There simply wasn't going to be unity, and we shouldn't expect unity on a question of such enormous magnitude: whether we had a right to throw off the yoke of English power and govern ourselves (i.e., change our entire economic and political existence). John Adams reminded us of just how divided Americans were at the time. Indeed, John Ferling notes that "[Adams] remembered . . . that 'all the great critical questions' down to the spring of 1776 had been decided by the slimmest of margins. Not infrequently, he recalled, the passage of pivotal measures had hinged on the vote of a single delegate."[39]

Our Revolutionary Intensity Grows

Obviously, the political and economic stakes surrounding the run-up to the Revolution were extremely high. The risks were enormous for the colonists regardless of what side of the issue they took. The leaders of the Revolution and the Patriots following them were committing treason—punishable by death. Without an organized army, let alone a navy, they considered fighting and ultimately decided to fight the most powerful army and navy in the world. Through all of that, people were using government decrees and forces, or rebelling against their use, to decide the fate of many things. In periods of such incredibly high drama and politics, along with the use of raw power and resultant consequences, we should expect that consensus was *not* possible—and so it was for America. In short, as we marched toward revolution, we were squarely within a *Persistent Division Dynamic*.

The pre-Revolutionary decade featured extreme actions, rough language, and strident people—common features we shall see in our periods of great division. British government officials were hanged in effigy in Boston from something called the Liberty Tree and carried in mock funeral processions by the Sons of Liberty—all in the center of town.[40] Government offices were destroyed, as well as, the homes of government officials,[41] and that was *before* the first shot of the Revolution! Some of the most strident players made history on both sides of the issue, such as Samuel Adams, who at least one historian said "controlled" Boston with his "trained mob."[42] Another said Adams had "few equals as an agitator," "with a reputation as a violence-soaked incendiary," whose pen "stung like a horned snake."[43] Adams's "seductive whispers" were said to leave "unsuspecting listeners 'closely attached to the hindermost past of Mr. Adams as the rattles are affixed to the tail of a rattlesnake.'"[44] It was Adams who sensationalized the early conflict in his writings and ensured the flame of revolution would not die out;[45] and yet, paradoxically by today's standards, eventually Adams would be called "the great forerunner of the race of American politicians" by Henry Cabot Lodge.[46]

Of course, Adams was not alone either in his passion, intensity, or writing in an age when the "media" made a decisive impact.[47] Thomas Paine would write a "fanatical" pamphlet called *Common Sense*.[48] Paine wrote extensively with a wide readership. His essays had "unmatched passion and verve."[49] He was said to have an "explosive personality."[50] The passion of his writing, evidenced in his *Common Sense*, included comments about the English such as "Even brutes don't devour their young, nor savages make war upon their families." Of some moderates, he said, "Men of passive tempers look somewhat lightly over the offences of Britain." Offended by such people, Paine declared some to possess the "heart of a coward and the spirit of the sycophant." With such invective and more, Paine "transformed" King George, who previously was not the object of public derision, into a tyrant in the eyes of the American people.[51]

As *History* knows, Paine's *Common Sense* was more than successful and "cut right through the half-and-half arguments" proposed by moderates that favored negotiation with England.[52] Strident though his words may have sounded, in a country of just two-and-a-half million people, *Common Sense* "sold over 100,000 copies and virtually everyone had read it or heard about it." It even garnered the approval of George Washington.[53] To others, it was the most successful and influential pamphlet ever published,[54] and "blazed the path of independence in America."[55] It was so influential, that no less than John Adams would say, perhaps jealously so, that "history is to ascribe the American Revolution to Thomas Paine."[56]

✱   ✱   ✱

It is time to ask yourself, How would the words of Patrick Henry, Thomas Paine, and Samuel Adams be received today in the modern media? They were plainly refusing to compromise. Undoubtedly, today they would be shouted down with disdain as extremists. Some did just that at the time.

Regardless, their dangerous and often exaggerated speech, which at the time was not free speech, was essential to our intellectual revolution, *Our Revolutionary Thoughts*, not to mention the coming war. It played such a key role that it can rightly be asked: Without their intensity, would we have the American form of *Liberty* that gave us the free speech guaranteed by the First Amendment? The answer is more than likely no. Their radicalism was key to giving us a Constitution more important and influential to history than the existing English form of government. In that light, we see once again that *History* demonstrates that partisanship can be an indispensable ingredient to important change where moderation simply would not succeed. That dynamic we have called the *Refusal to Compromise Dynamic*, and Patrick Henry, Thomas Paine, and Sam Adams would be representative of successes of that dynamic.

★ ★ ★

Keep in mind that the intensity of the times, to be sure, was not one-sided. There were passionate and even brutal people fighting for the loyalist side as well. In fact, "Loyalist rhetoric demanded that the patriot leaders be put to the sword, and those in rebellion have their houses destroyed and their possessions plundered. 'It is just that they should be the first victims to the mischief they have brought upon us.'"[57] Opposing Thomas Paine were the likes of James Chalmers—a pamphleteer in his own right. Forced by fear to write anonymously under the name Candidus, Chalmers denounced Paine's *Common Sense* as "quackery." In a pamphlet called *A Friendly Address to All Reasonable Americans*, author Thomas Bradbury Chandler was not friendly at all. Instead, he derided colonists by stating that "Ever since the reduction of Canada, 'we have been bloated with a vain opinion of our own importance.'"[58] Overall, from 1774–1776, "more original loyalist material was published than at any other time, including the great pamphlets of Daniel Leonard ('Massachusettensis'), Thomas Bradbury Chandler, Samuel

Seabury, Charles Inglis, and Joseph Galloway."[59] As we shall see, Loyalists picked up their guns in defense of England as well. David Fanning was one who fought on the Loyalist side and engaged in "terror and counter terror" against the governor of North Carolina, Thomas Burke, who sided with the Patriots. Thomas Brown fought for the Loyalist side in South Carolina as well—just to name two.[60]

Today we may say that Henry, Adams, and Paine were on one extreme wing of the debate while James Chalmers and Daniel Leonard were on the opposing extreme wing. Not everyone, however, was a "winger" or an agitator. Beyond the Olive Branch Petition, many wanted to put the brakes on runaway emotion and politics. Less "extreme" actors in our own Continental Congress included Joseph Galloway from Pennsylvania. Initially, Galloway was not in favor of convening a rebel Continental Congress because of its uncertain potential. When it did convene, the "moderate" Galloway hoped it would act with "Temper and Moderation."[61] Galloway eventually would offer a "conciliatory plan that would create a grand council overseeing matters of taxation and legislation in association with a royally approved governor-general."[62] Recalling John Adams' words about slim margins, we find that Galloway's middle-of-the-road plan was rejected by a vote of just six to five. On such a narrow and partisan vote did our history turn.

If we again consider the Olive Branch Petition, that last attempt at reconciliation, we find that the original committee to draft it was comprised of such luminaries as Benjamin Franklin, John Rutledge, William Livingston, and our future first Supreme Court Chief Justice, John Jay. They too could be considered moderates for that moment in time. When the Continental Congress turned down their first efforts, no less than Thomas Jefferson was added to the committee, along with another "moderate," John Dickinson. Jefferson took the lead by offering another draft. Dickinson, however, thought Jefferson's draft too strident, and therefore, Dickinson revised it to the split approval of the Continental Congress. As we know, however, the ultimate partisan, King George, rejected the petition and later declared the colonists to be in open rebellion, clearing the way for the Declaration of Independence and more highly partisan actions by the likes of Franklin and Jefferson.

★   ★   ★

King George's rejection of the conciliatory Olive Branch Petition had the effect of escalating the revolutionary fervor among our leaders and colonists. Even so, Americans were never uniform in their support of the decision to rebel and were uncertain even when they did. As the Revolution progressed, things would in some ways get worse before they got better on the way to *Washington's Unifying Moment*. The economic divisions that arose because of the embargoes would take new forms, and the factionalism and religious divisions, which were present before the war, would take on new and larger dimensions as fellow colonists exchanged their pens for muskets.

As we consider our Revolution born amidst great uncertainty and what we will find to be brothers fighting brothers, we need to keep an eye on the divisions among Americans that existed during the Revolutionary War and those that remained at the war's end. Although our Congress was relatively unified during the war, the difficulties and uncertainties of the war would more than test the resolve of our entire nation to be. It remains a wonder how we got through those times that tried men's souls.

Our Revolution of Uncertainty and Brother Fighting Brother

George Washington, in addition to his other qualities, was said to be a realist. He saw things "as they were, not as he would wish they were."[63] In addressing the troops the day before the Battle of Long Island in late August of 1776, Washington laid out the stakes of political rhetoric turned to battle—a choice between freedom and subjugation.

The time is now near at hand which must probably determine whether Americans are to be freemen or slaves; whether they are to have any property they can call their own; whether their houses and farms are to be pillaged and destroyed, and themselves consigned to a state of wretchedness from which no human efforts will deliver them. The fate of unborn millions will now depend, under God, on the courage and conduct of this army. Our cruel and unrelenting enemy leaves us only the choice of brave resistance, or the most abject submission. We have, therefore, to resolve to conquer or die.[64]

Washington could more easily frame the issue "to conquer or die"—high stakes indeed—than know the outcome of the mission. The real question facing Washington and the Patriots was how they could conquer the largest, most professional, and best-equipped army and navy in the world. Washington would have to go to battle with inferior fighting forces and a lack of hard currency, and facing fierce weather conditions. As if that was not enough, Washington dealt with lingering and new divisions among Americans. Among those familiar lingering issues were the actions of the commercial class. During the war, some engaged in war profiteering and did business with the British, often to the detriment of the Patriots. Loyalist activity remained a significant factor, included high-profile traitors, and would continue to wax and wane depending on the state of the war. As the war changed from words to bullets, the Loyalist issue would intensify as Patriots faced the difficult prospect of fighting Loyalists who were their brothers, fathers, and fellow colonists in what could fairly be called our first civil war. At the same time as all of the aforementioned, the Patriots faced the difficult and unprecedented task of creating state governments and a federal government.

All of those dynamics combined led to an atmosphere of doubt and uncertainty—not to mention division—but not just privately in the

minds of Washington, Congress, or the army. Instead, all of those difficulties and more played out in great detail in the many newspapers that
alternately reported on and enhanced the very palpable uncertainty of
the age. We certainly know from history that Washington and the Patriots prevailed—but not without very high costs that would set the stage
for the next conflicts among the victorious colonists. They would take
the form of enormous debt, worthless currencies, overactive state governments, and a huge fight over ineffective Articles of Confederation. In
other words, there was still a long way and a lot of troubled waters before
we would reach *Washington's Unifying Moment.*

In the next few pages, I will not be providing an exhaustive history of
the Revolution nor the trouble the Patriots endured during the Revolution—let alone recount all of the ups and downs of the fighting. Instead,
it will be useful to our understanding of what difficulties Washington
faced in unifying the country as our first president if we understand
that the Revolution was fought, at all times, squarely within a *Persistent
Division Dynamic,* and that the difficulties of the war strengthened the
dynamic. We shall see that consensus was not prevalent and could not
be. The extent of those divisions and troubles are not often remembered.[65] So let us look at the Revolution broadly with that in mind.

The Daunting Task of Fighting Great Britain

We need to remember that at the time the "shot" was "heard round the
world," there was not a national Patriot government. Nor was there a
single currency used by the colonies at the time they declared their independence more than a year later. There wasn't even a single entity that
had the power to collect taxes from the still-separate colonies in order
to raise an army. Instead, there were thirteen separate colonies—and
they did not necessarily see eye to eye on issues such as trade, taxes, and
their mutual borders. They also faced their own serious economic problems. Under those circumstances, it is also easy to understand why there

was no American army and no American navy. In the years before the Revolution, when it came to security needs and armed conflicts, armed Americans relied chiefly on themselves and neighbors—and the army of Great Britain (which included Americans). Once independence was declared, Americans had to quickly organize an army, a navy, and even their governments—and pay for them—in order to fight a war against their former protectors—the best army and navy in the world.

The British, by contrast, enjoyed considerable advantages over the Patriot forces. As the Revolution got underway, those advantages included superior wealth, a population three to four times that of the colonists', an organized and tested army of superior numbers, seasoned commanders, a navy, and mercenary fighters at their disposal.[66] Simply stated, it was "the best-trained, best-equipped, most formidable military force on earth."[67] Of Great Britain, Lois Clinton Hatch wrote in her book *The Administration of the American Revolutionary Army*, published in 1904:

> The Seven Years' War had greatly increased her dominion and influence. She had a considerable army, an excellent navy, and was accustomed to combining land and sea operations. British cruisers could interrupt the foreign trade of the colonies, to whom commerce was almost a necessity, since America was not a manufacturing country; British fleets could facilitate a landing in every harbor of the extended coast; and Canada furnished a base for an attack by land. Everywhere the colonies lay open to invasion; from Eastport to Savannah there was not a single fortified town.[68]

All of that is not to say that the British didn't have disadvantages. Indeed, "conducting a war across a 3,000-mile ocean was almost impossible. Coordinating supplies and battle plans was a nightmare when it took six to eight weeks for ships to travel from Europe to America."[69] Perhaps most telling, England "had no fundamental national interest in fighting the war. If they won, it merely brought more political problems. If they lost, it hurt little but their pride."[70] In practice, that meant there was a "missing spark" on the English side, or, put another way, "a vital element of national commitment was lacking in the British war effort."[71]

The Patriots did have some advantages. "The crucial advantage that Americans believed they possessed was not natural but moral."[72] They were not only fighting for their own property, but fighting for the broader rights to be free and for the right of self-determination, and not just for themselves. Many agreed with Washington when he said that "the fate of unborn millions" was at stake. Even so, the Patriots faced severe logistical problems and they understood the odds they faced. Indeed, "none who favored independence was blind to the uncertainty of the future."[73] Even Washington questioned, at the time of his commission as commanding general, whether he was fit for the task ahead, with "a realistic idea of how immense that responsibility would be" and knowing he would be leading "an undisciplined, poorly armed volunteer force of farmers and tradesmen."[74]

Washington's first engagement, immediately after being commissioned by Congress, was to rush to Boston and lead the siege of Boston Harbor. Washington saw firsthand what he already knew, namely that "at the start of the siege there had been no American army. Even [then] it had no flag or uniforms. Though in some official documents it had been referred to as the Continental Army, there was no clear agreement on what it should be called."[75] Despite its subsequent victory, "there would never be a truly integrated American military. . . . The Continental army did evolve into the United States Army, but throughout the war it existed alongside state regiments and even more numerous militia regiments and companies. They all set their own standards: terms of enlistment, rates of pay, inducements to serve, nature and amounts of equipment."[76]

★   ★   ★

The trials of our War for Independence validated the early concerns. "For eight years Congress would struggle to feed, clothe, equip, and shelter its soldiers."[77] Part of that struggle related to a lack of money. Prior to declaring independence, America's number-one trading partner was England. With very limited domestic manufacturing, America relied on that trade not only for goods but also for the ability to make, earn, and save money. Self-financing of the war would not be possible because America had a "tiny moneyed elite"[78] and, according to William Graham Sumner, the war resulted in an "enormous" financial "chasm."[79] Worse yet, with independence would come a British economic embargo, a massive reduction in trade, and a scarcity of hard currency. As a result, Congress looked to the states and any willing country, mostly France, for help.

The states, however, had their own financial and economic woes. In Virginia for example, the total currency outstanding dropped from £230,000 in 1764 to £105,000 in 1771 and £55,000 by 1773.[80] Our Great Depression of the 1930s was caused in great part by a reduction in the money supply of approximately 32 percent. By comparison, Virginia's loss alone was 75 percent and, even though people bartered their goods and wares, Virginians suffered because of the loss of currency and poor harvests, among other things. The other states had similar troubles. Those bad economic times meant that in 1775 and 1776, none of the states levied taxes at all.[81] Under those circumstances, congressional pleas for money from the individual states to fund the war "often went unanswered."[82]

Although France provided America with loans, they would not be nearly enough and France would eventually balk at further loans.[83] Indeed, Benjamin Franklin, who was in France seeking its support at the behest of Washington and Congress, "warned his colleagues in Philadelphia of France's growing weariness at the Congress' incessant requests for money."[84] So great were the financial concerns at the time that Robert Morris, a congressman and among the greatest private financiers of the Revolution, "believed that the sinews of war were financial. In his estimation bankruptcy was a greater threat to the nation than the British army."[85]

With money scarce from the outset of the war, and the states themselves often unwilling to contribute, Congress resorted to printing money. The name they chose for the money was the "Continental." Initially, the Congress printed $2 million. "Within eighteen months it had put $25,000,000 into circulation and was printing new issues every fortnight."[86] "By the end of 1779, $241.6 million" in Continentals had been issued, producing what some would say was the worst inflation in American history,[87] depriving "[C]ongress of its only fund."[88] That inflation combined with "shortages occasioned both by the loss of British trade and the enemy's ever-tightening naval blockade, threatened economic collapse."[89]

All of those hardships would gravely impact the effectiveness and morale of the Patriots fighting for General Washington—not to mention the effect of the weather. Leading up to the Revolution, poor weather exacerbated the economic conditions of parts of the colonies.[90] During the war, weather sometimes played havoc with troops, as it did at Valley Forge. "The sufferings of the troops during this winter were more severe than at any other period of the war, with the possible exception of the winter of 1779–80."[91]

Henry Cabot Lodge tells the story in vivid detail:

> In the frost and snow he withdrew to Valley Forge, within easy striking distance of Philadelphia. He had literally nothing to rely upon but his own stern will and strong head. His soldiers, steadily dwindling in numbers, marked their road to Valley Forge by the blood from their naked feet. They were destitute and in rags. When they reached

their destination they had no shelter, and it was only by the energy and ingenuity of the General that they were led to build huts, and thus secure a measure of protection against the weather. There were literally no supplies, and the Board of War failed completely to remedy the evil.[92]

Left to such deprivation, despite writing "literally hundreds of begging letters to Congress and state governments,"[93] Washington did exactly what he didn't want to do: impose forcibly on American citizens for supplies and risk losing their support. It is likely that John Adams had such things in mind when he surmised, as independence was being declared, that "much affliction lay ahead," and that "America shall suffer Calamities still more wasting and Distresses yet more dreadful."[94] Indeed, the army had "11,000 men when it entered Valley Forge at Christmas 1777. By February 7,000 soldiers were too ill for duty. Altogether, 2,500 died that winter. Another 1,000 men deserted."[95]

The problem of desertion, brought on by poor and inconsistent pay, in addition to poor conditions and lack of food, certainly was not limited to Valley Forge. The annual desertion rate for the entire war was a staggering 20 percent.[96] It was so rampant that Washington lamented that troops were "here today, gone tomorrow, without assigning a reason or ever apprising you of it."[97] Beyond desertions, Washington faced mutinies that "could hardly fail to wound American pride, for it cast dishonor either on the government, or on the soldiers."[98] Even beyond mutinies, of course, there was "the most serious crisis of the Revolution"—Benedict Arnold's treason.[99] Through all of it, "Washington's own constancy became necessary to sustain the Revolution."[100]

Washington's frustration with obtaining supplies was not solely directed at the states and Congress. Private citizens raised his ire as well, and in two different ways. The first related to private citizens conducting business with the British when it was done to the detriment of his efforts. The second problem was war profiteering.

We need to keep in mind that prior to the war and the signing of the Declaration of Independence, Americans were British subjects. They traded not only for British manufactured goods but also for their clothing. John Hancock, the first and most prominent signer of the Declaration of Independence, was a bit of a "dandy" and spent extravagant amounts on English clothes and goods in his lifetime.[101] George Washington considered himself to be an English gentleman. Prior to the war, he traded tobacco to the English and purchased many English goods, including "the latest fashions [from] London," and his "favorite cheeses—double Gloucester and Cheshire."[102] The desire for British goods was certainly not limited to them. "American consumers were used to purchasing British products, and this preference did not disappear with the outbreak of hostilities."[103]

After the war started, however, extensive trading with the enemy, including needed food, hurt the Patriots and, at times, enraged Washington.[104] Why would Americans do such things? Part of the motivation was that the British paid in their stable currency—pounds sterling, whereas Americans paid in rapidly depreciating Continentals. While Chernow believed Washington to present "a rare case of a revolutionary leader" who recognized the "fallibility" of Americans acting in their own best interest,[105] Washington was still more than angered by the practice and was not afraid to use what many today would consider to be "extreme" language to describe them and their actions.

Washington variously referred to them as "pests of society," "murderers of our cause," that were "preying upon the vitals of this great Country and putting every thing to the utmost hazard."[106] To Washington, they were nothing more than "Speculators, various tribes of money makers, and stock jobbers of all denominations," seeking "their own private emolument, without considering that their avarice, and thirst for gain must plunge every thing (including themselves) into one common Ruin."[107] Overall, Washington believed at times during the Revolution that "virtue and patriotism are almost kicked out of the United States."[108]

The fact also remained that Americans trading with the British hurt the war effort. As Stuart Brandes points out in his book *Warhogs: A History of War Profits in America*, "Goods shipped to the enemy not only strengthened them . . . but also weakened the American effort in that there were fewer goods available to the patriots."[109] According to Brandes, it was not possible "to determine exactly how much trading with the enemy occurred."[110] What was observable, however, and what is important with respect to our discussion, was that "trading with the enemy bred distrust"[111] among the colonists. Overall, amidst such troubles, it is not difficult to imagine that the continuing Revolutionary War, like most any war, fueled political division, not just between the British Loyalists and the American Patriots but also within the ranks of Americans and their Congress.

Our First Civil War

In a very real sense, as many historians have written, the Civil War was not the first civil war fought in America. That distinction belongs to the Revolutionary War. By now we should understand that our War of Independence could never have been a story of united American colonists fighting a British army and navy that had freshly landed on American shores. To the contrary, many Loyalist colonists were never in favor of splitting from England. In time, they would fight on behalf of the British, which meant they would go to war with their fellow colonists. The fighting among the colonists would be so intense that at least one historian believes that "the Revolution, in reality, was not just one of America's civil wars; it may well have been the most bitter."[112]

Nowhere was that more true than in the South. In general, the Southern colonies were thought to be less "insurrectionist."[113] As a practical matter, that meant there were a higher number of Loyalists in those colonies who would side with England. In fact, the British, as part of their Southern Strategy, between 1778 and 1781, believed that Georgia and the Carolinas could be separated from the other colonies, and they designed a strategy to do just that.[114] It also meant that in "the South many fell victim in the raging civil war after 1779."[115] Incredibly, "103 battles were fought with no one but South Carolinians on *both* sides."[116]

According to American General Nathanael Greene, the fourth general chosen for the Southern Command, after the failures of Robert Howe, Benjamin Lincoln, and Horatio Gates,

> The animosities between the Whigs and Tories of this state renders their situation truly deplorable. There is not a day passes but there are more or less who fall a sacrifice to their savage disposition. The Whigs seem determined to extirpate the Tories and the Tories the Whigs. Some thousands have fallen in this way in this quarter, and the evil rages with more violence than ever. If a stop cannot be put to these massacres the country will be depopulated in a few months more, and neither Whig nor Tory can live.[117]

G. Kurtz and James H. Hutson in their book *Essays on the American Revolution* tell us of South Carolina that

> neither side had the capability of fully protecting its supporters among the civilian population, and a ferocious guerrilla war spread throughout South Carolina and into Georgia and North Carolina. Areas thought to have been pacified quickly slipped out of control, sometimes because loyal forces fought their own little wars of counter-terror against rebels, rebel sympathizers, suspects, and anyone else they disliked.[118]

Reading further we find that

a loyalist observer, who had defected some time before
from the rebel side, described South Carolina as "a piece
of patch work, the inhabitants of every settlement, when
united in sentiment, being in arms for the side they liked
best, and making continual inroads into one another's
settlements." During this civil war, there was little difference between loyalists and rebels in terms of organization, tactics, or the use of terror.[119]

That description of "patchwork" applied to many of the colonies
and the honeycombed, divided loyalties within their borders. Kevin
Phillips, in *The Cousins' Wars: Religion, Politics, and the Triumph of
Anglo-America*, describes why that was so: "The best explanation is that
more than dissatisfaction varied from colony to colony. So did culture
and preferences in religion."[120] Phillips describes "regional nuances," ethnic divisions, and even the varying loyalties of the American Indians in
his exhaustive work.[121]

Thomas McKean, chief justice of Pennsylvania, told us that at one
point, Pennsylvania "was not a nation at war with another nation, but a
country in a state of civil war."[122] Writing of Pennsylvania, John B. Frantz
and William Pencak in their book, *Beyond Philadelphia: The American
Revolution in the Pennsylvania Hinterland*, tell us that

> Pennsylvania's Revolution was also a profoundly civil
> war in the counties along the Delaware, in Philadelphia,
> and on the frontier, where internal violence accompa-
> nied political strife. Only in the central region was there
> no clash over who was to rule locally. And people there
> united to oppose the indifferent colonial government
> they overthrew. To be sure, this civil war took differ-
> ent forms in different parts of the state: class conflict in

Philadelphia, settlers versus Indians in the Juniata Valley, Pennsylvanians versus Yankees in the Wyoming Valley, the central counties versus the eastern, and Quakers and loyalists versus other dissenters and patriots in Bucks and Chester. Despite unifying elements of ethnic conflict, commercial evolution, and intense popular mobilization, Pennsylvania's American Revolution was as diverse and unique as the colonial experience that preceded it.[123]

Massachusetts, the state that led the revolutionary effort in many respects, was not immune from civil war either. From James S. Leamon's book *Revolution Downeast: The War for American Independence in Maine*, we learn that

the British occupation had momentous ramifications for Massachusetts and its easternmost counties. Massachusetts mounted a major expedition to dislodge the enemy but suffered a disaster so complete as to leave the state bankrupt, virtually defenseless, and more divided than ever. The British at Bagaduce, having defied the best efforts of the rebels, became a rallying point for loyalists from Maine and Massachusetts who hitherto had no alternative but passivity or flight. Stimulated by the British presence, many chose to stay and fight, and in doing so they transformed the Revolution in Maine into a bitter civil war.[124]

It is hard, after reading those accounts, not to conclude that the Revolutionary War was as much a civil war as a war of independence—the most stark evidence of the *Persistent Division Dynamic* affecting the fledgling country possible. Certainly to the British, it was a civil war.

Henry Belcher, writing from a British perspective, entitled his book about the Revolution, published in London in 1911, *The First American Civil War*. The Marquis de Lafayette, so integral to the success of our Revolution, thought it a civil war as well.[125] We must come to a similar conclusion and also understand that the Patriot victory changed world history but left bitterness among Loyalists in America—one more challenge for Washington on the way to his *Unifying Moment*.

Politics Leading to Even More Division During the Revolution

So far, in this discussion of the American Revolution, we have seen that Americans struggled in making their decision to go to war with England. It was a decision made in difficult economic times and promised even more difficult and divisive times ahead. We also know that Americans were not only fighting the British; they were fighting themselves in a civil war. Our own times tell us that war can make for difficult political times. During the Revolution, those difficulties took the form of political fights not only between Americans themselves, but between Congress and the Patriot army, Congress and the states, and Congress and Americans at large. Again, the decision to go to war, and the process of fighting it, mired us in the *Persistent Division Dynamic*.

Beyond those political battles, which would be significant in any age, Americans and their fledgling politicians faced the enormous task of creating, under duress, thirteen state governments and a national government, as well. It was a set of tasks without historical precedent and produced its own set of divisions for Americans.

Washington, the Continental Army, and Congress

During the war, Washington regularly had to beg Congress for money and supplies. That, however, was not the only cause for disagreement between Washington and Congress. Initially, Congress attempted to micromanage the war. For example, Congress "at first refused to approve of a general war, and tried to confine the fighting to the vicinity of Boston."[126] It chose Washington's generals, required its permission for major engagements, told him to defend the defenseless New York, and even dictated whether Washington could assign chaplains to army units.[127] On the issue of their micromanaging, Washington thought them to be "amateur experts," who, "when they are at a distance, . . . think it is but to say, 'Presto! Begone' and everything is done. They seem not to have any conception of the difficulty and perplexity attending those who are to execute."[128] There were other operational issues between Congress and Washington as well. Over time, Washington employed a large and effective spy network to help win the Revolution. Congress, however, wasn't always his partner in that endeavor. In fact, Washington often had to "bypass Congress, which couldn't be trusted to keep secrets"[129]—a problem not foreign to our own times.

Not surprisingly, the relationship between Washington and Congress was often dependent on how the war was going for Washington and his army. Dissatisfaction with Washington began to appear in 1777 because "Washington had been beaten at Brandywine; had lost Philadelphia; lost the forts on the Delaware; and failed at Germantown."[130] Even so, General George Washington, who certainly was more concerned about the military prognosis, "did not fear military defeat so much as he believed the effort to attain independence might fail due to political shortcomings."[131]

When the war was going well, Congress went to the opposite extreme. They let him make more and more tactical decisions and make the all-important choice of Nathanael Greene to take over the southern theatre of the war after Congress had made four inferior choices for that task.[132] The support of Washington even ran to "hero worship" in good times. But even that caused political problems and envy, as evidenced by John Adams, who wrote to his wife in a letter dated October 28, 1777, "I have been distressed to see some of our members disposed to idolize an image which their own hands have molten. I speak of the superstitious veneration which is paid to General Washington."[133]

In victory, of course, Congress celebrated Washington; and many of their disagreements would be forgotten. Prior to victory, however, only Washington's dedication to the cause allowed him to persevere. That was not the case for the average Patriot soldier.

The army, as a whole, held Congress in far greater contempt than Washington did in his worst moments. Initially, and in the rush to war, American Patriots joined the effort of their own accord. After all, the "shot heard round the world" came before Congress first met in May of 1775, and local Patriot militias led the early siege of Boston Harbor without the help of a Congress yet to convene. As the war continued, however, and men's souls were truly tried, both Washington and Congress understood that victory was simply not possible without a professional army.[134] That professional army, however, required resources of which Congress had precious little. Even so, "money and benefits, particularly cash bounties, not emotional appeals, became inducements to serve, and so Congress and the states, sometimes in competition, rushed to offer promises of pay, bounties, and land to those who would enlist or stay in service."[135]

Unfortunately, "congress and the states had saddled themselves with commitments they could not possibly honor and upon which they soon waffled."[136] Not surprisingly, as we saw previously, "broken promises ate away at morale."[137] Two examples provide a glimpse of the issue beyond simple desertions or the mutinies that "ranged from a few disaffected individuals to the rising of entire regiments."[138]

The first occurred in 1781. That year "began under circumstances very unfavorable to the American cause, for it opened with by far the most formidable mutiny that had yet appeared in the American army."[139] It actually occurred among men who "had done good service in suppressing the mutiny of Connecticut troops in the previous year. Their pay, however, was a whole year in arrears. They were left nearly naked and exceedingly destitute of provisions, and an ambiguity in the terms of their enlistments gave rise to a fierce dispute with their officers."[140] They were even offered "a complete amnesty and British protection," and a promise "to pay all the arrears due to them from Congress, without exacting any military service" by a British general—an offer they refused.[141]

> Some officers were killed or wounded in attempting to suppress the mutiny, and the non-commissioned officers and privates, numbering about 1,300 men, left the camp at Morristown with their firearms and with six field-pieces, and marched to Princetown, apparently with the intention of proceeding to Philadelphia. General Wayne, who commanded at Morristown, fearing lest they should plunder the inhabitants for subsistence, sent provisions after them. The mutineers kept together in a disciplined body, elected their own temporary officers, committed no depredations, and proclaimed their full loyalty to the American cause, and their readiness, if their grievances were redressed, to return to their old officers.... [And although the] mutiny was quelled with much less difficulty than had been feared, . . . a great part of the Pennsylvanian troops now disappeared from the American army, and a dangerous precedent was established of wrongs redressed by revolt.[142]

Sure enough, years later, even in the afterglow of winning the Revolution, that episode would nearly be repeated when eighty or more soldiers marched toward Philadelphia to protest lack of pay. "Congress asked state authorities to call out the militia to protect them," but the request was refused with the warning that the Pennsylvania state militia could not be relied on to protect Congress, and on "that note the congressmen fled to Princeton, New Jersey, putting the Delaware River between them and the soldiers."[143] It is unimaginable today to think of Congress being driven from the capital. To think that it happened in the wake of victory indicates the depth of the divide at the time. That divide would not simply go away, because the issue of pay and welfare of the soldiers could not simply go away. It would be a harbinger of future problems Washington would have to quell on the way to his *Unifying Moment*.

The American People and Congress

Relations between Congress and the American people suffered during the war as well. We must remember that Americans were fighting for freedom amidst severe economic hardships made worse by the war. To make matters even worse, "almost every freeman of military age soldiered in some capacity in the course of the war,"[144] and for many the "war had destroyed their homes and shops; they had been forced to billet soldiers and surrender their crops to feed the army," and "their paper money was worthless."[145] As a result, many Americans were complaining "that their own economic losses equaled or surpassed" the losses of the officers of Washington's army.[146] During difficult periods of the war, such as 1782 leading into 1783, "among the general population, Americans, sick of war, were directing their ire at an impecunious and feeble Congress."[147] Americans' view of Congress was that at best it was ineffectual,[148] if not disdainful.[149] Army Major John Armstrong, who was quite vocal in his day, "referred to Congress as full of 'fools and rascals.'"[150] "All of this was leading, according to some of the more optimistic intelligence reports, toward an increased desire on the part of disillusioned rebels to reconcile with the Crown."[151]

By 1781, and "after the new paper money plan proposed by Congress in March 1780 had failed, . . . Congress finally gave up paper money as a means of financing itself and began to struggle with the problem of getting an independent income."[152] "Congressional committees met, talked, reported, and then met to talk and report again. Scheme after scheme was proposed" and the result of those "discussions and of the desperation of Congress was the adoption of an amendment to the Confederation which was submitted to the states for ratification. That was known as the 'Impost of 1781.' In February, Congress asked to be allowed to levy a duty of five per cent on the value of all goods imported into the United States."[153] As you should be able to imagine by now, "Americans rose in protest,"[154] and "radicals who saw the impost as an invasion of states' rights, fought the measure tooth and nail, particularly in New England and most especially in Rhode Island."[155] "The opposition was more general & violent in Connecticut," according to Daniel Webster.[156] Webster reported that "inflammatory publications roused the people of many towns to call meetings, & discussion. . . . It was alleged that . . . [the impost] was unjust: that the officers of the army had not suffered more by the war than other citizens."[157] Webster feared civil war and anarchy in Connecticut over the proposed tax.[158]

Once again we see that significant government action, a tax, begot high partisanship (a *Partisan Catalyst Dynamic*)—and that disagreement would not end with war (a *Persistent Division Dynamic*). Instead, it would carry over into the war over the adoption of the Constitution, including Rhode Island's decision not to send a delegation to the Constitutional Convention and to be the last state to adopt the Constitution after a considerable delay.

Congress, the States, Political Differences, and the Articles of Confederation

Once independence was declared, thirteen separate nation-states were created overnight. No one had a firm idea of where American democracy was headed at that point—but this much was certain: there was a war to fight, individual state governments to construct, a national government to construct, and difficult economic and financial circumstances plaguing all.

As we briefly consider those issues, it is important to keep in mind that the best of the best did not rush to be congressmen. Instead, the best of the best began writing state constitutions and winning state offices, such as Jefferson and Madison, who returned to Virginia, and in the process, proving where people of the time considered the center of political power and activity to be (i.e., the states). After all, "much of the real power resided with the states,"[159] and to be governor of Virginia was to be far more powerful than president of a Continental Congress, which had no taxing authority and needed the approval of states to act.

By contrast, according to historian William M. Fowler, "for the most part Congress was a kaleidoscope. Members came and went with an alarming frequency. States often did not have enough members present to vote" (under the Articles of Confederation, which required two members to be present in order to vote).[160] The ineffectiveness of Congress during the war vexed Washington, who "was dismayed that the states now shipped off their mediocrities to Congress while more able men stayed home"[161] and, according to Washington were 'framing constitutions, providing laws, and filling [state] offices."

We have already seen that the "states neglected and ignored" congressional pleas for money.[162] Throughout the war, states reserved the right and most often did appoint officers for their own regiments.[163] Meanwhile, the states were slow to send additional soldiers when asked and didn't apprise Washington or Congress of their plans.[164] Much of that had to do with the financial problems states were having during the war. Some of that had to do with the fact that separate colonies were not altogether unified. Until just a "few years before the Revolution, no real sense of American nationality existed among the colonists."[165] Indeed, the "war exposed the fragility of the Union. Sectional divisions temporarily suppressed in Congress reemerged in the ranks of the military ... [and] mutual distrust and jealously lingered, surfacing at crucial moments in the war."[166] For instance, "Samuel Adams, who railed at New Jersey's 'shameful' performance in failing to adequately respond to Cornwallis' invasion, blamed the reconciliationists for the citizenry's poor showing. Dickinson and his allies, he charged, had 'poisoned the Minds of the People' with their incessant prattle about being reunited with Great Britain."[167]

In addition to those dynamics, there was the considerable distraction of the states needing to create their own governments. Keep in mind that it "was the first time in the world's history that a large group of communities had begun the formation of their own governments under written constitutions."[168] Obviously, such an undertaking would not be easy under any circumstances, let alone war, and at times it would be very contentious.

> The labor of writing the State constitutions in 1776–77 was one of forbidding magnitude. In the State that was the very keystone of the Union, Pennsylvania, the party animosities aroused during this task brought on a convulsion which threatened civil war. In another rich and powerful State, New York, the perplexities of constitutional theorizing gave birth to several institutional monstrosities that it required two generations of bitter experience to wipe out. In still other States, such as North Carolina, the glaring imperfections of the new government half disabled it during the Revolutionary struggle.[169]

In constructing their constitutions, the states did indeed become "a collection of independent republics,"[170] and would remain so even after the adoption of the Articles of Confederation. The drafting of the Articles began shortly after Independence was declared—yet it would be five years before they would be formally adopted by the thirteen states. "John Dickinson of Pennsylvania had drawn up a draft in July of 1776, a week after the Declaration of Independence," and "every inch" of it would receive scrutiny.[171] Indeed, the debate over the proposed new government proved "far more acrimonious than anyone had anticipated—so bitter, in fact, that on the eve of the British invasion of New York in August, Congress tabled the issue. Fearing that the attendant rancor and division would impair the war effort, it did not take up the proposed constitution again until the spring, by which time the military crisis of 1776 had passed. Even so, it did not send the document to the states for ratification until after the decisive American victory at Saratoga, when the populace brimmed with confidence that the war was as good as won."[172]

The American victory at Saratoga occurred in the fall of 1777. As it turned out, however, that victory did not mean that the war was "as good as won." The fortunes of the war would turn more than a few times before the Americans won. In the meantime, "only Virginia was prepared to sign the Articles right away,"[173] and did so in December of 1777. Over the next three and a half years, however, the remaining states would take their time to approve of the Articles. In doing so, claims to western lands proved critical. When New York and Virginia made concessions on that point, Maryland approved of the Articles in March of 1781. During all that time, although there was no document that bound the colonies, there was a Congress that acted like an approved government with respect to the conduct of the war and to the printing of money and with respect to foreign relations.

In its November 17, 1777, "Letter Transmitting Proposed Articles of Confederation" to the states, Congress acknowledged the disparate and divided nature of the country at the time:

> Permit us, then, earnestly to recommend these articles
> to the immediate and dispassionate attention of the

legislatures of the respective states. Let them be candidly reviewed under a sense of the difficulty of combining in one system the various sentiments and interests of a continent divided into so many sovereign and independent communities, under a conviction of the absolute necessity of uniting all our councils and all our strength, to maintain and defend our common liberties.

While the defense of common liberties was of great concern to many in Congress, the independent nature of the colonies defined the Articles. "The thirteen articles presented in 1777 declared a 'firm league of friendship' and a 'perpetual union.'"[174] Under the Articles, "congress had responsibility, but no authority."[175] Congress would not have the power to tax or regulate overseas trade,[176] and it took nine of the thirteen states for proposed legislation to pass, with two members of each state being present in order for a state to cast a vote. Often, however, two members weren't present, causing considerable delays. Almost from the outset, our Founding Fathers, including Washington and Madison, wanted a more centralized government than the Articles of Confederation provided.[177] The uneasy nature of the Confederation would cause Jefferson to write, "I know of no danger so dreadful and so probable as that of internal contests. And I know no remedy so likely to prevent it as the strengthening of the band which connects us."[178]

At the end of the war, Washington was more stark about our prospects. He said that the states were united "by a rope of sand."[179] That tenuous connection between the states under the Articles would not hold. In the next chapter we shall see how, in the aftermath of the war they won, and the Articles that bound them, Americans remained within a *Persistent Division Dynamic*. Their victory and new government were born of years of strife and division as much as fighting on the same side. They had fought and divided over English rule, over deciding to rebel, over how to rebel, over the cost of rebelling, and over what forms of government they should enact. Their divisions were not limited to politics but ran to economics and religion as well. In each case, partisanship ran high as the rights and nature of man were decided either with guns or explosive rhetoric fitting for such high stakes. There were colonists on both sides and some even risked the middle. As we go forward, we shall see those dynamics playing out again and again.

In chapter 3, "Our Constitutional Divide," named for the period that defines our divisions over adopting a constitution, we can complete our look at this period and our understanding of how the adoption of a new Constitution would cut new wounds of American division. Those wounds would heal for a time under *Washington's Unifying Moment*, but not before.

CHAPTER 3

Our Constitutional Divide

The whole country is alive with wrath.
—A report in *The Independent Gazetteer*

*I would rather be a free citizen of the small republic of
Massachusetts, than an oppressed
subject of the great American empire.*
—A Federalist

*Should the States reject this excellent Constitution,
the probability is . . . the next will be drawn in blood.*
—George Washington

The American Constitution is the most successful governing document in history. No other single document has served as the foundation for successful governing for so long, or for so many, with so few amendments. Its enormous success, however, does not mean that it was always celebrated or unifying. Quite to the contrary, the adoption of the Constitution, which occurred under difficult circumstances, produced intense rhetoric and partisanship, as evidenced by the quotes above— all for a simple reason: the proposed Constitution offered profound changes affecting the very foundation of the state and federal governments, their relationship to each other, and most importantly, their relationship to the blood-torn colonists who were now Americans.

Keep in mind that the Constitution was adopted just eight years after the struggle to ratify the Articles of Confederation. Americans faced two broad categories of issues in taking up the question, for the second time in less than a decade, of how to govern themselves and future generations. First, the decision had to be made as to whether the existing form of the national government was sufficient. Americans would answer that in the negative but it would take time for them to come to that conclusion—much like they took time to make the decision to break from England. That was the easy part—also like the decision to break from England as compared to the question of how to win the war. The second, and more difficult, broad question that had to be answered was what should be done about our insufficient government? That included the question of whether the Articles of Confederation should be amended or abandoned altogether for a new Constitution—and, if a new Constitution was in order, what should be our form of government and how should it be adopted? Those were no small issues to decide, especially for those who had recently fought a war over the right to be free and were ready to fight each other over their current differences.

By now, we should come to expect high partisanship when government becomes the favored forum to decide such high-stakes issues. Sure enough, there were many highly partisan moments fueled by highly partisan actors—some of whom may surprise you. How partisan were they? Well, for the first and only time in our history there would be a political fight between one party, the Federalists, and what would become known as their literal and diametric opposition, the Anti-Federalists. The political parties would exercise aggressive tactics and intense rhetoric not unlike those that were employed to inspire our Revolution. There were also those seeking compromise for compromise's sake and some who wanted no controversy at all. In the end, the Constitution would be adopted and the light at the end of the dark rhetorical tunnel would be Washington—who would bridge *Our Constitutional Divide*. Before we can cross that bridge, however, we must come to understand the depth of the momentous issues being faced and decided, by and through government, along with the resultant partisanship and division.

The Historical Setting of Our Constitutional Divide

As the 1780s unfolded, post-Revolutionary America was coming to grips with profound problems. Prior to the Revolution, Americans lived under stable government and superpower protections. That was no more. Instead, in the fog of war, Americans quickly designed state governments and a confederation they hoped would govern in keeping with their revolutionary ideals—all the while fighting their onetime masters amidst very difficult economic times and now unprotected borders.

You may ask, what experience did they have in such matters of making governments—let alone under those circumstances? According to Alexander Hamilton, Americans "began this revolution with a very vague and confined notion of the practical business of government."[180] Pulitzer Prize–winning historian David McCullough went a step further when he said our Founding Fathers were "winging it." We should not be surprised by such assessments. After all, as the Anti-Federalist writer Brutus said, "History furnishe[d] no example of a free republic, any thing like the extent of the United States" of the 1780s.[181]

The Americans were not only having to deal with the leftover problems from the war, but also dealt with incredibly difficult and divisive new problems, including oppressive private and public debt, a heavy tax burden, and states with runaway legislatures passing endless laws to deal with the difficult economic times. Historian Gordon S. Wood wrote that the Founding Fathers "were never in charge of events or circumstances. Everything was moving and changing much too fast."[182] Those problems and the dynamics alluded to in the quotes at the start of this chapter brought America to the edge of political divisions that could have led to warfare among the states. Under such pressure, the original designs of our national government turned out to be far from ideal.

★   ★   ★

On October 19, 1781, Lord Cornwallis surrendered at Yorktown, Virginia. The British Prime Minister Lord North resigned in disgrace early the next year because of the British defeat, and England began evacuating its troops from America. It would take a year, until November 30, 1782, to be precise, before England and the United States would sign preliminary Articles of Peace. It was still another year until the formal peace treaty, the Treaty of Paris, was signed on September 3, 1783. The triumph of victory, however, gave way to a harsh reality for Americans. Historian Woody Holton, in his compelling book *Unruly Americans and the Origins of the Constitution,* notes:

> Today the Revolutionary War is seen as clearing the way for the unprecedented prosperity that has made the United States the envy of much of the world. But for the Americans who fought the war, the decade that followed it was disastrous—as bad, according to some modern analysts, as the Great Depression of the 1930s.[183]

Some of the difficulties encountered during the Revolution carried over after the war, including loss of trade with England and a worthless currency. Also contributing to the difficult economic times was loss of the economic output Americans might have undertaken if they had not been fighting.[184] Added to that would be the destruction caused by the war, the economic impact of slaves who found their freedom either through fighting or "declaring their own independence," and continued conflict with Indians on the Western frontier.[185] There was also the problem of government debt.

The Continental Congress incurred comparatively huge debts to fight the Revolutionary War. Congress financed its share of the war expense in essentially three ways: (1) printing money, (2) getting loans, and (3) issuing debt certificates, or what we would consider government bonds today. America, under the Articles of Confederation, acted with less than full faith and credit in all three regards. As for the currency, the Continental was made worthless by issuing too much of it without any real backing. It literally went out of circulation by 1781 with "no attempt ever made [by Congress] to compensate its holders."[186] Thus, to a certain degree, Congress used Monopoly money to fund part of the war without ever having to back it. Congress also procured millions in loans to support the war effort. Two years after the Treaty of Paris was signed, however, Congress defaulted on the loan from France—its main creditor. In addition, Congress never paid interest on the loan from Spain.[187] As for the debt certificates, which were used much like money in that they were often exchanged for supplies, their value dramatically decreased over time because holders of the debt did not believe Congress would be able to make good on their repayment obligations.[188] As a result, Congress was able to finance the war through less-than-honorable means, and at the end of the war, its debt was said to have a face value of $27 million (a huge sum at that time)—although as originally issued, the value of the debt was several times higher than that.[189] At the end of the war, Congress and the United States had a new and farther-reaching problem, which played a significant role in the adoption of the Constitution: America was not considered creditworthy.

Part of the reason Congress defaulted on loans and couldn't back its fiscal obligations, although difficult for us to fathom now, was that under the Articles of Confederation, Congress could not directly tax the American people. Nor could it force the states to contribute tax monies. Instead, Congress could only issue "requisitions" for money, voluntary requests in practice, and hope that the states would comply. It was up to the individual state whether, and in what amount, to do so; and, as we have seen, the states were unresponsive, if not unable, to positively respond to Congress's many calls for money.

That was due to the economic conditions in the states and the fact that public debt was not confined to Congress. The individual states were burdened with incredibly large debts as well. By 1779, the thirteen states combined "had issued approximately $210 million in debt securities in order to finance their participation in the Revolutionary War. Much of this 'money' was in the hands of foreign states and foreign citizens. Additional debt was purchased at a substantial discount from the initial creditors by domestic speculators."[190]

In an attempt to retire state debts, the post–Revolutionary War states did what most governments are wont to do—tax, and tax, and tax. Indeed, amidst what we shall see were frequent elections, the states levied oppressive and many times inequitable taxes that were "wretchedly imperfect" and were "favorable to a number of opulent members in every legislature."[191] Returning to our reading of *Unruly Americans and the Origins of the Constitution*, we find that in order "to finance their war against British 'taxation without representation,' Americans had committed themselves to higher taxes than they had ever faced as British colonists. After the war, taxes in most states remained *three to four times higher* than colonial levels."[192]

Predictably, the high government debt and high levels of taxation led to a stagnant post–Revolutionary War economy. Compounding the economic troubles caused by the high debt levels and high tax levels, along with depreciated currencies and lost output, England renewed its imposition of a trade embargo on the United States, which vastly reduced American trade. All of that led to the post-war depression.

★　　★　　★

Politics in the post-war period were just as challenging for the Americans as their economic hardships. Prior to the Revolutionary War, each of the colonies had its own government. Seven had governors appointed by King George without constitutions, three were proprietary provinces run by famous families, two had charters and controlled their own executive branches, and the remaining colony, Massachusetts, had a charter and a Crown-controlled executive. After 1776, that experience translated into colonial governments that did not so much start from scratch but, instead, evolved from their colonial past into state governments. That evolution would not be easy, however. The Patriots' inexperience, born amidst the "vague" notions that Hamilton referenced, resulted in a rather arduous and sometimes testy constitutional process. What emerged from that process were thirteen sovereign states with constitutions of varying sorts—all of which relied on *frequent* popular elections. Eleven of the thirteen new states had an upper house. In six of those states, the members of that upper house were elected *annually*, as were eleven of the thirteen assemblies.[193]

Those newly formed states, with their frequently campaigning, elected politicians would produce a cavalcade of laws just after their formation, and into the 1780s, in response to their economic difficulties and their clamoring constituents. A great deal of those laws dealt with the plight of American farmers. In many states, farmers were usually the most heavily burdened with debt and high taxes, yet were without the currency to pay them. They relentlessly petitioned their legislatures seeking relief through "reforms that would ease the payment of debts, reduce taxes, publicize the expenditure of state funds, and pare down the powers of the court of common pleas." American farmers also made such other demands as "tender laws," which allowed the payment of debts through bartering, and/or allowed the issuance of paper money to alleviate the effects of the shortage of gold.[194] In response, "during the half-decade that preceded the adoption of the Constitution, every state legislature granted at least some tax and debt relief."[195] But that was not all they did. Caught between proponents who said they were not doing enough (usually those concerned about debtors) and those that

said they were doing too much (usually those concerned about creditors), the state legislatures took up and passed laws on countless issues.
Some states issued their own paper currency, which was widely seen as
helping debtors who had no gold to pay taxes and for whom depreciated
money would make it easier to pay their debts. States also fought over
and passed laws over larger issues, including the frequency of elections,
amending their constitutions, the size of legislative districts, the location
of capitals, and who had a right to vote.

Within a decade, however, those actions of the frequently campaigning and elected officers—perhaps as a glaring byproduct of their
inexperience—would cause great concern among the likes of Hamilton,
Madison, and many others. James Madison raised his concerns in a letter to Thomas Jefferson and referred to the "mutability" and "injustice"
of "the laws of the states." Along with the "encroachments of the States
on the general authority, sacrifices of national to local interests, [and
the] interferences of the measures of different States,"[196] "Alexander
Hamilton . . . affirmed that many Americans—not just himself—were
'growing tired of an excess of democracy.' Others identified the problem as 'a headstrong democracy,' a 'prevailing rage of excess democracy,' a republican frenzy, 'democractical tyranny,' and 'democratic
licentiousness.'"[197]

Beyond that excess of democracy over issues going on within the
states, which would become the focus of many of the Founders, there
was also the problem of states feuding. As we know, "under the Articles
of Confederation, Congress was little more than a loose-knit council
in which each state retained so much 'sovereignty, freedom . . . power,
jurisdiction and right.'"[198] Those autonomous states were exercising
their newfound power. In the process, we find that

> most of the states were feuding over boundaries and
> territorial claims and seldom agreed on anything. Eight
> states had armies. Pennsylvania's militia had actually

fired at settlers from Connecticut in northeastern Pennsylvania. Connecticut sent Ethan Allen's Green Mountain Boys to defend the settlers, and [Daniel] Webster's friend Oliver Wolcott drew up a constitution that declared the area independent and created a new state called Westmorland.[199]

Harlow Giles Unger, in his book *Noah Webster: The Life and Times of an American Patriot*, tells us that "the result was near anarchy. Each state printed its own currency, imposed duties or embargoes on goods from other states, and tried to control immigration from neighboring states."[200] Connecticut, for example, "had resorted to the creative measure of voting a 5 percent impost on all goods imported from abroad—or from Rhode Island."[201] So fractious was the period that Alexander Hamilton believed that there was a distinct risk of civil war among the states during this time.[202]

★   ★   ★

The bad economic times and the dynamic of overactive adolescent governments made for a tinderbox. Much like the Stamp Act was a catalyst for *Our Revolutionary Thoughts*, one event would prove to sharpen the focus of the time and lead to political change; that event was Shays' Rebellion. Colonial farmers suffered among the worst after the Revolution. They were saddled with debt and faced lawsuits at the hands of their creditors. According to David P. Szatmary, in his book *Shays' Rebellion: The Making of an Agrarian Insurrection*,

> Before turning to clubs and muskets, New England farmers pleaded peacefully for relief. Between 1784 and 1787, yeomen in seventy-three rural Massachusetts towns—more than 30 percent of all communities in the

state—sent petitions to the General Court in Boston seeking relief.[203]

For many, the scope of relief provided by the legislatures of New England was not enough and so they changed tactics: "When their representatives rejected their remedies . . . the people retaliated by striking at the instruments of government near at hand—the courts."[204] The courts were the object of such frustration because of the many, many debt collection lawsuits prosecuted against farmers and their fellow debtors by the creditor class—a class of people farmers and others believed had the favor of the legislature. The farmers retaliated by literally taking up arms and taking over courthouses. For instance, "a mob of about 1,500 [a simply huge number in those days] gathered in Northampton [Mass.] and took possession of the courthouse in order to prevent the sitting of the county courts. . . . The insurgents wanted no court business transacted until the people's grievances had been redressed,"[205] which produced enough results to encourage much more of the same throughout New England. In fact, for three months in the fall of 1786, the courts were completely shut down in five Massachusetts counties.[206]

Imagine, if you will, armed mobs of such relative size effectively controlling the courts of today in your county. At the start of 1777, Massachusetts more than took notice and endeavored to raise an army to combat the increasing size and effectiveness of the mobs. One of the leaders of the rebellion, considered by some to be *the* leader, was Daniel Shays. "He had served over five years in the Revolution, attaining the rank of captain before he was mustered out in 1780."[207] For Shays and his followers, however, the governments formed in the wake of revolution were not acceptable—not because of an excess of democracy, but because they were doing too little! According to Shays and others, the governments had refused the pleas of too many debtors and in effect were doing the bidding of a privileged few.

At the height of discontent, in January of 1787, Shays and his mob marched upon an armory in search of supplies for his men and his cause.

> In the late afternoon of January 25, Shays' men drew up a few hundred yards from the arsenal. General Shepard sent twice to inquire about their intentions and to warn them that he was prepared to fire upon them to defend the arsenal. According to Shepard's account, Shays demanded barracks and stores. When Shays' forces drew even nearer, Shepard ordered two rounds sent over the heads of the advancing wave. When this did not deter them, a third shot fired into their center killed three men outright and fatally wounded a fourth.[208]

If we keep in mind that the Boston Massacre, which involved five deaths and the trial of nine British troops, helped touch off the American Revolution just seven years before, we can gather a sense of the impact not just of that day, which was actually strategically minimal, but of the ongoing process and buildup of frustration, dissent, and armed action. As for Shays' forces, they scattered in response, which proved to be a terrible loss for the morale of Shays and his followers. A court soon declared Shays' efforts to be part of a "horrid and unnatural Rebellion and War ... levied against this Commonwealth." The overall rebellion soon would be put down and the incidences of armed mobs would dwindle away. The effect of the rebellion, however, had far-reaching implications well beyond an armory.

The rebellion caught the eye of Thomas Jefferson, then serving as the ambassador to France. It was in response to that rebellion that Jefferson declared, in all seriousness, that "A little rebellion now and then is a good thing. ... It is a medicine necessary for the sound health of government. ... God forbid we should ever be twenty years without such a rebellion." Other leaders were not nearly as sympathetic, let alone supportive.

Abigail Adams, wife of John Adams, chastised the mobs as "ignorant, restless desperados, without conscience or principles." As for Jefferson's comments, she chastised him as well by writing that "instead of that laudable spirit which you approve, which makes a people watchful over their liberties and alert in the defense of them, these mobbish insurgents are for sapping the foundation, and destroying the whole fabric at once." She was not alone in that view. Alexander Hamilton was alarmed by Shays' Rebellion and joined James Madison and others in the call for a stronger government to combat such insurrections from occurring in the future—and no less than George Washington was summoned out of "retirement" to attend a convention with the argument that a stronger government was necessary.[209] In other words, an *Escalating Partisanship Dynamic*, action and reaction, was well underway.

★   ★   ★

The economic and political problems of the 1780s were serious matters. As the 1780s wore on, in fits and starts, the desire arose to take another look at this American form of *Liberty* that had been won. Serious people raised essentially two questions: First, what could be done about the weak nature of the Confederation to address the pressing issues of government debt and foreign affairs? Second, the question was being raised as to whether the loosely tied states were preserving our liberty or endangering that liberty. Those were two very distinct issues raised by diverse problems. Keep in mind that prior to the Revolution, in the push for independence, the colonists' ire was focused mostly in one direction—at England and those loyal to it. England was the source of the laws and military action, and therefore, it was England that had to be opposed. After the Revolution, however, there were thirteen different state governments, which attracted the frustration of Americans.

Although Congress defaulted on debts, including to veterans, it was not the main focus of discontent, because Congress had very little authority and, as we have seen, little law-making ability. The newly freed colonists did not look primarily to Congress for redress—they looked to the states. As such, the instability affecting American government at the time was not very centralized.

Of course, the design of the Articles of Confederation was to deliberately create a decentralized national and state government system. After rebelling against a central authority, it could hardly be expected that Americans would opt for a single, centralized government. Decentralized authority, however, is inefficient. In the wake of the Declaration of Independence, although decentralization was intellectually preferred, it presented a problem, as we have seen, in fighting the war and dealing with national debt. Beyond that, as Will Durant wrote, "it was of no use to talk of 'states' rights' when the economy was ignoring state boundaries."[210] As a result, almost from the outset, there were those who wanted to strengthen the Confederation and to support a national economy; that meant giving more power to Congress. They included Alexander Hamilton, who wanted that as early as 1780.[211]

Two efforts were made to grant Congress increased taxing authority by amending the Articles. "In 1781 and again in 1783, Congress asked the states to let Congress collect duties on imports (an "impost") so it could at least pay its debts."[212] "To Robert Morris, the superintendent of finance, the amendment proposal was only a first step toward more extensive federal taxation, which would include a land tax, a poll tax, and an excise on spirits."[213] Amendments to the Articles of Confederation, however, "required the unanimous ratifications by the state legislatures and Rhode Island refused to ratify the first impost amendment,"[214] claiming that "the tax would weigh hardest on the commercial states, that the tax collectors would be employees of the federal government unaccountable to Rhode Island, and that the tax itself would represent a 'danger to public liberty' from the power of the federal government."[215]

Later Virginia would rescind its approval[216] and the proposed Amendment of 1781 was dead. Congress offered a different impost Amendment in 1783 to the states.

> The Impost of 1783, regarded by leading nationalists as completely inadequate, proposed that Congress be granted the right to levy a 5 percent *ad valorem* duty on all imports, in addition to specified duties on certain articles. To make the amendment less objectionable to state rightists, the proposal limited the grant to a twenty-five-year period. In addition to the impost, the states were asked to contribute $1.5 million annually to the continental treasury, also for a twenty-five-year period. This time both Rhode Island and Virginia ratified, but New York did not. Its refusal to do so is hardly surprising, considering that duties on imports through New York City provided the state government with its major income. By the spring of 1787, the Impost of 1783 was to all effects dead.[217]

That amendment process and its failure, along with Shays' Rebellion, played key roles in convincing our Founders that change was necessary. The difficulty of governing ourselves, excessive public debt, fighting between states, legislative acts that undermined the rights of private property, fights over boundaries, and problems with currency—each of them highlighted, in a different way and from a different source, the instability and inadequacies of our governing systems. Those times really did try men's souls, and, as a result, our nation's leaders would push for change—but there would be a fight.

★   ★   ★

In 1785, "Washington described the Confederation as 'little more than an empty sound, and Congress a nugatory body.'"[218] According to Washington, "If you tell the Legislatures they have violated the treaty of peace and invaded the prerogatives of the confederacy they will laugh in your face. . . . I am told that very respectable characters speak of a monarchial form of government without horror."[219] Sure enough, Americans were openly questioning whether life after the Revolution was better than life under the British Crown, and "according to a . . . report, Nathaniel Gorham, the president of the Continental Congress, even sounded out Prince Henry of Russia on becoming King of America."[220] As for the practical matter of improving government, we know that Hamilton pushed for more centralized authority as early as 1780. Similarly, Noah Webster, in 1785, called for a government that would feature "a supreme head, clothed with the same power to make and enforce laws" as the states."[221] Washington exchanged correspondence with numerous leaders including James Madison, John Jay, Henry Knox, and others about the problems of government and potential changes.[222] Eventually, there would be a "convention" of sorts in Annapolis, Maryland, which was called for the purposes of discussing trade between states. In the end, Hamilton, purportedly at Washington's urging who wrote of a "general convention . . . for the purpose of revising and correcting the defects of the federal government," pushed through a resolution calling for another convention to do just that, i.e. to "render the Constitution of the federal government adequate to the exigencies of the union."[223]

That convention began in May of 1787. By September of 1787, they had completed their work. The convention that was called by Congress "for the sole and express purpose of revising"[224] the Articles of Confederation, instead offered a complete replacement of the Articles. There would be winners and losers if the content of the new Constitution was to be adopted. For instance, the nation's creditors, and there were many, would breathe a sigh of relief if the Constitution was adopted, because of the inclusion of the "contract clause"—one of the main provisions insisted upon by the Founders to bring stability to the nation's commerce by presumably halting the states' disregard of private contracts. Equally, if not more dramatically, the relationship between the states and the federal government would change because the reach and the authority of the federal government would change. In other words, the Founders were suggesting another wide-ranging change in the rights of Americans. Naturally, what followed was a remarkably spirited and partisan debate over whether the convention had a right to dispose of the Articles and even to write a new constitution, and whether and how a new constitution should and could be adopted. Disagreement and partisanship were rampant. *History* would expect no less.

The Heights of Our Constitutional Divide

We have already seen some of the rhetoric of the 1780s. The width of our divisions, at that time, was considerable. Some of it was reflected in the high level of partisanship rhetoric. It was much more than that, however. It also included hardball political tactics. For now, as you read some of this rhetoric, imagine the commentary in the mouths of a modern-day politician—but not just any politician. Imagine it being said by our most prominent leaders and ask yourself how they would be received in the modern media and among everyday Americans.

About the state of affairs under the Articles of Confederation, George Washington wrote that the "General Government [was] now suspended by a Thread, I might go further, and say it is really at an End."[225] Washington wrote that American affairs "were drawing rapidly to a crisis,"[226] and likened the Confederacy to a "house on fire" that would be "reduced to ashes."[227] Benjamin Rush "even thought that the American people were on the verge of 'degenerating into savages or devouring each other like beasts of prey.'"[228] Madison, exasperated after attempting to cure the ills of the Articles, believed America was "notoriously feeble" under the Articles of Confederation,[229] and John Jay, the future first

Supreme Court Chief Justice, wanted to completely change our federal government.[230] Henry Knox thought amendments to the Articles would be "a step backward 'assisting us to creep on in our miserable condition.'"[231] The delegates of the Annapolis Convention approved a report saying that the seriousness of the defects in the Articles "had reduced the United States to a situation 'delicate and critical,'"[232] and Edmund Randolph, the new governor of the largest state, Virginia, believed "that every day dawns with perils to the United States," while Patrick Henry all but walked away from politics in disgust at that time.[233]

Perhaps summarizing it all for those of that view, Noah Webster "warned that the Articles of Confederation had left the American states in disunion, on the verge of anarchy, with each at liberty to fight its neighbor."[234] Webster declared,

> [There is] no sovereign to call forth the power of the continent to quell the dispute or punish the aggressor. . . . Either the several states must continue separate, totally independent of each other, and liable to all the evils of jealous dispute and civil dissension—nay, liable to a civil war upon any clashing of interest, or they must constitute a general head, composed of representatives from all the states, and vest with the power of the whole continent to enforce their decisions. There is no alternative.[235]

Of course, there were alternative views about the state of the Union. James Monroe worked to have the Articles of Confederation amended on a number of fronts, including giving "Congress powers over interstate trade, foreign commerce, and foreign affairs."[236] That was in part because Monroe knew that "southern and northern states were deeply divided and civil war over the status of the western frontier seemed a distinct possibility."[237] For his part, Thomas Jefferson, in his communication with Washington, "dismissed as 'light' the 'inconveniences' of the

Articles of Confederation."[238] Even more dismissive were the likes of historians such as Charles Beard, who later wrote that the crisis was "conjured up" by the Federalists.[239] Who was right is not so much the point as for the reader to realize the nature of the times. They moved even George Washington, *the* colossus astride the American political stage, to rhetoric that was anything but restrained or moderate. The rhetoric of some of the other Founders, some of which I have referenced, falls into the same category. Others were more restrained, and, as we saw with the lead-up to the Revolution, there was a broad range of views from what many would characterize as moderate to extreme.

A good deal of the reason our Founders were so glum had to do with this issue of the excess of democracy, and their rhetoric on the subject reflected their high tension.

> The abuses of the state legislatures, said Madison, were "so frequent and so flagrant as to alarm the most steadfast friends of Republicanism," and these abuses, he told Jefferson in the fall of 1787, "contributed more to that uneasiness which produced the Convention, and prepared the public mind for a general reform, than those which accrued to our national character and interest from the inadequacy of the Confederation to its immediate objects."[240]

Writes Holton:

> Noting how frequently control of the Pennsylvania legislature passed from one party to the other, one writer warned that "annual elections, the choicest gem in the cap of liberty, are subject to very imminent danger of becoming a Pandora's box, replete with evils perhaps as pernicious as those annexed to despotism."[241]

Meanwhile, George Richards Minot, "a Harvard-educated lawyer and well-connected member of the Massachusetts political establishment," lamented that "the poor patriots who had fought the war 'could not realize that they had shed their blood in the field, to be worn out by burdensome taxes at home; or that they had contended, to secure to their creditors, a right to drag them into courts and prisons.'"[242] On the other end of the spectrum, in New Jersey, at least one state legislator was told it was his "business to help the feeble against the mighty, and deliver the oppressed out of the hands of the oppress[or]."[243] Meanwhile, in a sentiment of the time and preview of fights to come, a New Hampshire paper raised the invective by printing: "Honesty is not engrossed by the fortunate, neither is wealth the test of wisdom; else whence those lucky rogues, those wealthy fools, who roll in chariots?"[244]

In the wake of Shays' Rebellion, we saw how Jefferson casually declared that "a little rebellion now and then is a good thing." Abigail Adams ripped Jefferson and the "mobbish insurgents" and their acts that Jefferson took so lightly. Samuel Adams, for his part, was far less charitable. After John Hancock, then governor of Massachusetts, obtained "full pardons from the General Court for all participants in Shays' Rebellion, and . . . put through legislation that prevented creditors from seizing clothing, household goods, or tools of trade as security for debt," he "incurred the inevitable wrath of Sam Adams,"[245] whose efforts Hancock had financed in the past. According to Harlow Giles Unger, "Once the farmers' champion, Adams now demanded nothing less than death for the leaders of Shays' Rebellion—much as Parliament had demanded his death for participating in the Boston Tea Party."[246] In doing so, Adams fulfilled the historical maxim that yesterday's radical not infrequently becomes today's conservative.

Beyond Adams, other "radical Whigs echoed his call for retribution. Even twenty-year old John Quincy Adams, already mesmerized by his older cousin Samuel, railed against Hancock for allowing men to 'commit treason and murder with impunity.'"[247] The statement from John

Quincy Adams tells us quite a bit. There you have a future president and a member of a prominent family that included the future second president, John Adams, and, of course, Sam Adams. In a sign of the times, John Quincy Adams felt no apparent restraint in taking on, in strident terms, a sitting governor of perhaps the second most important state in the Confederacy at the time.

Perhaps the real reason Adams felt such freedom was that, in context, his statement was not all that strident. After all, his comments had followed an armed rebellion that was part of "the wave of revolts that swept over the new nation in the 1780s."[248] The taking up of arms is the ultimate partisan action and Americans had proven that they were not shy about such actions during the Revolution and even in victory and supposed peace.

It must be said that *History* remembers some of these men as our first presidents and our Founders. They are celebrated men and deservedly so. Yet, even they were driven to extremes at times. They became caught up in the *Escalating Partisanship Dynamic*—not because they were extreme by nature, but because they and others were drawn to a fight over the rights of man taking place in the public forum of government. By now we should accept that without government action initiating the fight, such partisanship would not occur. The cause is the use of government power: the mother of *Partisan Catalyst Dynamics*. The result often includes partisanship—intense though it may appear.

If the post-war troubles of the Confederacy prompted partisanship, the calling of the Constitutional Convention and the completion of its work certainly would not end it. If you recall, Chief Justice John Marshall told us, "At length, two great parties were formed in every state, which were distinctly marked, and which pursued distinct objects, with systematic arrangement."[249] That political divide, with fighting over the rights of creditors and debtors, would take on amplified and national dimensions once the Constitutional Convention produced our Constitution, instead of amendments to the Articles of Confederation. Some partisans were incensed that the Convention had exceeded the mission Congress assigned to it. Other partisans were aghast at the powerful, centralized government that the Founders recommended. During the nine-month public debate over the Constitution, between September of 1787 and June of 1789, in a very public fashion, *Our Constitutional Divide* would reach its rhetorical heights.

As we consider *Our Constitutional Divide*, let us note that coming out of the Convention would be a circumstance that had never occurred in American politics and has not since. There would be a party and an antiparty—Federalists and Anti-Federalists. The undeniably high political stakes of the time produced such opposing views that the partisans would be known by opposite names. It is hard, other than taking up arms like we did in the Civil War, to get much more partisan than that. *History* knows few examples of such diametric parties—although it includes our own example and that of Florence, Italy, in the early 1300s, where the Black Guelphs, supporters of the papacy, were the political opposites of the White Guelphs, who were against papal influence.

A Remote Chance It Would Do Some Good

Amidst that economic and political turmoil, the Founders produced a Constitution. Congress had only asked them to revise the Articles of Confederation. Instead, they endeavored to redefine the American experiment with *Liberty*. They started in May of 1787, and finished in September of that year. Between May and September, the Convention was witness to a Virginia Plan, a New Jersey Plan, Charles Pinckney's plan, and even a British Plan proposed by Alexander Hamilton. Representative power was debated along with executive power, suffrage and slavery, the selection of senators, the appointment of judges, and much more. There was a preamble and seven Articles but no Bill of Rights. Remarkably, what is now considered a triumph seemed to bring little satisfaction to the Convention participants who supported the Constitution.

In what was hardly a ringing endorsement, Washington, the first to sign the new Constitution, famously wrote: "I wish the constitution . . . had been more perfect, but I sincerely believe it is the best that could be obtained at this time; . . . the adoption of it . . . is in my opinion *desirable*."[250] Gouverneur Morris, close friend of Washington, who physically wrote much of the Constitution,[251] "had objections but would support the Constitution 'with all its faults' as 'the best that was to be attained.'"[252] Benjamin Franklin "consented to the Constitution 'with all its faults, if they are such.'"[253]

It was the work of "mutual deference and concession" according to the Convention delegates.[254] For James Madison, the overall goal was to establish "a firm *national Government*."[255] That was necessary because "it was generally agreed that the *objects of the Union* [sustainable liberty] could not be secured by any system founded on the principle of a confederation of sovereign States."[256] That work of deference and concession was a "material" improvement, but Madison "felt the new government was going to be too weak" and "had not corrected the problem that bothered him most: 'sacrifices of national to local interests.'"[257] Alexander Hamilton also thought the Constitution was too weak, desiring instead "a central government that appointed the states' chief executives [i.e., governors] as well as officers of the state militias."[258] Hamilton, however, said he would sign the Constitution despite his misgivings "because the alternatives were 'anarchy and Convulsion on the one side,' and, on the other, a remote chance that Constitution would do some good."[259]

Those modest reactions, from those who would become the chief proponents of the Constitution during the ratification debate, were rather dull compared to the initial comments of those who opposed it. Three important Constitutional Convention delegates famously refused to sign the Constitution. Their judgment was stark. Virginia's George Mason, the onetime member of the Virginia House of Burgesses and from whom Washington sought counsel on public and private matters,[260] declared that "I would sooner chop off my right hand than put it to the Constitution as it now stands."[261] Virginia's Governor Edmund Randolph—also of the largest state—deemed it a "foetus of monarchy." Finally, a governor of another large state, this time New York, focused his ire on the issue of the failure to follow Congress's mandate to revise the Articles. Clinton "called the proposed constitution an illegal usurpation of power."[262] In other words, right out of the gate, the governors of two out of the three most important states in the Confederacy, New York and Virginia, came out verbally and *stridently* firing at the Constitution.

Keep in mind that previously New York played a key role in dooming the Articles of Confederation by refusing to approve of an amendment to the Articles. Now, Governor Clinton "seemed prepared to secede rather than allow his state to ratify the Constitution and cede his sovereignty to a national government."[263] Not to be outdone, Patrick Henry, who turned down being a Convention delegate, accused "the authors of the Constitution of having usurped powers and staged a coup d'état by violating the mandate of Congress."[264]

> In fact, Henry had so many objections that he had neither the time nor the patience to enumerate them. . . . Henry's objections, however, were legion. Predicting tyranny as inevitable, he railed at the failure of the Constitution to limit national government powers. "Congress," he predicted, "will have an unlimited, unbounded command over the soul of this commonwealth," with powers to pass any laws it deemed "necessary and proper," as stated in Article 1, Section 8. The president would have free rein to exercise whatever he defined as "executive power."[265]

James Monroe thought such views to be born of "antifederal prejudices"[266] and there would be plenty with that view. We well know that Madison, Hamilton, and others made use of the press—often anonymously—to make their case for the Constitution. Their work would become known as *The Federalist Papers*. The opponents of the Constitution did the same in what became a very vibrant, public, and partisan debate over the meaning of liberty—a debate reprinted by scores of newspapers throughout the states and which made spectacular *Our Constitutional Divide*.

Among the more strident detractors was Samuel Bryan, son of a Pennsylvania Supreme Court justice, who wrote under the pseudonym "Centinel." On January 23, 1788, he made the case that the Founders, far from saving liberty, were committing treason. Centinel argued his point in the *Independent Gazetteer*, published in Philadelphia—the very home of the Constitutional Convention—as follows:

> Fellow-Citizens, Conscious guilt has taken the alarm, thrown out the signal of distress, and even appealed to the generosity of patriotism. The authors and abettors of the new constitution shudder at the term *conspirators* being applied to them, as it designates their true character, and seems prophetic of the catastrophe: they read their fate in the epithet.
>
> In dispair [sic] they are weakly endeavoring to screen their *criminality* by interposing the shield of the virtues of a Washington, in representing his concurrence in the proposed system of government, as evidence of the purity of their intentions; but this impotent attempt to degrade the brightest ornament of his country to a base level with themselves, will be considered as an aggravation of their *treason*.

Understand that he was speaking of Washington, Madison, Hamilton, and Franklin among others! Again, imagine such rhetoric being used today at such a high level. Centinel was far from being alone in his use of high-pitched rhetoric against the Founding Fathers of the Constitution. "An Officer of the Late Continental Army" offered this advice:

> Consider well before you take an awful step which may involve in its consequences the *ruin of millions yet unborn*. You are on the brink of a dreadful precipice; in the name therefore of holy liberty, for which I have fought and for which we have all suffered, I call upon you to make a solemn pause before you proceed. *One step more, and perhaps the scene of freedom is closed forever in America*. Let not a set of *aspiring despots, who make us* SLAVES and *tell us tis our* CHARTER, wrest from you those invaluable blessings, for which the most illustrious sons of America have bled and died; but exert yourselves, like men, like freemen and like Americans, to transmit unimpaired to your latest posterity those rights, those *liberties*, which have ever been so dear to you, and which it is yet in your power to preserve.[267]

The *Independent Gazetteer* would offer on February 27, 1788, that "time and investigation . . . will prove that there has been a *deep laid scheme to enslave us*." According to Richard Henry Lee, in a letter to George Mason dated October 1, 1787, "As it is, I think 'tis past doubt, that if it should be established, either a *tyranny* will result from it, or it will be prevented by a *civil war*." It was made far and wide. According to Cato, in his third article published in the *New York Journal*, October 25, 1787, "Its principles, and the exercise of them will be *dangerous to your liberty and happiness*."[268] *Americanus VI*, written by John Stevens, Jr. and published in *Daily Advertiser*, New York, January 12, 1788, argued that "this consolidated Government will be an *iron handed despotism*." In his first article, Centinel argued that "it [was] the most daring attempt to establish *a despotic aristocracy* among freemen, that the world has ever witnessed."[269] David Redick, in a letter to William Irvine, which was published on September 24, 1787, perhaps summed up the opposition sentiment by stating that "the day on which we adopt the present proposed plan of government, from that moment we may justly date the loss of *American Liberty*."[270]

★   ★   ★

The once modest proponents of the Constitution, the Founding Fathers, did not just sit back in the face of such attacks. Knee deep in a clear *Escalating Partisanship Dynamic*, they reacted. Though they were understated in their support of the Constitution coming out of the Convention, they swiftly rallied their spirits to fight hard for its ratification—so much so that they were not above using extralegal ways to get their way.

We need to remember that prior to the Constitutional Convention, politics within the separate states had broken down into basically a two-party system. During the 1780s and before, the political participants honed their political skills inside and outside the halls of government fighting over the issues we have discussed. They also had taken the brave step of breaking from England and then fighting a war. So by the time it came to a ratification fight, they were not only experienced political operatives—they had political courage. Beyond that, they were not shy or necessarily scrupulous with the political tactics they used to get their way.

Indeed, our Founders were the first to use questionable political practices to achieve their goals of a stronger, more centralized government. Do not forget that the Articles of Confederation had been adopted by the thirteen states. The Articles had very specific provisions for the amendment of the Articles. Rather than follow the will of the people as reflected through the sovereign states, the Founders that are so celebrated today chose to *blatantly ignore the existing rule of law*. They proposed a complete replacement of the Articles that required only nine states to enact instead of the thirteen required to amend the Articles. That was the first of many strategic, and questionable, tactics they would employ to get their way. The name they chose, Federalists, was another. "Federalism," of course, is the belief that government should be decentralized; the locus of power, on balance, should reside with the states. In what amounted to a deft marketing move, "the nationalists, after doing their best to destroy federalism in the Convention, cleverly assumed the name Federalists and called their opponents Antifederalists."[271] The so-called Anti-Federalists were anything but against a state-centric system of government. Consider again the quote I cited at the outset of this chapter: "I would rather be a free citizen of the small republic of Massachusetts, than an oppressed subject of the great American empire." That statement was made by a pamphleteer who called himself "A Federalist." His sentiment was a true "federalist" sentiment. He wanted power to reside with the individual states, not a large central government. He and others like him, however, were rhetorically outflanked by the proponents of the Constitution, who, at the very outset, falsely advertised their views.

As for the tactics used to obtain actual ratification votes from the states, Benjamin Franklin, of all people, ignored all principles of self-government by leading the delegation out of the Constitutional Convention and marching into the Pennsylvania Assembly hall in the same building. Interrupting the Assembly's proceeding, he all but promised that Philadelphia would be the new federal capital if Pennsylvania was first to ratify the Constitution. He urged state legislators to call a state ratification convention immediately, *without debate*.[272]

It is worthy to note that "Franklin stood to reap enormous profits if the new government established the capital in Philadelphia."[273] How much that played a role, we may never know, but what followed his pronouncement was a remarkable story of hardball political tactics perhaps unrivaled since in American government. In response to Franklin's maneuver,

> angry backcountry Antifederalists ... refused to appear in the Assembly and left it two members short of a quorum. Speaker Thomas Mifflin, the wealthy Philadelphia merchant, ordered a sergeant of arms and a clerk to find at least two absent members and order them to the hall. A mob of Federalists followed the two to the boarding house where many Antifederalists lodged and *physically dragged two assemblymen back to their seats* in the State House, where, despite their shouts of protests, *sentries physically restrained them* while Federalists voted to hold the ratification convention on November 20.[274]

Imagine such a scene today, if you can. At the time Franklin and his fellow Federalists made their move, Robert Whitehill, "the representative from inland Cumberland County," "estimate[d] [that] not one Pennsylvanian out of twenty knew anything about the Constitution."[275] Whitehill was one of the representatives that was aware of Franklin's proceeding, but stayed away.[276] According to Pauline Maier, in her essential read on the subject, *Ratification*, the technique of "postponing a vote by not showing up—had been used in the past by both sides in Pennsylvania politics."[277] The Federalist strategy of moving quickly was part of what Maier calls "The Big Rush." The Federalists were more organized than their opponents in the beginning and sought to press their political advantage.[278] Indeed, "Pennsylvania ratified because of the superior organization of friends of the Constitution, large numbers of whom, holders of continental debt, looked to the new government for its redemption at par value."[279]

Those hardball tactics were not confined to Pennsylvania politics.

Rhode Island, which refused even to send delegates to the Constitutional Convention, and which refused to agree to an amendment to the Articles of Confederation, when "confronted with an actual threat of a commercial boycott by the new Congress, reluctantly followed" the other states and adopted the Constitution.[280]

In addition to the Big Rush and the use of power politics, the proponents of the Constitution took an all-or-nothing approach. During the Constitutional Convention, the subjects of free speech, freedom of the press, and religion were debated. However, protections for those issues did not make it into the Constitution. The simple argument that was made during the Convention, and after, was that additional protections were not needed because this new national government was not being given any power to affect those issues. Therefore, the argument went, there was no need to state the obvious (i.e., to state more than that Congress could "make no law" concerning those issues). How very differently many feel today about that argument or the need for more definitive language actually prohibiting Congress from making laws on those subjects.

Once the ratification process was underway, many didn't buy that facile explanation. Numerous state politicians wanted to amend this Constitution, which was suddenly thrust upon them, to include such protections and more. The Founders, however, knew that enlarging the debate over ratification to include possible amendments would result, at the very least, in endless debate and likely no ratification at all. As such, the Founders initially took the position that "they must adopt *in toto* or refuse altogether for it must be a plan . . . formed by the United States, which can be agreeable to all, and not one formed upon the narrow policy and convenience of one particular state."[281] That tactic, and notion that states couldn't offer amendments to the proposed Constitution, became the subject of many heated debates throughout the states.

As resistance mounted to both, and the prospects for ratification appeared to wane, "in the Massachusetts convention in February their all-or-nothing strategy finally collapsed. Facing a major defeat, [the Federalists] had to enter into a gentlemen's agreement to propose amendments through the First Congress."[282] The same held true for Virginia. "Largely because of Madison's abrupt shift in support of the Bill of Rights, the Virginians voted 88 to 80 to ratify the Constitution."[283] In other words, in order to get ratification from two of the three most important states, Massachusetts and Virginia, beyond their use of hardball tactics and tough rhetoric, the supporters of the Constitution resorted to blatant deal-making to obtain their slim margins of victory.

The use of hardball tactics by the Federalists, however, came with a political price. "On Saturday, September 29, the same day [the Pennsylvania] Assembly adjourned, sixteen of the seceding members signed an address to their constituents that would be republished throughout the states, awakening suspicions not only of the Constitution's supporters but of the Constitution itself."[284] "In the days and weeks that followed, Antifederalists in the backcountry protested the Assembly's actions, *attacking Federalists and burning effigies of Federalist leaders and copies of the Constitution.*"[285] At the same time, a Cumberland County reporter for Philadelphia's *Independent Gazetteer* wrote, "The whole country is alive with wrath and it is spreading from one county to another so rapidly that it is impossible to say where it will end or how far it will reach."[286]

Patrick Henry's anger reached new heights over Madison's deal-making. Henry responded by "crushing Madison's bid for the US Senate with warnings to the Assembly of civil war and 'rivulets of blood' flowing through Virginia, if it elected Madison or any other Federalist to the US Senate."[287] Virginia went on to appoint two Anti-Federalist US senators, and Madison was left to run for Congress with James Monroe as his opponent. The deal-making caused political troubles among their own, as well. "Irate Federalists ... called Madison [the Father of the Constitution] a *turncoat* for pledging to work for passage of a bill of rights, and even some moderates thought him disingenuous."[288]

Obviously, the Anti-Federalists were not without their resources.

Virginia's George Mason, who refused to sign the Constitution, publicly made the argument that the Constitution would give the new Congress endless power.

> Mason's dissemination bore quick fruit. In mid-October, "Old Whig," a Philadelphia pamphleteer, was referring to "that undefined, unbounded, and immense power" in the Necessary and Proper Clause and saying that, read together with the Supremacy Clause, it gave the power to "make all such laws which the Congress shall think necessary and proper." The next day "Brutus," a New York pamphleteer, was charging that the Necessary and Proper Clause, when combined with the Supremacy Clause, would lead to the annihilation of state governments and to the "complete consolidation of the several parts of the union into one complete government."[289]

Even so, in part because of the sway, if not demands, of Federalists, "only twelve of over ninety American newspapers and magazines published substantial numbers of essays critical of the Constitution during the ratification controversy,"[290] while "essays on behalf of ratification had no trouble getting printed."[291]

Even so, the "Antifederalist campaign gradually swayed public opinion against the ratification of the Constitution,"[292] and their tactics would garner the contempt of the top Federalists. "Washington accused [Richard Henry] Lee and other opponents of the constitution of using 'every art that could inflame the passions or touch the interests of men' to defeat ratification."[293] In response to the actions of the New York Governor Clinton to defeat ratification, the man who wrote the Constitution, Gouverneur Morris, "condemned Clinton as part of a 'wicked industry of those who have long habituated themselves to live on the public and cannot bear the idea of being removed from power and profit of state government, which has been and still is the means of support-ing themselves, their families, and dependents.'"[294] Such name-calling was not limited to Morris or Clinton. "The Constitution's supporters described 'Antifederalists' as state officials who feared for their jobs and so attacked the Constitution for selfish reasons. Even their commitment to the Revolution was called into question by writers who associated those who criticized the Constitution with the Loyalists who opposed independence."[295]

*   *   *

By now, we should be able to see that the Constitution, so revered by so many today—and rightfully so—was hardly universally accepted at the time. Again, the reason was quite simple. The Founders proposed to create a whole new system of government. Important rights were sub-ject to significant, if not dramatic, change. Faced with such prospects, those who perceived themselves winners and losers became engaged in the process just as you would if government came unannounced to your home to tear down your fences or told you that you had to give up some cherished possession. For those who had fought the Revolution so recently, and had sacrificed so much, the cherished possession was American *Liberty* itself, their fence, the line they didn't want govern-ment to cross.

*   *   *

Rhetoric. Power politics. Hardball tactics. They are the wares of politi-cians when much is at stake, and so it was during the 1770s and 1780s, when Americans decided to rebel against England, fight a war, tax them-selves, and create governments. That fighting and partisanship was not confined to those on the margin. Our Founding Fathers were among the most partisan and used some of the roughest tactics and extreme rhetoric. Their antagonists, the Anti-Federalists, did the same. Neither wanted to compromise. Yet, the Founders got their Constitution and the Anti-Federalists got their Bill of Rights.

Should our greatest leaders have been more compromising? Should we reconsider our reverence for them because of their actions? Should we hope for a better species of leaders than Washington, Franklin, Madison, and Henry? While it may be comforting for some to look with disdain on similar actions today and blame participants for their tactics, the fact remains that history is filled with such examples. We are better off, going forward, being philosophical about the nature of men with "all their faults, if they are such." We should come to understand the cause of such rancor—the use of government power—rather than resort to the useless and misguided arrogance of disdain for the partisan.

Finally, before we reach *Washington's Unifying Moment*, one more point should be made. The actions of Americans during that seminal period involved choices. Congress took a vote and rebelled. A choice was made. They fought a war and there was an outcome. They adopted state governments and two very different national governments. Each of those decisions was made over time and after much fighting. There was escalating partisanship and lasting division. Over time, however, the hard feelings would recede and the fever of a *Lasting Division Dynamic* would be broken. That was true for several reasons. First, the major decisions of the day wound up being closed-ended decisions—meaning the issue was capable of a clear resolution. We now have a United States and there is a Constitution. Second, and as a result of the first, the process that led to division did not linger. The fact that tens of thousands of Loyalists who did not want to live without British rule left the country after the war had an ameliorating effect. Third, and just as important if not most important, people could return to their lives relatively unfettered by government. Despite the dire warnings of Patrick Henry and his fellow misnamed Anti-Federalists, government did not immediately become a monolith. The power of the states was not immediately lost in all regards. Governments were still only involved in a very small percentage of the lives of those Americans. There was no Department of Education and no Environmental Protection Agency. Federal regulations were nearly a century away. The revolutionary governments were only spending a percent or two of the national income even if the national government had more power than before. That meant people had a chance to go back to their ordinary lives largely free of the reach of government. Unlike today, the dividing factors of government action during the 1770s and 1780s came and went.

That is not to say that the adoption of the Constitution cured all ills of the time by any means. Indeed, by the time the Constitution was finally adopted, the nation was weary. It was divided in countless ways over the prior two decades. Public and private debt remained and taxes were a burden. But once Americans put down their guns and their pens, to a greater extent than before, the decades ahead became stories about the pursuit of life, liberty, and happiness.

One significant reason that was so was George Washington. Today we can look in calm retrospect at how the strife that was America settled down after *Our Constitutional Divide*. At the time, however, it was more than unsteady. No one quite knew how the new government would work. It would take an extraordinary leader to calm the waters and to make Americans—and their fractious and ambitious leaders— unite behind a common goal. As Thomas Jefferson said, there was only one man who could unite America. Once again, it was time for George Washington, and it was time for his *Unifying Moment*.

CHAPTER 4

Washington's Unifying Moment

The tidal pull of Washington . . .
—**Richard Brookhiser**

We have now been through two chapters of discord—even amidst incredible triumph. For the Americans that lived it, it was the better part of twenty extraordinary and difficult years. During that time, they faced bad economic times, fought a war, and even fought among themselves over countless issues. Partisanship ran high en route to victory and the establishment of the federal government and state governments. Our new nation had uncertain boundaries, both politically and geographically. As we embarked on this constitutional experiment, the first of its kind in history, there were far many more questions than answers. Despite all of their disagreements, Americans almost universally were in agreement on one issue, or rather, about one person. Federalists. Anti-Federalists. Congressmen. State leaders. Soldiers. Farmers. Creditors. Debtors. Northerners. Southerners. As to the importance to America and its need for George Washington, they were all Americans and they all agreed—almost to a man.

How was it possible that one person could forge such a consensus? How could one person unite such discord? How could one person be the unanimous choice for general of the Continental Army, for president of the Constitutional Convention, and for president of the newly constitutional United States—arguably the three most important positions in early American history, if not ever?

The answers are as straightforward as George Washington himself. First, Washington was larger than life. In stature and fame, no one measured up to Washington, which gave him a unique opportunity to realize his goals for the nation. Second, Washington had extraordinary character. His political selflessness combined with his natural and humble leadership not only defined Washington but also defined the Continental Army and inspired the nature of the presidency as outlined in the Constitution. Third, and just as importantly, Washington was a visionary. He was possessed of an extraordinary and single-minded vision of a United States, which existed in him greater than, and likely before, anyone else. Combined in the person of Washington, those things made the presidency real and made possible a nation conceived in *Liberty*.

The Fame of George Washington

There has been no comparable figure in American history to George Washington—political or otherwise. He was beloved during his time and has been ever since. Given the difficult political and economic times in which he lived and served, that is not only an extraordinary accomplishment, it is also likely historically unique. As we consider that aspect of Washington, his fame, it is rather difficult for the modern reader to grasp how revered Washington was during his day. If we note that Washington first became president in 1789, we can begin to understand the magnitude of the country's affection toward him when we find out that Americans started celebrating his birthday ten years earlier, in 1779, during the Revolutionary War, and "calling him 'godlike' for the constancy of his devotion to the nation."[296] It is all but impossible to imagine such a circumstance happening again.

Keep in mind that during Washington's time, "fame was an accolade reserved for those who had served their fellow countrymen with distinction. Virtue, disinterested self-denying service for the good of the commonwealth, was the means by which one laid claim to fame."[297] Washington began to earn such fame during his service in the French and Indian War. He was but twenty-two. Of course, at the time Washington was fighting on behalf of the British against the French and Indians, and "in 1754, Washington had become famous throughout America ... [and] for the next two years, his name seemed to hold particular attraction for the Boston press. Despite the greater influence of policymakers in the East, in 1754 Washington was at the center of the action, and he became somewhat of an icon during this opening stage of the war. His name appeared in the Boston newspapers in 1754 as many times—48—as all other military officers combined."[298]

In 1755, Washington built on that reputation while he was an aide-de-camp to the British Major General Edward Braddock. In a precursor of future military battles in the Revolution, Braddock rejected Benjamin Franklin's and Washington's advice on fighting the Indians, whose style was in stark contrast to the European style of standing in formation and fighting.[299] The Indians and their French allies appeared for a moment from behind trees, got off their rounds, and then disappeared only to reappear again somewhere else. The British suffered a horrible defeat and Major General Braddock was killed.

As for Washington, who warned against such possibilities but was ignored,

> Washington at the outset flung himself headlong into the fight. He rode up and down the field, carrying orders and striving to rally "the dastards," as he afterwards called the regular troops. He endeavored to bring up the artillery, but the men would not serve the guns, although to set an example he aimed and discharged one himself. All through that dreadful carnage he rode fiercely

about, raging with the excitement of battle, and utterly exposed from beginning to end. Even now it makes the heart beat quicker to think of him amid the smoke and slaughter as he dashed hither and thither, his face glowing and his eyes shining with the fierce light of battle, leading on his own Virginians, and trying to stay the tide of disaster. He had two horses shot under him and four bullets through his coat. The Indians thought he bore a charmed life, while his death was reported in the colonies, together with his dying speech, which, he dryly wrote to his brother, he had not yet composed.[300]

According to Washington biographer Ron Chernow, "In a stupendous stroke of prophecy, a Presbyterian minister, Samuel Davies, predicted that the 'heroic youth Col. Washington' was being groomed by God for higher things. 'I cannot but hope Providence has hitherto preserved [him] in so signal a manner for some important service to his country.'" Meanwhile an Indian chief that had seen Washington in battle "concluded that some great spirit would guide him to momentous things in the future."[301]

Years later, "Washington's renown reverberated through the colonies" again—this time with the passing of the Fairfax Resolves.[302] In response to the British port bill of 1774, which was part of the Intolerable Acts, Washington became distinctly partisan. The Fairfax County committee, which he chaired, passed a series of resolutions, including one that stated that "taxation and representation are in their nature inseparable."[303] The Resolves were printed in the *Boston Gazette*. According to Chernow, during this period, the partisan Washington "allowed his heated opinions to bubble up and boil over as his pronouncements grew more vehement. . . . [In] the summer of 1774 he had no qualms about expressing open militance. He scoffed at the notion that the forthcoming Congress should submit more petitions to the king when so many had failed: 'Shall we, after this, whine and cry for relief?'"[304] Here again, Washington himself reminds us of the power of, and often the need for, partisanship.

The premonitions of the minister and the Indian chief reached new heights when Washington became Congress's unanimous choice for general of the Continental Army in 1775.[305] When he was chosen, "he was informed that 'all America' wanted him."[306] "Washington received a festive send off from the Philadelphia populace," and was greeted by "cheering masses" in New York on his way to Boston.[307] Later that year, a twenty-two-year-old slave named Phillis Wheatley famously made Washington the subject of a poem that praised Washington "literally to the skies and ends by wishing him 'a crown, a mansion, and a throne.'"[308] In 1777, "the battle of Princeton gave Washington far-reaching fame as a strategist."[309] By 1778, despite two years of a difficult war that included many lost battles, having to abandon New York and Congress fleeing Philadelphia, Washington was being called "our political father," and that year an almanac called him "father of his country."[310] A town in Massachusetts took the matter one step further when it renamed itself in his honor in 1778.[311] As for physical stature, according to Henry Cabot Lodge, Washington "was tremendously muscled, and the fame of his great strength was everywhere."[312] And by 1779, the Supreme Executive Council of Philadelphia commissioned his portrait and wrote of the idolization of Washington by members of Congress.

After the Revolutionary War, Washington "retired" from public life, so to speak. In truth, his fame would not allow it as "legions of hopeful tourists made a pilgrimage" to Washington's home at Mount Vernon.[313] However, the "endless stream of visitors had become a mixed blessing. The hero of the Revolution was expected to provide, at his own expense, hospitality to enumerable visitors."[314] As for Washington's military fans, Philip Mazzei, Jefferson's Florentine-born friend, wrote, "There is not one single officer on the whole continent who will forsake the pleasure of spending a few days with his General. . . . The result is that his house is continually filled with strangers who bring with them an even larger number of servants and horses."[315]

All of the above, of course, occurred a decade *prior* to Washington becoming president. In time, Washington would be "elected to preside over the Constitutional Convention of 1787, [but would say] little in public in the four-month-long session. He didn't have to . . . [because of his] enormous prestige."[316] Many have said that the proposed office of presidency was too powerful. However, as the debate over the Constitution unfolded, and the nature of the new office of the president came into being, the "delegates were willing to extend such power to the president because they 'cast their eyes towards General Washington as President.'"[317] While modeling a presidency on the greatness of one man seems improvident, even Madison "was not deeply concerned about presidential 'perfidy' and was content to confer to the president power of the military. This was because George Washington was the model (and likeliest candidate) for the office."[318]

Once the Constitution was completed, Washington was the first to sign it. That raised an essentially already settled question: Who should be the first president of the Republic? There was a single answer: "Washington had united Americans in war and now—as the hands-down favorite for the new country's first executive—in peace."[319] "Washington's [friends] had long since predicted that he would be the first president if the Constitution was ratified,"[320] and Madison predicted as much to Jefferson.[321] Newspapers "clamored" for him,[322] such as the *New Hampshire Gazette*, which declared, "Should the new Constitution be adopted, George Washington will undoubtedly be President."[323]

> Immediately after the ratification process was complete, [Washington] received letters urging him to accept the presidency that was to be offered to him. It was not a question of running. . . . Lafayette wrote to him that the executive seemed to be more powerful than it should be

in a republic; thus, the country would be in good hands only if he should assume office. "You Cannot Refuse Being Elected," the French-American general declared.[324]

Lafayette also told Washington, "You only Can settle that Political Machine";[325] and "'Without you,' Henry Lee, Jr. wrote from New York, the new government would 'have but little chance of success.'"[326] Gouverneur Morris added that "should the Idea prevail that you would not accept the Presidency it would prove fatal in many Parts."[327]

Once he was unanimously elected, Washington "prepared to leave Mount Vernon for the temporary national capital of New York, aware that he would have to endure celebratory canon fire and widespread idolatry, as young girls scattered flowers along the route and amateur poets enlarged his victories into godlike triumphs. He was widely referred to as a 'saviour.'"[328] After taking office, Washington told his vice president, John Adams, "It would be advantageous to the interests of the Union for the President to make a tour of the United States . . . to become better acquainted with their principal characters and internal circumstances, as well as to be more accessible to numbers of well-informed persons."[329] "Thousands cheered as he approached each stop, with officials falling over each other to greet him and veterans fighting their way to the front of crowds to salute him."[330] "Doomed to his own celebrity, he tried to submit with the best possible grace."[331] During his first term as president, his "fame" was now such that many "people, including Jefferson, expected that Washington might be president for life, that he would be a kind of elective monarch—something not out of the question in the eighteenth century."[332]

★　★　★

That is a fair, if not understated, glimpse of Washington's fame. Harlow Giles Unger tells us that at the Second Continental Congress,

"Washington was the most visible delegate: at six feet, four inches, he towered over most of the others."[333] He might as well have been speaking of Washington's entire career. There simply was no one else of his stature at the time. Washington's accomplishments provide obvious clues to the source of his notoriety—but not the whole story of his fame. Yet another extraordinary aspect of George Washington was how he handled the praise and fame that was heaped upon him. Surely any politician would have succumbed to his ego at some point along the way and turned his fame into something personal rather than virtuous—not Washington, however. Washington had extraordinary public and private character. He was virtuous in the classical, selfless sense. Combined with his notoriety, Washington's character would permit him to accomplish unprecedented and revolutionary things.

The world knows of Washington's honesty.[334] We also have read that David McCullough said, "What Washington was above all was a leader" with a "commanding presence,"[335] which he matched with "priding himself on staying cool-headed."[336] We can add to those assessments by noting that the fearless Washington often "rode at the head of his troops."[337] He "was not in the habit of receding from a fixed purpose," and had an "absolute moral fearlessness"[338] along with the fact that a "close attention to detail . . . always characterized him."[339] Ambitious, yes, but "Washington never tired in his efforts at moral improvement"[340] or improvement in general: "George Washington's military career presents the most outstanding illustrations of a characteristic peculiarly his own, that he did not mark time in any of the important positions of his life. His passion for education caused him to concentrate upon hard study, to acquire the necessary knowledge to excel, whether it was surveying, farming, building forts, shipping produce, or leading armies."[341] As a commander, "one of his hallmarks . . . was unremitting vigilance,"[342] often adhering "to an unwavering daily routine"[343] in the battlefield. Finally, "sobriety, gravity, and steadiness were the qualities [James] Madison had come to expect of the leadership corps in the new national system he visualized and Washington embodied them all."[344]

Washington, it seems, could do nothing else but use those qualities and traits for the public good. "Washington . . . felt the force of the classical idea and throughout his life was compulsive about his disinterestedness. . . . He was continuously anxious that he not be thought greedy or 'interested.' He refused to accept a salary for any of his public services, and he was scrupulous in avoiding any private financial benefits from his governmental positions."[345] That is why John Marshall could rightly conclude that Washington devoted "himself to the duties of his station, . . . pursuing no object distinct from the public good," and that "no man has ever appeared upon the theatre of public action, whose integrity was more incorruptible, or whose principles were more perfectly free from the contamination of those selfish and unworthy passions, which find their nourishment in the conflicts of party."

It seems it was always so for Washington, and his pursuit of the public good took several forms. Prior to the start of the Revolution, in response to a British provocation, a partisan Washington pledged to "raise 1000 Men, subsist them at my own Expence, and march myself at their Head for the Relief of Boston."[346] We know that Washington refused a salary for his service in the Revolution—and we should keep in mind that he served eight and a half years as general—longer than a modern presidency can legally last, and he did so without pay as soldiers all around him complained about their pay. John Adams, for one, admired Washington's willingness to risk his enormous fortune by supporting the rebellion.[347] Keep in mind that at that time, Washington was committing treason and not only could expect the loss of all of his considerable possessions but also his life. After the war, Washington balked at receiving the Virginia Assembly's "gift of 150 shares in the James River and Potomac canal companies."[348] Instead, Washington held the shares in "trust" for charitable schools.[349] According to historian Gordon S.

Wood, "This was no ordinary display of scruples such as government officials today show over a conflict of interest: in 1784–85 Washington was not even holding public office."[350] Once he became president, Washington continued in that regard by furnishing the first home of the president "at his own expense."[351] While waiting for the presidential mansion, "Washington refused the loan of a finer house owned by Governor George Clinton," as he explained to Madison, in part because he wished to be placed in an independent situation."[352] Washington was charitable beyond his public roles as well. "He gave his old army buddies large interest-free loans that he never expected to see repaid; he gave his weaver a loan to bring his wife and children from England, even though the man could never possibly afford to repay him. And he quietly paid for the schooling of cash-poor relatives and friends."[353]

Beyond being charitable, privately and publicly, Washington made the American experiment work because he constantly did the right thing—where perhaps no one else could or would. Consider that as the Revolution was winding down, and Washington's stature was at a peak, "some of his senior officers had urged seizing congress and setting up a military dictatorship."[354] It was not the first time "dictatorial" power for Washington had been suggested.[355] At that moment and that time, Washington stood in the breach of history. History could have gone one way or another—but not in Washington's mind. Instead, "Washington, horrified, had confronted them. He urged them to 'place full confidence in the purity of the intentions of Congress.' Again, at Princeton, he warned his departing troops that 'unless the principles of the federal government [are] properly supported and the powers of the union increased, the honor, dignity, and justice of the nation would be lost forever.'"[356]

At the end of the war, standing even taller in the eyes of Americans and the world, Washington again did the historically unimaginable; he willingly relinquished his power for the greater good. He did so by going to Congress by his own accord. "He was, he said, presenting himself 'to surrender into their hands the trust committed to me.' He was resigning to a 'respectable nation' the 'appointment I accepted with diffidence.'"[357] As he did so, "everyone in the house sensed history unfolding before them. For the first time since ancient Rome, a commanding general with absolute power in his grasp had, in Monroe's words, left 'sovereignty vest in the people.' It was unprecedented in modern civilization."[358]

Washington's "voice broke as he neared the end of the three-and-a-half minute talk, but by now many other people in the room were also choked up. . . . The spectators all wept and there was hardly a member of Congress who did not drop tears."[359] Washington told them, "Having now finished the work assigned me, I retire from the great theater of action and bidding an affectionate farewell to this august body, under whose orders I have long acted, I here offer my commission and take my leave of all the employments of public office."[360] For that, "like others who had fought in the war, [future President James] Monroe was deeply moved by Washington's address. 'The manner in which he took his leave . . . was such as evinced the high sense . . . of his merit.'"[361]

Washington, to be sure, had more than merit. He was "the greatest man in the world," or so King George III may well have argued. Washington was being offered tributes "to [his] Excellency for all you have suffered and all you have effected for us" from the likes of Thomas Jefferson.[362] More importantly, he had the trust of Congress and of nearly every American. When they trusted him to be general of the Continental Army, Washington had earned that trust and returned that trust. The same held true for his service as president of the Constitutional Convention. It was that trust that led members of the Constitutional Convention to extend such power to the office of the president, because they "cast their eyes towards General Washington as President."[363] It was also that trust that led to Washington's unanimous election as president by the Electoral College, whose electors were chosen by the states that, not long ago, were in political disarray.

In sum,

at the time Washington was probably the only representative of the established order to whom Americans
would delegate any significant amount of political
power. The courage, honesty, diligence, and acumen
with which he had fought the Revolution dispelled fear
on the part of his countrymen that he would abuse their
trust. When Washington became chief executive, their
trust in him was transferred to the government. When
Washington achieved success in office popular endorsement for republicanism was guaranteed.[364]

Washington's election, by itself, was a unifying moment for the
young nation—but it was not the only aspect of his unifying moment.
His fame and character, as important as they were, would not have aided
in the unity that ultimately occurred unless they were tied to Washington's single-minded vision of a *United* States that he pursued at all times.
For instance, during the Revolution, Washington "tried to dissolve state
differences into a new national identity, telling his men that the troops
being raised from various colonies were "now the troops of the United
Provinces of North America and it is hoped that all distinctions of colonies will be laid aside."[365] He also "habitually referred to America as
a 'rising empire.'"[366] It was that determined vision, combined with acts
to make that vision come to pass, that caused people then and now to
celebrate him as the father of our country.

★   ★   ★

When we consider Washington's vision, it is important to note that it
was born not just of idealism but of practicality, as well. According to
historian Paul Johnson, when Washington "attended the first Continental Congress in Philadelphia in 1774, he had visited more of America than any other delegate."[367] The Revolution would then take him

to "nine of the thirteen states and [he] got to know large parts of the country with painful intimacy but also with glowing regard for their potential."[368] Washington began thinking of that potential long before the American Revolution. His experience in the French and Indian War, including having "to deal with destructive competition among" the colonies, not to mention "short-sighted politicians," made Washington think in terms of a stronger central government.[369] His work as a surveyor, along with his service in the war, had already given Washington an extraordinary, firsthand view of much of America, and as "early as 1769 he tried to promote the use of lock canals to improve natural waterways like the Potomac and Ohio."[370] It was part of Washington's "ambitious plan that would connect the [Potomac] river with 'a rising empire' in the western country.... His plan for Potomac commerce required not just endless locks but portages through the mountains of what is now West Virginia."[371] It also included "a plan for a joint stock company that would receive charters from Virginia and Maryland and make the river navigable from Tidewater Virginia to the Ohio Country," which Washington pushed through the Virginia House of Burgesses.[372] When business interests in one state "momentarily stalled" the project, Washington saw that "American states instead of cooperating with each other were competing and placing obstacles in each other's paths,"[373] and "it provided Washington with yet another early example of the need for inter-colonial cooperation."[374] "Washington's diaries show that as soon as the war was over he turned again and again to canals. In September 1784 he travelled across the Alleghenies partly to inspect his western lands but also to plan canal routes (and roads) to link Ohio tributaries to the Potomac."[375]

"Washington argued that the national government should at least be surveying its vast new western Territories, especially the tributaries of the Ohio River, so that the west could be opened up to even larger numbers of settlers and traders."[376] In a letter to the Marquis de Lafayette, Washington "saw his role in opening up a route to the west by water in grand terms."[377] Washington wrote, "I wish to see the sons and daughters of the world in peace and busily employed in the more agreeable amusement of fulfilling the first and great commandment—'increase and multiply'—as an encouragement to which we have opened the fertile plains of the Ohio to the poor, the needy and the oppressed of the Earth. Anyone therefore who is heavy laden or who wants land to cultivate may repair thither and abound as in the Land of Promise with milk and honey. The Ways are preparing and the roads will be made easy."[378]

According to James Madison, in a letter sent to Thomas Jefferson,

> The earnestness with which he expresses the undertaking is hardly to be described, and shows that a mind like his, capable of great views, and which long has been occupied by them, cannot bear a vacancy, and surely he could not have chosen an occupation more worthy of succeeding to that of establishing the political rights of his country than the patronage of works for the extensive and lasting improvements of its natural advantages; works, which will double the value of half the lands within the Commonwealth, will extend its commerce and link its interests with those of the western states.[379]

Historian Harlow Giles Unger tells us that the Annapolis Convention, which led directly to the Constitutional Convention, was an "outgrowth" of Washington's grand design that would "unite the nation with an unbreakable economic, as well as geophysical and political, bond."[380] Despite their common victory, however, after the Revolution, the states did not have unbreakable bonds. To the contrary, they were on the verge of fighting amongst themselves again. Washington believed that "the primary cause of all our disorder lies in the different state governments, and in the . . . incompatibility in the laws of different states and disrespect to those of the general government." The result, he declared, had left "this great country weak, inefficient, and disgraceful . . . almost to the final dissolution of it."[381] As Madison told us, that dynamic drove many to call for a more powerful central government. Returning to Washington, when it came to the Constitutional Convention, held in the wake of Shays' Rebellion, his vision of a truly *United* States was in jeopardy, and therefore, "he made it known he would support any 'tolerable compromise'"[382] while he hoped for the "widest possible agreement."[383] During the ratification process, publicly Washington was largely silent "so that he did not appear to be running for the presidency,"[384] but he "moved stealthily in the background."[385] Not surprisingly, given his stature, that was more than enough. Indeed, Gouverneur Morris's assessment was that Washington's name attached "to the new constitution has been of infinite service,"[386] and according to Willard Stern Randall, in his biography of Washington, his support for the Constitution was "the margin of victory"[387] for its passage.

★   ★   ★

The new nation now had a new Constitution and a unifying person to head it. Historian Paul Johnson writes that the "American Constitution was the work of an oligarchy of able men, the Founding Fathers. But there is a case for arguing that the most influential of them all was Washington, not by his voice—but by his public silence, his presence, and his record of republican virtue and decisive action speaking louder than words."[388] Washington's fame, character, and vision did as Jefferson said: Washington "united the confidence of all America, and was the only person who did so." To give you some context to Washington's achievement, much has been said of Lincoln's cabinet. A much-heralded book was written called *Team of Rivals: The Political Genius of Abraham Lincoln*. In the book, the author Doris Kearns Goodwin extols Lincoln's ability to create and then work with a cabinet of men who wanted to be president. There is obvious merit to Goodwin's argument, but Lincoln's effort in no way can compare to Washington's feat. During his presidency Washington was served by John Adams, Thomas Jefferson, James Madison, James Monroe and John Quincy Adams. No other president can remotely lay claim to a record of having the succeeding five presidents to himself play a supporting role to him—not to mention countless other Founding Fathers. Such was the tidal pull of Washington and a key aspect of *Washington's Unifying Moment*.

Washington's Unifying Moment Continues During His Presidency

The unanimously elected George Washington set about his presidency to further his primary goal of creating a nation.[389] Washington was well aware that "whatever" he did "established a precedent."[390] In Washington's words, "I walk on untrodden ground. There is scarcely any part of my conduct which may not hereafter be drawn into precedent."[391] Overall, his actions and policies were designed to create confidence in America and to garner loyalty to its new government.[392] That is why, when asked his preference for a vice president, Washington wanted a "true Federalist"[393]—belying claims he was against parties, per se, and demonstrating that he wanted supporters of the Union in office. In making his appointments, he stuck to a policy of "utmost impartiality" so as to "strengthen the government's legitimacy. 'If injudicious or unpopular measures should be taken . . . with regard to appointments,' he told his nephew Bushrod, the government itself would be in the utmost danger of being utterly subverted."[394] Washington then proceeded to turn down that nephew's request for an appointment.[395] In general, his appointments, including to the first "cabinet," were made so that all views would be represented,[396] thereby avoiding early divisions, which naturally arose from the exclusion of important voices. That was no more true than in the appointment of Alexander Hamilton, a strong proponent of centralized federal power, as the first Secretary of the Treasury, and the appointment of Thomas Jefferson, a strong proponent of states' rights, as Secretary of State—soon to be the position thought to be *the* entre to the presidency. When Washington sided with Hamilton over Jefferson on the issue of Hamilton's finance plan for the country—a controversial plan that involved the federal government exercising substantial power—Washington did so because his experience convinced him that the newly united states could not succeed in the absence of a "strong and fiscally sound national government."[397]

Beyond those examples, in an effort to bring the nation closer together, in "the earliest days of his administration,"[398] Washington undertook not one, but four official tours of the country.[399] Those tours gave "hundreds of thousands" of Americans the chance to see him.[400] The first tour, by this president from the South, was a politically wise and unifying trip to New England.[401] In keeping with his character and desire to unify the nation by his trip and to "avoid alienating Boston's highly charged political factions, Washington refused the invitation to stay at the governor's mansion, saying he had declined all such invitations to private homes and had slept in public houses during his entire journey."[402] Later, Washington would tour the South. Washington wanted that tour to have "the same effect to the Southward as it did Eastward."[403]

When faced with the difficult problem of a renewed war between England and France, Washington immediately opted for a policy that would prevent the citizens of the newly united states "from embroiling us with either of those powers"[404] even though it was an unpopular position. He did so, in large part, "to allow the government to take hold."[405] Washington understood that a nation fresh off a revolution, which included such large components of a civil war, likely could not withstand participation in another war, which would divide loyalties, if not sap the country of resources. Henry Cabot Lodge credited Washington's policy by writing that it "was a great work of far-sighted and native statesmanship" that ultimately resulted in the Monroe Doctrine twenty-five years later,[406] and kept America at peace and able to expand internally.

In keeping with expectations of the country and the trust reposed in Washington, Washington was reelected unanimously in the Electoral College for the second time, a distinction he alone holds for one election, let alone two. That is not to say that politics and factions had not begun to take hold in America. As we will discuss in the next chapter, partisan fighting had emerged over such issues as a national tax on whiskey and a central bank. Strong infighting had begun to emerge between cabinet members—especially between Hamilton and Jefferson. Madison was no longer the confidante he once was and Adams's support was also no longer the same. Notwithstanding the growing ambitions of those future presidents and cabinet officers, there was no doubt in anyone's mind that Washington would be reelected once he publicly made his choice.

Washington's final unifying act came in the form of what he did not do. Washington chose not to run for a third term, which was certainly available to him and for which he was lobbied to accept. Washington, however, was "intent on teaching his last lesson about transferring power in a republic."[407] Not long after, "Jefferson followed in Washington's footsteps, and in so doing he emphasized Washington's precedent."[408] In truth, Washington's entire career served as an example. The manner in which he conducted himself as a general shaped the manner in which the Continental Army conducted itself. Chernow tells us that "his stewardship of the army had been a masterly exercise in nation building. In defining the culture of the Continental Army, he had helped mold the very character of the country, preventing the revolution from taking a bloodthirsty or despotic turn."[409] We have seen how his "prestige" guided the Constitutional Convention and how he acted with dignity during the ratification process. His presidency then set innumerable precedents and made the theoretical constitution a practical reality.

It is impossible today to know how fragile America was at each of the major junctures of its early history, including deciding to go to war, fighting a war, adopting a constitution, and implementing a federal government. Historians have now and again analyzed Washington's actions and judged his effectiveness and have done so with some criticism. Certainly Washington was not perfect. At each of those seminal moments, however, the largest figure presiding over the process was George Washington. At each of those unprecedented junctures, Washington acted for the good of the nation and whenever "petty partisan disputes swirled around him, he kept his eyes fixed on the transcendent goals that motivated his quest."[410] In the final analysis, Washington, far more than anyone else, guided America through a gauntlet of uncertainty. He elevated us above our escalating partisanship, and for a time quelled lasting divisions. In doing so, the true unifying moment we can ascribe to George Washington may well be the United States as we know it. The lesson he left for every leader who followed, and of critical importance to the *Divided Era,* was the value of a strong vision forged by character and determination. We will need such a vision, character, and determination again if we are to rise above the *Divided Era.*

CHAPTER 5

The Secret Behind the Era of Good Feelings

Who has been deprived of any right of person or property?
—James Monroe,
from his first inaugural speech

James Monroe ran unopposed for his reelection in 1820. His "renomination was such a forgone conclusion" that few attended the convention at which he was nominated for reelection.[411] The opposition party Federalists had all but disappeared and didn't nominate a candidate. There was no campaign, and Monroe got every Electoral College vote except one. He truly was presiding over what became known as the *Era of Good Feelings*—the name given to the period covering his presidency—a period of very limited partisanship.

In the wake of the War of 1812, Monroe's elections and presidency were a welcome respite from conflicts and difficult partisan politics. Washington had to deal with the challenge of forming a government and inter-cabinet fights. As we shall see, Adams and Jefferson dealt with partisan issues and emerging parties. Madison faced a difficult war. It can truly be said, on the other hand, that there was less political division in the *Era of Good Feelings* than during any other presidency. To understand why that was so is to also understand why, in many ways, Monroe's presidency was a political period 180 degrees opposite from America today. American politics in the Bush/Obama era is a study in active government. Today, our governments spend more than one of every three dollars spent annually and promulgate countless decisions and regulations every day. In doing so, the rights of Americans and their businesses necessarily are curtailed with each such act. Meanwhile, First Amendment rights related to freedom of expression and religion along with the right to bear arms, supposedly guaranteed by the Second Amendment, are rarely long from public dispute. As government and the competition for its spoils catalyze Americans today to fend for their rights at every level of government, partisanship has become a constant, not the exception.

The presidency of James Monroe was anything but that. Overall spending by federal and state governments measured less than 4 percent of the economy. Government was so limited that Monroe could rightfully ask when inaugurated: "Who has been deprived of any right of person or property?" That was so because our federal government under Monroe did remarkably little—much to the disappointment of historians who prefer, if not lionize, activist presidents like the Roosevelts and their governments. Monroe was a president with Anti-Federalist roots. The Congresses that served under Monroe did virtually nothing to deprive Americans of their rights and passed few significant pieces of legislation during Monroe's eight years in office. Monroe enjoyed the political opportunity that the self-imposed decline of the Federalist Party gave him. Unlike almost any other politician in our history, however, Monroe chose not to press his advantage. He *chose* not to legislate Americans into disputes. Instead, Monroe would get credit for opening up the West to Americans as they pursued life, liberty, and happiness. In the absence of an active government, partisanship waned to the point of our second, and our last, unopposed presidential election in 1820.

Partisanship in the New Republic

In order to understand the cause of Monroe's *Era of Good Feelings*, it will be important to understand the partisan dynamics of the presidents who served before him. We know the four decades leading up to James Monroe's first election were hectic, intense years. Americans declared their independence, fought a revolution that was at times a civil war, set up state governments, fought over a constitution, and then established a federal government. The process of setting up a federal government, of course, was unprecedented and many times it was understandably contentious. In several key ways, the nature of our republic took its form during the presidencies of Washington, Adams, Jefferson, and Madison. Washington laid the cornerstones of our system of government, which now and again proved difficult because new institutions were being created nearly out of whole cloth. Adams' presidency took a deeply partisan turn and introduced us to contested elections. Jefferson's presidency featured the first significant reversal of a predecessor's policies (i.e., Federalist policies); it also solidified the nature of a two-term presidency and at times tested the limits of presidential power. Madison presided over our first war as a nation. Understandably, those political dynamics—which necessarily involved government action—led to partisan moments.

When Washington took office, there was no government as we know it. There were the memories and experiences of the colonial governments, as well as an untested piece of paper—the newly adopted Constitution. There were no protocols for a new republic, let alone functioning cabinet offices. Washington really did have to establish precedents, and among them were the basic operations of our federal government. That process started with the first session of the First Congress, which was not aligned by a party system. Those serving in the First Congress were largely supporters of Washington and his vision—and there was, with respect to "both leadership and membership, a strong continuity between the Constitutional Convention and the First Congress."[412] At their first session, they undertook basic acts such as achieving a quorum, electing officers, counting the electoral ballots, and passing an act on how and when to administer certain oaths. Their first session also included establishing the Department of Foreign Affairs, now known as the Department of State. They established the Departments of War and Treasury as well. Along with those acts, the First Congress set up our federal court system in the form of a Judiciary Act, which formulated our Supreme Court as well as our District Courts, Circuit Courts, and District Attorneys. In their second session, among other actions, the First Congress passed the Patent Act, the Copyright Act, and the Federal Crimes Act, and set up the first census. Those proved to be largely unpartisan, if not uneventful, actions taken by Congress.

As you would expect, however, the First Congress had to tackle more difficult issues as well. Not surprisingly, some of those more difficult tasks involved finding ways to fund the new government. Fresh off a revolution precipitated by direct taxes, the notion of an income tax was never a consideration of the Founding Fathers. Nevertheless, the new government needed funding, lest the Constitution and the new federal government suffer the same fate as the ineffective Articles of Confederation and its Confederacy.

To get funding, Congress turned to the accepted method of raising revenues during that era: tariffs—taxes imposed on certain goods entering the country. If an incoming product was taxed, the domestic producer of the same product gained a competitive advantage, i.e. protection over the imported product burdened with taxes. The consumers of protected products, on the other hand, had to pay higher prices that resulted from the lack of competition and/or the taxes that came with the imported product. James Madison, the leader of the first House of Representatives, offered the first bill on that thorny subject, which, by its very nature, promised to pick winners and losers—the protected and the unprotected. As such, it was also guaranteed to attract strong opponents, and the powerful Alexander Hamilton was one of them.

Hamilton carefully analyzed Madison's bill and came to the opinion that it would start a costly trade war with Britain because of the restrictions on British goods that Madison proposed. Hamilton also thought that Madison's version of the bill would result in lost British trade and credit—something the young country sorely needed for its ailing economy. Madison pushed his bill through the House but it failed in the

Senate. In time, a bill would pass both houses of Congress but only after significant input and partisan lobbying by business and farming interests whose economic fate was being decided by government. Once again, *History* was witness to government action fostering self-interested and partisan reactions (i.e., a *Partisan Catalyst Dynamic*).

The final bill avoided the feared trade war with Britain and provided a certain level of protection for northern manufacturers in the form of tariffs imposed on many imported manufactured items. However, it also saddled southern farmers—who purchased many imported goods, and therefore, favored lower tariffs so they could obtain cheaper goods—with "a disproportionate share of the tax burden of the new government."[413] We shall see, during our review of the Civil War and of the *Gilded Age*, just how partisan the issue of tariffs would become. For now, however, the issue did not derail Washington's first term. It did, on the other hand, set the table for future disputes between the North and South and resulted in an important breach between Hamilton and Madison during Washington's first term.

*   *   *

Next up, with respect to the issue of the new government and its finances, was the question of debt. The varied states and the federal government had a lot of it. So the new "Congress called upon [Alexander] Hamilton to prepare a report on the status of American debt outstanding and on the possibilities of its assumption by the new Federal Government."[414] Hamilton's comprehensive report separated out "the public debt outstanding into three main categories—the Continental and Confederation foreign debt, the Continental and Confederation domestic debt, and the Revolutionary state indebtedness."[415] Hamilton's solution, on the other hand, was to consolidate all of that debt and to have the federal government assume it all—a remarkable suggestion given the times. Not surprisingly, his "Report on Public Credit generated controversy from the beginning," and given its far-reaching implications, it was "not uniformly accepted."[416]

In order to pay off the proposed consolidated debt, Hamilton also proposed that the federal government take away the power of coastal states to impose their own tariffs—a power they exercised after the Revolution—and, instead, give that power to the federal government. Beyond the obvious concerns of those states losing revenue and power, the Southern states, which relied heavily on slavery and were aware of Northern sentiments on that issue, were especially wary of such a concentration of power in the federal government.[417] In Congress, James Madison renewed his differences with Hamilton and "led the opposition to Hamilton's Plan for assumption of states' debts."[418] Madison used his influence to have the House vote down "the assumption plan, thirty-one to twenty-nine; and two weeks later voted to discontinue debates on that issue altogether."[419] It was Madison's position that the prudent states, which had little remaining debt, would be penalized by a plan that bailed out those states that weren't as fiscally prudent,[420] a sentiment echoed in those states that had paid down their debts. Predictably, the new nation was at odds over the proposed action by the federal government. In the end, however, none other than Thomas Jefferson, who fought tenaciously at the cabinet level with Hamilton over his plan, brokered a deal between Madison and Hamilton, and Hamilton's assumption plan was adopted.

As you might expect, however, the First Congress was not through taxing the American people. The First Congress wanted another tax in the form of something called the Whiskey Act. It was passed a year into Washington's first term. In the estimation of the new Secretary of the Treasury, Alexander Hamilton, and others, the existing tariff bill was not producing sufficient revenue for the new government—clearly proving that the imposition of the first tax is never that of the last tax. In response, the First Congress passed a bill that placed a "luxury" tax on spirits, which Hamilton and Congress believed would be the least objectionable kind of tax. That estimation did not mean, however, that it wasn't objectionable. Indeed, Hamilton and Congress grossly underestimated the reaction to the new tax. Over time, resistance to the tax grew to the point such that "through the fall and winter of 1791 and into the summer of 1792, efforts to enforce collection of the tax in western Pennsylvania ceased. In Kentucky not a cent was collected—the excise there was effectively dead on arrival. Similar results occurred in northwestern Virginia and in North Carolina. Refusal to pay and violence met the tax collectors in South Carolina."[421] Over time, those mere protests by Americans turned violent and eventually into the Whiskey Rebellion. As told by Thomas Slaughter, in his book *The Whiskey Rebellion: Frontier Epilogue to the American Revolution,*

> At daybreak on July 16, 1794, about fifty men armed with rifles and clubs marched to the house of John Neville, regional supervisor for collection of the federal excise tax in western Pennsylvania. They demanded that Neville resign his position and turn over to them all records associated with collection of the tax on domestically distilled spirits. He refused. Shots were fired. In the ensuing battle five of the attackers fell wounded. One of them later died. Neville and his slaves, who together had defended the premises from secure positions inside the house, suffered no casualties. The mob dispersed.
>
> The following day a crowd of between 400 and 800 locals returned to the scene. This time Neville protected his home with the help of the slaves and eleven soldiers from Fort Pitt. Again the two sides exchanged fire. Neville escaped under cover of a thicket. One or two of the aggressors fell dead. One soldier may have died, three or four were wounded, and two deserted during the course of battle. The remaining guards surrendered after the

mob torched the house and outbuildings. The mansion, barns, slave quarters, and most storage bins burned to the ground.[422]

The parallels between the Whiskey Rebellion and Shays' Rebellion, events separated by just eight years, are entirely evident in reading that passage. Before the Whiskey Rebellion was over, thousands would join in the protest, in addition to refusing to pay the tax. "In response, President Washington nationalized 12,950 militiamen from New Jersey, Pennsylvania, Maryland, and Virginia—an army approximating in size the Continental force that followed him during the Revolution—and personally led the 'Watermelon Army' west to shatter the insurgency."[423] "From that time on, there was no problem collecting the excise tax on liquor"[424] but not without lasting circumstances even after President Jefferson repealed the tax.

As shocking as it may seem today that American citizens undertook an armed rebellion—the ultimate partisan reaction—in response to a tax, the intensity of their reaction was not that radical given the context of the times. After all, not long before, many of those same people fought the Revolutionary War over a similar direct tax imposed on them by the British. They lost family, property, and wealth fighting against a direct tax. Without that whiskey tax, without a tax on their freedom, there would have been no such rebellion. In other words, the actions of government precipitated the action of the partisans. While few would condone such a response today, it remains important to understand the causal effect that leads to division and partisanship.

The Whiskey Act, Hamilton's Plan, and the imposition of tariffs proved to be among the most contentious issues Washington faced in his first term. In many respects, there was no way for Washington to avoid taking significant action. After all, starting a government requires action—and actions of such magnitude are sure to attract competing views and catalyze partisanship. Fortunately for the country,

Washington's stature allowed for such divisiveness among his cabinet and key advisors, as well as the new nation, even while he was bringing the country together into the United States. Because of his stature and dedication to his vision, under Washington's watch, outright party sentiment was slow to emerge—but it did emerge. In Washington's second term, the Senate remained pro-administration but the House veered away. In response, Washington came to favor the Federalists more openly[425]—not so much because he wanted party division, but because he favored those who favored the completion of his vision. The next president, however, lacked Washington's stature and America would be introduced to the hazards of party politics.

★   ★   ★

John Adams had the impossible task of following George Washington in the presidency.[426] Washington was the 6'4" military hero and a visionary who had traveled the country en route to unifying it. No one could fairly measure up to Washington. Adams, by contrast, was but 5'7"—with no military experience—and spent his time in Congress. Adams's very job, prior to being vice president, was to immerse himself in the legislative competition of picking winners and losers—not spend all his time trying to unify a nation. By the end of Washington's term, neither Adams nor any other political figure seeking the presidency enjoyed universal acclaim. As a result, America was treated to its first contested presidential election. Keep in mind that election rules in America were "evolving" at the time of the 1796 presidential election.[427] "The Electoral College had grown to 136 voters, each casting a ballot for president and vice president. Electors in nine states were still selected by their legislatures, but in other states they were chosen by popular vote."[428] Without a dominant political figure, the results looked like this: Adams, the Federalist nominee, won 71 electors, "carrying most of the eastern seaboard."[429] Jefferson, the Republican nominee, won 68 with votes from the South and West; Thomas Pinckney, from South Carolina and the Federalist nominee for vice president, received 59; Aaron Burr, the Republican nominee for vice president received 30; and "Samuel Adams, John Adams's relative and his tutor in revolutionary tactics, received 11 of the 48 write in votes."[430] In other words, "whereas Washington was elected with a full measure of public confidence, Adams was a three-vote electoral college choice."[431]

According to Stephen G. Kurtz in his book *The Presidency of John Adams: The Collapse of Federalism,* "The Adams administration was born to trouble." Kurtz's reference is to the fact that the Adams presidency was dominated by the storm clouds of war with France from its outset. "The first formal meeting that President Adams had with his advisors was devoted to a discussion of how best to deal with the diplomatic crisis with France. The French government had refused to meet with Charles C. Pinckney when he arrived at Paris as James Monroe's successor, and the problem of avoiding war was one that haunted the Adams adminis-tration from start to finish."[432] Previously, "Adams had made no secret of his hostility to the French Revolution. . . . As president, however, Adams wanted to pursue Washington's policy of avoiding an open rupture."[433] It would not be easy. There still remained a significant split among many Americans. Some were thankful and partial to France, such as Jefferson and Madison. Others harbored British sentiments, like Hamilton. Their views mirrored the split among Americans at large. The combination of Adams's lack of comparable stature, the actions of France, and rising domestic sentiment made Adams's task incredibly difficult.

Further complicating Adams's presidency was the changing dynamic among the Founders related to serving the presidency. We have seen that Washington had the support of virtually every major political fig-ure at the outset of his presidency. The desire to serve the administra-tion was high among the nation's elite for the first president. After eight years, however, that desire had dissipated. During Washington's second term, Jefferson, Hamilton, Knox, and Randolph, Washington's original cabinet, had left. Finding their replacements proved difficult even for Washington—a problem with which Adams was acutely aware as vice president.[434] According to Kurtz, "Many men who might have filled Federal positions with distinction refused to do so out of weariness with public life. . . . By the time Jefferson and Hamilton retired from public life the novelty of the Federal government had worn off."[435]

For those reasons and others, the presidency was simply not as powerful under Adams as it was under General Washington. That proved to be an open door for party development and partisanship. Jefferson, the leader of the emerging Republican party and accustomed to fighting Hamilton and even disagreeing with Washington, had no trouble taking on Adams—the man who beat him by just three electoral votes. Jefferson wanted the United States to lean toward France with respect to its revolution and in its disputes with England. In a letter to a friend, which wound up being published in a New York newspaper, Jefferson, who lived in France for a considerable period, chastised the ongoing failure of our government to support the French revolutionary efforts. He wrote that the executive and judicial branches of government were filled with "timid men who prefer the calm of despotism to the boisterous sea of liberty."[436] According to A. J. Langguth, in his book *Union 1812, the Americans Who Fought the Second War of Independence*, "Perhaps Jefferson referred principally to Hamilton and Adams, but since he did not name the men he was denouncing, a reader might deduce that he included Washington among the 'apostates who have gone over to these heresies, men who were Samsons in the field & Solomons in council, but who have had their heads shorn by the harlot England.'"[437] Even prior to the soon-to-be third president's criticism, the future fourth president, James Madison, who had retired from Congress, refused Adams's request to lead a delegation to France—even after Adams had publicly named Madison.[438] Adams requested Jefferson's help in the process and when Madison declined, as Jefferson predicted he would, it was said that it "was the last time Adams spoke with Jefferson on any matter of policy."[439] How far the nation had come in just eight years! Washington had the support and admiration, at one point or another, of the next five presidents. Adams was under fire from or at odds with the next two presidents from the outset of his own presidency. As part of that dynamic, clear party lines were being drawn, aided by presidential ambitions and growing policy differences—both of which were intensified by the difficult prospects of war.

Adams's hopes for unity were further dashed when the infamous X, Y, Z Affair broke. In March of 1798, "Adams revealed that a diplomatic mission to France had failed when three French officials—known as X, Y, and Z in state papers—demanded bribes, a huge loan, and an American apology as the price of doing business" with France.[440] The breakdown in relations played out in partisan terms as Jefferson and the Republicans charged that Adams's handling of the crisis with France was a failure.[441] Meanwhile, the "Congress of 1798 geared up for war, spurred on by a ferocious speech by Adams against France."[442] As with most any pre-war period, the stakes and partisan reactions quickly escalated and Congress took extraordinary measures. Indeed, the "Federalists had sufficient votes to pass twenty bellicose measures, which broke off trade with France and allowed the seizure of French ships, setting off what was termed a 'Quasi-War.'"[443]

Hysteria gripped parts of the United States, including fears French sympathizers would burn Philadelphia.[444] Adams, although popular among many Americans for his actions,[445] was ridiculed in the press and that led his Congress to enact "four pieces of legislation popularly known as the Alien and Sedition Acts.... The bills invested the president with extraordinary powers at the expense, Republicans argued, of the liberties of a free people."[446] Adams's signature on the legislation meant "the speaking of one's mind—a foundational freedom—could result in fines of up to $2,000 and up to two years in prison."[447]

The acts remain perhaps the most partisan legislation ever enacted in American history. Predictably, in the words of Jon Meacham in his book *Thomas Jefferson: The Art of Power*, "so began a furiously divisive time of intensity and vitriol. Jefferson and the Republicans believed they were no longer expecting but were instead experiencing the end of American Liberty.... The prosecutions under the new laws were egregious. Republican editors were arrested, indicted and tried for publishing pieces the Adams Administration deemed seditious."[448] A Vermont congressman endured the same fate.[449]

Jefferson and Madison were completely divided from Adams over that incredible government act of eviscerating the First Amendment. They responded to the Alien and Sedition Acts dramatically if, at times, only secretly.

> Each prepared a set of legislative resolutions condemning the Alien and Sedition Laws. Jefferson sent his to John Breckinridge of Kentucky. Madison sent his to John Taylor of Caroline, Virginia's agricultural thinker and the Republican party's most influential pamphleteer. On November 16, 1798, Kentucky's legislature resolved that "whensoever the General Government assumes undelegated powers, its acts are unauthoritative, void, and of no force." On December 24, Virginia voted a similar condemnation and, like Kentucky, called on the other states to join the protest.[450]

With those resolutions was born the "nullification" theory of state and federal politics. Under that theory, states could nullify the acts of the federal government like the attempts we see today in certain states over Obamacare, executive orders and federal gun legislation. In their time, Jefferson and Madison were quite plainly stating that if the federal government went too far, then the states had the right to preserve their own sovereignty—the right to legislative rebellion against such a power grab. When states took such action, that meant that the federal

Alien and Sedition Acts had made partisans out of entire states. George Washington quite well understood the far-reaching implications of that dynamic and those resolutions. He responded by stating that the resolutions, if pursued, could dissolve the Union.[451] That is, of course, a fair reading of the run-up to the Civil War.

As for John Adams and the presidency, it is more than likely that he did not deserve the presidential hand that was dealt to him. He was an essential figure to American independence who skillfully handled many political moments in the run-up to independence. Some of his actions, part of an *Escalating Partisanship Dynamic*, including signing the Alien and Sedition Acts, however, were gross overreaches by the federal government. They guaranteed that the growing partisanship of the age would increase, not decrease, and would cause lasting division. His actions also led to him being challenged in his bid for reelection, and there was much at stake in that election fight. "For six years the Congress of the United States had been solidly Federalist."[452] The laws passed by those Congresses were more than objectionable to the Republicans, who wanted to take the country back to its "first principles."[453] "To the Federalists, if Jefferson defeated Adams, upending a government of 'order,' he would introduce in its place a government of dangerous 'experiment,' with the country devolving into atheism and anarchy. To Republicans, of course, 'order' had slaughtered liberty."[454] With the future direction of the young nation's federal government at stake, it is not surprising to find that the second presidential contest, between Adams and Jefferson, was more fiery than the first. The Republican Jefferson, and his running mate Aaron Burr, excoriated Adams for his handling of foreign affairs— even though Adams followed Washington and kept us out of a war with France. They also went after Adams for his domestic policies, which included deficit spending and taxes. The third major issue upon which they seized was the Alien and Sedition Acts. For their part, the Federalists branded Jefferson as an un-Christian deist and portrayed him as far too sympathetic to the out-of-control French Revolution.

After its first real negative campaign, on Election Day, the nation was ready to move on from Adams, who placed third in the voting of a system that still had all Electoral College voters voting twice—once for president and once for vice president. However, unlike when Washington was elected, there was not a successful effort to ensure that the vice presidential candidate would not get the same number of votes as the presidential candidate. Jefferson and Burr tied with seventy-three votes. As a result, for six days in February—three months after the election—the presidency hung in the balance during House proceedings before the election was decided in favor of Jefferson.

In the final analysis, the Adams presidency was hardly an *Era of Good Feelings*. Indeed, Adams and his party—in a highly partisan way—criminalized opposition to his presidency. The Republicans' response to that catalyst, that egregious government act of abridging people's rights, was what we should now expect: division and understandable partisanship. Politically, the excesses of Federalists played a key role in Adams's defeat and earned him the dubious distinction of being the first one-term president in our history—something that would not be repeated again until the presidency of his son, John Quincy Adams, whose term as sixth president also lasted only one term, in part because of his inability to quell rising partisanship. Without question, the decision to restrict the rights of Americans played no small role in stoking partisan flames and ultimately deciding John Adams's fate.

★   ★   ★

If Adams's presidency was "born to trouble" because of the tension with France and all its attendant challenges, Jefferson's presidency would benefit as it receded. Adams was preoccupied with keeping us out of war with France. Even so, in preparation for the possible war, Adams raised taxes, bolstered the military, and ramped up spending. Every one of those policies, especially for a country wearied by war and fights over taxes, was met with partisan objections. Jefferson, by contrast, was able to cut taxes and reduce the size of the military. By reducing the scope of government (i.e., by reducing the number of things government did, and by reducing the taxes government took from Americans), Jefferson's presidency would be comparatively less divisive than Adams'—at least until the European war landed on our shores again.

As for Jefferson's first term, after the bitter campaign, the new president sought unity in his inaugural address—a now familiar request, although in Jefferson's time it was as new as the country itself. In that address, Jefferson famously declared that "every difference of opinion is not a difference of principle. We have called by different names brethren of the same principle. We are all Republicans, we are all Federalists." Jefferson also made it clear that "nothing shall be spared on my part to obliterate the traces of party and consolidate the nation if it could be done without abandonment of principle."[455] While Jefferson would have preferred such unity, for the "common good," as he said in his inaugural speech, he nevertheless considered the results of the election a "mandate for change."[456] The results on which Jefferson based that belief were that "for the first time the U.S. Senate would contain a majority of Republicans; the House of Representatives would be composed of a nearly two-thirds Republican majority."[457] That new Congress, however, would not be seated for eleven months—until December of the next year, as was the practice of the day. The old Congress, dominated by Federalists, would have one last say and was able to get in one last, highly partisan piece of legislation on its way out the door. It was called the Judiciary Act of 1801, and it increased the size and scope of the federal judiciary and gave many Federalist judges lifetime appointments. By passing that, along with Adams's signature, the Federalists took one last partisan shot and hoped to cement a Federalist legacy for our government.

Jefferson would have none of that. He wanted to change the course of the young government—a desire that would be met with the partisan objections of those who guided its early course: the Federalists.

For Jefferson, "building a new American future required redeeming the excesses of the Federalist past, and Jefferson issued presidential pardons for some of the printers convicted under the Sedition Act."[458] It would also mean replacing a historic number of federal officeholders/bureaucrats—46 percent of them—"the strong majority of which were Federalists."[459] Jefferson also brought a different philosophy to governing America. Never happy with the power of the federal government Washington, Hamilton, and Adams had created, Jefferson convinced Congress to repeal all internal taxes,[460] including the divisive Whiskey Act that necessitated armed enforcement during Washington's presidency. Jefferson also had Congress undo the Judiciary Act of 1801, which increased the federal judiciary, with the Judiciary Act of 1802, which reduced it. In contrast to the Congresses under Adams, which passed numerous pieces of divisive legislation, Jefferson's Congresses did less. Jefferson's desires along those lines are quite apparent when you read passages from his "Messages to Congress"—which, since the time of FDR, we now know as State of the Union addresses.

In his first Message to Congress, which he delivered on December 8, 1801, just over a year after he was elected, the frugal Jefferson called on Congress to "reduce expenses to what is necessary." Jefferson "delivered" that message in written form instead of appearing in person. Jefferson purposely broke with the precedent set by Washington and Adams because he felt going in person was too monarchial. In a country that had just emerged from a ruling monarchy, many Americans, including Jefferson, viewed policies that centralized power with the federal government as dangerously similar to a monarchy, in addition to having concerns about those who outright preferred Washington to be a monarch of some degree or another. Jefferson went so far as to refer to certain important opponents who favored a strong central government as "Monocrats," a word that "means government by the one."[461] In contrast to the government they built, Jefferson called for a government that recognized that "the States themselves have principal care of our persons, our property, and our reputation."[462] In a direct commentary about his predecessors' actions, Jefferson told America that "we may well doubt whether our organization [the federal government] is not too complicated, too expensive; whether offices and officers have not been multiplied unnecessarily and sometimes injurious to the service they were meant to promote."[463]

Jefferson wanted to reduce government and taxation wherever possible. With regard to military spending, he chastened Congress by writing that "sound principles will not justify our taxing the industry of our fellow citizens to accumulate treasure for wars to happen we know not when." Overall, he told Congress that

> Considering the general tendency to multiply offices and dependencies and to increase expense to the ultimate term of burthen which the citizen can bear, it behooves us to avail ourselves of every occasion which presents itself for taking off the surcharge, that it never may be seen here that after leaving to labor the smallest portion of its earnings on which it can subsist, Government shall itself consume the whole residue of what it was instituted to guard. In our care, too, of the public contributions intrusted to our direction it would be prudent to multiply barriers against their dissipation by appropriating specific sums to every specific purpose susceptible of definition; by disallowing all applications of money varying from the appropriation in object or transcending it in amount; by reducing the undefined field of contingencies and thereby circumscribing discretionary powers over money, and by bringing back to a single department all accountabilities for money, where the examinations may be prompt, efficacious, and uniform.[464]

In his message to Congress delivered on December 15, 1802, again in written form, Jefferson touted the paying down of the public debt "merely by avoiding false objects of expense."[465] He spoke of tax collectors now "out of commission" because of the repeal of internal taxes that he signed into law.[466] Each year thereafter, Jefferson would report to Congress his administration's progress in paying down the national debt. So much was his success that by December 2, 1806, Jefferson was openly asking Congress what to do with an impending surplus. Jefferson acknowledged that some "would certainly prefer" to continue the current impost/tax rates to pay for "the great purposes of the public education, roads, rivers, canals, and such other objects of public improvement." However, the legally frugal Jefferson surmised, "I suppose an amendment to the Constitution, by the consent of the States, necessary, because the objects now recommended are not among those enumerated in the Constitution, and to which it permits the public moneys to be applied." It would not be the only time Jefferson would speak of enumerated powers and reduced spending.

In those ways and sundry others, Jefferson was the first president who sought to reduce the size and scope of the federal government, and a rare president to achieve it. In doing that, Jefferson clearly understood that government action was often divisive. In a nutshell, Jefferson explained the very historical dynamic on which this book rests when he wrote of Washington, DC, "*Here are so many wants. So many affections and passions engaged, so varying in their interests and objects, that no one can be conciliated without revolting others.*" In other words, government was in the business of picking winners and losers—a process that was fraught with competition and one sure to divide people.

Notwithstanding Jefferson's general desire to reduce the scope of government, he was not always legally frugal. Many historians note that Jefferson actually expanded the power of the executive branch—even as he called for smaller government. Among the more startling actions taken by Jefferson, and not enumerated in the Constitution, was the

Louisiana Purchase. Just two years into his presidency, Jefferson was offered a deal of a civilization's lifetime—a deal to purchase a quantity of land that would nearly double the size of the United States and remove France from our western border—all for a relative bargain and without war. Jefferson simply couldn't resist, even though he knew he was on dangerous legal ground.

Jefferson at first thought that the purchase would need a constitutional amendment to complete. Apparently, in a hurry to sign the treaty for its acquisition, Jefferson convened his cabinet to discuss the legal ramifications of the treaty after he signed it.[467] In his 1803 message to Congress, Jefferson acknowledged the issue along with the added public debt by writing, "Should the acquisition of Louisiana be confirmed and carried into effect, a sum of nearly $13 million will then be added to our public debt." His unprecedented action met with not unexpected opposition. Jefferson was said to be hypocritical for doing what he assuredly would have said Hamilton had no right to do—not to mention Jefferson's flip-flopping on the need for an amendment after his cabinet talked him out of the need for it. A Federalist senator from Massachusetts, Timothy Pickering, was so angered by the power grab that he "suggested secession and the formation of a northern confederacy."[468] Critics in Congress had their say as well.

In the House of Representatives were many Old Republicans, and they proceeded to give Jefferson some palpitations. When New York Federalist Gaylord Griswold called for papers to prove that France, and not Spain, had a title to Louisiana, Majority Leader John Randolph tried to crush the request by an immediate vote. With a 3–1 Republican majority, he won by a mere two votes, 59–57. The next day Griswold was on the attack again, arguing that the territory could not be admitted without a constitutional amendment. In the ensuing debate, the Republicans sounded like Federalists, touting the implied powers of the government.

More threatening was the argument of Federalist Roger Griswold of

Connecticut. He admitted that the Constitution's implied powers gave the government the authority to acquire Louisiana. But the Jeffersonians could not incorporate the people of the territory into the Union, as the treaty required them to do. Louisiana could only be governed as a colony, the way the British ruled Jamaica or India.

Majority Leader Randolph scoffed at this argument and declared that the implied powers of the Constitution entitled the federal government to incorporate Great Britain or France into the Union if the opportunity arose. With this all-but-total repudiation of strict construction, Randolph called for a vote on the treaty. The Republicans rediscovered party discipline and voted 90–25 to approve the treaty and appropriate the purchase price.[469]

There were other flash points of divisions during Jefferson's term as president as well. They included Jefferson's decision to use the navy against the Barbary States without consulting Congress.[470] There was his constitutional showdown with his cousin John Marshall in the seminal case of *Marbury v. Madison*, which is known to history as the case under which the Supreme Court claimed forever the right to review and strike down actions of Congress. It was a judicial power unenumerated and proof that the desire to centralize power does not belong to legislators or presidents alone. There was also the Embargo Act of 1807, which Jefferson signed into law in response to violations of US neutrality by the British and the French in their ongoing war. That, too, brought cries of possible secession from the north because of the very negative effect on their trade with Europe. It was yet another example of high partisanship brought on by government action.

Notwithstanding Jefferson's executive branch power grabs and the Embargo Act and the understandable consternation they set off, all in all, the federal government was doing less, in key respects, under Jefferson than under Washington and Adams. Washington had to establish the federal government, and Adams and the Federalists chose a difficult path under the pressures of the potential war with France. Jefferson, by and large, did not face those dynamics and, over his years in office, asked Congress to do less on average.

Even so, with the direction of the country at stake, the Federalists remained vigilant partisans despite being legislatively ineffective. Jefferson, on the other hand, proved to be a very effective president politically. He easily won reelection—162 electoral votes to 14 over Federalist Charles Pinckney. Jefferson's policies of reduced spending and taxes worked well. His landslide reelection was not the only story. In the words of Jon Meacham, "Thomas Jefferson was the most successful political figure of the first half century of the American republic. For thirty-six of the forty years between 1800 and 1840, either Jefferson or a self-described adherent of his served as president of the United States: James Madison, James Monroe, Andrew Jackson, and Martin Van Buren. (John Quincy Adams, a one-term president, was the single exception.) This unofficial and little-noted Jeffersonian dynasty is unmatched in American history."[471] Indeed, Jefferson's policy changes set the stage for his successors and the *Era of Good Feelings*. Before we can get to that time, however, American politics and the presidency of James Madison would be challenged by the War of 1812.

★   ★   ★

The political success of Thomas Jefferson overall certainly helped the fortunes of his close political ally James Madison, whom Jefferson endorsed for the presidency. Although Madison defeated Charles Pinckney 122 to 47 votes in the Electoral College, Madison's victory was strained because the next president of the United States, James Monroe, and others ran against him. Even though Monroe didn't fare well in this go around—he received no electoral votes—it was evidence that the country was not unified at that time. Perhaps the most significant reason the race was far closer for Madison than Jefferson's reelection was because of the Embargo Act of 1807.

In the early 1800s, England began seizing American ships on the high seas. As her hostilities with France increased, in 1806, "England declared all French ports blockaded. France retorted with a similar fulmination. Amidst their crisis, English war vessels coasted along our shores to overhaul our ships; and even entered our harbors in chase of prey."[472] In response, President Jefferson proclaimed an embargo against England and France. However, the "embargo was specially injurious to New England shipping. . . . The Massachusetts legislature, which at first endorsed the measure, in its next session condemned it."[473] Eventually, it adopted a report declaring Congress's attempt to enforce the embargo as 'not legally binding" and a New England convention was planned for purposes of secession.[474] The New England states also disputed the federal government's right to require them to lend troops or tax them to combat the hostilities with England. At one point, it was said that "New England was practically in rebellion. It had seceded from united national action, and had set up a war confederacy."[475]

If we remember that the Federalists were always strongest in the Northeast, and Jefferson's party in the South and West, we can understand how the Embargo Act created geographical political divisions. It also revived the fortunes of the Federalists who opposed Jefferson's embargo policy. Once Madison took office, the similarities between Madison and Adams became more apparent than those between Madison and Jefferson. Madison and Adams "both highly admired the men they replaced as chief executive. Both were smaller men in stature and force of personality than the presidents they followed. . . . Both inherited cabinet members and agendas from their predecessors."[476] There was one more important similarity between the two: the war between England and France took center stage at the outset of their presidencies. For Adams, it defined his presidency. For Madison, it would lead to the newly formed United States' first war, fought on American soil, notwithstanding his inaugural address declaring neutrality in the ongoing dispute between England and France.

Domestically, Madison continued Jefferson's practice of a limited legislative agenda. That meant that the First Congress of James Madison's presidency did not pass significant domestic legislation. That did not mean, however, that all was right for Madison or the country. Instead, Madison faced a growing foreign policy crisis and his early Congresses passed legislation related to that. Just prior to leaving office, Jefferson's last Congress repealed the Embargo Act of 1807—a source of considerable and continuing division in the United States. It was replaced three days prior to Madison's inauguration with the Non-Intercourse Act. That act still restricted trade with England and France but reopened trade with neutral countries. However, it too was ineffective, at least with respect to keeping America buffered from the conflict between France and England. In some respects, it made the English believe America's resolve was weakening because, as a practical matter, it allowed for trading with England and France in neutral ports,[477] even though both France and England continued to interfere with American commerce, including seizing Americans ships.

A year later, as hostilities continued, Congress enacted Macon's Bill Number 2, which ended the embargo with respect to France and England for a short period. It also offered the incentive to either of them that if they ended their hostilities toward America, America would stop trading with the other country. Ultimately, that carrot approach did not work either, and because "British and French interference with American maritime trade continued unabated, Madison prepared for armed conflict."[478] When he finally made a declaration of war against England, our "principal enemy,"[479] and sought congressional approval, Madison received important bipartisan support from former Federalist President John Adams. Knowing the difficulty of the situation and of opposition complaints, Adams posed the question: "How it can be said to be unnecessary is very mysterious. I have thought it both just and necessary, for five or six years."[480] Adams's support for Madison, however, did not mean that all or even a majority of Federalists, let alone the country, were in support of the war. The Federalists in Congress "supported Republican measures that expanded the army, prepared the militia, and explored innovative financing should hostilities occur. Federalists could only go so far, however, and in early 1812, they opposed additional taxes to refurbish the military and new commercial sanctions against Britain. When the decision for war loomed in June, they violently opposed the declaration."[481] They were not alone. "One-quarter of House Republicans either opposed the war or abstained from the vote altogether. It was hardly the act of a unified party. In the Senate, the division was worse. The upper chamber debated for more than two weeks before endorsing a declaration of war on June 17 with a close vote of 19–13. These gloomy indications of national division at the start of the war continued during it, and an acutely divided national legislature frequently struggled, sometimes unsuccessfully, to meet the demands of waging the conflict."[482]

For our purposes, a long recount of those struggles is not necessary. Suffice it to say that unlike World War II, which saw our country come together, the War of 1812—which lasted two years, not one—did not bring the country together. Instead, Congress was beset by "perpetual disagreement."[483] The war took a toll on Madison politically. He became the first president to be reelected with a smaller percentage of the popular vote than his first election—one of only four to have that distinction.

As for the view from New England, the English blockade had "so seriously impaired New England's financial health that the region plunged into economic depression," and "Federalist opposition to the War of 1812 finally resulted in the Hartford Convention in late 1814."[484] As we have seen, there were Federalists in New England who already spoke of secession. As such, it could fairly be said that the "Hartford Convention had been in a formative process for fourteen years. Among New England Federalists were some who were not good losers—politicians who had not yet come to understand the niceties of majority rule. They distrusted in other hands the power they would so gladly wield

themselves."[485] That distrust, so very blind, led to a convention rife with
rumors of secession even as the course of what had been an uneven war
at best, including the burning of the White House, was turning in favor
of America. "From his home in Quincy, Massachusetts, former president John Adams judged the Convention as 'ineffably ridiculous.'"[486]
The Convention, which held its deliberation in secret without con-
temporaneously published records, produced seven demands. They
included constitutional amendments such as limiting future presidents'
tenures to one term; removing the three-fifths representation clause
related to slaves, which benefitted the South numerically in Congress;
and requiring each successive president be from a different state. The
latter of which was meant to break the developing Virginia Dynasty of
presidents including Washington, Jefferson, Madison, and the possible
presidency of James Monroe to come.

The actions and timing of the Convention participants could not
have been worse in retrospect. First, the "public did not approve the
secrecy of the meeting," and "perhaps because of their secrecy, what they
did was thought to be much more treasonable than was indicated by the
mild report."[487] Second, it was obvious that the demands of the Convention reached far beyond the war at hand—it was a laundry list of political
gripes. "Here were New Englanders apparently more at odds with their
own government and constitution than with the British and their policies. Indeed, the more extreme Federalists had actually gone to Hartford
prepared to threaten secession and a separate peace if they did not get
their way."[488] After the Convention, they sent "ambassadors" to Washington, DC, with their demands. Before they got there, however, news
of a signed peace treaty between England arrived in that city, along with
news of Andrew Jackson's stunning victory in New Orleans. According to the Secretary of the Treasury Albert Gallitan, writing at the time,
"The War has been productive of evil and good, but I think that the
good preponderates. . . . The War renewed and reinstated the National
feelings and character which the revolution had given, and which were

daily lessened. The people now have more general objects of attachment with which their pride and political opinions are connected. They are more American: they feel and act more as a Nation, and I hope that the permanency of the Union is thereby better secured."[489] Thus, when "the ambassadors from Hartford arrived in the midst of the ensuing celebrations, they quickly muted their demands, . . . [and] irreparable damage to the Federalist Party had been done."[490] Indeed, the "persistent Federalist complaints about the war, occasional defiance of the government, and this final deed at Hartford all seemed a pattern of persistent disloyalty and flagrant troublemaking. The rest of the country was in no mood to tolerate such behavior while celebrating the victory at New Orleans and the achievement of peace. The Federalists were doomed."[491]

There were numerous legacies of the Madison presidency, including renewed American pride and success in what some historians have characterized as the Second War for Independence. For the purposes of our analysis of the *Divided Era*, the most important legacy was that the Federalist Party all but disappeared as a viable party. The next election featured the lopsided election of another Virginian, James Monroe, by an Electoral College count of 183 to 34. Overall, the experiences of the first four presidents of the United States set the stage for Monroe's presidency. Washington unified the country, established a working government, and held off partisanship as long as he could. Presidents Adams and Madison, and to a lesser extent Jefferson, had to deal with very difficult foreign policy concerns. Adams and his Congress dominated by Federalists overreacted. Jefferson literally undid most of their overreach and set in place a more limited government both philosophically and as a practical matter. Madison became our first wartime president. All of those dynamics were precedent setting and difficult for the new nation. Even so, by the time of Monroe's inauguration, the nation had settled down, so to speak, militarily, economically, and politically.

A great deal of politics is timing, and Monroe had the good fortune of serving after the trials and tribulations of the first four presidents. The collapse of the Federalists meant that Monroe would serve a good deal of his presidency without an organized opposition, leaving him in much the same position, at least politically, as General Washington. Also like Washington, Monroe won reelection in an unopposed election. He would preside over the *Era of Good Feelings* with enormous potential to act given his congressional majorities and unrivaled stature. The secret of his success, however, and that of the nation, was in Monroe's decisions *not* to act.

Preserving Rights— Not Legislating Differences

According to our sixth president, John Quincy Adams, young James Monroe "was bred in the school of the prophets, and nurtured in the detestation of tyranny."[492] Only five years old at the time of the Stamp Act, Monroe "commenced his military career, as his country did that of her Independence, with adversity. He joined her standard when others were deserting it."[493] John Quincy, the son of Federalist President John Adams, and the man who served as Monroe's secretary of state for the better part of eight years, tells us that "at the Heights of Haerlem, at the White Plains, at Trenton [Monroe] was present, and in leading the vanguard, at Trenton, received a ball, which sealed his patriotic devotion to his country's freedom with his blood."[494] James Monroe took the oath of office as president with a "ball" in his shoulder or what we know as a bullet today. He was, as Harlow Giles Unger wrote, the "Last Founding Father."[495] After his service to and for the Revolution, over the next forty years, Monroe "gave himself to the nation, . . . assuming more public posts than any American in history." [496] Indeed, working backwards, not only was Monroe a two-term president, but prior to that, Monroe was the US Secretary of War, the US Secretary of State, the four-term Governor of Virginia, the US Minister to Spain, the US Ambassador to France and Britain, a US Senator, a US Congressman, and a state legislator. Monroe is the only American in our history to hold two cabinet posts at the same time: US Secretary of State and US Secretary of War during the Madison administration. In that way and others, Monroe was "the most visible . . . [and] most powerful figure in the last months of the Madison Administration."[497] Given all of the above, when "the second Madison administration was over, the people of the United States naturally looked to James Monroe as their President."[498] It also meant that Monroe was ready to serve with unparalleled experience. That experience included watching the previous four presidents. Monroe took lessons from each of them. He also took office with a rather defined political philosophy forged from his real life experiences. According to James P. Lucier, Monroe "was a man of intellect, but not an intellectual, if by the latter term we mean one who deals in abstraction for theoretical sake. Monroe was an active man who wrote to report upon or defend the practical actions in which he was engaged. But since he acted upon a settled body of principles, his writings constitute an admirable unity of outlook, an unfolding vision of the American nation and its destiny in history."[499]

Monroe was determined to realize that destiny by unifying the nation in two distinct ways. First, it meant physically working to bring the nation together much like Washington had done. It also meant not dividing the nation with legislative agendas. Indeed, the hallmark of Monroe's presidency would be opening the West and allowing people to pursue life, liberty, and happiness by preserving, not infringing upon, their rights.

The outset of the Monroe presidency was much like that of our first president, with "the most elaborate" inauguration since Washington.[500] The nation was ready after the distress of the prior years. Then, just like Washington, in "the late spring he set out on a tour of the United States,"[501] for four months! It was "a tour of inspection and observation through the middle, eastern, and western states; it being his desire to become acquainted with the people and learn their wants, to ascertain how the machinery of government, remote from the central power, performed its functions."[502] "During this journey he also became the first president to visit the West; his presence on the other side of the mountains seemed to reassure and encourage settlers that they, too, were members of the Union. He cultivated the nationalism that had grown with the Louisiana Purchase and fanned the flames of manifest destiny."[503] Although he hoped he could do it like "a private citizen," again displaying sentiments like Washington, in "what proved to be an expression of deeply felt national pride and genuine love and admiration for Monroe, thousands—sometimes tens of thousands—greeted him at every stop and turned the tour into a triumphal procession."[504]

The age was defined, so to speak, after his visit to Boston. It was reported that 40,000 people greeted him, including "4,000 children— half of them boys in blue coats and buff pants, resembling Monroe's own Revolutionary War colors. The other 2,000 were girls in white dresses with either a red or white rose symbolizing the two political parties and their reconciliation under Monroe."[505] According to Harlow Giles Unger, in his book *The Last Founding Father*, "The press hailed his visit for its effects in allaying 'the storms of party.'"[506] For instance, "the *Columbian Centinel* declared that [Monroe's] visit would 'remove the prejudices, and harmonize feelings, annihilate dissentions, and make us *one people* . . . rest assured that the president will be president, not of a party, but of a great and powerful nation.'" The *Columbian Centinel* declared that the Monroe presidency was the beginning of an "Era of Good Feelings."[507]

As Monroe recognized in his inaugural speech, he was blessed to take the office with the country at peace. With such an incredible reception by the public at large and no real opposition party, Monroe also became a colossus astride the political landscape. He would have been able to enact an agenda of his choosing with his party in firm control of Congress. As he disclosed in his inaugural address, however, Monroe's agenda was to ensure that government was limited. That agenda did not require congressional haggling or approval and didn't risk public division. It also was the key to perhaps the least partisan era of our country's history.

When it came to Monroe's cabinet, he also followed Washington's lead in an effort to unify the nation. Indeed,

> much of Monroe's agenda centered around issues of inclusion, and he did not want the U.S. citizenry to assume that only Virginians were able to lead the country. As his secretary of state and implied successor, then, Monroe chose a New Englander: John Quincy Adams. Adams not only had defected from the withering Federalist Party to join the Republicans, but also was the son of the second president of the United States. . . .
>
> Monroe balanced the northern appointment with a southern one (William H. Crawford as secretary of the treasury). He completed his cabinet with John C. Calhoun as secretary of war, Benjamin Crowninshield as secretary of the navy, and William Wirt as attorney general. New York governor Daniel D. Tomkins served as Monroe's vice president for both terms, which added to the geographic breadth of the executive branch. Monroe relied on his cabinet to inform and advise him. When opinions differed between officials, he listened to the different sides of the debate much as Washington had done.[508]

Monroe's first inaugural address also stressed our shared values and the need for unity, as was the custom of the day. According to Monroe, the "American people ha[d] encountered great dangers, and sustained severe trials with success. They constitute one great family with a common interest. . . . To promote this harmony, in accord with the principles of our Republican Government, and in a manner to give them the most complete effect, and to advance in all other respects the best interests of our Union, will be the object of my constant and zealous intentions."

How would he do that? Providing a glimpse of the future, in that same inaugural address, Monroe then went on to keep "the practice of the distinguished men who have gone before me, to explain the principles which would govern them in their respective administrations." For Monroe, the highest principle was "self-government," and to what "effect"? Monroe rhetorically answered his own question with a series of questions. "If we look to the condition of individuals what a proud spectacle does it exhibit! On whom has oppression fallen in any quarter of our Union? Who has been deprived of any right of person or property? Who restrained from offering his vows in the mode which he prefers to the Divine Author of his being? It is well known that all these blessings have been enjoyed in their fullest extent."

For the president with Anti-Federalist roots, the preservation of rights was the key to his governing philosophy. That was his goal. It was his understanding of his role among the distinguished men who held his office.

★　★　★

I started out this chapter by stating that Monroe's presidency was a political period 180 degrees opposite from America today. Today's presidents and their governments have different goals. They were not nurtured in the detestation of tyranny. Instead, they grew in the era of social engineering when government and their presidents did things proactively and in response to events and perceived wrongs. Rights, to them, are of lesser concern than in days gone by. That could not be more evident than when you read the State of the Union addresses of our modern presidents versus those of James Monroe. Today, the State of the Union addresses are laundry lists of social programs and

Christmas wish lists of spending, that the modern president, Republican or Democrat, wants government to enact. They are starting points for legislative negotiations with the understanding that something will be enacted. They set off new rounds of the competition for spoils, and, quite often, signal that more taxes will be necessary. That was not the case during the Monroe presidency.

A review of Monroe's Messages to Congress provides a stark contrast to those of the modern presidents. In his first Message, Monroe gave first priority to the state of affairs with Europe. Given Monroe's extensive foreign policy credentials, and the ongoing issues with England and now Spain as it related to Florida, it is not surprising that Monroe would address those issues first. When he eventually turned his attention to the internal concerns of our country, rather than provide a list of things he wanted government to do, like Jefferson, Monroe gave an account of the public debt and how it would be retired—as he did in each of his Messages to Congress. In other words, enlarging government was not the primary goal of his domestic agenda. Paying down the public debt to zero was paramount—a goal Jefferson disciple Andrew Jackson would complete. Returning to Monroe, he then turned his attention to the ever-present requests of Congress to spend money on extensive internal improvements. Recall that Jefferson refused their similar requests in the absence of a constitutional amendment. Madison did the same and vetoed the "internal improvements" spending bill known to history as the Bonus Bill in the waning days of his administration. Madison noted in his veto message that the bill was "an act to set apart and pledge certain funds for internal improvements... for constructing roads and canals, and improving the navigation of water courses, in order to facilitate, promote, and give security to internal commerce among the several States, and to render more easy and less expensive the means and provisions for the common defense." Madison stated plainly that "it does not appear that the power proposed to be exercised by the bill is among the enumerated powers, or that it falls by any just interpretation with the power to make laws necessary and proper for carrying into execution those or other powers vested by the Constitution in the Government of the United States." He also rejected the argument that it was constitutional under the clause "to provide for common defense and general welfare" because it "would have the effect of giving to Congress a general power of legislation instead of the defined and limited one hitherto understood to belong to them."

In a letter to Madison, dated November 24, 1817, Monroe signaled his intent to stand with Jefferson and Madison on the subject, stating that "I am fixed in the opinion, that the right is not in Congress and that it would be improper of me, after your negative, to allow them to discuss the subject & bring a bill for me to sign, in the expectation that I would do it." In his First Message, delivered December 2, 1817, Monroe kept his word, stating:

> The result is a settled conviction in my mind that Congress does not possess the right. It is not contained in any of the specified powers granted to Congress, nor can I consider it incidental to or a necessary means, viewed on the most liberal scale, for carrying into effect any of the powers which are specifically granted. In communicating this result I can not resist the obligation which I feel to suggest to Congress the propriety of recommending to the states the adoption of an amendment to the Constitution which shall give to Congress the right in question. In cases of doubtful construction, especially of such vital interest, it comports with the nature and origin of our institutions, and will contribute much to preserve them, to apply to our constituents for an explicit grant of the power. We may confidently rely that if it appears to their satisfaction that the power is necessary, it will always be granted.

Monroe also made it clear that a limited government, rightfully constrained as it was, should also reduce taxes whenever it could. Monroe told Congress and the nation:

> It appearing in a satisfactory manner that the revenue arising from imposts and tonnage and from the sale of the public lands will be fully adequate to the support of the civil government, of the present military and naval establishments, including the annual augmentation of the latter to the extent provided for, to the payment of the interest of the public debt, and to the extinguishment of it at the times authorized, without the aid of the internal taxes, I consider it my duty to recommend to Congress their repeal.
>
> To impose taxes when the public exigencies require them is an obligation of the most sacred character, especially with a free people. The faithful fulfillment of it is among the highest proofs of their value and capacity for self-government. To dispense with taxes when it may be done with perfect safety is equally the duty of their representatives.
>
> In this instance we have the satisfaction to know that they were imposed when the demand was imperious, and have been sustained with exemplary fidelity. I have to add that however gratifying it may be to me regarding the prosperous and happy condition of our country to recommend the repeal of these taxes at this time, I shall nevertheless be attentive to events, and, should any future emergency occur, be not less prompt to suggest such measures and burdens as may then be requisite and proper.

To a great degree, those were the principles that guided James
Monroe's success in his first term. It was a hallmark of truly limited government, not the activist government of today. Early in Monroe's first
term, the "internal duties were . . . abolished by act of Congress,"[509] congressional desires for funding of "internal improvements" failed under
the threat of a Monroe veto,[510] and even in the throes of the Panic of
1819, Monroe remained steady. The Panic is historically recognized as
America's first peacetime financial crisis with eerie similarities to the
financial crisis of 2008. At the time, the regulation of banking was left
to the states,[511] and those banks fueled western land speculation. When
the "economic 'bubble' suddenly popped, with hundreds of banks shut-
ting down, and thousands of depositors and investors wiped out,"[512] the
Era of Good Feelings and Monroe's limited government philosophy were
put to the test.

At the time, there were more than a thousand banks. Highlighting
an issue that would dominate *Our Gilded Age of Division*, namely, what
type of currency could America have, each such bank issued its own bank
notes. One such bank, with no more than $45 in investor capital, issued
over $800,000 in bank notes.[513] The severity of the economic downturn
has been debated in history with some claiming it was a "long-lasting
depression" to a likely more reasoned analysis saying it produced "a
brief business slowdown."[514] Regardless of which assessment is correct,
the fact remains that the response of the Monroe Administration was
not to enact an 1819 version of a Dodd-Frank mega-regulatory bill,
which was passed after the 2008 financial panic—a bill that many today
believe is holding back economic growth. When federal revenues did
decline during the Panic of 1819, as they are wont to do depending on
the fortunes of the economy overall, Congress did enact higher tariffs.
Monroe and his Congress, however, stayed within the constructs of the
Constitution and refused to undertake a federal takeover of the banking system—a decision which stands as a stark, 180-degree contrast to
our federal government of today.[515] Of course, history has recorded that

America recovered from the Panic of 1819 without extensive government intervention.

Perhaps one indication of the real condition of the economic times, and the public's assessment of Monroe's response, came just months later "when James Monroe stood for reelection at the end of 1820 . . . [and] no one opposed him."[516] "The federalists presented no candidates at this election; indeed, they had become almost merged in the republican party."[517] "Of 235 electoral votes, Monroe received 231, with three abstentions and only one elector casting a dissenting vote to prevent Monroe from matching George Washington as the only President to have won unanimously."[518] The mortified recipient of the one vote, John Quincy Adams, would write of the election results that "party conflict has performed its entire revolution and that unanimity of choice which began with George Washington has come around again in the person of James Monroe. In the survey of our national history, this latter unanimity is much more remarkable than the first."[519]

Perhaps what made Monroe's unifying success all the more incredible was that he accomplished it not only in the wake of the Panic of 1819 but also just after the partisan debate that we know as the Missouri Compromise. In one of the many preludes to the Civil War, when "the Maine district, a part of Massachusetts, with the state's consent, requested admission to the Union as a separate state, southerners howled over the potential of further tilting the sectional balance, but perceptive observers saw in Maine an opportunity for a quid pro quo."[520] That dynamic and so-called opportunity eventually resulted in the Missouri Compromise passed during Monroe's reelection year.

History knows that Compromise as a deal between the divided slave-state and antislavery factions in Congress. The Compromise admitted Maine as a "free state" and balanced its admission by admitting Missouri as a "slave state," in addition to creating a demarcation line at the parallel 36°30′ north. No less than Thomas Jefferson underscored the divisive nature of the Compromise when he famously wrote to Senator John

Holmes that "this momentous question, like a fire bell in the night, awakened and filled me with terror. I considered it at once as the knell of the Union. It is hushed indeed for the moment, but this is a reprieve only, not a final sentence. A geographical line, coinciding with a marked principle, moral and political, once conceived and held up to the angry passions of men, will never be obliterated; and every new irritation will mark it deeper and deeper."[521] In time, as we shall see in the next chapter, "Our Partisan Heights—The Civil War," Jefferson would prove to be correct. Nevertheless, the difficult subject and Compromise were addressed without derailing Monroe's landslide reelection.

Thus, the story of Monroe's first term was not that of an activist Congress or government, despite the desires of Speaker of the House Henry Clay, whose spending plans were frustrated by both Madison and Monroe.[522] James Monroe benefitted from America being at peace and the demise of the Federalist Party. Rather than press that advantage legislatively, Monroe stuck to his principles. He avoided dividing the nation with a strong legislative agenda, Instead, he continued to favor the preservation of rights. While that may not have garnered Monroe favor among historians given his uneventful first term, his first term is historical proof of the basic maxim of this book stated in the reverse: *a lack of government action, or attempts by government to curtail rights, will result in reduced partisanship.*

Instead of curtailing rights or being an activist president, the story of James Monroe's presidency was that of enlarging America, and much of that was done through opening the West to Americans. During his first year in office, Alabama would become a separate territory from Mississippi, and Mississippi would then become the twentieth state. Illinois then followed Mississippi to statehood in 1818. During his reelection year, the Land Act of 1820 made it easier for Americans to purchase federal lands. In Monroe's second term, the United States also took possession from Spain of what would become the Florida Territory based on a treaty signed during his first term. Missouri and Maine were also admitted as states. The nation, and therefore the Monroe presidency, obviously could benefit from that natural growth outlet. Rather than restrict that outlet, like we find today when it comes to Americans accessing their own energy sources, Monroe fostered that growth and reaped the political rewards that came with it. Monroe dedicated a good portion of his fifth Annual Message to Congress, the first of his second term, to that issue. Monroe noted that "possessing as we do the raw materials in such vast amount, with a capacity to augment them to an indefinite extent," would allow America to become a "manufacturing country." Monroe saw that as a strength of the nation and a means to bring us together. According to Monroe, "It can not be doubted that the more complete our internal resources and the less dependent we are on foreign powers for every national as well as domestic purpose, the greater and more stable will be the public felicity. By the increase of domestic manufactures will the demand for the rude materials at home be increased, and thus will the dependence of the several parts of our Union on each other and the strength of the Union itself be proportionally augmented."

The story of James Monroe and his presidency, however, was not all triumph. First, Monroe's victory over partisan politics could not last forever. Although it was Monroe's goal to diminish partisanship and parties in our system, the lack of partisanship between parties, in this case brought on by one-party rule, eventually meant that divisions would occur within Monroe's own party. That dynamic was increased as Federalists folded into Monroe's party. That issue was historically highlighted when Monroe was excoriated by the future eighth president of the United States, Martin Van Buren—literally for not being partisan enough. Van Buren chided Monroe for the "Monroe Heresy" of appointing former Federalists to government positions, and even worse, failing to handpick a presidential successor.[523] It was said that Monroe's refusal to "interfere in the matter of selection ... encouraged a large group of would-be candidates to disregard party unity . . . [and] assured a breakup of Republican ranks."[524]

It should be noted, however, that notwithstanding Van Buren's "intense dislike" of Monroe,[525] Van Buren's words underline a central point of this chapter. "The President, he wrote, had introduced *no disturbing public questions*. The tariff was not a problem; the issue of internal improvements was 'speculative'; the United States Bank was going its separate way without regard for the government or the people; no embarrassing questions had arisen in foreign affairs."[526] By stating that Monroe had "introduced no disturbing public questions," the contemporary Van Buren validates the historical record, and the point of this chapter, that Monroe did not push a strong legislative agenda that divided America. Van Buren's comment that the issue of internal improvements was "speculative," a word that does not indicate immediacy or materiality, is further evidence of the limited agenda pursued by Monroe.

Nevertheless, "Monroe's suggestion [of a constitutional amendment to allow Congress to pay for internal improvements] seemed too slow and complicated for the eager legislators. . . . They had little time for due procedure as they watched the West expand and commerce move with it. Roads and canals were needed to help the nation keep up with its unprecedented growth. Eventually, Congress wore down the president. He signed two internal improvement bills into law before the end of his second term."[527]

Those bills were signed, notwithstanding the broader veto by Monroe in 1822, of a congressional appropriation of "$6,000 to repair the Cumberland Road in April 1822."[528] Monroe's twenty-five-thousand-word veto message to Congress, unprecedented to this date, is among the most thoughtful documents on any subject ever written by any president. According to Monroe, "There were two separate and independent governments established over our Union, one for local purposes over each State by the people of the State, the other for national purposes over all the States by the people of the United States." Going further, within his veto message, Monroe acknowledged the critical point for any argument in favor of the limited nature of our federal government. Monroe wrote plainly and clearly by stating that the "National Government begins where the State governments terminate." Within those words lies the essential nature of the Tenth Amendment—the notion that states have primary authority which defines the boundaries of the federal government—not the other way around. Beyond that, Monroe stressed that the "real sovereignty is in the people alone." According to Monroe, after the Revolution, sovereignty "passed directly to the people of each Colony and not to the people of all the Colonies"; "from the Crown it passed directly to the people." Again, with those words Monroe succinctly states the essentials of limited government (i.e., that government was not the creator of rights). Instead, government was granted certain powers after those powers were bestowed on the people of the colonies—not a country as a whole.

Despite Monroe's complete argument, "Congress eventually found a compromise route by passing the General Survey Bill, which appropriated $30,000 and authorized the president to use the Army Engineering Corps," to do in part what Congress could not do.[529] Monroe signed it and according to some, "Monroe slid down the slippery slope Madison had predicted, and the 'general welfare' stretched beyond the Republicans' wildest imaginations." [530] The result of that, of course, was more division and partisanship, including the making of the Democrat Party as Robert V. Remini argues in his book *Martin Van Buren and the Making of the Democratic Party*.

Finally, no discussion of Monroe, or his presidency of the *Era of Good Feelings*, could be complete without referencing the seminal *Monroe Doctrine*. It was, of course, the goal of every president that preceded Monroe to keep America out of the disputes of the European powers. Recall that for Washington it was a necessity to keep Americans from dividing themselves over the dispute between France and England, and in the process dividing America, perhaps hopelessly, before it had the chance to be truly unified. Adams, Jefferson, and Madison wanted the same to one degree or another, but obviously Madison's America succumbed to the conflict and Adams' presidency was consumed by it— even in the absence of an actual war. It would be Monroe who would lay down a marker that sustained American policy for the ages. Although a complete discussion of the doctrine is well beyond the scope of this book, "the Monroe Doctrine was a statement that the systems of despotism of the European powers could not be applied to the Western Hemisphere."[531] Any attempt to do so would be considered "a threat to the United States."[532] Again speaking plainly, Monroe declared: "The occasion has been judged proper for asserting a principle . . . that the American continents, by the free and independent condition which they have assumed and maintain, are henceforth not to be considered a subject for future colonization by any European power." Going on to state that the United States would not interfere with "existing Colonies and dependencies of any European power," Monroe declared that any future European power attempt to subjugate a country of the Western Hemisphere would be "the manifestation of an unfriendly disposition towards the United States." With that, the "Monroe Doctrine ushered in a thirty-year span in which the United States remained free of serious international involvement, a welcome change from the years of quasi war and direct war former presidents had known."[533] Of course, that is precisely what Washington would have wanted and pushed for when he set forth his Neutrality Proclamation and Monroe's fervent desire when issuing his doctrine. For our purposes, Monroe's policy was also designed to allow America to avoid divisive entanglements abroad, which could result in division at home. Fortunately for Monroe, his "speech drew universal acclaim across America" and "it dispelled American fears of imminent attack by foreign powers and unleashed a surge of popular energy that strengthened the nation economically and militarily."[534]

★   ★   ★

As we close out consideration of James Monroe and the *Era of Good Feelings*, the point of this chapter, indeed this book, is not to exalt or to excoriate any one president or party. The point is that it should be manifest by now that partisanship and division are natural byproducts of government action. Suffice it to say that the greater or more significant the government action, the higher the potential for greater or significant division. We have seen how the high-stakes nature of declaring independence, fighting a revolution, adopting a constitution, forming a government, and fighting a war led directly to understandable division. By contrast, the *Era of Good Feelings* demonstrates that a smaller number of significant government actions, and the preservation of rights, results in less partisanship and less division. There is no other logical conclusion to make, given that by all historical accounts the *Era of Good Feelings* was a period of very low partisanship and, not coincidentally, government did comparatively less during that period of time in favor of allowing people to pursue prosperity privately. In our next chapters we shall see partisan effects of the ultimate in government action: the Civil War and the federal government's establishment of state governments during *Reconstruction*. For now, however, we should give James Monroe his proper due for disclosing to us the secret of the *Era of Good Feelings*.

CHAPTER 6

Our Partisan Heights:
The Civil War

I will suffer death before I will consent . . . to any concessions or
compromise which looks like buying the privilege of taking possession
of this government to which we have a constitutional right.
—**Abraham Lincoln**

The South can never know peace
and security again in the Union.
—**South Carolina Congressman**
William Porcher Miles

The Civil War, in the minds of many Americans and historians, was the most seminal event in American history. "At the cost of more than 750,000 dead and that many more wounded, it guaranteed the preservation of the Union and abolished the institution of racial slavery."[535] One of the essential narratives of the Civil War is the incredible lengths, from secession to war, the people of the South went to in order to protect their perceived rights from the threat of government action—and how far the people of the North and their governments would go, including going to war, to enforce their view of the Constitution through government action. With so much at stake, matched with unprecedented government action and escalating partisan reaction, the United States endured the most partisan period in its history, and it was partisans that defined the debate and ended slavery.

Deciding Our Fate with Guns, Not Ballots

The Civil War occurred in considerable part because America had become divided along geographic, cultural, and partisan lines like no other time in our history. In some important ways, we were two different countries economically and socially—North and South. Although there were other key differences, at the center of our divisions was slavery. The Southern economy and way of life was built on it and very much depended on it. Southerners were intent on keeping it that way. Most Northerners were of a different mind. For a country amid Manifest Destiny, they wanted to limit slavery from expanding beyond the South into additional states and Territories yet to become states. Indeed, as we passed into the 1850s, a country not yet one hundred years old, the "immediate crucial issue was the place of slavery in the national Territories; the longer term question concerned the character of the Union and who would wield power of it."[536] The issue would not rest there, however. As the impact of Lincoln's election unfolded, soon the very abolition of slavery would take center stage.

From the inception of the country to the fateful election of 1860, Southern presidents and slaveholders had run much of the country. While they did so, the institution of slavery was not in jeopardy of being abolished and the Southern way of life, therefore, was not in jeopardy either. However, demographics were changing nationally, and with that, so too was the Northerners' view of slavery's place in America and what to do about it. Aware of that, "Southern leaders were fearful the ever-growing population of the free-state bloc would reduce the existing bloc of slave states to minority status in the Union,"[537] and use its growing political power against the South. Those changing dynamics and differences reached a focal point with the 1860 presidential election. As a direct response to the election of Abraham Lincoln, many people in Southern states agreed with the sentiment of South Carolina's congressman, William Porcher Miles, expressed at the outset of this chapter. They no longer believed that their way of life and the institution upon which it was built—slavery—could be protected if they stayed in the Union. Egged on by partisans so intense, history would know them as "fire-eaters," many Southerners believed that Republicans and their president wanted nothing less than to change their way of life and use the federal government to do it.

Fearful of such change and the government action it might take to do it, Southern states took the dramatic and unprecedented partisan step of seceding from the Union during what became known as our great *Secession Crisis*—the greatest example of an *Escalating Partisanship Dynamic* in our history. The crisis took place largely in between the time of Lincoln's election in November of 1860 and his inauguration in March of 1861. As the crisis unfolded and the talk of a war grew, a pattern similar to what we witnessed in the run-up to the Revolution emerged, with partisans on both sides and those seeking compromise in the middle.

Obviously, there was the broad division between the Deep South states that seceded after Lincoln's election and the states of the North. Between them geographically and politically were the "border" states, with ties to the North and the South that took a wait-and-see approach and sought compromise. Our divisions, however, were not limited to differences between the states. The precarious position of the border states led to intense political division within those border states as well. There also was intense division among those in the North, within the Republican Party, which was based almost exclusively in the North, and even among Lincoln's cabinet. There was intense division among the Democrats as well. The Democratic Party split into two parties, North and South, during the 1860 election over the best way to protect Southern rights. Beyond those divisions, the commercial class once again opposed the prospects of war as disruptive to business, and the media of the age was both witness to and an advocate of the partisan rancor.

All over the country, the high stakes led to bitter partisanship. After Lincoln's election, intense and determined "fire-eating" partisans of the South pushed for and got secession to protect perceived Southern rights, and Northern Republicans staked out uncompromising positions as well—Lincoln among them. In the middle was a cast of many prominent "conciliationists," who sought compromise among those uncompromising partisans. Between the time of Lincoln's election and the start of the Civil War, numerous efforts were made to bridge the divide. On all sides, the American people not only participated by voting in that fateful election, they were also engaged, like few other times in our history, in attempts to influence their party leaders *after* the election. The rhetoric and actions of many Americans, inside and outside of government, reached partisan heights and invective simply unimaginable by today's standards because the stakes facing Americans at the time could not be overstated.

Indeed, according to Russell McClintock, in his work, *Lincoln and the Decision for War*, "it was during [the Secession] crisis that citizens of free states finally defined the fundamental nature of the American Union, a task at which their Revolutionary forebears had deliberately and tragically balked."[538] Of course, McClintock is referring to the fact that our Founders, many of them judging it not possible at the time, failed to extend freedom to all Americans (i.e., they failed to abolish slavery at the time of our Founding). The Civil War did that and more. Speaking of the Civil War and the years and actions that followed, Mark Twain said they "uprooted institutions that were centuries old, changed the politics of a people, [and] transformed the social life of half the country,"[539] and to do so, along the way, there had to be much partisanship and division. Indeed, without the partisanship and intransigence of leaders like Abraham Lincoln, slavery would not have ended in the 1860s.

While historians have argued whether slavery would have or could have been abolished without the Civil War and whether the South would have seceded over tariffs regardless of the slavery issue, the fact remains that Secession, the Confederacy, and slavery's abolishment all occurred at that time and place, and it is the legacy of those who refused to compromise. The ensuing war became the ultimate partisan action of American history wherein we decided the fate of the nation with guns, not ballots.

Our Divided Nation

The America of 1860 was no longer the nation of the *Era of Good Feelings*. President James Monroe had been determined to end partisanship and party differences. His unopposed 1820 reelection was a good indication that he met his goal. During Monroe's two terms, the opening of the West accelerated and Americans sought prosperity, to a great degree, without clashing with each other. Most importantly, government did not get in their way and our politicians did not legislate us into differences. Forty years later, that was no longer the case. America was a different place. The North differed even more from the South. Northern prosperity was being built, to an important and ever larger degree, on the idea of "free labor"—free men working for a wage, and on the manufacturing that government had protected over the years. Southern prosperity, on the other hand, had been and was continuing to be built largely on slave labor. Even though the entire American economy benefitted from the abundant agricultural exports of the South, attitudes were quickly changing toward slavery, the foundation of the Southern economy, and Southern culture. For decades, the issue of whether slavery should be expanded beyond the existing Southern states produced political division—part of our longest *Lasting Division Dynamic*. Recall that President Monroe endured such a fight in his reelection year, 1820, the resolution of which was known as the Missouri Compromise. The Compromise of 1850 defused the issue again with a trade-off, which, among other things, admitted California as a free state and, as a concession to the South, strengthened the Fugitive Slave Act of 1793 with the Fugitive Slave Act of 1850—both of which required the return of escaped slaves.

As the election year of 1860 approached, whether slavery should be extended beyond the South was not only the dominant political issue—it had become *the* issue. Ominously, in the view of the South, a "Republican victory in 1860 would do more than cost the slave-holding South control of the national government. It menaced, some believed, the foundations of Southern life—a system of labor and race relations based on Negro slavery."[540] As our country split on the escalating issue, the division that came with it, and the prominence that our political parties reached fighting over it, can no longer be surprising to us. Before we turn to that dynamic, however, let us first survey some of the differences and divisions of 1860 America.

The Growing Contrast: North and South

By 1860, the US population had grown to more than thirty-one million. "The fourteen Southern states, excluding Delaware, contained only 11,751,000 inhabitants,"[541] meaning the Northern states had almost twice the population of the South. The "industrializing and eagerly commercial North was increasingly different from the overwhelmingly agricultural South."[542] Although the entire nation remained predominantly agricultural, including the North, "the industrial sector of the economy was expanding rapidly"[543] and unevenly between the North and the South. More than 90 percent of the nation's manufacturing was in the North.[544] Moreover, "the North manufactured 97 percent of the country's firearms, 96 percent of its railroad locomotives, 94 percent of its cloth, 93 percent of its pig iron, and over 90 percent of its boots and shoes . . . [and the] North had twice the density of railroads per square mile."[545]

By contrast,

> in 1860, the 14 Southern states harvested 5,385,000 bales of cotton, 187,161,000 pounds of rice, 231,000

hogsheads of cane sugar, 375,266,000 pounds of tobacco, 49,168,000 bushels of wheat, 65,000 tons of hemp, and 433,009,000 bushels of corn, and the region also contained 20,637,000 hogs and 12,686,000 cattle. This represented a hundred percent of the cotton, rice, and cane sugar, 86 percent of the tobacco, 29 percent of the wheat, 89 percent of the hemp, and 52 percent of the corn that was produced in the United States as well as 62 percent of the hogs and 50 percent of the cattle that were counted in the 1860 census.[546]

Those incredible numbers also meant that the South produced "two-thirds of all the commercially grown cotton in the world and about four-fifths of the cotton that Great Britain's mammoth textile industry consumed every year."[547] Incredibly, between 1830 and 1860, the South's cotton industry accounted "for about half the value of all the United States' exports."[548] Descriptive of the nature of the Southern economy at the time, 90 percent of the cotton produced in America was based on Southern slave labor, as was "more than half of all the South's tobacco [and] almost all of its sugar, rice, and hemp."[549] The Southern economy, as you can see, was dominated by agriculture and its agriculture was highly dependent on slaves.

Incredibly, nearly one in three living in the South were slaves. At that time, those nearly 4 million people had what has been estimated to be a $3 billion market value. That amount was said to be greater than the value of all Southern farmland and 300 percent of the "construction costs of all the railroads that then ran throughout all of the United States."[550] According to the Southern Presbyterian Minister Charles Colcock Jones, slaves were "the source in large measure of our living, and comprise our wealth,"[551] and they paid for "our education, our food, and clothing, and our dwellings, and a thousand comforts of life that crowd our happy homes."[552]

Slavery was not only essential to the Southern economy—it was also essential to the Southern way of life. "The Deep South ... had been a true slave society ... for twice as long as it had belonged to the union of states."[553] In the words of Bruce Levine, in his book *The Fall of the House of Dixie*,

> Slaveholding was not *simply* an economic necessity. It was not only the source of their wealth and physical comfort. It was not merely one possible enterprise, one possible investment, among many. It was, instead, the unique basis of the particular outlook, assumptions, norms, habits, and relationships to which masters as a social class had become deeply and reflexively attached. It defined their privileges and shaped their culture, their religion, and even their personalities.[554]

To dramatize the point, Levine goes on to tell us that "Abel P. Upsher, ... a judge of the General Court of Virginia, and later a U.S. Secretary of State, enunciated the point clearly. The 'domestic slavery' that formed 'the great distinguishing characteristic of the southern states,' he explained, also 'exerts a powerful influence in moulding and modifying both their institutions and their manners.'"[555] "Anything that contributed so tremendously to prosperity could hardly be regarded as an evil. Instead of being ashamed of slavery, the average Southerner began to look upon it as a great religious, social and moral blessing."[556]

By contrast, slavery had already lost its prominence in the North years before. Historically, the "legalization of slavery had been a matter left entirely to the individual states to decide for themselves; for most of the eighteenth century slavery had been condoned throughout the American colonies, but had been abolished in the northern states in the last quarter of the century, starting with Vermont in 1777."[557] "Some slaves remained in seven of the eleven free states as late as 1820, though they were numerically significant in only two of them."[558]

As we can see, the economic and cultural life of the North and South were divergent and becoming more so every day. Their differences, however, did not end there. As slavery diminished in the North, the views of Northerners turned increasingly against slavery and those that supported it. By contrast, Southerners still believed as Virginian John Randolph had declared decades before: slavery "is to us a question of life and death."[559] In 1860, that was true, more than ever. Those divergent views crossed economic, constitutional, philosophical, and religious grounds. As we continue to consider those differences and how they would play out, it is impossible not to see at every juncture and in every corner just how intense the partisanship and invective would become.

By the 1850s, "commercial values and the 'capitalist ethos' pervaded Northern society."[560] With that came the view that "free labor" was more productive than slave labor. "During the 1850s, leading northern newspapers sent correspondents into the slave states to give their readers first-hand descriptions of southern life and of the debilitating effects of slavery on the southern economy."[561] They also encouraged slaves to run away.[562] At the same time, the "economic superiority of free to slave labor became a major argument of the Republicans in their attempt to win northern votes."[563] According to Eric Foner in his book *Free Soil, Free Labor, Free Men: The Ideology of the Republican Party before the Civil War*,

> If the free labor outlook gave Republicans a model of the good society, it also provided them with a yardstick for judging other social systems, and by this standard, slave society was found woefully wanting. The most cherished values of the free labor outlook—economic development, social mobility, and political democracy—all appeared to be violated in the South. Instead, the southern economy seemed stagnant to Republicans, the southern class structure an irrevocably fixed hierarchy, and southern society dominated by an aristocracy of

slaveholders. To Republicans, the South appeared as an alien and threatening society, whose values and interests were in fundamental conflict with those of the North.[564]

That sentiment was echoed by religious leaders as well. The Reverend Joseph Eldridge of the Congregational Church in Norfolk, Connecticut, provided a sample of that when he sermonized that "slavery [was] doomed to expire. Not merely is the intelligence and the conscience of the civilized world against it, but Christ the Redeemer is also against it."[565]

From a constitutional perspective, "the North, increasingly driven by emancipationists, thought of the Constitution as a document which, when applied in its spirit, would eventually ensure that all people in America, whatever their color, black or white, whatever their status, slave or free, would be equal before the law."[566] Consistent with that, "many Republicans insisted that equality of rights and opportunities was a cardinal principle of their party; [William] Seward, for example, stressed that the Republicans stood for 'one idea... the idea of equality—the equality of all men before human tribunals and human laws.' And Lincoln summarized the egalitarian aspects of the free labor outlook when he declared, 'In due time the weights should be lifted from the shoulders of all men... *all* should have an equal chance.' To the self-confident society of the North, economic development, increasing social mobility, and the spread of democratic institutions were all interrelated parts of nineteenth century 'progress.'"[567]

According to Paul Johnson, in his work *A History of the American People*,

> The Southerners, by which I mean those who dominated the South politically and controlled its culture and self-expression, had a quite different agenda. They believed the Constitution could be used to extend not

so much the fact of slavery—though it could do that too—but its principle. Moreover, they possessed, in the Democrat Party, and in the Taney [Supreme] Court, instruments whereby their view of the Constitution could be made to prevail.[568]

Echoing that, William J. Cooper tells us in his work *We Have the War Upon Us* that Southerners, bolstered by the Dred Scott decision, "overwhelmingly" believed that they had a constitutional right to bring slaves into the Territories.[569] As for the Republicans of the North, from day one they had taken the opposite view and "even in the face of Dred Scott they refused to back away."[570] The importance of that last point, in the *Divided Era*, cannot be overstated. Notwithstanding a Supreme Court decision in favor of the South, and which was not out of line with the historical norms of the time, Republicans became increasingly hyper-partisan on the issue within that *Escalating Partisanship Dynamic*. Republicans were outright defiant of that decision and the Republican Party platform of 1860 continued to call for no slavery in Territories. For perspective, try to imagine such a response to a Supreme Court decision today, or consider the magnitude of the media backlash to the desire of some Republicans to defund Obamacare in 2013, notwithstanding a Supreme Court decision upholding it.

It must also be noted that "slavery was not the only issue between the North and South. Indeed, it is possible that an attempt at secession might have been made even if the slavery issue had been resolved. The North favored high tariffs, the South low tariffs; the North, in consequence, backed indirect taxation, the South direct taxation."[571] For decades those tariffs "directly aided the economic development of the northeastern states, where most of these fledgling enterprises concentrated, while it drove up prices on manufactured goods everywhere. The South, therefore, saw no immediate benefit from the tariff and many there believed that northerners had effectively taxed southerners on the North's behalf."[572] Indeed, "during the 1850s, tariffs amounted to 90 percent of federal revenue [and] Southern ports paid 75 percent of tariffs in 1859."[573]

We also cannot forget that those tariffs had been causing division in America since our Founding and in the years before the Civil War, tariffs were as divisive as ever. This was no small issue to the South. "A precursor for a War Between the States came in 1832 when South Carolina called a convention to nullify tariff acts of 1828 and 1832, referred to as the 'Tariffs of Abominations.'" Action and reaction. This time, however, "a compromise lowering the tariff was reached averting secession and possibly war."[574]

Closer in time to the Civil War, the statements of Republicans and/ or Northerners concentrating on slavery were not taken at face value in the South. Indeed, many "Southerners believed deeply in their hearts that the moral indignation of the North was spurious, masking meaner economic motives. As Mississippi's Jefferson Davis put it, 'You free-soil agitators are not interested in slavery... not at all.... It is so you may have a majority in Congress of the United States and convert the government into an engine of Northern aggrandizement... because you want... to promote the industry of the North-East states, at the expense of the people of the South and their industry.'"[575] Jefferson Davis, of course, was soon to be president of the Confederate States of America and his comments were reflective of many Southerners and the high tensions and spiteful rhetoric of the time. It is in that light that their partisanship and intense rhetoric must be viewed.

Our Most Divided Election Begets Secession

The chasm between the North and the South over the issues of slavery and tariffs and the growing cultural and economic divide produced the most divisive election in our nation's history, dramatic change, the Secession Crisis, and ultimately the Civil War. The political result of the 1860 election was that "a long history of sectional strife culminated in the victory of the Republican Party"[576] and, for the first time in our history, a "new party with a solely northern constituency"[577] held the White House. What a difference that would prove to be. In response to the election results, outgoing President James Buchanan said that Lincoln's election created two geographical parties.[578] The voting pattern of the 1860 election validated his assessment.

> In the eighteen free states ... Abraham Lincoln won 54 percent of the popular vote and nearly every electoral vote. In the fifteen slave states ... Lincoln received just 2 percent of the popular vote and captured a total of two counties; his name did not even appear on the ballot in the Deep South cotton belt.[579]

Overall, Lincoln became president with only 39 percent of the popular vote and without carrying a single Southern state. By modern standards, Lincoln's plurality victory with just 39 percent of the vote—the second lowest in our history—would be considered a historically divided result, and so it would be in 1860. Seeing the results as an opening, the South's political and physical reaction to Lincoln's election was swift and dramatic. "It began in direct response to the outcome of a national election, specifically to the triumph of a particular party,"[580] and it started with South Carolina:

> The South Carolina legislature immediately called a convention to take the state out of the Union. Within six weeks, six more legislatures in the lower South had done the same. Each convention had voted by a substantial margin to secede. As they did so, their militias seized federal forts, arsenals, and other property. In February of 1861, a month before Lincoln's inauguration, delegates

> from these seven states met in Montgomery, Alabama,
> to form a new nation they called the Confederate States
> of America. . . . Spokesmen for the eight upper-South
> and border slave states still in the union threatened also
> to go out if the government tried to "coerce" the seceded
> states.[581]

Obviously, no other election in American history produced such escalation of partisanship. Heading into the election, Jefferson Davis, employing his usual sharp rhetoric, said that the election of an antislavery president "would constitute 'a species of revolution' transferring power 'into the hands of our avowed and implacable enemies.'" [582] So disposed toward secession was Davis that he believed that Mississippi "would have the positive 'duty' to bolt from such a Union."[583] After the election, Davis not only declared for secession—he advocated the same to Congress. Davis believed that "the primary object of each Slaveholding State ought to be its speedy and absolute separation from a Union with hostile States."[584] To Congress, Davis said the South's need for "the labor of African slaves" warranted secession. Meanwhile, the Confederate Secretary of State, Robert Toombs from Georgia, wanted his diplomatic staff to tell its European counterparts that "for the cotton South to remain within the United States would have 'threatened not merely to disturb the peace and security of its [the South's] people but also to destroy their social system.'"[585] To put a fine point on it, according to Howell Cobb, a member of President Buchanan's Cabinet who resigned during the Secession Crisis in support of the South, and someone who had supported compromise before but no more, "Southerners [were] risking their property and their society."[586]

As for the sentiments of some of the individual states, Alabama was rather blunt and "specifically assign[ed] blame for its decision on 'the election of Abraham Lincoln . . . by a sectional party, avowedly hostile to the domestic institutions, and the peace and security of the state.'"[587]

In Georgia, the "Mayor of Savannah defiantly raised a toast that carried an implicit warning to the incoming administration: 'Southern Civilization—It must be maintained at any costs and at all hazards.'"[588] Again, in the minds of the South, the election and its possible consequences appeared to them to be a "question of life and death." Facing potential government action that could bring death, they became the ultimate partisans, rhetorically and in action.

The South Sets the Terms of the Partisan Debate

As a result of the immediacy of the Secession Crisis after Lincoln's election, and before any meaningful discussion could be held on the issue of slavery in the Territories, let alone the direction of the country, the Deep South states chose the issues that would consume the Lincoln presidency: What should be done about secession? Was it constitutional? Whether it was or not, what would Congress, Lincoln, and the Northerners do in the face of it? Obviously, those were unprecedented questions facing not just a president, but also the entire nation.

President Buchanan declared that it was unconstitutional for a state to secede.[589] He also sought to reassure the Southern states that the North would not invade the South.[590] Buchanan, however, was almost as powerless as he was unpersuasive at that point. As a result, despite an inauguration four months away, after his election, most of the nation looked to Lincoln, if not for answers to those questions and issues, at least to determine what he would do about them.

Of course, the Deep South states that seceded did not listen to President Buchanan or wait on President-elect Lincoln with respect to the issue of the constitutionality of secession. Many in the South believed in true federalism. They believed the Founders designed a confederation, which left states free to come and go at their will. They also believed that Northern Republicans were attempting to impose their "moralistic" views on the South.[591] According to Virginia Senator Robert M. T. Hunter, the issue was the "preservation of the constitutional rights of the South."[592] As to what the North might do about secession, the prevailing view among Southern leaders was that the use of force "would destroy republican government."[593]

It is worth noting that the issue, leading up to the 1860 election, was not abolishing slavery in the United States per se. "Americans, Republicans included, overwhelmingly believed that the Constitution protected slavery in the states where it existed."[594] Once the Secession Crisis began, however, the central issue facing the country changed dramatically. It became what to do about the disintegrating Union. For Northerners, the question was truly "whether to compromise with the South in hopes of preventing disunion and, that failing, whether to use force to maintain national authority."[595] The South's decision to secede forced the North's hand, elevated the preservation of the Union to the most important issue, and eventually made war "all but inevitable."[596]

The Crisis Breeds Partisan Division Among Friends and Foes Alike

Like the *Persistent Division Dynamic* of the Revolution, consensus on another civil war would never be possible. Division was everywhere as it had been before the Revolution. It is worth noting how far from Monroe's presidency and the absence of an active party system we were by 1860—by then "well-organized parties had become an integral part of the American political tradition."[597] Those parties and their supporters and partisans were at the center of the unfolding crisis.

As for what to do in response to secession, in the North, "keen political rivalries and widely divergent attitudes and beliefs polarized residents of the free states."[598] The same division existed among Republicans in Congress. For instance, Senator William Pitt Fessenden of Maine "demanded facing down 'the Slave Power' by demolishing its attempted intimidation of Republicans by talk of disunion."[599] By contrast, according to two mid-West Congressmen, Schulyer Colfax of Indiana and Samuel Curtis of Iowa, "Our Republicans shall and should be conciliatory and forbearing." Republican Samuel Chase of Ohio completed the spectrum of early views among Republicans by urging "his party to steer clear of all issues relating to the Union [and] to the sectional question."[600]

The Democrats were even more divided. Unable to reach consensus on the multiple issues slavery presented at the time, despite two presidential nominating conventions leading up to the 1860 election, the Democrat party split nearly in half, becoming a party of Northern Democrats and a separate party of Southern Democrats. In the aftermath of the 1860 election, "defeated and divided, the Democrats found themselves in opposition, with the task of putting their party back together."[601] Buoyed by control of the Senate and the belief the next election would result in Democrat gains, some Democrats believed that could "stifle the Republicans."[602] Despite that appeal, there was no Democrat unity on that point or what to do next. After the election, while "northern Democrats pledged their fervent support for their southern comrades—to gain equal rights for the South—they simultaneously made clear their devotion to the Union. Secession was not an acceptable option; they would lend no assistance to disunion."[603]

"In the South, radical secessionists saw this moment, the election of a northern president heading a northern party by northern voters, as their opportunity to disrupt the Union,"[604] and so they did and rather quickly—although that did not mean there was complete unity in the South. The story of Alexander Stephens best demonstrates that point. Stephens was a Southern Whig politician when he was elected to the Georgia legislature before moving on to the US Congress, where he served between 1843 and 1859. Among the most prominent politicians in Georgia, as well as an ardent supporter of slavery, Stephens nevertheless resisted secession all the way to the Georgia vote for secession in

January of 1861. Considered a moderate on the issue of secession as a result of his prior stance, if not a Unionist, the need for Southern unity saw Stephens, from the very large state of Georgia, become Vice President of the Confederacy. Even so, the secession movement was swift in the Deep South.

By contrast, "attachment to the Union remained stronger and lasted longer in the upper South, where both personal and commercial ties with the North were firmer and slavery was growing less important to the economy."[605] Beyond that, the "political weight of non-slaveholders was also greater there, and their ties and loyalty to large masters less firm. Because they were physically closest to the North, the states of the upper South also feared that civil war would most immediately expose them to attack and devastation."[606] Kentucky exemplified the problems and conflicts of its kindred border states of Missouri, Maryland, and Delaware. "Kentucky strongly opposed Lincoln and supported Southern rights, by 119,194 votes to 27,002, or seven out of nine Kentuckians."[607] In his book *Divided Loyalties: Kentucky's Struggle for Armed Neutrality*, James W. Finck points out well just how difficult the post-election times were for Kentucky. "After the election, the vast majority of Kentuckians continued to reject separation as the cure for their troubles."[608] Kentucky wanted and "needed to show that, while it would not submit to Republican bullying, it did not see secession as a useful weapon."[609] Kentucky's Governor Magoffin "believed his state had an even greater reason to fear Northern fanatics than Alabama because of Kentucky's closer proximity to the North . . . [and] still saw a chance for compromise."[610]

Shortly after the election, Magoffin devised what, in many respects, amounted to a foreign policy to deal with the changing dynamics after the election:

> First, Kentucky's loyalties were with the South and slavery. Second, geography put Kentucky in a dangerous location. Third, Kentucky wanted to stay in the Union

if at all possible. Fourth, Kentucky's leaders believed compromise was the answer. Lastly, only after every attempt had failed to preserve its people's rights within the Union would Kentucky consider secession.[611]

Of course, Kentucky was at risk for much more than just fighting on its own soil—as if that would not be enough. There was the risk that slaves would abandon Kentucky farmers for the protection of the North. Compounding that concern, the "secession of the lower South caused a depression in Kentucky,"[612] a state that "produced crops and livestock needed by the people of both North and South."[613] Its desire not to be run over by the North ("seven major railroads from . . . three Northern states into Kentucky offered convenient logistical routes for invasion"),[614] and mindful of its economic interests, for Kentucky, the "best possible outcome would be not to choose sides at all and for that reason Kentuckians pushed for a compromise and peace."[615]

Division Beyond the North Versus South, Republican Versus Democrat

In addition to the differences between and within the parties, as well as the geographic divisions, the fragmented run-up to the Civil War featured yet another characteristic of divided eras: third parties. Of course, the Republican Party was a third party at its inception in 1854 and a rival to the more established Democrat Party and Whig Party. The Republican Party came into existence in the cradle of division that was slavery. As we have seen, for their part, the Democrats split before the 1860 election into the Northern Democrats and Southern Democrats. Beyond those unstable divisions, the challenging times also saw the birth of the Constitutional Union Party whose members had a "commitment to the Union above all else."[616] Situated largely and literally "on the border between North and South, in what one termed 'the temperate zone of politics,'... they characterized the secession movement as a 'wicked frenzy'... [while] they found mightily distressing 'the declaration of unceasing warfare against slavery as an institution, as enunciated by the Representative men' of the Republican party, for it unsettled the political world."[617]

Beyond the warring parties, there was also the business community to consider in this fractured puzzle. Much like during the run-up to the Revolution, the business community wanted business as usual and that meant no war. According to historian William J. Cooper, "No group was more eager for settlement than the northern business community," for whom Southern agriculture was also big business.[618] Russell McClintock, in his book *Lincoln and the Decision for War*, tells us that "many wrote anxious letters to Southerners and Republicans alike, pleading with them to find some reasonable adjustment of their differences."[619] In December of 1860, "some two thousand merchants and bankers" met in a gathering that was "deigned to highlight the breadth of support for compromise or conciliation."[620] Despite their pleas, much like merchants who sought reconciliation with England prior to the Revolution, the commercial class of the 1860s didn't get their way despite what would be considered moderating, centrist ways—which in reality were expressions of their self-interests jeopardized by the threat of war.

The media had its say as well and expressed partisan views that sometimes mirrored, and other times fostered the divisions we have already seen. Of course, the media of 1860 was largely confined to newspapers and periodicals. They also tended to be far more overtly political than the newspapers of today, including numerous papers run by "prominent political figures."[621] Indeed, such overtness was the norm as the nation featured many "party newspapers."[622]

Donald E. Reynolds, in his book *Editors Make War: Southern Newspapers in the Secession Crisis,* lets us know that amidst the growing division, most papers either didn't or could not remain nonpolitical. In the South, "virtually all of the so-called independent Southern newspapers expressed as much dislike for Lincoln and his party as the political sheets."[623] Moreover, "Northern papers considered dangerous to Southern interests, such as William L. Garrison's *Liberator*, had long been proscribed from the South . . . [and during] the secession period, other Northern newspapers which were critical of Southern institutions had very little circulation in the South."[624]

In the Upper South, as the Secession Crisis unfolded, there was a quick progression from moderation to a more hard line. According to historian Harold Holzer, "At first, pro-Union journals in the Upper South did urge caution. . . . But soon enough, separatist rhetoric began drowning out the moderates," some of which eventually joined the secessionists[625] much like Benjamin Franklin did after the failure of the Olive Branch Petition.

While some newspapers of the Deep South "vacillated, . . . the great majority of Southern-rights journals of the lower South showed little hesitation in endorsing secession. The election of Lincoln by a sectional vote, in utter disregard for the South's feelings, was the final insult, they declared. If the South accepted the 'Black Republican,' secessionist papers warned, he would exclude slavery first from the Territories and later from the South itself."[626] A North Carolina paper warned: "We proclaim it now, *and mark us if it is true—if we submit now to Lincoln's election, before his term of office expires, your home will be visited by one of the most fearful and horrible butcheries that has cursed the face of the globe.*"[627]

> With invective almost unimaginable today, the Charlotte *Daily Bulletin* published the following about Lincoln: "The head and front of the Abolitionists actually claims for the negro social and political equality with you and me. . . . I would prefer to live under the government of a wise and enlightened King than that of a Black Republican fanatic like old Abe Lincoln whose whole political life is a *deadly hostility* to us and our

institutions."[628] A Georgia newspaper went one very dangerous step further when it "posted a $10,000 reward for 'Hannibal's [Lincoln's vice president] and Abe's heads without their bodies.'"[629]

The North likely had a broader spectrum of views expressed in newspapers for a longer period of time, which reflected a North more divided than the South on what to do as Secession took hold. "The leading moderate Republican papers included Samuel Bowles' Springfield *Republican*, the (Columbus) *Ohio State Journal*, and the Cincinnati *Gazette*, while the *National Era*, edited by Gamaliel Bailey, expressed the views of the radicals. Democratic-Republicans were represented by William Cullen Bryant's New York *Evening Post*, John Wentworth's Chicago *Democrat*, and the Chicago *Democratic Press*, while Henry J. Raymond's New York *Times*, and the Philadelphia *North American and United States Gazette* reflected the outlook of Republican conservatives."[630]

Horace Greeley's *Tribune*, however, "with its combined daily and weekly circulation of 287,750 in early April of 1861, was possibly the most widely influential newspaper that America had ever produced."[631] Greeley's paper was the unofficial voice of the Republican Party. Personally, Greeley agreed in theory that the South could succeed, but had "expressed the hope that 'the moderate men of the South' would 'cheerfully' acquiesce to Republican Rule,"[632] even though Greeley's newspaper was the leading antislavery newspaper in the country. Meanwhile, other "New York newspapers went into overdrive urging caution."[633] "A New York correspondent quoted the great English commander the Duke of Wellington . . . , 'Anything is better than civil war.'"[634] Thurlow Weed, "long a prominent figure in New York state politics" in addition to being a Whig and then a Republican leader, was also the editor of the *Albany Evening Journal*.[635] Weed wanted "to soften the tone of the Republican press." Weed used his newspaper to publicly advocate for averting the crisis by "extending the Missouri Compromise line to California."[636]

Obviously, the escalating partisan tide was against those who urged caution whether in the North or the South. In time, the inevitability of war forced their views and their hands. For our purposes, the dynamic of partisans versus moderates and those seeking compromise amidst such division—an *Olive Branch Dynamic*—should be familiar to us now.

Intense Rhetoric and Gridlock Among Americans and Our Leaders

The stakes leading up to the Civil War were as high—if not higher than—those leading up to the Revolution. The South believed they had everything to lose. The North believed itself to be morally right. The South began to secede. The North was mobilizing itself after the election intellectually as to how to confront secession. Soon they would have to mobilize militarily. As we have seen, partisan embers and fiery rhetoric lit the way along that dark road.

During the Secession Winter, "since each side was convinced that the other's proposals could only end in ruin, advocates of both sides raged at what seemed the other's willful blindness, if not outright treason. Much of the energy expended during the crisis was spent in rancorous display of finger-pointing." [637]

Fire-eaters fanned Southern flames of secession in addition to secessionist newspaper sentiments. "The central argument of the fire-eaters was that the Republican contempt for the South would grow as Republican electoral power grew."[638] As early as 1850 they pushed for disunion and wanted "to reopen the African slave trade."[639] Their leaders, including Lawrence M. Keitt, Louis T. Wigfall of Texas, Mississippi's John Quitman, J. B. De Bow of Louisiana, and Edmund Ruffin of Virginia, argued that the "Republican critique of the South . . . was a humiliating, degrading affront to their status 'both as "real" men and "true" Christians.'" Republicanism was "much more than a threat to slavery"—it was an "intolerable slap in the face." In February 1857, believing that he had been insulted by Congressman Galusha Grow of Pennsylvania during debates over slavery in Kansas, Keitt physically attacked Grow, whom he referred to as that "Black Republican puppy," on the floor of the House of Representatives, sparking a "general melee in front of the speaker's podium in which dozens of congressmen fell upon each other." Keitt, who already had a reputation as a "gallant," now "earned the sobriquet 'Harry Hotspur of the South.'"[640] Again, such a scene is almost unimaginable today but reflected the high-stakes tensions of the Secession Crisis.

Strong feelings or rhetoric were hardly limited to the South or congressional representatives. Frederick Douglass reacted to Southern secession by railing: "Shame upon this cowardly, guilty, and fantastical method of dealing with the stupendous crime and curse."[641] Lincoln himself, whose hand was being forced by secession, used charged rhetoric during the crisis, including stating that "by no act or complicity of mine shall the Republican party become a mere sucked egg, all shell and no principle in it," and that "he would sooner go out into his backyard and hang himself." He would "regard any concession in the face of menace the destruction of the government itself" and would "suffer death" before he would consent to a compromise.[642] In other words, in the face of the greatest crisis facing the Union to date, Lincoln was not afraid of employing intense rhetoric. More than that, he was overtly partisan and uncompromising at times.

Nothing Lincoln said, however, compared to the hate mail he received. That mail included

> editorials in pompous language, referring to him as the Illinois ape, a baboon, a satyr, a negro, a mulatto, a buffoon, a monster, an abortion, an idiot, etc. There were threats of hanging him, burning him, decapitating him, flogging him, etc. The most foul, disgusting and obscene language was used in the press which were the

organs of the Southern *elite par excellence*.... Nor had the limner's art been neglected: in addition to several rude sketches of assassination, by various modes, a copy of *Harper's Weekly* was among the collection, with a full length portrait of the President-elect; but some cheerful pro-slavery wag had added a gallows, a noose and a black cap.[643]

Even worse, "on January 26, 1861, after visiting Lincoln in his temporary office set up in the Illinois state capitol building in Springfield, a man by the name of Joshua Allen wrote his mother: 'He has got stacks of preserved fruit and all sorts of such trash which he is daily receiving from various parts of the South, sent him as presents. He had several packages opened and examined by medical men who found them all to be poisoned.'"[644] Such were the extremes of the escalating pre–Civil War partisanship.

Recall how close the votes in Congress were prior to the Revolution. Division was everywhere and between everyone over the most difficult issue the new nation had ever faced. Another civil war also predictably led to political gridlock among our leaders. The lame-duck President James Buchanan, still president for the months between November and the inauguration in March, had lost his gravitas and did not want to take a misstep that could lead to war.[645] Lincoln, on the other hand, would not be president for four months and chose to be largely silent—believing people knew where he stood on the issue; and he did not want to muddy those waters or let the press misconstrue his words. "Congress quickly deadlocked between members who wished to entice the Southern states with concessions to slavery and those who refused to bow to the threat of disunion."[646] Fostering that gridlock, "Southern fire-eaters strutted; Republicans crowed. In contrast, anguished men on both sides of the Mason-Dixon Line struggled to find a way toward reconciliation."[647]

The gridlock did not mean that the partisans were inactive. Quite to the contrary, the period in between Lincoln's November election and the time he took office in March saw a flurry of activity by leaders and partisans as well as moderates seeking compromise. Chief among those seeking compromise was Kentucky Senator John J. Crittenden. On December 18, 1860, he introduced what history knows as the Crittenden Compromise, which not surprisingly favored the South but still made "a deep impression on Northern opinion."[648] According to Arnold Whitridge in his book *No Compromise! The Story of the Fanatics Who Paved the Way to the Civil War*, Crittenden "was the spokesman for the great majority of the nation . . . who had not given up hope of preserving the Union without resorting to war."[649] Under his proposal, the Missouri Compromise line would be extended to the Pacific, and he "wrapped up his series of compromises in a final amendment which forbade any future tampering with the Constitution in so far as it applied to slavery."[650] In other words, even the person viewed as the great compromiser of the time was unyielding in a critical respect.

In offering his "compromise," Senator Crittenden played the role of Continental Congressman Joseph Galloway, who had hoped for "Temper and Moderation," during the run-up to the Revolution. Recall that Galloway was fearful of a convention that could get out of hand. For his part, Crittenden hoped that an "angry debate" in Congress would not ensue.[651] He said he would "search out, if it be possible, some means for the reconciliation of all the different sections and members of this Union" and believed that there was "not a Senator . . . who [was] not willing to yield and to compromise much in order to preserve the government and the Union of the country."[652] A month after the election and before secession took hold, the Congress took up the compromise with committees in both the House and the Senate.

Ultimately, however, compromise was not the order of the day.

"Republicans were fundamentally obdurate in opposing any compromise touching the territories."[653] As Southern states seceded, and their representatives and senators departed, the Republicans used their growing majority to block any votes on compromise bills.[654] Those "vigorous partisans"[655] were bolstered by "rank-and-file Republicans"[656] who, in late December, "helped to convince congressional moderates to back away from compromise."[657] Indeed, so active were many citizens, "the Northern debate over disunion was nothing so much as a political campaign."[658]

Lincoln, mindful of all of that, staked out principled—and often uncompromising—positions with regard to secession even if he showed a certain degree of flexibility on the issue of slavery, except as it related to the Territories. As the secession advanced among the Deep South states, and "the day after Alabama joined the 'stampede,' Lincoln rejected the idea [of compromise] more firmly than ever." Lincoln, despite incredible pressure, would have none of it and in response to a plea to compromise from the Pennsylvania Republican James T. Hale, Lincoln wrote in uncompromising fashion:

> We have just carried an election on principles fairly stated to the people. Now we are told in advance, the government shall be broken up, unless we surrender to those we have beaten, before we take the offices. In this they are either attempting to play upon us, or they are in dead earnest. Either way, if we surrender, *it is the end of us, and of the government.* They will repeat the experiment upon us *ad libitum.*[659]

In the final analysis, at each end of the spectrum, President Lincoln and partisan Republicans on the one hand, and the partisans of the South on the other hand decided the outcome of the Secession Crisis from deep within a *Refusal to Compromise Dynamic.* As for Lincoln's part, until his death, America's most prominent citizen and president was proving, by modern standards, to be not only partisan and uncompromising, but also incendiary in his rhetoric. The actions and reactions of many Southerners, as we have seen, more than matched the actions and rhetoric of Lincoln. In a matter of months, those in the middle, average citizens and legislators alike, were completely overwhelmed by the forces tearing the country apart. Congress suffered to a large degree from a "paralysis"—with moderates unable to fashion a compromise—until the start of the war in South Carolina.[660] In the North, however divided the people were before, they unified, Republican and even most Democrats, with the firing upon Fort Sumter.[661] With that, partisan politics had passed from ballots to guns and the United States would never be the same.

★   ★   ★

If we pause at this moment, we should be able to accept that the Civil War, inclusive of its unprecedented death toll and upheaval, was likely the seminal event in American History. That the stakes were impossibly high should now be self-evident. We also now know that the issues of slavery, tariffs, secession, and the potential for a Civil War produced a dynamic similar to that which we endured prior to the Revolution. The approaching revolution fostered bitter division between the Patriots and the English, tension between the colonies, and division among the colonists. Many colonists, including our Founders, at least initially urged reconciliation and compromise with England, while others pushed for unconditional independence nearly from the outset. The business community warned that war would hurt the economy. Meanwhile, those loyal to the Crown stood their ground. The partisan press of the time alternately supported and fostered public opinion on both sides and in the middle. All along, there was intense, escalating partisanship and political invective. The same script could be read in the run-up to the Civil War. The same types of divisions, partisanship, rhetoric, conciliatory efforts, and more were present in 1860 and early 1861.

In both cases, consensus was simply not possible because of the magnitude of the differences and the nature of the issue. As a result, the main protagonists and antagonists *could not* compromise. They clung to their beliefs and their guns and in both cases those uncompromising partisans changed history. The South saw the election of Lincoln and the preservation of slavery literally as a life-or-death matter. In the months before the Civil War, their actions, rightly or wrongly, were precipitated by the perceived threat of government action and, as we now know, the greater the action, the more intense the partisanship. For its part, the North's view of slavery and America had changed. Despite a Supreme Court ruling upholding slavery in the Territories, Northern Republicans politically rejected the Supreme Court ruling—a ruling uniformly condemned today by Republicans and Democrats alike. Instead, Republicans continued to press for the abolition of slavery in the Territories. Despite prior compromises on the issue, the advancing times meant that individuals and states that pushed for compromise in the past were not willing or able to compromise again. The new Northern-based government proved to be the final catalyst for that change and the ultimate example of the dynamic that government action produces partisanship. In the next chapter, "Our Gilded Age of Division," American politics would be transformed, government action would still be significant, and partisanship would be ever present. For now, the period between Lincoln's election and the Civil War, the Secession Crisis—a period of less than six months—provides us with our history's most stark examples of *Partisan Catalyst Dynamics, Escalating Partisanship Dynamics, Olive Branch Dynamics, Persistent Division Dynamics*, and ultimately, the positive effect of a *Refusal to Compromise Dynamic*.

CHAPTER 7

Our Gilded Age
of Division

Every Rebel guerilla and jayhawker, every man who ran to
Canada to avoid the draft, every bounty-jumper, every deserter,
every villain, of whatever name or crime, who loves power more
than justice, slavery more than freedom, is a Democrat.
—Future Republican President James
Garfield campaigning in 1866

If disaster results from the inaction of the Congress,
the responsibility must rest where it belongs.
—Democratic President Grover
Cleveland, 1877

The Civil War ended in 1865. A century earlier, Carl von Clause-
witz said war was "an expression of politics by other means." Certainly, the Civil War was America's most violent political expression and
marked the height of our political divisions. In its wake, there was tre-
mendous economic and political ruin in the bitter and defeated South,
including the literal burning to the ground of some of its major cities
and the crumbling of its political institutions. Meanwhile, the North
was economically and politically ascendant. Thus, even though the
Union was saved, which was the principal purpose of the war,[662] the
Civil War did not end the physical differences between the North and
the South—let alone their political and cultural divisions.

In that aftermath and destruction, the federal government faced "as complex problems as ever taxed the capacity of government."[663] Those problems included how to reconstitute Southern political institutions while at the same time ensuring that slavery was truly extinguished—a goal which did not emerge until significantly after the Civil War started. Both goals, if they truly were to be achieved, required a change in Southern views, in addition to the physical rebuilding of the South and its governments. The principal means our Northern-dominated federal government proposed to achieve those goals was known as *Reconstruction*. It was by far the most ambitious government-led social engineering program in our history. Through *Reconstruction*, and by utilizing a mix of heavy-handed military and political action, new governments would be imposed on the defeated South.

Not surprisingly, large numbers of Democrats, and the South in general, resisted the North's use of such considerable power for such ends. The resultant and new conflict was so dramatic that it could well be considered an "expression of war by other, i.e. political, means." Understandably, partisanship between the North and the South was renewed and divisions deepened. We shall also find that the extraordinary use of federal government power, including the creation of military districts and governments—sometimes accomplished by unprecedented if not unconstitutional presidential acts—not only caused divisions between Republicans and Democrats and between the North and South, but also split the previously united Republican Party.

In time, *Reconstruction* would give way, during the 1870s, to the main subject of this chapter—the *Gilded Age*. During that age, the divisions the Civil War and *Reconstruction* fostered were then added to those caused by our continuing fights over tariffs, protectionism, and the form of our currency, among other issues. Altogether, the competition to grasp power and the desire to use such power and to choose the winners and losers cemented broad differences into place and produced one of the most partisan periods in our history—the *Gilded Age*. If the

Era of Good Feelings, which featured an uncontested presidential election, was the near opposite of our current *Divided Era*, we shall find that the *Gilded Age*, with all its partisanship and rancor, most closely resembles our current age.

Not coincidentally, and likely more than any time in our history, during the *Gilded Age* our political parties rose to dominate the American political landscape. Indeed, by the time we reached the *Gilded Age*, it was also considered by many to be the golden age of the two-party system. Like no other time before or since, parties determined the candidates, got voters to the polls for their candidates, and even controlled their politicians' agendas. Party loyalty became a must. It was enforced ruthlessly and, for much of the *Gilded Age*, rewarded with post-victory patronage. Even though the Republican and the Democrat parties were at their most powerful over their own, their power was limited externally by an important dynamic. Much like today, during the *Gilded Age*, the American electorate was nearly equally divided between the major parties. Indeed, from "the mid-1870s to the 1890s, the two major parties were in such close balance that there was no national majority party and neither party could easily enact its proposals into law."[664] Modern observers might well refer to that in the same way they do our *Divided Era* of politics—as gridlock. We shall see that the *Gilded Age* can therefore provide important parallels and possible lessons for us today.

The *Gilded Age* also featured vibrant third party activity. The inability of either party to dominate, matched with ongoing significant government action, meant that third parties, such as the Greenback Party, exerted important influences on the major parties and public policy. All told, the *Gilded Age* featured "extraordinarily high levels of participation in voting... and overflowing attendance at political parades and rallies"[665]—and from residents on down the line: partisanship, wrangling, and vitriol were the order of the day—something that we must now come to expect. Before we can appreciate the intensity of the *Gilded Age* in full, however, we must pay brief attention to the most ambitious

government social engineering attempt in our history: *Reconstruction*—
the new divisions it fostered and the old divisions it deepened.

The Decimated South, Reconstruction, Social Engineering, and Division

"The war *is* over, General Grant had proclaimed. But Ringo, the freedman in William Faulkner's *The Unvanquished*, remained wary. 'Naw,
suh . . . This war ain't over. Hit just started good.'"[666] Politically, that was
not fiction. General Lee may have accepted the loss for what many in
the South still call the War of Northern Aggression; most Southerners,
however, hardly surrendered their views or converted to the northern
point of view overnight—if ever. To the contrary, after the Civil War
there were "eleven states that . . . seethed with hatred and resentment,"[667]
in addition to remaining culturally at odds with Northern views.

According to Carl Shurz, a Republican senator from Missouri who
toured the South and reported back to President Andrew Johnson,
"Southern whites . . . were 'thoroughly hostile to the tendencies of this
revolution,' especially the implications of a free labor system and race relations."[668] They took that view despite the comments of the likes of Confederate General James Longstreet that Southerners were "a conquered
people" who must face that hard truth "fairly and squarely," including
by "moderation, forbearance, and submission."[669] Conquered though
they may be, some Southerners continued the Civil War by other means,
including "Rebels who went about burning houses and murdering their
foes." In time, "former Unionists" would become "pitted against the Ku
Klux Klan, what many have labeled 'the terrorist arm of the Democratic
Party.'"[670] Southern Blacks, suddenly freed, faced a similar fate. The continued resistance was so significant that while "facing local governments
unwilling to defend them, Unionists suspected that . . . although the
Union had been victorious at Appomattox, . . . 'they would not be victorious at home.'"[671] In other words, many were concerned that the North

wouldn't win the peace. Indeed, many felt that if significant follow-up action wasn't taken, and Northern troops simply returned home, the South would revert to its pre-war ways entirely.

The continued resistance obviously meant the nation wasn't unified by the South's loss. In fact, to some, the Civil War "created Southerners" or as "Robert Penn Warren famously put it, 'only at the moment when Lee handed Grant his sword was the Confederacy born.'"[672] That birth occurred in despair. War correspondent Whitlaw Reid, who toured the South just after the war, would say this of what he found:

> All men were overwhelmed and prostrated under the sudden stroke of a calamity which the fewest number had anticipated. Many had believed the war hopeless, but nearly all had thought their armies strong enough, and their statesmen skillful enough, to extort from the North terms that would soften away, if not conceal, the rugged features of utter defeat. They expected the necessity of a return to the Union, but they hoped to march back with flying colors, with concessions granted and inducements offered that would give them the semblance of a victory. Studious encouragement had been given from the Rebel capital to such hopes; and outside of Virginia there were scarcely a dozen men in a State who comprehended the straits to which the Confederacy was reduced in the winter of 1864–65, or were prepared for the instantaneous collapse of the spring.
>
> The first feelings were those of baffled rage. Men who had fought four years for an idea, smarted with actual anguish under the stroke which showed their utter failure. Then followed a sense of bewilderment and helplessness. Where they were, what rights they had left, what position they occupied before the law, what claim

they had to their property, what hope they had for an improvement of their condition in the future—all these were subjects of complete uncertainty.[673]

While the "North enjoyed on the whole a considerable degree of industrial and commercial prosperity during the war,"[674] it was anything but that for the South. According to William Archibald Dunning, in his work *Reconstruction: Political & Economic, 1865–1877*, in the heart of the Confederacy, a "long, devastating war followed by the sudden end of slavery had upended Southern society and thrown its communities into chaos," and that "chaos was universal."[675] Dunning further noted that

> the problem of reconstruction in these states involved on the one hand the question of mere existence, how to provide the necessities of life for the population, and on the other hand the vital question of civilized existence, how to constitute governments adequate to the social needs. For in none of the rebel states did the war leave either an economic organization that could carry on the ordinary operations of production, or a political organization that could hold society together. During the continuance of hostilities the military and naval operations of the Union forces almost destroyed the commercial system of the South, and thus reduced the life of even the well-to-do classes to a pitifully primitive—almost barbarous—level.[676]

Keep in mind that to a significant degree, that destruction was the goal of the Union Army toward the end of the war. After being fought almost exclusively in Southern states, the war's decisive end was brought on in large part by General William T. Sherman's campaign through the South—a campaign that included literally burning to the ground entire Southern cities, including the city Confederate President Jefferson Davis said was the heart of the Confederacy: Atlanta. Charleston, where the Civil War was started, was described as a "city of ruins, of desolation, of vacant houses, of widowed women, of rotten wharves, of deserted warehouses, of acres of pitiful and voiceful barrenness."[677] Sherman's stated goal was to break the back of the South, and he did. Reflecting on the aftermath and summing up the challenge facing the country after the war, a prominent American author of the time, Charles Eliot Norton, stated that "though the South has sullenly laid down its arms, it has not laid down its hate . . . we have not yet secured a moral Union, a civil unity; we have the harder part of our task before us."[678]

★   ★   ★

Historically, bitterly defeated peoples are loathe to assimilate in the image of their conquerors, and so it was and would be for the American South. At the end of the Civil War, America had a politically crippled, economically impoverished, culturally divided, and, in many parts, angry South. Despite saving the Union through war, we were still a divided nation—if not more so. Most Americans understood that. In Washington, DC, most Republicans also understood that the country would never be one again if they simply picked up and went home—home being the North—and left the South to rebuild itself. The question, therefore, was what to do about it. Simply deferring to private action was not an option in Lincoln's mind nor those of the Republican-dominated Congress. Instead, they were intent on using extraordinary and *unprecedented* government power, including passing far-reaching laws and installing state governments, all over Southern objections, and using Union troops to enforce their use of power—troops that did not leave the South until 1877, twelve years after the Civil War had ended.

Reconstruction would be the most ambitious attempt at social engineering in American history for several reasons. Philosophically, the victorious North, driven largely by Republican leaders in Congress, wanted Southerners to adopt and enforce Northern views of what American society should be—a necessity in their minds to ensure slavery was truly extinguished. Imagine being told you had to abandon your views—views held for centuries by generations of your family—not over time, but right then and there by the victors who had killed your neighbors in battle, if not burned your homes. It was in that light that the North wanted Southerners to change their ways. To achieve their philosophical goal, Republicans "strove to bring about a fundamental reordering of society in the South,"[679] including to the nature of government in the Southern states and their constitutions. Obviously, government-imposed solutions of such magnitude, especially when they involve cultural issues, necessarily lead to political division and intense partisanship among the participants.

★   ★   ★

Reconstruction would occur in essentially three phases. The first phase had Abraham Lincoln as its dominant figure, and started at the outset of his presidency.. After his death, the second phase garnered the historical term of Presidential Reconstruction largely under Lincoln's replacement, President Andrew Johnson. The efforts of Lincoln and Johnson have been characterized as a more lenient brand of *Reconstruction* compared to what came next.[680] After the 1866 elections, more partisan Republicans took control of *Reconstruction*. They imposed more onerous government action on the defiant South and that deepened our divisions as the South continued to push back, in escalating fashion, against the unprecedented and, in their view at least, escalating government action.

> For Lincoln, the question of Reconstruction required an
> answer from the moment he took the oath of office on

March 4, 1861, and that fact helps explain the trajectory that Reconstruction would follow as an era and a policy. Historians usually trace the beginning of Reconstruction to Lincoln's signing of the Emancipation Proclamation on January 1, 1863, or to Lee's surrender to Grant on April 9, 1865. But when Lincoln took office, his first task was indeed to reconstruct a divided Union.[681]

Once the bitter and deadly Civil War was over, Lincoln and others realized that the "complications of reconstruction were greater than those of the war itself."[682]

Sadly, Lincoln was assassinated on April 14, 1865—just six days after Lee surrendered at Appomattox and just more than a month after his second inaugural. Obviously, Lincoln's *Reconstruction* efforts were severely limited, at first by the ongoing war, and then by his death. Prior to his death, in what would become a serious point of contention, Lincoln took the lead in *Reconstruction* efforts, believing them to be "mainly a presidential function"[683] and part of his role as Commander in Chief. Lincoln's efforts were driven to a significant degree by his ideological vision of what America must become, and his "first approach to *Reconstruction* combined government and political policy with military action."[684] Beyond fighting the Civil War, Lincoln's *Reconstruction* policies utilized legislative efforts including signing into law the Confiscation Acts, which safeguarded fugitive slaves. Later, Lincoln acted through executive order in the form of the Emancipation Proclamation, which freed slaves in the states still under Confederate control as of the date of the Proclamation, January 1, 1863. Southern states excluded from that Proclamation were Tennessee, Kentucky, Missouri, Maryland, and Delaware. Prior to that, acting again through the office of the presidency, not Congress, Lincoln and his army installed military governorships in rebel states under total or partial Union control. Those states were Tennessee, North Carolina, Louisiana, and Arkansas.

Beyond those efforts, efforts imposed by military force, was the extremely difficult task of reintegrating Southerners and Southern states back into the Union. Ultimately, that was a critical, central goal of *Reconstruction*. The magnitude of that issue, as we shall see, and the notion that we could forgive to one degree or another the rebels and their states, were no small affairs. Indeed, they would prove to cleave the dominant Republican Party—a party that was previously united in saving the Union and in winning the war.

President Lincoln led the way on this treacherous but necessary issue. Acting through executive action, "to any citizen willing to take an oath of allegiance (an oath the president wrote himself), Lincoln offered a 'full pardon' and the restoration of all property 'except as to slaves.'"[685] In other words, and incredibly to some, Lincoln was willing to offer "amnesty" to Southern rebels who had taken up arms against the Union. Imagine that thought today with regard to the fight over illegal immigration. As potentially divisive as Lincoln's position was, the more difficult question, however, was how to readmit entire Southern states back into the Union. On that question, Lincoln and many Republicans in Congress strongly disagreed. Lincoln's approach did not demand much of the South states for the right of reintegration into the Union. Republican leaders in Congress wanted far more of the South. Not surprisingly, historians and commentators view Lincoln's position as being "moderate" and the Republican leaders in Congress as being "radical."

In 1863, Lincoln was the first to come up with a plan for the reintegration of southern states. He proposed it for Louisiana. Under the Proclamation of Amnesty and Reconstruction, what Lincoln called his "ten percent plan,"[686] a state could establish a government and "be recognized as the true government of that state" if a minimum of 10 percent of a state's electorate took Lincoln's oath of allegiance. It is important to note that under his plan, Lincoln was not offering federal protections (e.g., a greater federal presence—policing or otherwise—for the Southern states that adopted his plan). Instead, it would be the state constitutions that would enact emancipation and "the freed people had only those rights granted to them by each state."[687] In other words, Lincoln was allowing the former Confederate states a degree of leniency if not autonomy.

When he announced it, Lincoln's plan received favorable reviews in several important Republican newspapers.

> Horace Greeley was completely delighted. No presidential message since George Washington's day had given "such general satisfaction." The proclamation was wise and humane, and the *New York Tribune* could not see how anyone in the South could refuse its offers. Henry Raymond's *New York Times* was in wholehearted agreement. The program of reconstruction was "simple but perfectly effective," and the closer it was examined the more it would be found "completely adapted to the great end desired." In fact, "feasibility, justice, consistency, and security" were its recommendations. The *New York Evening Post* undertook the closer examination and emerged with the glowing conclusion that "it would be almost ludicrous pedantry to criticize the President's message."[688]

The Democrat press was reflexively less favorable and viewed it as a political ploy. Some saw it as part of an effort to continue to control the South through the vote of a small number of partisans favorable to Lincoln's *Reconstruction* designs and/or supportive of the Union.[689] Democratic leaders such as the Democratic governor of New York, Horatio Seymour, saw it that same way.[690] Indiana's Democratic Congressman Henry W. Harrington, on the other hand, attacked Lincoln from a different angle when he stated that Lincoln "made treason the foundation of reconstruction, the main pillar of universal liberty. Men who had been three years in arms against the United States could have forgiveness 'provided only that they are content to be the slavish instruments of Mr. Lincoln.'" Northern Democrats also attacked Lincoln for his "extraconstitutional" acts during his prosecution of war such as "increasing the size of the army on his own authority, spending funds without congressional appropriation, arresting and exiling opposition leaders, emancipating slaves in the Confederacy, and creating new southern state governments."[691]

Obviously, as with most issues of that magnitude, consensus and civility were hard to come by—even for Lincoln. Nevertheless, Tennessee, Arkansas, and Louisiana took up Lincoln's offer and complied prior to the end of the Civil War.[692] Congressional Republicans, however, in a sign of division to come, refused to seat the representatives from those newly constituted states. In other words, they did not support Abraham Lincoln, their own party's president, on this issue—even during a war fought on our own soil! Imagine, if you will, what consternation that would cause today in the halls of Congress, in the media, and among voters.

The "radical" Republicans wanted more out of the South than Lincoln did, including a majority of each state taking the oath of loyalty, not just Lincoln's ten percent.[693] They proposed as much in the form of the Wade-Davis bill, which also included federal emancipation and protections for the newly freed, and therefore, a greater role for the federal government in the South.[694] However, their Republican president refused to sign the bill and it died via Lincoln's pocket veto. The Republicans saw Lincoln's Proclamation, as did many Democrats and Southerners, as dictatorial and a usurpation of congressional power under the Constitution to determine when a state could be admitted to the Union.[695] Lincoln's use of such power, and even *Reconstruction* itself, split the Republican Party. Andrew Slap, in his book *The Doom of Reconstruction: The Liberal Republicans in the Civil War Era*, describes the tension for the liberal Republicans who were troubled by the use of such power in this manner:

The long-perceived threat of the Southern slave system to republican government led them to support
reconstruction of the South. Reconstruction, however,
required uses of federal power that they admitted could
be seen as tyrannical. While they ironically supported
military rule to safeguard republican government, by
the late 1860s they also increasingly feared that wartime
changes in the North threatened that very system.[696]

So deep was the rift within the Republican Party that, as the *Gilded
Age* got underway, liberal Republicans split off and formed a third party
called the Liberal Republican Party. In 1872, they opposed the radical
Republicans and the reelection of President Ulysses S. Grant.

Returning to *Reconstruction* under Lincoln, all of the above is not to
say the radical Republicans and Lincoln were always at odds. In early
1865, for instance, Republicans in Congress and Lincoln agreed on the
Bureau of Refugees, Freedmen, and Abandoned Lands Act. Under that
law, aid to freed Blacks on issues such as housing, health care, education, and employment was administered by the US Army.[697] The Act
also permitted the Army to lease and sell confiscated land. Of course, we
must not forget the Thirteenth Amendment. Barely two months after
Lincoln's reelection, in January of 1865, the lame-duck House of Representatives approved the seminal Thirteenth Amendment, which freed
all slaves. Although it was quickly adopted by the Republican-dominated Northern states, it would take until December of 1865 to be
approved by enough states—clear evidence of the existing *Persistent
Division Dynamic*. Lincoln did not push to make emancipation a centerpiece of his 1864 reelection and, in fact, it was a somewhat "muted"
issue during the fall campaign.[698] With a Republican "mandate," however, in the form of gaining control of the Senate and House in the 1864
election, and growing public sentiment, Lincoln nudged the proposed
amendment forward in his State of the Union in December of 1864

by asking: "There is only a question of time as to when the proposed amendment will go to the States for their action. And as it is to so go, at all events, may we not agree that the sooner the better?"

In the final analysis, however, despite congressional passage of the Thirteenth Amendment, Lincoln's stature as president, his commanding of a successful war effort, and his pending and then actual reelection, even his fellow Republicans, from the party Lincoln made, parted company with him over who had the right to exercise the unprecedented power being used. Congress wanted to exercise more of it and they wanted Lincoln to exercise less of it. The divisions within the Republican Party, not to mention the *Persistent Division Dynamic* between the North and the South, also meant that, by the time of Lincoln's death, *Reconstruction* was not an achievement he could claim.

★   ★   ★

President Johnson did not fare well politically over the *Reconstruction* power struggle either. "As the only southern senator who had remained loyal to the Union in 1861, Johnson was appointed military governor of Tennessee by Lincoln."[699] Johnson then became vice president of the United States—a position not of great stature in that time. Indeed, few remember the name of Lincoln's first vice president, Hannibal Hamlin, despite his unusual first name. Even though he served as vice president under Lincoln, Johnson "never became a Republican."[700] To the contrary, during his career he was allied with the Democratic Party of Tennessee on his way to becoming its governor,[701] and was a slaveholder until midway through the Civil War.[702] As such, when he became president of the United States, Johnson lacked the trust of the increasingly more partisan Republicans in Congress.

Johnson's difficulty with congressional Republicans increased as he pursued his own comparatively lenient *Reconstruction* policies, which included granting amnesty for all Southerners not previously pardoned. Johnson's initial policies led a Southern Republican congressman to write that "his extreme favoritism to open Enemys of the Government here has made and is fast bringing back a state of anarchy."[703] Johnson did, however, abolish the governments of the Southern states and gave "power instead to existing Unionist governments in four states; Arkansas, Louisiana, Tennessee, and Virginia, and to men appointed as provisional governors elsewhere. In the latter seven states elections were then held to create entirely new state governments, which the President subsequently required to rescind their secession ordinances, abolish slavery, repudiate the Confederate war debt, and ratify the proposed *Thirteenth Amendment* to the federal constitution [which freed the slaves]."[704] According to Martin E. Mantell, in his work, *Johnson, Grant, and the Politics of Reconstruction,* by the fall of 1865, those "conditions had been almost totally accepted by the South, although in some cases strong executive pressure had had to be applied in order to secure compliance. Even this, however, proved to be insufficient for the majority of northern voters, and Johnson's program in turn went down to defeat."[705] Indeed, despite Johnson's efforts, and the efforts of Secretary of State Seward, who declared on December 18, 1865, that the Thirteenth Amendment had been adopted by a union of thirty-six states, including the Southern states, nevertheless the Republican-dominated 39th Congress had already proclaimed earlier that month that "no legal state governments" existed in any Southern state except Tennessee. As such, they refused to seat the new Southern congressmen—obviously calling into question Seward's proclamation, which still stands today, that the Thirteenth Amendment ending slavery was ever truly, constitutionally adopted.[706]

In the wake of the defeat of Johnson's plans, the real legislative victories belonged largely to the increasingly emboldened congressional Republicans. In what was a clear marker of persistent division and Southern resistance, in April of 1866, Republicans in Congress had to override President Johnson's veto of their Civil Rights Act, which stated "there shall be no discrimination in civil rights or immunities among the inhabitants of any State or Territory of the United States on account of race, color, or previous condition of servitude." That same year, the Republicans in Congress adopted the Fourteenth Amendment, which famously provided that "no State shall make or enforce any law which shall abridge the privileges or immunities of citizens of the United States; nor shall any State deprive any person of life, liberty, or property, without due process of law; nor deny to any person within its jurisdiction the equal protection of the laws."

Soon congressional Republicans would undertake even more dramatic action, amidst an *Escalating Partisanship Dynamic*, including the passing of the Tenure of Office Act and the Army Appropriations Act—both pure power grabs—which collectively were meant to prevent the firing of a cabinet member, Secretary of War Stanton, a holdover from the Lincoln Administration and to strip Johnson of commander-in-chief powers.[707] Johnson's dismissal of Stanton anyway would lead to his impeachment, the first in our nation's history, by the "radical" Republicans.[708] In 1867, they passed not one, but three Reconstruction Acts, all over the vetoes of President Johnson. The First Reconstruction Act, known as the Military Reconstruction Act, divided most of the South into five military districts with a Union general in charge of each—with the exception of Tennessee, which had adopted the Fourteenth Amendment.[709] All combined, under the Acts, Congress asserted the right to decide the nature of the Southern governments and their constitutions. Congress also demanded, as a price for readmission to the Union, that the Southern states adopt the Fourteenth Amendment and disenfranchise high-ranking Confederates.

The magnitude of the assertion of congressional power cannot be underestimated. First Lincoln, then to a lesser degree Johnson, and now, in even greater detail and scope, the Republican Congress wanted to dictate to the Southern states how to form their state governments. Recall that Jefferson and Madison wrote the Kentucky and Virginia

Resolutions, respectively, that stood for the proposition that states could resist the imposition of federal laws upon the states. Jefferson outright stated that the governments could "nullify" the effect of the federal laws. States like Georgia took that to heart and passed a law threatening anyone with the death penalty if they sought to enforce a certain federal action. Now Georgia was being told not only that it could not nullify the federal laws, but also that it had to adopt Congress's laws under the threat of military action—laws that the Supreme Court would later affirm.

After voter registration was overseen by the military, including that for Black men, courtesy of the Acts, in 1868, seven Southern states complied with the congressional demands with Blacks voting in great numbers, including making up a majority of registered voters in South Carolina and Mississippi and 15 percent of the offices in the South after the 1872 election (a larger percentage than in 1990).[710] A year later, the Fifteenth Amendment would pass the Congress in an effort to guarantee Blacks the right to vote with the following language: "The right of citizens of the United States to vote shall not be denied or abridged by the United States or by any State on account of race, color, or previous condition of servitude."

Despite their legislative victories, all under the name and cause of *Reconstruction*, the reality in the Southern states was not that of sudden political agreement, let alone equality. Many Southerners, including their early post-war governments, continued to resist *Reconstruction*— at times violently and virulently so. In 1865, among the first of the Black Codes was enacted in Mississippi. In general, Southern states used Black Codes to significantly curtail the freedoms of the newly freed Southern Blacks, including restricting their rights to bear arms[711] and tying them to labor contracts that subjected them to conditions not much better than before the Civil War.[712] Once tied to those contracts, Blacks under the Mississippi law, for instance, were subject to the following legal threat: "Every civil officer shall, and every person may, arrest and carry back to his or her legal employer any freedman, free negro, or mulatto who shall have quit the service of his or her employer before the expiration of his or her term of service without good cause." In Texas, Blacks could be fined for "leaving home without permission,"[713] and into 1867, boarding public transportation could result in arrests for Blacks.[714] All the while, Black soldiers faced "endemic harassment from White Southerners."[715] The very real threats to the newly freed Blacks, however, did not end there.

The same year that saw Lincoln's assassination at the hands of a strong proponent of slavery, in 1865, also saw the Ku Klux Klan created in Tennessee by ex-Confederate soldiers.[716] Using nothing short of terrorist tactics, including beating and murdering their opponents, all in an effort to prevent Blacks from gaining the equal rights with Whites, and instilling fear in Blacks.[717] In addition, America witnessed interracial riots across the South,[718] including the Memphis Riots of 1886. Those riots started with tensions between Irish immigrants and newly freed Blacks. They then progressed to a shooting altercation between former Black Union soldiers and White policemen, and then a rampaging by Whites, including policemen, through Black neighborhoods.[719] When the carnage was all told, by a joint congressional committee, a dozen buildings had been burned, women raped, and forty-six Blacks killed along with two Whites.[720] That same year, New Orleans endured a race riot as well,[721] which saw thirty-four Blacks killed as well as three Whites who obviously disagreed with Black equality.[722] In the years after emancipation, it was claimed that as many as fifty-three thousand Blacks had been murdered in the South.[723]

Beyond that violence and threat of violence, "Southern courts were nullifying the Civil Rights Act and the states were continuing to prohibit freedmen from keeping and bearing arms."[724] The Southern states also delayed providing sufficient support to the Fourteenth Amendment for two years as a means of resistance to the federal impositions of the Republican-dominated Congress.[725]

★   ★   ★

It is worth pausing at this point to seek perspective on the tension and division caused by *Reconstruction* in the wake of the Civil War. The raw feelings of Southerners, whose homes, if not culture, were burned to the ground by the Union Army were more than prevalent in the years that followed the war. At that moment in time, in the wake of the triumph of one side, it was not humanly possible for the division of the last decade to simply end. The *Persistent Division Dynamic* was bound to continue. Beyond that, from the Southern perspective, victory alone in the war was not enough for the North. The post-war actions by the North convinced many Southerners that the North wanted the total domination of the South in the manner that Jefferson Davis warned before the war. By contrast, the dominant party, the Republicans of the North, strongly believed that a new order had to be created in the South lest they relapse into the type of society still hostile to free labor, if not worse.

In an example of a pure *Escalating Partisanship Dynamic*, as the North exercised that domination militarily, and sought to impose a new order in Southern governments, we have seen how many Southerners resisted that process legislatively, in the courts at times, and quite violently at other times. Again, from the Southern perspective, as the federal government exerted even more control, Southern resistance became more inflamed. For the Republicans in Congress, on the other hand, continuing if not growing Southern resistance—and the South's desire to decide their own fate and live as they had before—was all the cause they needed to impose even more laws to ensure Northern ideas won the peace. Indeed, when the radical Republicans passed the First Reconstruction Act, on March 2, 1867, it declared that

> no legal State governments or adequate protection for
> life or property now exists in the rebel States of Virginia,
> North Carolina, South Carolina, Georgia, Mississippi,

Alabama, Louisiana, Florida, Texas and Arkansas; and
whereas it is necessary that peace and good order should
be enforced in said States until loyal and republican
State governments can be legally established.

In response, the Democrats' 1868 platform "condemned the Recon-
structions Acts as 'unconstitutional, revolutionary, and void.'"[726] Meanwhile, their 1868 vice presidential candidate called for the ouster of
Republican officials in the South and to "allow white people to organize their own governments."[727] Keep in mind that the Fourteenth
Amendment, guaranteeing rights through due process, also was deemed
necessary by Republicans because it was apparent that simply freeing
the slaves, pursuant to the Thirteenth Amendment, was not achieving
the outcome that they wanted. Then Southern resistance to the Fourteenth Amendment and the Civil Rights Acts led to the Reconstruction
Acts. In time, the Fifteenth Amendment, "guaranteeing" the right to
vote, became necessary as well, because of Southern resistance. In other
words, the sides were clearly drawn and the actions of the other side, but
not their own actions, were deemed divisive and worthy of reaction—
again, an *Escalating Partisanship Dynamic* if ever there was one.

Beyond that self-perpetuating dynamic that featured intense government action, we should reconsider the notion that the Republicans in
Congress were "radical." If we placed the respective views of Lincoln,
Johnson, Republicans, and Southerners on a continuum of what laws
should have been passed at any given moment, it is by now obvious that
many congressional Republicans wanted numerous and more aggressive
federal laws, and Southerners, by and large, wanted few, if any—and
what laws were to be passed should be their own state laws. Lincoln
and Johnson tried to strike a balance between the two. According to
many historians, they were moderate, if not lenient, by comparison to
the "radical" Republicans and Southerners. If we consider some of the
latter, surely the actions of the more violent Southerners, like the Ku

Klux Klan in their murdering of Blacks, earned them the proper condemnation of *History*. The actions of those that passed the Black Codes also find few proponents today.

For our purposes, however, the more interesting designation is that of the congressional Republicans as "radicals" for their actions. History book after history book refers to those Republicans as radical. Today that word carries a very negative connotation, and they certainly were considered strident in their day even within their own party. Yes, on the one hand, authorizing the military to effectively install governments in the South was well beyond extraconstitutional. On the other hand, Presidents Lincoln and Johnson undertook similar actions, yet they have been designated in time as having had the more "moderate" approach. However, it was those same *radical* Republicans who refused to compromise with Lincoln and Johnson, and then passed the 1866 Civil Rights Act and the Thirteenth, Fourteenth, and Fifteenth Amendments in response to highly partisan if not murderous acts undertaken by certain Southerners. Who today would argue that the Fifteenth Amendment, which guaranteed Blacks the right to vote, should not be a part of our Constitution? Or that the "Due Process" guarantee of the Fourteenth Amendment should not be the law of our land? Indeed, today the Fourteenth Amendment is quite useful for many who want to extend what are considered today to be more liberal or progressive legal and/or social positions.

Given all that we know, should the Republicans of the *Reconstruction Era*, clearly one of our more divided eras, have been less, well, radical? Once the war was over, and they were presented with that host of problems, should they have compromised and allowed the South to persist in passing Black Codes or in nullifying the Civil Rights Act of 1866? Or to let them administer justice as the Southern courts were wont to do? Would we even have a Fourteenth or Fifteenth Amendment if they had compromised with Lincoln or Johnson? It is likely that the judgment of time will answer all of those questions in the negative. If that is so, should we not also realize that their partisanship, viewed radically in time, actually resulted in significant and important change—change that may not have occurred without their partisanship? If the answers to those questions are yes, then once again, we are witness to the historical significance of partisanship—a *Refusal to Compromise Dynamic*—and the important change that it can bring.

As we leave our discussion of *Reconstruction*, and move into the *Gilded Age*, we must keep in mind the absolute raw nature of the times. Party politics would reach new heights over the next twenty years along with political participation. Government was still deciding very large issues—though not as large as a Civil War or *Reconstruction*. Without those bloodstained memories, however, if not fresh wounds, the *Gilded Age* would not have seen its political heights.

Our Gilded Age of Division

The *Gilded Age*, which began in the wake of the Civil War, takes its name from none other than Mark Twain, who used it as the title of his 1873 novel, in which the greed and corruption of the age was derided.[728] In almost every way, it was a transformative era. Economically, technologically, socially, and of course politically, America changed dramatically during the *Gilded Age*. The enormous changes, inequities, and growth meant that there was fertile ground for the politician, his party, and their supporters to become involved; and involved they were. Indeed, it can fairly be said that the "political parties dominated American political decision making to a greater extent than ever before or since. Parties firmly controlled virtually all access to public office, all aspects of elections, and all aspects of policy making"[729]—and there were plenty of issues over which they could do battle.

In the wake of the Civil War and *Reconstruction* divisions, American politicians grappled once again with the issue of the proper role of government, tariffs, the nature of our currency, political patronage, and the enduring issues of the post-war South—now referred to as the South-ern Question. Toward the beginning of the *Gilded Age*, the Southern Question was of greater prominence. By the end of the *Gilded Age*, and the collapse of *Reconstruction*, economic issues took center stage and the Southern Question receded as a focal point. Again, *Reconstruction* was an enormous and unprecedented social engineering program. The use of federal government power under *Reconstruction* was also unprece-dented. The party that pursued it, the Republicans, did not simply shed their activist government tendencies when *Reconstruction* began to fail and eventually was abandoned. To the contrary, "they set about fram-ing a national economic program of tariff protection, a stable currency, and aid to business aimed at feeding a material development that would benefit the whole nation and its citizens."[730] The Democrats, by contrast, "clung to their party's Jeffersonian belief in small government and states' rights."[731] They also "doubted that government-generated bounty would be equitably shared. They attacked government activism and cast them-selves as the party of the people."[732] As a result, "Republicans and Dem-ocrats differed sharply over matters of public policy and offered voters real choices at the polls."[733]

During that period, voter turnout (absent women who didn't yet have the right to vote) averaged nearly 78 percent or "far more than in any subsequent period."[734] The "secret" behind the intense interest and partisanship was the opposite of the dynamic that occurred during the *Era of Good Feelings*. Recall that under President James Monroe, the opposing party, the Federalists, had severely damaged themselves and lost relevancy. Monroe, rather than legislate us into differences, pursued a very limited legislative agenda and co-opted many Federalists. Absent an active federal agenda, and therefore, a catalyst to invigorate opposi-tion, Monroe ran unopposed for a second term. By contrast, during the *Gilded Age*, both parties were motivated by the recent past. One party, the Republicans, was pursuing activist government and the other party, the Democrats, who had fought Republicans "tooth and nail for more than a decade,"[735] continued that fight. The combination of government acting on large issues and two parties providing a stark contrast—all in the wake of deep divisions—is the political story of the *Gilded Age*.

★ ★ ★

The *Gilded Age* is perhaps better known for its "massive economic and social transformations"[736] than its political dynamics. As described in the book *Massachusetts in the Gilded Age: Selected Essays*,

> From 1865 to 1900 the redirection of economic life from farm to factory spawned a new urban society that transformed the lives of all Americans by the twentieth century. This economic revolution was the result of the complex interweaving of a growing factory system; gigantic boosts in farm output due to mechanization; the development of a national transportation system that ended the reliance upon local markets; and the migration of peasants from American farms and European villages to the mushrooming, chaotic urban centers of America. The result was social dislocation, and both discontent and satisfaction with the fruits of industrial productivity.[737]

During the *Gilded Age*, the US population surged from just over 31 million in 1860 to over 76 million by 1900 and with that, along with technological advances, trade, and more, the economy grew by some accounts as much as 400 percent.[738] As for wages, "one study finds that real non-farm earnings rose more than 60 percent between 1870 and 1900. Another shows that wages grew, in real terms, from $1.00 daily in 1867 to $1.90 daily in 1893."[739] From 1896 to 1901 alone, according to the US government, wages rose 10 percent and employment rose

20 percent.[740] As a practical matter, prior to the Civil War "the United States was a giant country made up of small-scale, local enterprises."[741] The Civil War, however, transformed our economy into a national economy, and by the end of the *Gilded Age*, the economy was experiencing domination by giant enterprises.[742] Indeed, the *Gilded Age* coincided or perhaps was defined by "The Triumph of Capitalism," as H. W. Brands writes about in his must-read book *American Colossus*.

While Twain and others derided the inequities that our nascent capitalism produced, it is important to note that "the field of professional philanthropy"[743] was created during this age with giants like John Eastman of Eastman Kodak giving away $125 million in his lifetime; Julius Rosenwald of Sears, Roebuck & Co. giving away $70 million;[744] Andrew Carnegie, who gave away more than $350 million—the equivalent of $67 billion today; and, of course, John D. Rockefeller who, "as a first-year clerk, . . . regularly donated 6 percent of his wages to charity,"[745] and would go on to give away more than $530 million in his lifetime—the equivalent of over $100 billion today.

Amidst all that societal upheaval and change, not to mention money, the nation's politicians, if not the nation, were ripe for yet another fight over the proper role of government. Chief among the issues for such a debate was the economy. Keep in mind that as of the *Gilded Age*, there was neither Federal Reserve nor a federal income tax. Those would not come for decades. There were no federal regulations until the late 1870s and they had minimal impact at the outset. As such, the ability of the government to be activist, at least with regard to the economy, was limited—but not nonexistent. Among the greatest tools at its disposal were land grants and loans for development made by the federal government and, of course, tariffs. The former allowed railroads to expand across the country and otherwise gave the opportunity to many Americans to settle westward and increase the nation's farming output.[746] The imposition of tariffs proved to be far more divisive than land grants.

Tariffs necessarily were about picking winners and losers and—as practiced during the *Gilded Age*—they did so to a considerable degree.

Recall that since our nation's birth, beginning with the Tariff Act of
1789, tariffs had been used to raise tax revenue for the federal government. It always was our federal government's main source of revenue
and since the beginning, plain and simple, we required the South to
pay far more in tariff revenue than the North. In fact, just before the
Civil War, according to economics Professor Walter E. Williams, "tariffs
amounted to 90 percent of federal revenue... [and] Southern ports
paid 75 percent of tariffs in 1859."[747] That never sat well with the South.
In fact, "it was tariffs, not slavery, that first made the South militant."[748]
Remember that a "precursor for a War Between the States came in 1832
when South Carolina called a convention to nullify tariff acts of 1828
and 1832, referred to as the 'Tariffs of Abominations.' [However,] a
compromise lowering the tariff was reached averting secession and possibly war."[749] Recall also that, in the run-up to the Civil War, a significant
number of Southerners cited tariff policy as reason to secede. When the
Civil War came, and the South seceded, the Confederate constitution
outlawed tariffs. In the North, on the other hand, tariffs were raised in
part to pay for the war and also to provide added protection to American industry.[750] Once the war was over, and the Union "saved," the fighting over tariffs resumed its old sectional ways and stayed at "the center
of fiscal debates for the remainder of the century."[751]

As for party politics, "over time, the protective tariff emerged as
the centerpiece of the Republicans' economic program"[752] and of their
political strategy, as well. By 1884, it was the main plank of their party
platform.[753] Republicans also raised campaign war chests off the issue,
as in 1888, "by coercing manufacturers into contributing if they wished
to have tariff protection."[754] In return, industrialists got the protection
from free trade that they sought and fattened coffers as well.[755] According to Quentin R. Skrabec, Jr. in his work *William McKinley, Apostle of
Protectionism*, "The strong Republican tariffs from 1860 to 1890 caused

a boom in American manufacture."[756] That significant trade protection helped steel production rise

> from 1.3 million tons in 1880 to 11.2 million tons in 1900 to 28.3 million tons in 1910. In 1898 the American steel industry surpassed Britain in pig iron production. By 1900, America was making more steel than Britain and Germany together.... [and] during the peak tariff years of 1896 to 1901 under President McKinley, steel production increased 111%, electrical equipment production increased 271%, and farm equipment increased 149%.[757]

Under such circumstances, future President William McKinley felt assured to tell the House of Representatives that "the only supporters of across the board tariff cuts . . . were feather-brained reformers."[758]

"Tariff politics reached its greatest crescendo between 1880, when [President] Garfield turned it into a Republican electoral sword, and 1897, when McKinley resolved the basic debate in the GOP's favor"[759] by signing another tariff bill that raised tariff rates yet again. For a long time, even though the issue divided the parties, especially at election time, the Democrats were, by and large, Republican-lite on tariffs. Democrats advocated for lower, revenue-focused tariffs,[760] but tariffs nonetheless. All that changed when they took a firm stand on the issue in 1887.[761] That was the year Democrat Grover Cleveland, in an unheard-of tactic, "devoted his entire third annual message," his State of the Union, to the issue of tariffs.[762] Over the objections of an advisor who said it would hurt the Democrats in the 1888 election,

> Cleveland called upon Congress to reduce the rates as soon as possible.... His language made Republicans and protectionist Democrats furious, many vowing political

revenge. Cleveland's words were potent in the time-honored way that president's and the people's representatives confront one another. If disaster results from the
inaction of Congress, the responsibility must rest where
it belongs.[763]

The disaster, of sorts, was occasioned on the Democrats. In the 1888
election, Republicans gained seventeen seats in the House of Representatives, taking control of the House, while Cleveland lost his bid for
reelection in a close and disputed election. The Democrats' stance on
tariffs played a significant role in those losses. Two years later, Republicans would pass what history knows as the McKinley Tariff Act—named
after the future Republican President William McKinley. "McKinley's
enthusiasm for protective tariffs was part of what led foes to call him
a front man for corporations, trusts, and plutocrats."[764] Front man or
not, McKinley's presidential candidacy, and fear for his populist opponent, William Jennings Bryan, "opened the purses of Carnegie, Frick,
Morgan, and Rockefeller in amounts of $250,000"[765]—a completely
unheard-of sum previously. All in all, tariffs were indeed big business,
not just economically, but politically as well during the *Gilded Age*.

★   ★   ★

Another potent economic issue during this period was whether United
States currency should be gold, silver, or greenbacks. According to
Kevin Phillips, in his biography of William McKinley, from 1873 to
1900 "no American issue throbbed more deeply."[766] It is worth recalling that we had political and economic disputes over currency during
and after our Revolution, which we discussed in chapters 2 and 3. Those
disputes occurred for several reasons. First, the Continental Congress
issued paper money, not backed by gold or silver, to fund the Revolutionary War. They did so in such great numbers that the Continental,

as it was called, became worthless. Many states did the same after the war. Second, and also to fund the war, Congress issued debt certificates, or what we consider bonds today. They too became devalued because the creditors holding the bonds, as well as the traders in such bonds, didn't believe America as yet had "full faith and credit" to pay its debts. Third, there was the issue of private debt—much of it held by farmers. Their creditors wanted that debt paid in hard currency (i.e., gold, which had real value). The debtors, on the other hand, favored paper money, which made it easier to pay back the loans because, while the principal of the loan was fixed, paper money was being printed at alarming rates, and therefore, devalued. Finally, the general scarcity of gold also made it difficult to conduct basic commerce. Nearly one hundred years later, the reasons to fight over currency had hardly changed.

Once again, wartime debt was a major driver of the issue economically and politically. The Civil War was funded, in part, by the federal government selling $2 billion in bonds. It also issued $400 million in legal tender notes, "greenbacks," which were unbacked by hard currency.[767] In other words, at the time we had a dual money system.[768] One of the most hotly debated questions was how to pay back the debts of the federal government. Should they be paid back with gold or with paper greenbacks? Not much later, advocates for coining silver would join the discussion. The answer as to which currency was best depended on one's station in life and location in America. In general, creditors wanted to be paid back in hard currency,[769] especially those in the Northeast for "whom gold was an economic religion."[770]

Debtors, on the other hand, many of whom were in the Midwest, West, and South, especially after the contraction of the US money supply in the decade after the Civil War,[771] wanted a more accessible currency—paper and/or silver, not just gold.[772] During the *Gilded Age*, the answer to that question was a very big deal for farmers in particular. In the same manner they did after the Revolutionary War, American farmers as a whole were carrying considerable debt. Worse yet, falling crop prices after the Civil War deprived them of the wherewithal to pay back debts.[773] Beyond that, once again, the amount of available currency was an issue. For those reasons, farmers "called for more paper money in circulation" so they could "buy goods at reasonable prices and make mortgage payments easily."[774] The debt issue for farmers and their creditors also took on a more modern look—and real societal division as well—because much of their debt was held by the farmers' newfound "enemy"—Wall Street.[775] Many producers in the iron and steel industries, hurt by an economic downturn in the mid-1870s, were in a similar predicament and also called for easier money.[776] Eventually, certain state governments—like Ohio, with its share of debtors and suffering industries—joined the push for the US government to resume using silver coins to ease economic problems.[777]

All those issues—how to pay back those wartime debts; whether to use hard currency or some lesser form; how to assure a sufficient money supply; and battles between creditors and debtors—would vex the economy and politicians for the duration of the *Gilded Age*.[778] The importance of the currency issues, as we can expect, would also cause intense division and partisanship not just between the major parties, but within them as well.[779]

For instance, suggestions that the debt would be paid back with something less than gold garnered this response in the 1868 Republican Party platform: "We denounce all forms of repudiation as a national crime; and national honor requires the payment of the public indebtedness in the utmost good faith to all creditors at home and abroad, not only according to the letter, but the spirit of the laws under which it was contracted."[780] The law to which those Republicans were referring was the Constitution. It gave Congress the power to "coin" money. Some Republicans interpreted that to mean that the federal government was required to pay its debts in gold and only gold. The president at the time, however, Republican Ulysses S. Grant, did not agree with those Republicans. He believed in the need for greenbacks to accommodate a growing economy even if he wanted to gradually retire them by exchanging them for hard currency.[781] In 1870, Republicans would openly battle their president and war hero, Ulysses S. Grant, on the issue; they even accused Grant of "packing" the Supreme Court in search of support for his mixed currency policies.[782] Beyond that division within the Republican Party, there was a division between Republicans from the East who favored hard currency policies and those elected in the Midwest and West, considered more liberal at the time, who advocated softer currency policies.[783] Over time, however, the hard money faction of the party took control and Republicans gravitated to an increasingly more hard money position. That certainly can be explained, in part, by the fact that Republicans had more significant ties to the banking community than the Democrats. In the end, proponents of hard currency won the ultimate currency battle with McKinley signing into law the hard currency bill known as the Gold Standard Act of 1900.[784]

For their part, the Democrats would have an equal amount of trouble, if not more, with the politics of currency. Sectional politics was at the center of some of their troubles, as well.[785] A decade after the Civil War, Democrats dominated Southern politics. The weakened Southern economy induced calls for expansive monetary policies, not hard currency policies. Southern Democrats supported those calls. Democrats in the West held views in concert with the prevailing politics of the West, which also called for expansionist policies. In the Northeast, on the other hand, most politicians favored hard money policies and many of them were Democrats. As such, the Democrats had a gold wing to their party and a silver wing.[786] By and large, however, Democrats supported softer money policies than their Republican counterparts. For instance, their 1880 platform plank called for "honest money, consisting of gold and silver, and paper convertible into coin on demand."[787]

As for intra-party fights, the Democrats suffered an even more bruising fight over currency than did the Republicans. It occurred during Grover Cleveland's first administration. Cleveland, after his 1892 election, was faced with an economic crisis. The crisis shook national and international confidence in the American financial system and featured a European run on gold. Faced with that crisis in confidence and that run on gold, Cleveland, who was from the gold wing of the party, pushed for the repeal of the Republican Sherman Silver Purchase Act of 1890. In practice, buybacks under that Act depleted federal gold supplies. After a bitter fight, Cleveland got his way. The vote, however, evenly split the silver and gold wings of his party: 22 votes for repeal and 22 against repeal. Rarely in our history has a party vote been split so dramatically and it is no surprise that it happened on such an important issue.

Of course, during the *Gilded Age*, it was far more likely that congressional votes over the currency issues would split the opposing parties. For instance, amidst economic troubles, Democrats won a substantial majority in 1874 elections. The lame-duck Republican majority, taking advantage of their Republican president, passed the hard money Species Resumption Act, under which unbacked US notes would be retired for gold. The Act had the effect of tightening the US money supply and favored creditors. The law was passed on a strict party line vote in both houses of Congress and was signed by President Grant.[788] In the 1880s, a currency bill would pass in the same fashion to be signed by another Republican president—this time it would be Benjamin Harrison.[789] Not shy of the partisan nature of the vote, Harrison wrote, "I have been asking for a Republican bill and this must be one for no Democrat voted for it in either House." [790] Finally, in 1900, the parties split again almost exactly along party lines to pass the ultimate hard money bill—the Gold Standard Act of 1900.[791]

Party line votes, however, were not the most spectacular theatre for differences between the parties over currency issues. That would come with the presidential election of 1896 and the squaring off between Democrat William Jennings Bryan and Republican William McKinley. As we have seen, the Republicans had been gradually moving toward a gold standard. As the 1896 election progressed toward the Democratic convention, the Democrats were more split on the currency issues. The gold wing of the Democratic Party had not yet settled on a candidate, leaving the "Missouri Representative Richard 'Silver Dick' Bland" as the spring front-runner.[792] At the Democrat convention, William Jennings Bryan, however, maneuvered his way to speak on behalf of silver.[793] He strode to the podium and roused the convention delegates by stating that the "humblest citizen in all the land, when clad in the armor of a righteous cause, is stronger than all the hosts of error. I come to speak to you in defense of a cause as holy as the cause of liberty—the cause of humanity."[794]

Bryan then took hold of the convention, his party, and nearly half a nation. Using populist rhetoric, he gave a speech whose strains can still be heard in the rhetoric of Democrats today. Bryan drew a vibrant distinction of two Americas, if not class warfare. His speech was one of the great speeches of American political history. It says in part:

> We stand here representing people who are the equals before the law of the largest cities in the state of Massachusetts. When you come before us and tell us that we shall disturb your business interests, we reply that you have disturbed our business interests by your action. We say to you that you have made too limited in its application the definition of a businessman. The man who is employed for wages is as much a businessman as his employer.... We do not come as aggressors. Our war is not a war of conquest. We are fighting in the defense of our homes, our families, and posterity. We have petitioned, and our petitions have been scorned. We have entreated, and our entreaties have been disregarded. We have begged, and they have mocked when our calamity came. We beg no longer; we entreat no more; we petition no more. We defy them!

The gentleman from Wisconsin has said he fears a
Robespierre. My friend, in this land of the free you need
fear no tyrant who will spring up from among the people. What we need is an Andrew Jackson to stand as
Jackson stood, against the encroachments of aggregated
wealth. . . .

There are two ideas of government. There are those
who believe that if you just legislate to make the well-
to-do prosperous, that their prosperity will leak through
on those below. The Democratic idea has been that if
you legislate to make the masses prosperous their prosperity will find its way up and through every class that
rests upon it.

You come to us and tell us that the great cities are in
favor of the gold standard. I tell you that the great cities rest upon these broad and fertile prairies. Burn down
your cities and leave our farms, and your cities will spring
up again as if by magic. But destroy our farms and the
grass will grow in the streets of every city in the country.

Having set the populist stage, William Jennings Bryan then marked his
place in political history with one of the great rhetorical finishes in the
history of political speech making:

If they dare to come out in the open field and defend the
gold standard as a good thing, we shall fight them to the
uttermost, having behind us the producing masses of the
nation and the world. Having behind us the commercial interests and the laboring interests and all the toiling
masses, we shall answer their demands for a gold standard by saying to them, you shall not press down upon

the brow of labor this crown of thorns. *You shall not crucify mankind upon a cross of gold.*

Bryan's words were said to be "messianic—a call to arms, not just to oppose the gold standard, but to save democracy and stand again, as Andrew Jackson had stood, against the encroachments of *organized wealth.*"[795] Bryan had drawn the societal contrast many Democrats felt. In unprecedented fashion, Bryan barnstormed the nation making countless speeches and capitalizing on the "excitement" that "rippled out of the convention hall and across the nation."[796] Although McKinley won that year, Bryan's speech and candidacy demonstrated the breadth and scope of *Our Gilded Age of Division.*

★   ★   ★

In addition to the economic issues of currency and tariffs lay the fight over political patronage and the difficult Southern Question. As for the latter, the end of *Reconstruction* and the start of the *Gilded Age* overlapped by many years. As we entered the 1870s, the nation as a whole, and the Republican Party in particular, were well worn, and tired of fighting sectional issues. After the disputed election of Rutherford B. Hayes in 1876, a compromise would be reached on the Southern Question. It was "an elaborate but tacit compromise, with Hayes' silent blessing, that averted violence and promised to end Reconstruction. Its salient points were well known" to a politically attune nation.[797]

A Republican president would remove federal soldiers from Louisiana and South Carolina, the last remaining unredeemed states, and recognize local rule; as part of a long-term program, Republicans would extend federal patronage to the South, construct levee and harbor

improvements, help complete the Texas and Pacific Railroad, and welcome the South into national life; southern
politicians would not obstruct certain Republican programs, would help elect Garfield speaker of the House
[and] obey the Constitution.[798]

Of course, that meant that Southern politicians had to guarantee the
rights of Blacks in the South, which hardly could be taken for granted.
Nevertheless, the new President Rutherford Hayes was of the belief that
"material progress" would do more for both Whites and Blacks than
"martial law," and that the "carpetbag governments had not been successful."[799] He allowed that the "complaints of the southern people were
just in this matter."[800] In other words, Hayes was admitting that *Reconstruction* had failed to a larger degree and, as a matter of national policy,
it was time to move on. However, just because Hayes, in his inaugural speech, said he wanted the "Southern people . . . to be made to feel
that they are a part of the great American republic," that didn't mean
the Southern Question was resolved. The war, sectionalism, and racism
were potent issues long after the war had ended. For instance, "Republican politicians, when they feared defeat, reverted to waving the *bloody
shirt*, both to consolidate their Northern following and to enlist the one
sure Republican element in the South, the Negro."[801] The "bloody shirt"
was a reference to Republican efforts to press voters to remember the
recent hardships of the Civil War and to remind them of the actions of
Democrats. Indeed, the "Republicans never tired of proclaiming that,
having saved the Union in war, they alone deserved to administer the
Union in peace."[802] Nor was it a "coincidence that in eight of the nine
presidential elections between 1868 and 1900, the Republican candidate was a Union veteran. The sole exception, James G. Blaine, lost in
1884."[803] Highlighting the continuing potency of the Southern Question, after his loss, Blaine "blamed the result on the political repres-
sion in the South, which 'has crushed out the political power of more

than 6,000,000 American citizens, and has transferred it by violence to others.'"[804]

Blaine was not entirely wrong in his assessment. Those in power in the South were said to practice "a far more virulent sectional rhetoric, inflaming the emotions of the war and Reconstruction for partisan purposes well into the twentieth century,"[805] and did so long before the 1884 election. Indeed, the election of 1876, which elected the president that effectively ended *Reconstruction* (the Republican Hayes), was also marred by violence across the South, which served to suppress the Black vote. Violence and rhetoric were not the end of the story of the suppression of the Black votes by Democrats either.[806] Ballot stuffing was undertaken in the South as well, to ensure the victory of Southern Democrats.

In an effort to combat all of those tactics, following the Civil Rights Act of 1866, as part of the *Escalating Partisanship Dynamic* of the time, "congressional Republicans enacted civil rights acts in . . . 1870, 1871, and 1875."[807] No amount of laws, however, seemed to be enough, and, in perhaps one final blow to the civil rights efforts of the day, the 1875 Act was struck down by the Supreme Court. Then Republican President Chester Arthur did call for "new legislation to secure the equal enjoyment of constitutional rights,"[808] but no further such acts would be enacted until 1957. In the meantime, Southern Democrats attempted to dilute voting rights laws at the federal level.[809] One measure of how the Southern Question persisted was the Republican Party platform of 1888, which charged that the "Democrats held the House of Representatives and the White House as a result of 'the suppression of the ballot by *criminal* nullification of the Constitution and laws of the United States.'"[810]

Two years later, House Republicans acted on such charges over criticism of Democrats that the Republicans' complaints about ballot frauds were "the wail of bitter disappointment."[811] However, the disputed vote totals in Southern states, including three Southern states with Black majorities in the 1888 election, found illogically low vote totals for

Republicans. In South Carolina, for instance, despite Blacks numbering 60 percent of the citizenry, only 17.2 percent of the vote was counted for the winning Republican President Benjamin Harrison.[812] The esteemed Henry Cabot Lodge then put forth what history knows as the Lodge Federal Elections Bill, which would have authorized federal oversight of elections within the states experiencing voting irregularities. The July 2, 1890, House vote for the Lodge Federal Elections Bill was 155 Republicans for it and 149 Democrats against it—no defections.[813] Senate Democrats then successfully killed the bill in the Senate. In other words, twenty-five years after the Civil War, American politics—if not the nation—was as divided as ever on the issue within the Southern Question. The Republicans thereafter slowly moved away from an emphasis on the Southern Question in favor of the economic issues, and the hope that they could appeal to even Southern voters on the issue of prosperity. For their part, the Democrats had a "Solid South" and were unwilling to loosen that grip that sectional politics gave them. In any case, for our purposes, the Southern Question continued to play a key role in *Our Gilded Age of Division*.

★   ★   ★

Yet another major issue of the *Gilded Age*, as if the country was not divided enough, was the issue of political patronage. Simply stated, during the *Gilded Age*, the business of politics was big business. In America today, we have a relatively permanent class of federal workers, more than 2.7 million, in the sense that nearly all of them are not subject to removal from their jobs by an incoming administration. The head of agencies and their deputies are subject to removal—but not the great body of federal workers. That was not true in the *Gilded Age*. During that latter half of the nineteenth century, the number of federal workers exceeded 150,000[814] and it was accepted practice that the victorious president's party appointed every one of them. Unimaginably today, "those appointed to government jobs, in turn, were expected to contribute a percentage of their salary to the party that had given them their job, just as party committees assessed nearly all candidates a percentage of the salary of the office they sought. Assessments from officeholders and candidates, in fact, constituted a major source of financing for campaigns and other party activities."[815]

In fact, the phrase "to the victor belong the spoils" originated from that system.[816] Of course, it doesn't take much of an imagination to see how such a system could lead to intense competition among politicians to win their elections, let alone the corruption that was sure to follow. Indeed, critics made the case that "spoilsmanship united personal and partisan advantage to create a system where the main purpose was winning office rather than doing anything with it."[817] That wasn't true, however, for all politicians and certainly not presidents. In fact, some used the blunt instrument of patronage to get their way. Earlier in this chapter, we discussed Democrat Grover Cleveland's pitched battle over currency. To get his way, Cleveland was said to have "identified enemies and denied them patronage, congressional authority, and party management."[818] It is worth noting, however, that Cleveland didn't always think that way. On the way to winning his party's nomination, Cleveland garnered the accolade of "Grover the Good" for taking on Tammany Hall—the ultimate political machine that was no stranger to the issue of patronage.

This issue was hardly a one-party problem. Republicans were accused of patronage abuse, as well. For instance, the Democrats' 1876 presidential candidate, Samuel J. Tilden, fulminated during his campaign that Republicans turned officeholders into "political mercenaries."[819] Republican President Chester A. Arthur, for his part, used patronage in his "approach to the southern question," using his "appointments to reward" supporters of his agenda.[820] Arthur did so even though he called for civil service reform in his first annual message.[821]

While the system had its fierce critics and those that demanded reform, that didn't mean the system didn't have its defenders. Indeed, according to George Plunkitt, a Democrat Party operative from New York, "you can't keep an organization together without patronage. . . . Men ain't in politics for nothing. They want to get somethin' out of it."[822] Plunkitt was hardly alone in his view on the nationwide system.

Even so, the calls for reform grew with the size of the federal government. President Rutherford B. Hayes wrote in 1877: "We must limit and narrow the area of patronage. We must diminish the evils of office-seeking. We must stop interference of federal officers with elections. We must be relieved of congressional dictation as to appointments."[823] In the way of reform, of course, were the many who depended on the system and benefitted greatly from the system. Indeed, "politicians understood the double threat in civil service reform, since it would deprive them of patronage and campaign funds."[824] Nevertheless, the abuse had grown to the point that President Arthur, who we know used the system for political gain, would push for reform, citing the "people's 'earnest wish for prompt definitive action.'"[825] Then, in a rare moment of bipartisanship on a major issue in the *Gilded Age*, the parties jointly passed the Pendleton Act, which provided for the selection of federal employees based on competitive exams rather than partisan affiliation.[826] The Act was the most significant civil service reform of the age, and over time, it would diminish patronage as an issue and even the importance of the political parties—but not all at once.

★   ★   ★

We have now reached the end of our discussion of four of the major issues that drove the political storms of the *Gilded Age*: tariffs, currency, the Southern Question, and patronage. That is not to say they were the only issues that were prominent during this period. William Jennings Bryan had raised the issue of "accumulated wealth" and class issues. The government spoils politically dispensed on the rich, the railroads, the trusts, the monopolies, and the banks, formed a large part of political discussion during this era as well. How to close budget deficits and even a fight over spending surpluses concerned the nation. Inflation, panics, bad economic times, and recoveries drove politics as well. Calls for prohibition were just getting underway during this period. Labor issues were beginning to emerge as well—and, of course, a battle over taxes. The first income tax was enacted in 1894 only to be struck down by the US Supreme Court. That too, was an issue that lent itself to division among the parties and the nation.

All in all, the *Gilded Age* was an age full of difficult times and issues that led to politicians wanting to use significant government power. Federal troops still occupied states even if we were not fighting a civil war. Instead, areas of the country were fighting in the halls of our government over currency, tariffs, and other economic issues. Politicians, not shy of using power after the Civil War and *Reconstruction*, continued to wield their newfound power. In doing so, our governments were picking winners and losers and our elections were fought over tooth-and-nail by an evenly divided nation. Amid that political maelstrom, before we leave the discussion of *Our Gilded Age of Division*, there are still other aspects of such an age to discuss—the political characteristics of deep division. Chief among them were the close elections and the divided government the age produced. Further, as with other periods in history where government is rather activist and the two major parties are not always responsive to needs beyond their own power, there was the prominence of third parties. Their influence, during this period, was at times perceived as able to tip the scales in one direction or another. We can also take one last look at the partisanship of that time. Once we do that, a comparison of the *Gilded Age* to our own *Divided Era* will come into focus.

★　　★　　★

With so much at stake during the *Gilded Age* we cannot be surprised at how intense the business of politics became. Tireless party activity was the order of the day, along with fighting over swing states, close and disputed elections, and post-election fights. We started this chapter by pointing out that the *Gilded Age* was also the golden age of the two-party system, and indeed it was. During the 1888 election, it was said that the "'whole face of the country is plastered with politics,' a visitor to the Indiana farm country reported. 'Seen from a train, the whole country might be thought the camp of some great army with the flags marking regimental headquarters.'"[827] While the issues drove the discussions and emotions of the day, it was the parties that drove the campaigns. "Elections were treated like battles in which the two main armies (parties) concentrated on fielding the maximum number of troops (voters) on the battlefield (polls) on election day,"[828] and "partisanship was something constantly drilled into followers of the rival organizations."[829] So important were the parties that for "voters, nearly all news about politics and governmental affairs came through the filter of party."[830] Even more than that, according to Robert W. Cherny in his book *American Politics in the Gilded Age, 1868–1900*, "parties controlled access to nearly all elective and appointive governmental offices."[831]

To accomplish all of that, the parties "boasted open and broad-based organizations that invited participation in ward, precinct, town, city, and county committees. These groups looked upward in a pyramidal structure of district, state, and national committees."[832] Of course, much of that effort was about Election Day. Long before Election Day, however, the campaigns assembled elaborate voters files including party preference, and "key demographic information, especially ethnicity and occupation."[833]

> During the month or so before the election, candidates
> and party dignitaries undertook speaking tours on behalf
> of the ticket. Local party organizations sponsored many

community activities—displays by marching clubs, barbecues, rallies, and torchlight parades. Speeches inevitably capped such events, often going on for hours, sometimes punctuated by campaign songs that glorified the party's candidates and disparaged the opposition. Party organizers intended such activities to whip up enthusiasm for the party and its candidates, reinforce the loyalty of the party's usual supporters, and attract first-time voters. All the hype and activities reached their climax on election day, when each party worked to mobilize its supporters to vote.... On election day, party workers labored over lists of the party faithful and made certain that all their supporters made the trip to the polls.[834]

Once voters got to the polls, how they voted was not left to chance. For much of the *Gilded Age*, there was no ballot furnished by the government. Instead, the parties distributed ballots to their voters as they arrived at the polling place. Those ballots were rarely blank. Instead, they were completely filled out. The voters then deposited that "ticket" into the ballot box.[835] That tightly controlled process ensured party-line votes. It wasn't until the 1892 presidential election that most states outside the South adopted a process of the government supplying blank ballots, and in the South it came years after. As the government ballot came into greater use, the role of the party was diminished accordingly, and over time that also diminished the power of the major parties.[836]

Those well-oiled, powerful, and brutally efficient party machines combined with an evenly divided nation and fights over major issues produced a string of close elections and divided government during the *Gilded Age*. Consider these voting percentage results from that period: the 1880 presidential election: Republicans 48.5 percent—Democrats 48.0 percent; the 1884 presidential election: Democrats

48.5 percent—Republicans 48.2 percent; and the 1888 presidential election: Democrats 48.6 percent—Republicans 47.2 percent.

Those results occurred in an age when "voter turnout typically surpassed 75 percent, and in some states it exceeded 90 percent" in presidential election years.[837] Those close elections produced not one, but two *Gilded Age* presidents, Republican Rutherford B. Hayes in 1876, and Republican Benjamin Harrison in 1888, who lost the popular vote but won the Electoral College vote. The *Gilded Age* was also a period of divided government. Indeed, five times in a twenty-year period control of the House of Representatives changed hands, and only three times between 1875 and 1897 did one party control both the House and Senate, and the presidency—the Republicans during the years 1881–1883 and 1889–1891, and the Democrats during the years 1893–1895.

The *Gilded Age* was also the era of the swing state. "The most important swing states were New York and Indiana."[838] Incredibly, "between 1872 and 1896, neither New York nor Indiana voted for the presidential nominee of the same party in two successive elections."[839] During that same period, "the two parties made twenty nominations for president and vice president: thirteen went to men from New York or Indiana."[840] New York was so important that Democrats nominated a New Yorker for "their presidential candidates four times out of five between 1872 and 1888, and . . . turned to Indianans for vice-presidential candidates three times during those same years."[841] One final point about New York and the tightness of our elections during the Gilded Age:

> In 1880, 1884, and 1888, the electoral votes of New York state were cast for the winning candidate. Had the other candidate carried New York in any of those contests, he would have won—and New York was very closely balanced between the two major parties. In those three elections, the winner and loser were, in effect, separated by only 1 or 2 percent of the New York state vote.[842]

The tight competition between Republicans and Democrats during those years, along with the important issues, also produced the "silver age for third and fourth parties."[843] As a general rule, third party activity in American history is tied to a perception that the two major parties of any given era are not solving or sufficiently addressing one or more pressing issues of the day. The run-up to the Civil War and its completion saw an upheaval of the parties. "In little more than a decade (1854 to 1865), the Democratic Party had divided, the Whig Party had dissolved, the American (or Know-Nothing) Party, and the Constitutional Union Party had been born and died, and the Republican Party had given way to the Union Party."[844] That dynamic did not completely disappear after the Civil War.

During the *Gilded Age*, the names of the third parties included the Populist Party, the Greenback Party or Greenbackers, the Prohibition Party, and something called a Mugwump. The Populist Party, considered to be one of the most important third party movements in American history,[845] reached out to all of the "aggrieved" during its political run.[846] The party's strength was in the West and the South.[847] The Populist Party definitively stood for "free and unlimited coinage of silver."[848] Obviously, the largely regional Populist Party's existence was due in large part to its clear stance on the currency issue—a clear contrast to the division that issue caused among the national Democratic and Republican parties. At its height, the Populist Party won 8.5 percent of the vote in the 1892 election along with 22 electoral votes. Its presidential candidate took considerable votes from the Republican candidate, incumbent President Benjamin Harrison, who garnered only 43 percent of the national vote that year in bad economic times.[849] The beneficiary that year of the Populist Party's success was the Democrat Grover Cleveland who won just 46 percent of the vote to win his second term—albeit not consecutively, after losing four years earlier to Harrison. Congressional Democrats benefitted as well, and "for the first time since 1858 . . . won not only the White House but also control of both houses of Congress."[850]

The forerunner to the Populist Party was the Greenback Party, which, as its name suggests, also rose to prominence over the currency issue. The Greenbackers pushed for the continued use of unbacked paper money for the benefit of farmers and debtors everywhere. They believed that the buyback of greenbacks would be deflationary, thereby reducing the money supply and weakening the economy further. The Greenback Party fielded presidential candidates in 1876, 1880, and 1884. In 1878, "they elected more than a dozen candidates to Congress and many more to state offices."[851] In 1876, the Greenback presidential candidate was no "rube," but instead a "millionaire pillar of iron industry"[852] named Peter Cooper.

As for the Mugwumps, it was said their name denoted "party bolters." They were a significant group of Republicans that left their party to support the Democrat Grover Cleveland in his 1884 victory over Republican James G. Blaine[853] over issues of trust and tariffs.[854] Mugwumps might well have thrown the state of New York to Cleveland that year. The Prohibitionist Party, which would not reach its heights until the next century, played a role in the 1884 election as well. The Democrats counted on them to siphon "anti-liquor" voters away from the Republican Blaine.[855] Indeed, the third parties of *Our Gilded Age of Division*, given the "even balance between Republicans and Democrats," and the potential for defections in the "doubtful states, haunted the calculations of the major party managers"[856] just as they do today.

★ ★ ★

Bold issues and even bolder parties, along with close elections, created a boiling cauldron during *Our Gilded Age of Division*. As we have seen, hyperbole was the order of the day and invective was used from presidents on down to party regulars. Even for a modest man, who was said to have "no enmity—naught but magnanimity,"[857] the times invigorated future President James Garfield to cry out on the campaign trail that "every Rebel guerilla and jayhawker, every man who ran to Canada to avoid the draft, every bounty-jumper, every deserter, every villain, of whatever name or crime, who loves power more than justice, slavery more than freedom, is a Democrat." Cleveland chided his opponents, and the strongest and most dignified president of the age, William McKinley, went so far as to call his opponents "feather-brained."

Beyond the invective, there was considerable corruption and dirty campaigning. Mark Wahlgren Summers, in his book *Party Games: Getting, Keeping, and Using Power in Gilded Age Politics*, tell us this not entirely uncommon story of *Gilded Age* corruption:

> When a Dartmouth law professor reported his findings about the expenses that the two parties had incurred in New Hampshire's 1888 state campaign, he dismayed one listener by setting the legitimate expenses at somewhere between $25,000 and $35,000 for each party and the vote-corrupting budget at $100,000 and $175,000, respectively. Protesting the professor's error, former congressman Luther F. McKinney declared on his own knowledge that the sums were far greater. "We all know there is corruption,' he told legislators; 'that there is no longer a free and honest ballot. The question asked concerning candidates is not, Who is the best man? But, Who has the means to buy the most votes?"[858]

There was also the stuffing of ballots, which included the use of "tissue" thin ballots "to allow one folded slip to contain a dozen more inside it." [859] So reckless was the practice of ballot stuffing that in the 1888 presidential election, twelve thousand more votes were counted than there were eligible voters in West Virginia.[860] Outright lying about the presidential candidates was fair game as well.[861] For instance, in the 1888 campaign, in which Benjamin Harrison lost the popular vote but

won a disputed electoral vote count over Cleveland, Democrats claimed
that Harrison stated that "a dollar a day was enough for any working-
man" and "any amount was too much for a striker."[862] For their part, playing on the manufacturing competition from England that Republicans
sought to blunt with protectionism, Republicans used fiction as well to
pass out "tens of thousands of cards with the Union Jack on one side and
quotes from English newspapers on the other, all assuring readers that a
vote for Grover was a vote for England."[863] Worse than that, it was also
said that "high-placed Republicans carried on a whispering campaign,
alleging that Cleveland beat his wife and went on drunken sprees."[864]

The American press had been partisan since the beginning of the
United States. That was true during the *Gilded Age* as well, although
toward the end, the number of independent newspapers was on the rise.
"Outside of the South, most towns had two organs, one Democratic, one
Republican; every major city had them both, along with other papers of
varying degrees of independence."[865] That partisan press participated in
campaigns not unlike the parties they supported and for good reason:
they too obtained spoils, in the form of government printing contracts,
depending on which party was in power. Knowing that, "editors urged
their readers to vote the whole party ticket and not to 'scratch' off a single name."[866] As for hyperbole, the 1888 campaign saw this from the
New York Sun, confirming that a quarter century after the end of the
Civil War, the reference to the "bloody shirt" was still meaningful:

> Vote out Republican disease,
> Vote out the nation's lasting hurt;
> Vote out four years of bloody shirt,
> Vote in four years of thorough peace.[867]

Playing on the issue of immigration and its potential impact on voting, "the *New York Herald* shrieked: 'CHICAGO'S MONGOLIAN
REPUBLICANS RAISE A CAMPAIGN FUND. THEY HOPE TO

VOTE SOME DAY. WORKING FOR HARRISON BECAUSE THEY CONSIDER HIM THEIR FRIEND.'"[868]

During the *Gilded Age*, politics was that blunt. Politics was blood sport of cause and effect, and nearly as often of quid pro quos. Perhaps one last measure of the intensity of politics between the Civil War, *Reconstruction*, and the end of the *Gilded Age* was that three of the four American presidents assassinated in our history, Lincoln, Garfield, and McKinley, were presidents during that time. Blood sport indeed.

★　★　★

It is time to place the *Gilded Age* in context with our own *Divided Era*. Enormous and consequential issues were decided during the *Gilded Age* even though government spending was as yet less than 10 percent of the national economy. What type of currency we used had a great effect on people—it drove the direction of the US economy. The patronage system meant jobs and power. Tariffs protected whole industries and required others to pay taxes. The Southern Question meant the Civil War was not politically over and that freedom hung in the balance for many. Beyond a simple desire for the power to decide such issues, the political parties and the press were also fueled by an equal if not greater desire for government spoils and money. Altogether, it meant that the *Gilded Age* was an age of dramatic partisanship. Indeed, to "those within the mainstream political culture, partisanship seemed as natural as the seasons, though nowhere near as variable."[869]

Historian Charles W. Calhoun concluded of the age that "in no other era in American history has citizen interest in politics and governance been more intense."[870] We can fairly conclude the same, all the time understanding that catalyst was government action—the desire to take such action, to control it, and to benefit from it. All in all, the importance of being in power reached new peaks from 1860 to 1900. As for Americans as a whole, it was understandably impossible for them to stand on the sideline during the Civil War while the nation's fate—and often their own—was decided. In the wake of the war, *Reconstruction* involved a dramatic use of political and military power, which sought to determine not only the nature of our governments but also the fate of race relations—if not our very culture. Once again, Americans could not help but be engaged in a process that promised *or threatened* to affect so many. Building on those unfinished battles, the major decisions being made to decide issues old and new, during the *Gilded Age*, meant that if your partisan competition was acting, it simply was not feasible to sit at home and watch that competitor succeed—because all too often success may well have come at your expense. During those forty years, government action affected people's lives like no other period in our history until today. That is where partisanship can be found—often out of necessity and at times necessarily uncompromising.

Of all the partisan periods in American history, the *Gilded Age* most resembles our own. Success during the *Gilded Age* meant a political party able to wield control and to dramatically benefit their friends through patronage, tariffs, currency issues, and the Southern Question, to name just the major issues. In each upcoming election, the potential for government to act anew *for* or *against* huge numbers of people—based on a history of doing so dramatically since the election of Lincoln—set off a furious competition during the *Gilded Age* to wield that power or block its use. Money, cheating, and lying, right along with good deeds, serious policies, and law—all were the currency of our elections as practiced by our politicians, the major parties, and the third parties vying for attention back then. In short, elections mattered and produced great and often immediate change.

In chapter 9, I discuss at length the comparison of today to the *Gilded Age*. For now, suffice it to say that we see that our governments have the power to dispense enormous benefits and detriments. From social welfare to industrial policy, our governments exercise enormous discretion over an increasing number of people—all well beyond what

Washington, Madison, Jefferson, and even Hamilton would have imagined during their fights over the "meaning" of the Constitution. The fights over tariffs during the *Gilded Age* have been replaced today with fights over income taxes and government subsidies for industry. Our former currency battles are now fought over social welfare programs; and the patronage issue, including the required kickbacks to the party that got someone a job, has evolved into issues about public employee unions, their job security, and compulsory union dues used for political purposes.

With so much at stake today, our governments that decide those significant issues, that tax so many, benefit so many, and employ so many—in short, governments that pick so many winners and losers—are understandably subject to an intense competition for their control. In that breach lays the heart of the *reason* we fight so much and even *how* we fight—just as we did during the *Gilded Age*. So we should not be surprised to see third party activity in our day—nor a presidential election decided one way by popular vote and another by the Electoral College. Today, the spending of seemingly large amounts of money on elections raises concerns but is hardly a new phenomenon. Voter fraud today is real but likely not as rampant as then. Our parties are hierarchical and growing in supporters and sophistication. Yet it was during the *Gilded Age* that extensive voter files first became a necessity.

In those ways and more, the *Gilded Age* helps us understand that what seems either new to us today, or perhaps only more urgent, is really just the same play with different actors and a slightly more modern script. In the final analysis, politics was an active blood sport during the *Gilded Age* because government was doing so much and what it was doing had real impact on people's lives. As we shall see in the coming chapters, that same dynamic drives our current *Divided Era*.

History knows that the intensity of the issues that drove politics during the *Gilded Age* receded over time. Civil service reform, undertaken in a bipartisan fashion, diminished the patronage issue as a significant flash point of partisanship. It also diminished the power, and therefore, the importance of the political parties as well. The Republican victory on the issue of our currency, with the Gold Standard Act, took that off the table for a number of years. The same could be said of the tariff issue. The Southern Question diminished for a time as well although not because the underlying issue of equality before the law was resolved. As a result, the number and significance of the issues taken on by government in the early 1900s did not match that of the *Gilded Age*. Overall, government spending, although growing slowly over time, was still around just 10 percent of the gross national product. Federal regulations were quite minimal and there was no federal income tax. All of that signified a less activist government as compared to the height of the *Gilded Age*, and a less activist government meant a less partisan nation. As we shall see, however, the partisanship and division within our own *Divided Era* cannot be resolved so quickly.

Before we get to that, however, let us understand in full how *The Power to Tax Involves the Power to Divide*.

CHAPTER 8

The Power to Tax Involves the Power to Divide

The power to tax involves the power to destroy.
—Chief Justice John Marshall

The robbery of one group of citizens by another,
even when the State, democratically controlled by the first group,
acts as its agent in carrying out the theft, remains—theft.
—Lady Rhys-Williams,
British Liberal Party then eventually
Conservative Party Member

[If the income tax] reaches a certain point,
perhaps you should revolt.
—Supreme Court Justice Antonin Scalia
in 2014

Every civilization, at one time or another, has to answer the question of the proper, or perhaps the tolerable, scope of government. How to fund that government must also be determined. Of course, that means levying taxes. What types of taxes to impose, on whom, and at what levels, are all questions that must be resolved. John Marshall's now historical dictum, quoted above, about the power to tax, was made with reference to such questions. As the Chief Justice of the Supreme Court, Marshall well understood the power of government—and, of all the

powers that a government can exercise, it is likely that none has caused
more controversy or rebellion throughout history than the power to tax.
In exercising the power to tax, *History* has shown that politicians have
been endlessly inventive as to how to tax people and that the first tax is
never the last tax. *History* has also shown that battles, real and rhetorical,
over tax burdens are a near historical constant.

Our own history includes perhaps the most famous, if not most
important, rebellion in history. It was fought over the nature and
amount of taxation. We are hardly alone. David Burg's *A World His-*
tory of Tax Rebellions: An Encyclopedia of Tax Rebels, Revolts, and Riots
from Antiquity to the Present provides a summary of some "4,300 years
of riots, rebellions, protests, and war triggered by abusive taxation and
tax collecting systems around the world."

For the purposes of the *Divided Era*, the issue goes beyond an understanding that taxes have been a source of rebellion. It is to understand
that the imposition of taxes necessarily involves a choice by government
as to *who* or *what* to tax and *how much* to tax them. In making that
choice, government burdens some and chooses not to burden others—
at least with respect to any one decision to tax. Since few actually prefer to be taxed, history is an open textbook of battles to avoid taxation,
among the rich, the poor, and those in between—either to prevent an
imposition in the first place or avoid them once they are made. That
Partisan Catalyst Dynamic of government choice—including the desire
by people to avoid taxation, and the competition it sets off—is divisive
by its very nature. Depending on the nature of a tax system, those divisions can reach dramatic heights.

In American today we have such a system. Indeed, a more divisive,
democratically imposed system could not be designed. Under our federal income system, roughly half of Americans pay federal income taxes
and the other half does not. Combined with a federal social welfare system that transfers away from taxpayers more than $1 trillion per year
largely to many who are not paying income tax, we literally have a tax

system that by design pits half of Americans against the other half—breeding now understandable resentment along the way. Recall that when tariffs were the main source of federal tax revenue, more revenue was collected from the South by as much as a 3-to-1 margin over the North. So significant was that imbalance that over time it bred historic, persistent division that played a significant factor in Southern dissent if not secession.

In plain terms, our current imbalanced tax system also has the potential to tear at the fabric of America. Indeed, our progressive federal income tax, which taxes people at a higher rate the greater their income, has become ever more the subject of political division. It is a central narrative in the class warfare discussion gripping our country. So much so that the argument can be made that fights over income taxes have replaced the tariff fights we had in the 1800s. We shall find that the income tax was born amid such controversy as well. Before we discuss that, however, let's consider the power to tax.

The Power to Tax

Woodrow Wilson, just over a decade before he became our twenty-eighth president, wrote that "government came, so to say, before the individual and was coeval with his first human instincts."[871] Funding issues must have been coeval as well. "The earliest and most widespread form of taxation was the *corvee*, compulsory labor provided to the state."[872] Of course, that form of taxation fell disproportionately on the poor.[873] As the complexity of societies and governments grew, so did the number and ways that governments taxed their people. Since we started as agrarian civilizations, early forms of taxes were imposed on land (e.g., a property tax, the raw crops grown on the land, the grains from those crops, the animals on the land, and the skin or wool of those animals). Beyond land, at times capitation taxes were imposed—a tax imposed on each person for simply being a person. Income taxes followed, and soon the tax man, who understood Benjamin Franklin's quip that "nothing is certain except death and taxes" long before Franklin uttered it, decided to combine the two by imposing the inheritance tax—or the "death tax" as some refer to it today. Beyond those taxes came sales, consumption, use, excise, value added, and service taxes and, as we have already seen, so did tariffs, or "duties" as they are sometimes called. Of course, we cannot forget the Stamp Tax.

Throughout the ages, the vanquished were required to pay "tributes," otherwise known as taxes, to their foreign masters. At other times, they were voluntarily paid to defer the cost of an alliance such as for the Delian League in the fourth century BC. There were temple taxes and tithing—taxes imposed on a person's religious expression. In France, of course, there was a winegrowers tax, and Bulgaria, not to be outdone, imposed a duty on grapes. Asia endured salt taxes and opium taxes along with silk taxes. China imposed a tax on bananas, Guatemala on indigo, and Spain on flour. In 2350 BC Babylonia/Sumer, a tax was levied for getting a divorce. When roads came into use, there were road taxes or tolls and, in time, gas taxes for the vehicles on those roads. Of course, we mustn't forget taxes on alcohol and tea. To those we can add taxes that at one time were imposed for having a beard, or for each window in a house, or even for owning a hat.

Beyond taxing a thing, *History* is also witness to taxing each form of the thing. There is, of course, the income tax. Even before it is received, income is subject to a withholding tax and a payroll tax and at times to a surtax, a windfall tax, a luxury tax, or a millionaire's tax. It is expanded to include a tax on the interest obtained from placing such already-taxed income in a savings account. Corporate income is taxed once and then taxed again when it is transferred to its owners—shareholders— in the form of a tax on dividends. Other times, governments impose value-added taxes, which tax items each step in the production process and often at the time of sale. In truth, just about everything that has come into being, or become popular or necessary, has been taxed at one time or another—think of cell phone taxes today and how quickly they came into being after the cell phone came into use.

The manner in which those taxes were collected has been an important story of *History* as well. While a monarch or elected government may have decreed the imposition of a tax, that may well have been the easy part. The collection of taxes has always been the harder challenge. For a long time it was more common that someone who wasn't actually on the government payroll performed that task. For instance, in our country's history, the Stamp Tax was to be collected by those commissioned by our government to collect the tax. During the Roman Republic, "tax farmers"—known as *publicani*—collected taxes. Other times the Republic relied on the privileged classes to do the same. However, since the collectors most often were paid based on the amount they collected, the system "effectively encouraged corruption and the maximizing of profits 'by wresting excessive and extortionate payments from . . . hapless and helpless victims.'"[874] Indeed, "tax collectors often brought soldiers or armed guards with them, ostensibly for protection but also useful for intimidating and punishing taxpayers."[875] Today we may see it as a measure of civility that our own system is restricted to audits and a legal process rather than a sudden knock on the door by someone flanked by guards.

The Power to Destroy

Throughout history, the power to tax has proven to be an irresistible power for rulers and politicians to use. Between funds needed for wars, ruling class privileges, government bureaucracy, and domestic programs, the scale of history is tipped demonstrably in favor of those politicians and rulers who wanted more tax revenue, not less. Not always versed in economics as much as urgency, they have often taxed people to the point of rebellion and things to the point of extinction.

If we accept that the more something costs, the less likely it will be produced, sold, or acquired—a foundational economic principle—we must also come to understand that rising tax rates have indeed had the power to diminish, if not destroy. For example, Edith Mary Wightman, in her work *Gallia Belgica*, instructs us of the bad effect a tax on traders had centuries ago in Gaul. According to Wightman, "Legislation of around 400 shows that the city guilds of Gaul were losing members who fled to the anonymity of the countryside, preferring . . . to live under the shelter of a rich rural patron rather than . . . pay the proper taxes."[876]

Avoiding high tax rates is indeed a time-honored tactic. Perhaps the worst such example was something that history knows as *agri deserti*. That was the "problem of abandoned land" in the "late antiquity" of the Roman Empire.[877] At its height, it was said that it "may have included as much as 20 percent of all arable land of the [Roman] Empire."[878] The cause? "The increased burden of taxation from the early fourth century onwards was regarded as having rendered agricultural production less profitable, prompting widespread abandonment of land."[879] Of course, there was a corresponding loss of economic activity as well—just as there was in response to a Roman poll tax in Egypt in 212 AD.[880] Staying with the Roman Empire, Will Durant describes life during Rome's socialist interlude under Diocletian as follows:

> Faced with increasing poverty and restlessness among the masses, and with imminent danger of barbarian invasion, [Diocletian] issued in A.D. 301 an *Edictum de pretiis*, which denounced monopolists for keeping goods from the market to raise prices, and set maximum prices and wages for all important articles and services. Extensive public works were undertaken to put the unemployed to work, and food was distributed gratis, or at reduced prices, to the poor. . . . "In every large town," we are told, "the state became a powerful employer, . . .

standing head and shoulders above the private industrialists, who were in any case crushed by taxation." . . .

The task of controlling men in economic detail proved too much for Diocletian's expanding, expensive, and corrupt bureaucracy. To support this officialdom— the army, the court, public works, and the dole—taxation rose to such heights that men lost incentive to work or earn, and an erosive contest began between lawyers finding devices to evade taxes and lawyers formulating laws to prevent evasion. Thousands of Romans, to escape the taxgatherer, fled over the frontiers to seek refuge among the barbarians.[881]

In China, tax avoidance took on the look of a religious revival. Between the year 460 and 577, an exemption from taxes and military service for Buddhist monks induced the number of monks to rise from the religiously plausible number of seventy thousand to a more profane total of approximately two million.[882]

In our own country's history, the inception of the income tax produced a similar dynamic. It was adopted by constitutional amendment in 1913, with a top tax rate of 7 percent. Within just four years, in an effort to fund our participation in World War I, among other things, the top rate was pushed to 77 percent. That meant that if you took the risk of making income, such as opening a business, and you made income that qualified for that top bracket, the federal government would take 77 percent of any such monies. Of course, the federal government was nowhere to be found if your business did not make money. Losses were your risk. It was only there to collect your profits, which, as it turns out, their high-rate policies diminished.

According to Andrew Mellon, the Treasury Secretary during the 1920s, the "history of taxation shows that taxes which are inherently excessive are not paid. The high rates inevitably put pressure upon the taxpayer to withdraw his capital from productive business." When he said that, Mellon was well aware that under "escalating wartime income tax rates, the number of people reporting taxable incomes of more than $300,000—a huge sum in the money of that era—declined from well over a thousand in 1916 to fewer than three hundred in 1921."[883] A significant reason for that decline, during that period of rising incomes, was a tripling of investments in tax-exempt securities. They were so large that the value of those investments was three times the amount of the federal budget.[884] In other words, people adjusted their behavior to the rising rates. They withdrew their capital from risky, taxable activities, for example, investment in the private market, and instead put their money in municipal securities that saw government paying tax-exempt interest *to them*. That process resulted in less government revenue because the economy was weakened by that withdrawal of capital from the private economy. After presidents Harding and Coolidge followed Mellon's advice and slashed the top rate down to 25 percent, capital moved back into the private sector (away from tax-free government bonds) and fueled the Roaring Twenties and a tax revenue increase of 61 percent— clear evidence that lower tax rates can lead to more revenue, not less.

Years later, during the Great Depression, the highest income tax rate was driven to 94 percent. That increase also hurt the private sector and deprived the federal government of revenues, as well. More recently, in 1991, amid a recession, a luxury tax was imposed on the sale of yachts. The theory of the tax was that if someone could afford to buy a yacht, they could and would pay the extra tax. However, as the *New York Times* reported, the tax significantly diminished the sales of yachts to the point of reducing revenues even further.[885]

Interestingly enough, while some politicians deny that higher tax rates diminish the creation of income, they are nevertheless ready to apply "sin taxes" to diminish the consumption of certain items. For instance, in the first half of the 1700s in England, there was said to be an "orgy of gin drinking to which the working classes in towns fell victims."[886] In response, the powers in charge devised a tax to reduce that consumption and the behaviors associated with it. A series of three Gin Acts that levied taxes "finally brought excessive consumption under some control."[887] Today such taxes are regularly applied to cigarettes, alcohol, candy, and soda—even grocery bags in California—among other items. Even in doing that, politicians go too far. Consider modern-day New York, where taxes on cigarettes are so high that a Tax Foundation study estimates more than half the cigarettes sold in New York are sold on the black market—thereby avoiding the tax man and fulfilling Mellon's warning that the "history of taxation shows that taxes which are inherently excessive are not paid."

Of course, the point of this portion of our discussion is not to present a comprehensive overview of the effect taxes have had on economic activity over the years. Instead, it is just to give some context to Chief Justice John Marshall's historical dictum that "the power to tax involves the power to destroy" if not used wisely. It must be said that much of tax history has been just that—unwise.

The Power to Rebel

How unwise? History is also replete with examples of peoples induced to rebel against the use of the power to tax. After our Revolution, during Washington's presidency, we can recall the Whiskey Rebellion fomented by our federal government's imposition of the tax "upon spirits distilled within the United States." The mere imposition of the tax, a direct tax not unlike that which was the catalyst for our Revolution, was enough to spark the Rebellion, and caused Washington and Hamilton to briefly nationalize state militias—in numbers larger than any army under Washington's direct command during the Revolution—in order to put down the Rebellion. Two centuries later, in 1978, California experienced a bit of a political rebellion in the form of Proposition 13, a property tax reduction initiative. Inflation during the 1970s resulted in rapidly rising property "values," but only on paper unless the property was sold. Property taxes rose along with those paper gains. Many homeowners, especially those on fixed incomes, were being pushed out of their homes because they couldn't afford to pay the rising taxes. Voters finally became enraged enough that they passed an initiative on the ballot that greatly reduced property tax increases year to year. It became a model for other states and produced similar laws, as many as three decades later. Candidate Ronald Reagan would ride the Proposition 13 wave of tax reductions to become president in 1980, and cut federal tax rates from 70 percent all the way down to 28 percent—also resulting in economic growth and a large increase in tax revenues.

We are hardly alone in experiencing such rebellions, political and otherwise. As you can imagine, Rome faced many a rebellion given the scope of the Empire, the costs of their military, the wars it prosecuted, and the taxes it imposed. Northern Africa rebelled during the time of Christ, as did Roman Germany. Egypt revolted several times, as did Judaea. Carthage rebelled, Thrace rebelled, Antioch rebelled, and Gaul did so numerous times.[888] Perhaps the most colorful of such rebellions was that of the Iceni, in Britain, in 60 AD. After a particularly harsh imposition of a new tax system, and the confiscation of property after the death of the local king, in what amounted to an even harsher death tax, the king's widow, Boadicea, led an enormous force in revolt—possibly as large as 230,000 people. Before a battle, Boadicea declared:

> You have come to realize how much better is poverty with no master than wealth with slavery. For what treatment is there of the most shameful or grievous sort that we have not suffered ever since these [Roman] men made their appearance in Britain? Have we not been robbed entirely of most of our possessions, and those the greatest, while for those that remain we pay taxes? Besides pasturing and tilling for them all our possessions, do we

pay a yearly tribute for our very bodies? . . . How much
better to have been slain and to have perished than to
go about with a tax on our heads! Yet why do I mention
death? For even dying is not free of cost with them nay,
you know what fees we deposit even for our dead. . . .
Only in the case of the Romans do the very dead remain
alive for their profit.[889]

Beyond Rome and the United States, the world has witnessed tax
rebellions in every age and in every corner of the globe. Peru faced a
tax rebellion at the same time we did.[890] There was a poll tax rebellion
in northern Brazil in 1906.[891] "In West Sumatra, a new taxation law
introduced by the Dutch led to a widespread anti-tax rebellion among
Islamic peasants in 1908. On the same theme, in another Malay state,
Trengganu, the Ulu peasants rose up to create a disturbance in 1928
in resistance to a new extra tax burden imposed by the British."[892] The
British also faced "rebellion in Sierra Leone in 1897–98 against a hut
tax."[893] Long after the Roman Empire, in 1385 Italy, the peasants of
Parma rebelled over taxes.[894] France, too, has had its tax revolts.[895] In the
early 1800s, the Dutch faced rebellion in Java where "rebel bands burnt
down toll stations and murdered tax collectors."[896] We also know that
Luther's Reformation, however spiritual, was not without its economic
and tax underpinnings.

Hundreds and hundreds more examples can be found in David
Burg's *A World History of Tax Rebellions: An Encyclopedia of Tax Rebels,
Revolts, and Riots from Antiquity to the Present.* Suffice it to say that it
is likely that nearly every civilization has experienced some form of tax
protest and many outright rebellions. Power exercised by a few often is
exercised to a greater degree than the larger population would like. The
power to tax is no exception, and in many ways provides history's most
frequent examples of the abuse of government power and, if our own
Revolution is an example, powerful responses to abuse.

Of course, rebellions—like our own—are usually started by a few and then attract others. Often, those few are part of a class, political, or societal faction upon whom a tax is imposed. That imposition, on that particular faction, was a choice made by those in power. By exercising that power in that manner, the *Power to Tax Involved the Power to Divide*.

The Power to Divide

As we have seen, government action means a choice as to who will get the benefit or detriment of that government action. Knowing that government is making such a choice, a competition between possible beneficiaries is often instigated. The competing camps not infrequently reflect division—sometimes significant division. Beyond their division, the process of collecting taxes can cause division, and, of course, the tax system itself can cause division.

In our own history, we must remember that after our Revolution, there was immediate division between the states and those who wanted to shift tariff revenue collection away from the individual states to the federal government as part of forming the new federal government. Once the Constitution was adopted, as we discussed in chapter 5, our very first Congress moved quickly to raise revenues through tariffs. A competition then quickly materialized between manufacturing interests on the one hand and farming/consumer interests on the other hand. James Madison and Alexander Hamilton did battle over the proposed tariff bill. James Madison, the Father of our Constitution, the first leader of the House of Representatives, and future president, pushed a tariff bill through the House. Notwithstanding all of Madison's stature, the importance and prickly nature of the tax resulted in the US Senate's refusal to pass his bill.

The tax that eventually passed instantly translated into sectional division for the entire United States. As we know, the decisive political power over the issue resided with the Northern states. Lacking the power to change the law, the South Carolina Nullification Crisis was fought over tariffs and South Carolina's desire not to be subject to that federal law. We also need to remember, again, that the South entertained thoughts of secession on the tariff issue alone. Overall, for more than 160 years, the use of tariffs—a tax—had the power to divide our country along sectional lines. It would not be until the 1930s, two decades after the income tax came into being, that tariffs faded from being a central tool for raising tax revenue, and therefore, lost their ability to significantly divide us.

Again, the United States is hardly alone when it comes to division and taxes. Taxes are the heart of sectional fights in several places around the world today. Take the case of Canada, which is energy rich like the United States. Oil discoveries in the Western province of Alberta have been a boon—especially to Alberta and to Canada as a whole. Not surprisingly, politicians quickly saw the potential for tax revenues flowing from the energy boom. Canada, like the United States during its tariff days, has a geographic, sectional, and therefore, political imbalance. The balance of powers lies in the Eastern provinces—not the Western. Sure enough, the national government made a push for laws and taxes that disproportionately favored the East over the West—certainly in the view of many Westerners. In response, an Alberta separatist movement arose.

In 2001, the Alberta Independence Party came into being with a platform advocating local control over "tax collection."[897] The interim leader of the new party said at its inaugural convention, "It's time to cut off the lifeline"—a reference to Alberta paying too much in tax revenue eastward. As many as 41 percent of Albertans have favored disunion. There is also a website called FreeAlberta.com that makes the case for why Alberta should not be subject to onerous federal laws and taxes. Beyond Canada's sectional differences, 89 percent of Venetians voted in 2014 to separate from the rest of Italy in an unofficial referendum. At the heart of their dispute are the fiscal policies of the government of

Italy, which include citizens in Venice paying more in taxes than they believe is fair. In northeast Spain, a similar movement exists among those living in Catalonia based on the same issues.

Long before complaints arose in the United States, Alberta, Venice, and Catalonia, tax systems caused division. In the Roman Republic, when the collection of taxes was "entrusted" to the privileged classes, "the brutal harshness with which they carried out their task . . . widened still further the gap between the *honestiores* [the wealthy and powerful] and the *humiliores* [the poor and weak]."[898] In Europe, for centuries, nobles were provided tax exemptions. Those exemptions obviously meant that the tax burden was imposed on the less fortunate and allowed the nobility to retain their riches—prolonging the distance and division between the classes. That friction between the classes, which was quite often present, was at times more than rhetorical, such as in France. Long before the French Revolution, those "exemptions evoked hostility and social protest against the aristocracy from peasants and craftsmen" in the sixteenth century.[899]

Our Tax Divisions Today

Tax policy in America today continues to be divisive but in ways different from those we faced at the outset of our country when tariffs were the tax of choice. Originally, of course, there were no income taxes in America. After breaking from England over "direct" taxes, which were akin to a modern-day service tax, the imposition of an income tax was not even a consideration, let alone a possibility. With the adoption of the Constitution, the issue over federal versus state collection of tariff revenue was resolved. Under Article I, Section 8, Clause 1—our Founders opted for a uniform, flat system of taxation. That section provides that "all Duties, Imposts and Excises shall be *uniform* throughout the United States." That meant that any one tariff or tax that was imposed had to be imposed to the same degree in each state. That was plainly an effort to not divide Americans over the imposition of taxes. About such taxes, Alexander Hamilton wrote in *Federalist No. 21*:

> The amount to be contributed by each citizen will in a degree be at his own option, and can be regulated by an attention to his resources.... If duties are too high, they lessen the consumption; the collection is eluded; and the product in the treasury is not so great.... This forms *a complete barrier against any material oppression of the citizens* by *taxes* of this class, and is itself a natural limitation of the power of imposing them.

Similar language could be found in Article I Section II, which provides that "direct taxes shall be apportioned among the several states which may be included within this Union, according to their respective numbers." That meant any direct tax instituted by the federal government would be collected on a per capita basis (i.e., each individual was to pay the same amount, regardless of income or existing wealth). Again the emphasis of the Founders was for a system that treated individuals equally regardless of their station or location. We do know from history, however, that the political imbalance between the North and South meant that, in practice, the South paid more in tariff taxes because they consumed more of the items that Congress subjected to tariffs than the North. In theory, however, long before protection for manufacturing was an issue, the Founders believed they adopted a system that would fall nearly evenly on all Americans.

As the funding needs of government grew, however, the ideal of uniformity gave way to the demands for more—more tax revenue, that is. That created the "need" for a new source of tax revenue. Income became that source. Funding for the Civil War was that first, major need for a new source of funds even though, at the time, the income tax was considered "a radical new step in the history of the nation."[900] The income tax that passed the Congress, and was signed by Abraham Lincoln in 1862, imposed a 3 percent income tax on incomes between $600 and $10,000, and 5 percent over that latter amount. Two years later the rates were raised to 5 percent on incomes between $600 and $5,000; 7.5 percent on income between $5,000 and $10,000; and 10 percent on income over that. In other words, the first income tax was a graduated income tax.

Before its passage, there was considerable consternation over the issue, including the propriety of a direct and graduated tax on individuals. The needs of the Civil War, however, carried the day. Indeed, House member William Sheffield of Rhode Island backed the bill and declared: "The people of Rhode Island are willing to assume the responsibility which may be properly and justly imposed upon them by the Federal Government for the purpose of speedily and effectually putting down that rebellion."[901]

Despite that overriding need, and the general consensus on the need for raising taxes, the process exposed section differences and the seeds of future division. As we saw in our discussion of the Civil War, wealth was not evenly distributed throughout the country. Plainly stated, in 1861, there was more wealth in the North and East, which featured more banking, manufacturing, and trade interests compared with the South and West. The South and West had overall lower incomes and, of course, more farmers faced with not unaccustomed debt. Not surprisingly, the discussion in Congress took on a regional flavor—as well as a class element. For instance, a "leading figure on the Ways and Means Committee," not from the Northeast, "articulated why he supported the income tax. 'The weight must be distributed equally—not upon each man an equal amount, but a tax proportionate to his ability to pay.'"[902] The *New York Herald* opined to the same effect that, under the new progressive tax, "millionaires like Mr. W. B. Astor, Commodore Vanderbilt, . . . and others, will henceforth contribute a fair proportion of their wealth to [the] support of the national government."[903]

As you can see, the very idea of a graduated income tax brought forth immediate arguments that people should not be treated uniformly. Some should be taxed differently. Some should pay more—some segments of society should be divided from the others and made to pay their fair share. According to Christopher Shepard, in his work, *The Civil War Income Tax and the Republican Party, 1861–1872*, the regional differences were reflected in the final House vote. "Many of those Republicans who voted against it were from Midwestern states and did not particularly like the tax on farmland and who wanted the income tax to collect much more revenue from the wealthy capitalist centers—namely, the cities of the Northeast."[904]

Incredibly, that first income tax was eventually repealed—a rather unheard-of concept these days. Of course at that time, you were more likely to find politicians like John Stratton, a House member from New Jersey, who stated, "I think that a Federal tax is always odious to the people; that a tax of any kind is always odious to the people."[905] Opposition to the income tax, on the grounds the federal government had no right to progressively tax a person's income, did result in a legal challenge. However, by the time the challenge reached the Supreme Court in 1880, it had already expired. Nevertheless, the Supreme Court ruled on the question raised by the citizen who was taxed, refused to pay that tax, and then lost his properties at the hand of the government. Incredibly, the Supreme Court in *Springer v. United States* ruled unanimously that "direct taxes, within the meaning of the Constitution, are *only capitation taxes*, as expressed in that instrument, *and taxes on real estate*; and that the tax of which the plaintiff in error complains [income tax] is within the category of an excise or duty." In other words, they separated the person from his income and believed that income was subject to a tariff of sorts, which did not have to be apportioned uniformly throughout the country.

The second income tax passed the Congress in 1894 as part of the Wilson-Gorman Tariff Act. The tariff aspect of the Act was controversial, as was the income tax portion. Despite the Democrats having 219 elected House members, with just 179 needed for a quorum, quorum on the bill was not made until "the deputy sergeant at arms arrested about thirty representatives"[906]—a tactic reminiscent of when the Pennsylvania Federalists did the same under Benjamin Franklin's watchful eye to secure an early vote for a state convention to adopt the Constitution. Such are the passions and protest that taxes can ignite. The bill finally passed, but largely on a party-line vote in the House with the Democrat majority prevailing. Democrat President Cleveland did not support the Act, but instead allowed it to become law without signing it.

Once again, the very idea of an income tax, that time a 2 percent tax on income over $4,000, engendered strong criticism beyond the quorum protest. For instance, the former governor of New York and now its senator, Democrat David B. Hill, spoke of it on the floor of the Senate. Despite his statement that it was "not time for partisan reproaches," Hill displayed his sectional bias, which rose above his party affiliation. He excoriated the income tax proposal as a "scheme," "unnecessary, ill-timed, mischievous—suddenly sprung upon the country in the hour of its distress, *un-democratic in its nature and socialist in its tendencies*—I enter the protest of the people of New York. They utterly dissent from any proposal to get revenue for the General Government by taxing incomes."[907] Hill was not alone in his views—views that demonstrated the divisive nature of the power to tax. According to Festus P. Summer, in his work *William L. Wilson and Tariff Reform: A Biography*,

> In population and money centers opposition to the personal income tax was even more vocal than opposition to tariff reform, and its opponents unlimbered every weapon in their arsenal. The tax was unconstitutional, inquisitorial, even monarchial; it was *class legislation* of the very sort which the Democrats professed to abhor and were committed to destroy; it was a war tax, a tax

on thrift, and, as James Mill had said, "a tax on conscience." . . . Bourke Cockran declared that the tax was
undemocratic because so few would be privileged to pay
it. . . . David A. Wells prophesied that if the income tax
were passed, it would never be repealed; it would be "but
the entering wedge for discriminatory taxation amounting finally to confiscation of all income or property over
a certain amount." If tariff reform was to be purchased at
such a price, the country would be unwise to consent to
the bargain. German political economy was at the bottom of it all, said Manton Marble. "A race unpracticed
in liberty is teaching American Democrats taxation and
Democracy." The personal income tax, the tax on the
income of corporations, the inheritance tax, and like
taxes were but first lessons in paternalistic government
of late come out of Europe.[908]

Our second income tax was also legally challenged. Just fifteen years
after its decision to uphold the income tax, a Supreme Court comprised of slightly different members, in a 5–4 decision, struck down the
nation's second income tax. In *Pollock v. Farmers' Loan Trust Company*,
after an exhaustive look at the words of the Constitution, and the "original intent" of the Founders, the Supreme Court declared:

> We are not here concerned with the question whether
> an income tax be or be not desirable, nor whether such
> a tax would enable the government to diminish taxes on
> consumption and duties on imports, and to enter upon
> what may be believed to be a reform of its fiscal and com-
> mercial system. Questions of that character belong to
> the controversies of political parties, and cannot be set-
> tled by judicial decision. In these cases, our province is to

determine whether this income tax on the revenue from
property does or does not belong to the class of direct
taxes. If it does, it is, being *unapportioned*, in violation of
the Constitution, and we must so declare. (italics added)

The reference to "unapportioned" came directly from the language
of the Constitution and it meant that the tax burden had to be spread
evenly across the states based on population, not disproportionately
based on the income of particular individuals. The manner in which the
Supreme Court decided the issue told the political classes that income
could be taxed if they were apportioned. However, apportionment
required census data and the fluid nature of income made that imprac-
tical. As a result, it would take a constitutional amendment approved
in 1913 to go around the Supreme Court—and the Founders' intent—
and establish a national income tax once, and perhaps, for all.

We must remember that between 1880 and 1913, the United States
was amidst the Industrial Revolution and the *Gilded Age*. It was the time
of Vanderbilt, Carnegie, Morgan, and Rockefeller. As Williams Jennings
Bryan said in his Cross of Gold speech, it was the age of "accumulated
wealth." A good deal of the history of taxation by politicians and rulers,
of course, is a history of taxing such accumulations, wherever they can
be found, for reasons necessary and otherwise. In that light, we shall find
that the Supreme Court as much set off the political fight for an income
tax as it did strike down a particular law.

★   ★   ★

The federal income tax we know today passed the Congress in 1913—
not long after the states adopted the Sixteenth Amendment, which permitted an income tax notwithstanding the US Supreme Court decision
and the Founders' intent. In making its decision, the Supreme Court

stated that whether the income tax was a good idea was left to the "controversies of political parties" and its decision created just that.

Against the custom of the time, the likes of William Jennings Bryan and others, politicized the Supreme Court decision striking down the income tax. Bryan deflected that criticism, at the 1896 Democrat convention, in his Cross of Gold speech, by stating: "They criticize us for our criticism of the Supreme Court of the United States. My friends, we have made no criticism. We have simply called attention to what you know. If you want criticisms, read the dissenting opinions of the Court. That will give you criticisms." More importantly, he nationalized the case for an income tax. According to Bryan,

> They tell us that this platform was made to catch votes. We reply to them that changing conditions make new issues; that the principles upon which rest Democracy are as everlasting as the hills; but that they must be applied to new conditions as they arise. Conditions have arisen and we are attempting to meet those conditions. They tell us that the income tax ought not to be brought in here; that is not a new idea. They say we passed an unconstitutional law. I deny it. The income tax was not unconstitutional when it was passed. It was not unconstitutional when it went before the Supreme Court for the first time. It did not become unconstitutional until one judge changed his mind; and we cannot be expected to know when a judge will change his mind. The income tax is a just law. It simply intends to put the burdens of government *justly* upon the backs of the people. I am in favor of an income tax. When I find a man who is not willing to *pay his share of the burden* of the government which protects him, I find a man who

is unworthy to enjoy the blessings of a government like
ours. (emphasis added)

The concern over accumulated wealth, let alone the desire to tax accumulated wealth, was not limited to Bryan or the Democrats. By now, the
idea of an income tax was gaining bipartisan support. Motivated by the
need for more revenue to fund the Spanish-American War, and wary of
the growth in the giant trusts headed by Rockefeller, Morgan, and others, Republican President William McKinley instituted an inheritance
tax "that reached a top rate of 15 percent for bequests over one million
dollars. Other provisions included a tax of 1 percent on all receipts over
two hundred thousand dollars of corporations refining oil or sugar (a
two-pronged jab at the sugar trust and Rockefeller's Standard Oil)."[909]
McKinley was also interested in reforms related to tariffs. However,
there was worry that could have resulted in a loss in revenues. This
peaked McKinley's interest in income taxes, and he was said to have
questioned Supreme Court Justice Harlan about Supreme Court rul-
ings on the income tax.[910] McKinley may have turned to an income tax
to replace lost tariff revenue. As we know, however, President McKinley
was assassinated and died in September of 1901. One result of his death
was that the talk of an income tax would temporarily take a back seat—
but not the concern over accumulated wealth.
McKinley's vice president, and therefore successor, was Teddy
Roosevelt. The ambitious Roosevelt had a much greater concern over
the giant corporations, also known as trusts, than did McKinley. During
his time as the governor of New York, Roosevelt sounded not unlike
William Jennings Bryan by making such comments as the "need for
'increasing a more rigorous control' of public utility companies that had
acquired wealth 'by means which are utterly inconsistent with the highest laws of morality.'"[911] Beyond that, Roosevelt believed that the "state
should be given power to inspect and examine thoroughly 'all the work-
ings of great corporations'—where necessary publishing its findings in

the newspapers."[912] Comments like that and others not only concerned Republican Party bosses in New York and beyond—it also concerned the heads of those great corporations. In an age when the "vice presidency, by long custom, conferred nothing but terminal anonymity on nearly all of those who held the office,"[913] they pushed the political process to make "TR" McKinley's vice president in the hopes he could do no further harm. The death of McKinley, however, meant those plans backfired.

While Roosevelt quickly moved to attack the giant trusts' monopolistic practices, it would be a while before an income tax would grab his attention. But when he won reelection in 1906, Roosevelt upped the ante of class-centered politics in support of a progressive inheritance tax. TR told the country that

> it is important to this people to grapple with the problems connected with the amassing of enormous fortunes, and the use of those fortunes, both corporate and individual, in business. *We should discriminate in the sharpest way between fortunes well-won and fortunes ill-won; between those gained as an incident to performing great services to the community as a whole, and those gained in evil fashion by keeping just within the limits of mere law-honesty.* Of course no amount of charity in spending such fortunes in any way compensates for misconduct in making them. As a matter of personal conviction, and without pretending to discuss the details or formulate the system, I feel that we shall ultimately have to consider the adoption of some such scheme as that of a progressive tax on all fortunes, beyond a certain amount either given in life or devised or bequeathed upon death to any individual—*a tax so framed as to put it out of the power of the owner of one of these enormous*

fortunes to hand on more than a certain amount to any one individual; the tax, of course, to be imposed by the National and not the State Government. Such taxation should, of course, be aimed merely at the inheritance or transmission in their entirety of those fortunes *swollen beyond all healthy limits.* [emphasis added]

No sitting American president had ever spoken in such terms and his sentiments would not end with the desire of a progressive inheritance tax. Roosevelt came out the next year in favor of an income tax. Acknowledging the difficulty in administering such a tax, given the most recent Supreme Court decision on the topic, Roosevelt declared that

great care would have to be exercised to see that it was not evaded by the very men whom it was most desirable to have taxed, for if so evaded it would, of course, be worse than no tax at all; *as the least desirable of all taxes is the tax which bears heavily upon the honest as compared with the dishonest man.*

Just over one hundred years had passed since the adoption of the Constitution, and gone was any sense, let alone the ideal, of uniformity. A US president, Theodore Roosevelt, echoing the arguments of lesser advocates from the past, was advocating a tax policy that specifically targeted a portion of American society—in their individual capacity. To be sure, the segment he targeted was a limited segment and no income tax was instituted during his term in office. Nor did Roosevelt's words or advocacy establish a hopelessly divided country on the issue of class or tax policy at the time they were said. They did, however, reinforce the existing divisions over the issue, and perhaps more importantly, given his stature and bully pulpit, they cemented the terms and provided the rhetoric for income tax debates that are *still* used to this day.

Roosevelt's handpicked successor, William Howard Taft, picked up where Roosevelt left off. Taft first engineered the passage of a corporation income tax of 1 percent on net corporate income in 1909, and then in 1913, came out in support of the Sixteenth Amendment, which authorized an income tax that would be beyond the reach of the Supreme Court. His efforts met with immediate and vitriolic resistance. "Richard E. Byrd, speaker of the Virginia House of Delegates made a particularly impassioned plea to reject the amendment, offering a potent rhetorical blend of state rights, limited government, and anti-tax convictions. Ratification, he warned, would open a new and dangerous chapter in American government."[914] Byrd predicted that

> a hand from Washington will be stretched out and placed upon every man's business; the eye of the Federal inspector will be in every man's counting house . . . The law will of necessity have inquisitorial features, it will provide penalties, it will create complicated machinery. Under it men will be hailed into courts distant from their homes. Heavy fines imposed by distant and unfamiliar tribunals will constantly menace the tax payer. An army of Federal inspectors, spies and detectives will descend upon the state . . . Who of us who have had knowledge of the doings of the Federal officials in the Internal Revenue service can be blind to what will follow? I do not hesitate to say that the adoption of this amendment will be such a surrender to imperialism.[915]

Today you can hear those same strains of Richard Byrd in the mouths of the opponents of the income tax. The "progressive" Teddy Roosevelt disagreed and proclaimed that "'the really big fortune, the swollen fortune, by the mere fact of its size, acquires qualities which differentiate it in kind as well as in degree from what is possessed by men of relatively

small means. Therefore, I believe in a graduated income tax on big fortunes.' In other words, uniform taxes, equal protection of the laws, and
full property rights do not apply to those people with fortunes that are
swollen. 'A graduated income tax on *big fortunes*' is needed, Roosevelt
insisted, as part of society's right to '*regulate the use of wealth in the public interest.*'"[916]

★　★　★

The nation had surely changed by the time of Teddy Roosevelt's populist
statements on income. When the last of our Founding Fathers, James
Monroe, was president, governmental expenditures were in the range
of just 3 percent of the overall economy. Jefferson and Monroe made
an effort of limiting, if not reducing government. There were no federal
regulations, no income tax, and we could have uncontested elections—
even at the presidential level. Americans were opening the West—which
meant some were literally getting farther away from the power of government. Between the time of James Monroe's Anti-Federalist leanings
and Teddy Roosevelt's declaration that society had a *right* to regulate
wealth, our population had exploded and we had endured a Civil War
and *Reconstruction*. With the Industrial Revolution, enormous wealth
had been accumulated and urbanization had become a core societal
dynamic. Governmental expenditures were now more than 7 percent
of the overall economy and heading higher. Amid all of that change and
often upheaval, there were inequities often highlighted by the proximity
and glare of the city—in contrast to the hardships of the farm, which
were more often borne with anonymity.

For the politician, inequity is too often the cover story for ambition, and accumulated wealth, the bank to be breached for his social
engineering. By historical standards, the desire to tax the *haves* for the
supposed benefit of the *have-nots* was neither new nor inventive; nor
was the populist rhetoric of the likes of Teddy Roosevelt. After all,

"Isocrates, old and rich, complained in 353 B.C.: 'When I was a boy wealth was regarded as a thing so secure and admirable that almost everyone affected to own more property than he possessed; ... now a man has to be ready to defend himself against being rich as if it were the worst of crimes.'"[917] By 1913, on a different shore, civilization had arrived there again.

In other words, Teddy Roosevelt had not invented populism nor appeals to class, let alone demagoguery or vilifying the rich. The taste for such rhetoric had been building for some time in America. Roosevelt simply borrowed from an older script. Our Founders were well aware of such political desires and efforts. They had not accidentally forged a system that required uniformity in taxation. But that was a different time—as the election of 1912 would demonstrate.

The Unbridled Power to Tax

By the time of the 1912 election, the Republican Party had been a half-century in the making and the Democratic Party even older. That represented relative longevity in our brief political history. The changing times, controversial policies, and one man's political ambition, however, meant that the 1912 election was rather unlike any that had gone before. Teddy Roosevelt bolted from the Republican Party and turned on his handpicked successor to run for what would have been an unprecedented third term under the banner of the Progressive Party. Joining the fray was the Socialist Party and its candidate Eugene Debs from the swing state (both politically and economically) of Indiana. The two took on Republican incumbent Howard Taft and Democrat Woodrow Wilson. The winner, Wilson, garnered just 41.8 percent of the vote and the incumbent Taft finished third—a first for an incumbent—with just 23.2 percent of the vote. The Socialist candidate Debs garnered a not historically insignificant 6 percent of the vote, but the ceaselessly ambitious Teddy Roosevelt grabbed 27.4 percent of the vote. Between Roosevelt and the Socialist Party, it was clear a chord had been struck and a new issue leveraged, an issue that lasts with us to this day—the societal argument for pursuing the wealth of some for the benefit of others; and the tool for such social engineering would be the power to tax.

If we fast-forward to the next Roosevelt, we find a similar approach to politics. Franklin Delano Roosevelt ran for the presidency amid the economic troubles of the 1930s. The Democratic platform that emerged from FDR's nominating convention actually called for a cut in federal spending and Roosevelt had accused Herbert Hoover, who had vastly increased federal spending to combat the prevailing economic troubles, of putting us on the road to socialism. Once in office, however, FDR increased federal spending not by Hoover's 25 percent, from roughly $3 billion to $4 billion, but from $4 billion to $39 billion—more than a 900 percent increase! In an effort to fund such ambitious spending, FDR not only continued Hoover's policy of high income tax rates— FDR pushed them even higher. Hoover had jumped the top federal rate from the 25 percent rate under Harding and Coolidge to 63 percent. Roosevelt then drove it to 79 percent and eventually 94 percent—a policy that hurt capital formation, and therefore, the economy. Even Democrats like Senator Tom Connally questioned the wisdom of FDR's policies when he stated that "we cannot get much more from the very high brackets, because as to them we have already reached the point of unproductiveness."

For FDR, however, it was much more than a revenue or economic issue. What we know today as class warfare "was the major campaign strategy for FDR during his whole presidency."[918] For instance, in the waning days of the 1936 campaign, and still facing double-digit unemployment, Roosevelt's strategy was laid bare when, two weeks before the election, "FDR announced that wealthy people had long been refusing '*to pay a fair share*' of the cost of government. Therefore, he boasted, 'we increased still further the taxes paid by individuals in the highest brackets—those with incomes over one million dollars a year. *Wasn't that the American thing to do?'"*[919] A year later, FDR quantified his political strategy by telling "two prominent Democrats, Senator Pat Harrison and Representative Robert Doughton, that if they would form a 'subcommittee to investigate tax avoidance,' that the *Democrats would gain 'at least 10,000,000 [votes]' by publicly exposing those who sheltered income*."[920]

In other words, FDR was using the income tax system at least as much—if not more—for the partisan and divisive purpose of winning votes as for collecting tax revenue. Although Roosevelt started by going after the rich, his desire to spend meant that his taxing ways could not stop with the rich. Roosevelt eventually signed tax laws that extended the income tax to ten times the number of Americans than were paying income taxes before his presidency. He also instituted the withholding tax in an effort to ensure the steady and consistent payment of taxes to the government. Again, the first tax is never the last and the older the civilization, the more wide-ranging the reach of the tax collector.

The Divisive Politics of the Modern Day Income Tax

Few people actually want to pay taxes. Having to pay taxes can cause ordinary people to become rather agitated—if not to rebel. If you add to the "odious" nature of paying taxes—seeing your neighbor not pay taxes, you have the makings of political division. Up to the time of FDR, the income tax was imposed on a rather small number of Americans. For instance, in 1916, just "1.1 percent of working age Americans even filed a tax return and roughly 17 percent of the 437,036 Americans who did file a tax return had no income tax liability."[921] The Revenue Act of 1942 changed all of that. With that Act, in addition to increasing income tax rates in general, a World War II Victory Tax was imposed on everyone making over $624 per year. Beyond that, the personal exemption was reduced from $1,500 per year to $1,200 and the child deduction was reduced from $400 to $350. The result of that was that a huge percentage of Americans were now paying federal income taxes. Indeed, "the number of tax returns jumped from 7.7 million in 1939 to 36.7 million in 1942. In 1945, the number of tax filers approached 50 million while the percentage of Americans who filed an income tax return neared 85 percent. By contrast, the percentage of nonpayers fell to 10 percent in 1945."[922] In other words, 90 percent of the people working in 1945 were paying at least some taxes. While imposing taxes is never popular per se, at least the system eventually imposed by FDR and his supporters in Congress, largely Democrats, affected most Americans, even if it was based on a graduated or progressive income tax. As we shall see, in that form, the system was less likely to be divisive between classes of Americans.

Since 1945, however, although it has fluctuated, the long-term trend has been toward a smaller percentage of people working and paying income taxes—and that trend has spiked in recent years. In 1960, 16 percent of those filing tax returns had no income tax liability, and in 2000, 25.2 percent of those filing a tax return paid no income taxes.[923] In 2009 that number peaked at 42 percent, and in 2010, the number was 41 percent and "many of these filers actually had a negative income tax burden because they were eligible for 'refundable' tax credits even though they had no income tax liability."[924]

The same IRS data can be expressed differently with respect to how the income tax burden is imposed on those filing taxes. Keep in mind that the top income tax rate in 1980 was 70 percent—the same as it had been from the time President Kennedy suggested reducing the top tax rate from 91 percent, which President Johnson enacted into law. In 1980, the top 1 percent of earners paid 19.05 percent of all income tax. The bottom 50 percent of earners paid 7.05 percent of all income tax. President Reagan reduced the tax rates for everyone, including reducing the top rate to 28 percent. At the same time, Reagan increased personal and married couple exemptions. The overall effect was to reduce the number of working taxpayers.

The tax rate reductions of President George W. Bush had the same effect of removing taxpayers on the bottom half of the income scale, and therefore, increasing the burden on the top half, as shown in Figure A, which represents the tax burden in 2009.

FIGURE A

TAX BURDEN OF AMERICANS BY INCOME PERCENTILE

Percentiles Ranked by AGI	AGI Threshold on Percentiles	Percentage of Federal Personal Income Tax Paid
Top 1%	$343,927	36.73
Top 5%	$154,643	58.66
Top 10%	$112,124	70.47
Top 25%	$66,193	87.30
Top 50%	$32,396	97.75
Bottom 50%	<$32,396	2.25

Note: AGI is Adjusted Gross Income. Source: Internal Revenue Service[925]

The chart expresses the effect three decades of federal tax policy has had on the imposition of tax burdens. As you can see, the burden of the top 1 percent has nearly doubled. The burden on the bottom 50 percent has dropped from 7 percent to just over 2 percent. Even more dramatic is the fact that due to certain tax benefits and transfer, the bottom 40 percent pays *negative 9 percent* of income taxes—which means they get money from the federal government instead of paying income taxes. For our purposes, the IRS data presents a clear picture of an income tax system that essentially has half of American workers paying taxes, and a trend that has been to intensify the burden on the upper half.

It is also important to note that at the same time the burden has been intensifying on the upper half, the amount America spends on welfare—essentially on those that tend to be in the bottom half—has dramatically increased. The Unites States has spent as much as $20 trillion on federal social welfare programs since President Johnson started the War on Poverty in the mid-1960s. After significant increases under President George W. Bush, there was an explosive increase in social welfare spending of 41 percent under President Barack Obama in his first term.[926] Indeed, under the Obama Administration, there have been a record number of people on food stamps such that, by the end of 2013, 20 percent of American households were on food stamps. That represents a doubling of the number of people on food stamps since 2004. At the end of 2013, there was also a record number of Americans on disability—nearly 11 million. By the end of 2014, one-third of Americans were receiving some type of means-tested assistance from the federal government—a number that excludes Social Security and Medicare.

Of course, the rise in the number of those receiving government benefits is not unrelated to the drop in the percentage of people in the workforce. The labor force participation rate in 2013 and 2014 was at a forty-year low. Beyond those difficult numbers, unemployment benefits have been extended from the traditional starting point of twenty-six weeks of benefits to the remarkable number of seventy-three weeks. Those bad employment numbers were a predictable byproduct of a stagnant US economy, which started in earnest in 2008 but has its roots in forty years of growing regulations. Stagnant economies, by themselves, result in political unease if not unrest. The sum total of those two dynamics of roughly half of Americans paying income tax and a huge percentage of Americans receiving government benefits during a stagnant economy magnifies tension between those two groups.

That division is evidenced in the ways we have now come to expect: intense rhetoric between the major parties, the rise of third parties, including the Tea Party and the Liberty Movement, along with the protests of the Occupy Movement. There are also continuing increases in the number of voters registering as "decline to state" or "independent." There is also the core division between those working and paying taxes, and those not paying taxes and demanding ever more government benefits.

As for the divisions and rhetoric between the parties, a key argument of the Democrats in the last decade has been that upper-income Americans should be paying their "fair share" of taxes (i.e., a greater portion of income tax). Of course, those who pay those taxes—along with a huge percentage of Republicans and other Americans—argue that, in 2013, the top 1 percent paid over 37 percent of the income taxes but made just 20 percent of the nation's income; and the top 5 percent paid more than 58 percent, etc. The Democrats argue in return that those people, nevertheless, made sufficient amounts that they should pay more.

As part of that Democrat push, recall that candidate Barack Obama campaigned by asserting, of the Bush tax cuts, that the "rich didn't ask for the tax cuts and didn't need them." He also promised a tax cut for 95 percent of Americans, thereby clearly pitting a portion of Americans against the majority of Americans—the tactic of FDR and Teddy Roosevelt before him. In his 2012 State of the Union address, given in a presidential election year, President Obama declared that "it's time to apply the same rules from top to bottom." Again and not unlike FDR, Obama was seeking votes by casting a sector of American society in a bad—and false—light. Of course, President Obama has repeatedly stated that "it's only right that we ask everyone to pay their fair share" and famously told Joe the Plumber, "I think when you spread the wealth around, it's good for everybody."

Soon-to-be Vice President Joe Biden, toed the Democrat line when he said in 2007, "We are giving people tax breaks who don't need it. The top 1 percent got an $85 billion a year tax break. It is not needed." In 2006, future Speaker of the House Nancy Pelosi stated: "There is no question these windfall profits and income created by the Bush administration need to be taxed at 100 percent rate and those dollars redistributed to the poor and working class." In 2004, the National Platform of the Democratic Party directly appealed to class differences on the tax issue:

Cutting taxes for middle class Americans. First, we must
restore our values to our tax code. We want a tax code
that rewards work and creates wealth for more people,
not a tax code that hoards wealth for those who already
have it. With the middle class under assault like never
before, we simply cannot afford the massive Bush tax
cuts for the very wealthiest. We should set taxes for families making more than $200,000 a year at the same level
as in the late 1990s, a period of great prosperity when the
wealthiest Americans thrived without special treatment.
We will cut taxes for 98 percent of Americans and help
families meet the economic challenges of their everyday
lives. And we will oppose tax increases on middle class
families, including those living abroad.

That same year, Hillary Clinton famously said, "We're going to take
things away from you on behalf of the common good." While running
for president in 2007, Hillary offered a tax plan that included "raising taxes on corporations and wealthy individuals." Obviously, those
plans, and the rhetoric used to support them, were not far from Teddy
Roosevelt's desire for a "graduated income tax on big fortunes" as part
of society's right to "regulate the use of wealth in the public interest."[927]
   For their part, as of the writing of this book, the Republicans had lost
the rhetorical upper hand when it came to advocating for pro-growth
tax policies. Candidate Ronald Reagan was the strongest advocate in
the last forty years for flattening the tax code, or reducing tax rates, as a
means to grow the economy and increase revenues—policies Democrat
John F. Kennedy championed, and Harding and Coolidge before him.
President George W. Bush also advocated tax rate reductions, and won
those reductions in the wake of 9/11 in 2001. Central to their argument
and policies for all of those presidents was that the economy overall—
and therefore all Americans—would benefit from the rate reduction

and resultant growing economy. Such a policy did not seek to pit Americans against each other. It was a unifying message in all four cases for policies that, in fact, significantly lifted the economy and employment.

Since the financial crisis of 2008, however, no national Republican has been able to successfully articulate the message of Harding, Coolidge, Kennedy, Reagan, or Bush. To the contrary, Republicans have virtually no response to the false claim that the Bush policies—including his tax rate reductions—led to the 2008 financial crisis. The Bush rate reductions—which reduced every tax rate to a rate lower than under Bill Clinton, and which removed many taxpayers from the lower end of the spectrum—did not and could not lead to an economic downturn. It is not possible for an economy to decline *because* people retain more of their earnings, thereby capitalizing on greater incentives to make money. Indeed, the Bush tax cuts were followed by robust growth and a record $700 billion increase in revenues. In fact, the four major income tax rate reductions in our history were all preceded by rough economic times, and all followed by increased economic activity, greater employment, and higher tax revenues. Nevertheless, the succeeding Republicans' presidential candidates—John McCain and Mitt Romney—were not able to make a forceful, unifying argument on tax policy. Overall, Republicans have fallen into a reactive—and negative—mode of blaming Democrats for inciting class warfare instead of having a positive message of their own. In other words, Republicans are left to partisan criticism themselves, while they decry the partisan criticism of the Democrats on the tax issue.

The playing field over the issue of taxes has not been left to the Republicans and Democrats alone. Starting in 2009, the rise of the Tea Party was fueled by resentment over out-of-control spending and rising taxes. Indeed, Tea Party members have turned the word *Tea* into an acronym meaning "taxed enough already." We shall discuss the importance of the Tea Party at greater length in the next chapter. For now, it is enough to note the current state of taxes is a central driver for the many Tea Party adherents and is one cause for their disaffection, and therefore, division with government in general and the major parties in particular. During the 2010 election, the influence of Tea Party activists played a critical role in Republican gains in the House of Representatives because voter intensity was greater on the right. The election of 2012, which featured Republican presidential candidate Mitt Romney receiving roughly the same number of votes as the 2008 Republican candidate John McCain, despite heightened opposition to President Obama, perhaps demonstrated a reduced influence of the Tea Party Movement. Of course, from the point of view of the Tea Party, the failure of Republicans to be decisive enough on the issues, including runaway taxes and spending reduced the desire of Tea Party members to support the national Republican Party effort.

In addition to the Tea Party, the Occupy Movement also feeds off the dynamic of tax policy turned class warfare. The Occupy Movement traces its roots to September of 2011, when a Canadian anti-consumerist, pro-environment group/magazine, *Adbusters*, called for a protest. The movement gained national attention when it hired a New York public relations firm, and Occupy Wall Street took hold. The focus of the Occupy Movement was not far from where candidate Barack Obama started when he suggested that 95 percent of Americans, who he said were struggling, should receive a tax break while the 5 percent of Americans who didn't need the tax break (i.e., didn't need their own money) should pay their fair share. Those percentages changed to attacks on the 1 percent and in favor of a slogan, "We Are the 99%"—signifying dissatisfaction with wealth distribution and income equality in America. The movement actually spread worldwide and took up camp in many American cities—violently so in some places like Oakland, California. The movement never reached the political participation level of the Tea Party, and while the encampments have gone away, websites and Facebook pages carry the message of the Occupy Movement even as its activities are reduced in scale.

The relative dissipation of the activities of the Occupy Movement does not mean that its central issue, income inequality, has been abandoned. To the contrary, the Democrat Party has continued to champion the issue in its rhetoric, if not its policies. In 2014, President Obama and many Democrats made income inequality, despite its significant rise under his administration, a main talking point as to why Democrats should be elected to office over Republicans. Obviously, President Obama was campaigning again on a strategy of pitting some Americans against others—an inherently divisive strategy. President Obama's solution to income inequality, of course, was an income tax system based on taking from some and giving to others—also an inherently divisive strategy.

Beyond the divisions of our personal income tax system as measured by who pays and who does not, there is the deeper issue of the IRS code overall. There is little doubt that the IRS tax code, and all its rules and exemptions, is the battlefield of one of America's most intense political competitions. Lobbying on tax issues is an industry unto itself and our tax codes, at the federal and many state levels, are testaments to political access and influence. Of course, it is a maxim of history that the more complex the laws, the more they benefit the rich, who can afford to hire consultants to navigate those laws. The nation's tax codes fall squarely within that maxim. Despite granting those tax breaks, politicians of both parties regularly make the case that the rich and corporations get too many breaks under the tax code. That too is a hallmark of political division in America today, courtesy of our income tax code.

The power to divide by tax policies is evident beyond the rhetoric and policies of the parties and the rise of third party movements. As we noted at the outset of this book, one of the deepening divides in America today is between so-called Red States and Blue States. As we shall see in the next chapter, there is a migration of like-minded people to states where they feel more at home ideologically. Conservative Californians moving to Texas is a prime and considerable example of that dynamic.

We should not be surprised to find out that tax policy plays a role in that dynamic, which means tax policy is significant in our Red state/ Blue state divide.

According to Art Laffer, Stephen Moore, and their coauthors of *An Inquiry into the Nature and Causes of the Wealth of States*, taxes play a considerable role in Blue States "getting bluer" and Red States "getting redder."[928] According to Laffer et al. in their exhaustively researched book, "Higher tax burdens, higher income tax rates, and higher corporate tax rates all have devastating effects on population and output growth."[929] As evidence, Laffer notes that "the average 10-year population growth of the nine zero income tax states was 8 percentage points higher than the average of the nine highest income tax rate states, or 14.6 percent and 6.3 percent respectively."[930] Indeed, "not one single state in the group of the nine highest earned income tax rate states had a ten-year population growth as high as the average of the nine zero earned income tax states."[931] Of course, the states with the highest income tax rates tend to be Blue States, like New York and California, while the states with the lower tax rates tend to be Red States, like Texas and Tennessee.

Perhaps the most vibrant example of all is the one-sided competition between Texas and California. Former Texas Governor Rick Perry regularly visited California during his tenure seeking to poach employers to no-income-tax Texas. Texas has netted such high-profile names as Occidental Petroleum and Toyota, as well as jobs from more than sixty California companies including Chevron, Apple, Facebook, Oracle, and eBay. Laffer, Moore, et al., point out, when considering the entire tax schemes of Texas and California, not just income taxes, that "California has tax rates that are roughly 65 percent higher than are Texas' rates." However, California only has tax revenues that are "about 25 percent higher than are Texas' tax revenues."[932] Under those circumstances, we should not be surprised to find that more people move from California to Texas than the other way around.[933] That dynamic does indeed result in a bluer California and a redder Texas. It also means overall, as a nation, the country is more divided between Red States and Blue States—as we shall discuss in the coming chapter.

Finally, the Internal Revenue Service under President Obama has become exceptionally political and divisive in the manner in which it has used the power to tax, beginning in 2010. There is no doubt that, following the lead of President Obama's divisive rhetoric, the IRS selectively chose how to enforce the IRS Code based on political party affiliation. A far lesser politicization of the IRS for partisan purposes garnered President Nixon an article of impeachment back in the early 1970s. Today, however, in the gridlock that is our *Divided Era*, there has not been a comparable committee like there was to get to the bottom of Watergate. To the contrary, since the IRS scandal broke, Democrats in Washington—and the media—have underplayed the magnitude of the IRS actions, which clearly targeted Tea Party groups and otherwise right-of-center political groups. The nature of IRS actions has absolutely increased partisanship across America and between the major parties. Beyond such normal division, however, lies a far greater rising division. As we shall cover to a greater degree in the chapters ahead, the IRS scandal is part of a growing division not just among Americans and their parties, but also among Americans and their governments.

The actions of the IRS have pitted many Americans against their government as part of a natural reaction to government taking action against certain Americans. Clearly, government action is the prime mover of this new division. Government under President Obama picks winners and losers based on partisan terms in unprecedented fashion. As a result of such divisive policies, and other government overreach, like the actions of the National Security Administration, among others, the number of Americans who believe that government is the greatest threat to their freedom is peaking. Governments and their overreach continue to grow, and if *History* is our guide, it is a dynamic unlikely to change. While the IRS may not show up to people's doors flanked by

mercenary tax collectors, there is little doubt that it is using the power
to tax aggressively—an aggression that undoubtedly led Supreme Court
Justice Antonin Scalia to wonder aloud in 2014 whether rebellion over
taxes was inevitable.

*　　*　　*

Before we move on to a broader look at our divisions, we can recognize
that all governments have sooner or later taxed their citizens. The extent
of the tax burden corresponds directly with the size of government.
More government equals more taxes. Larger government also means
a more complex tax code. Those with access and power, usually those
more well-off, draw those complex tax codes often to their benefit and
to the detriment of those with lesser access, usually those less well-off.
Like all other aspects of government, the creation and implementation
of an income tax code, sooner or later, is about picking winners and losers. Our Founding Fathers, who led our rebellion in part because of a
direct stamp tax of less than a penny on most transactions, attempted
to craft a constitution that featured a "uniform," and therefore fair, system of taxation. We well know, however, that in practice, the politicians
implemented laws that wound up picking winners and losers to a lopsided degree. The seeds of the Civil War were sown in the ill-conceived
tariff laws.

A hundred years later, when the income tax began to replace the tariff system, division accompanied the transition. The tax code became a
blatant tool for politicians to pit some Americans against other Americans. Some, like Teddy Roosevelt, wanted to use the tax system to
control accumulated wealth. Others, like Franklin Delano Roosevelt
and President Obama, use it not only for that purpose, but also for
political purposes.

For our purpose of coming to a greater understanding than simply
who should pay what, and regardless of where an observer falls along the

political spectrum, it is inescapable but to conclude that a system that taxes half of America and not the other half—not unlike the tariff system of pre–Civil War America—is on its face divisive, if not rebelliously so. Whether it remains so, and therefore, whether it continues to tear the original fabric of America, lies in the hands of our leaders. For now, however, it plays a central role in our *Divided Era*.

CHAPTER 9

Our House Divided

A house divided against itself cannot stand.
—**Abraham Lincoln**

A braham Lincoln, in June of 1858, famously warned us of the dangers of a house divided. Of course, then US Senate candidate Lincoln was speaking of our divisions over slavery in what would become an ominous premonition of things to come. America today is not nearly as divided as it was before the Civil War. However, our divisions are fast approaching that of *Our Gilded Age of Division*. Unless we come to grips with our growing division, inclusive of flames fanned by cries of wealth and income inequality, we shall dangerously surpass the divisions and tensions of *Our Gilded Age of Division*. Before I suggest possible ameliorations of our partisanship and division, let us consider the nature of the *Divided Era*.

The Catalyst for the Divided Era

The *Divided Era* did not occur spontaneously. Growing government laid the predicate for it to occur. Its time and place—the beginning of the 1990s—was by no means preordained. We shall see that it was the actions of leaders using government power that led to our division. It has continued and intensified for the same reason: the use of government power.

On a broader level, let us first address the issue of the cultural divide in America today. As we consider this issue, keep in mind that at the beginning of a civilization, its culture tends to be more homogenous and the core beliefs of its people within a more narrow range. Imagine a people pulling a cart in the same, steady direction even through difficult terrain. Over time, for sundry reasons and especially as wealth grows and if a population becomes expansionist or varied enough, a wider diversity of views becomes prevalent; often the culture becomes less defined and less confident of its place. Now imagine a people arguing over the destination of the cart and who has the right to be in it. That is certainly true of the American experience.

Our divide along those lines became prominent over the last half-century. Prior to that, even though we differed on the major issues we have discussed, and even though we fought our Civil War, to a larger degree, the ideal of American *Liberty*, given room to flourish amidst our *Manifest Destiny*, guided us and kept us on a similar cultural and ideological path.

By this century, America's population not only has grown immensely, American has become immensely rich. We have been largely freed of the struggle to secure the necessities of day-to-day life thanks to the toils of our ancestors. Amidst our many possessions and our ability to luxuriate, not unlike Rome and Greece at their height, we have become less disciplined as a people, our morals have loosened, and our religious devotion has waned. The quite American ideal of individual *Liberty*, incentivized by the promise of capitalist conquests, has lost its once universal appeal—let alone application. We saw the seeds of that sown in the fight over the imposition of the income tax dating all the way back to the Civil War and in the mouths of William Jennings Bryan, Theodore Roosevelt, and FDR. We shall see more of it as we discuss the growth in our governments in the pages ahead.

Although too large a topic for this book, it is clear that in America today there is a cultural divide between those who champion the older ethic, no longer taught in our public schools, and those more interested in an America that champions social justice for the group and the redistribution that entails, which is often taught in our public schools. That tension plays out in people's views of the proper role of government and the relationship between church and state.

In the competition between our political parties, within this last fifty years, that has sorted out to the point that the Republican Party has become the home of those who favor limited government and the more likely home of churchgoers and those socially conservative. For its part, the Democrat Party appeals to those more socially liberal, the more secular if not atheist, and those wanting a brighter, if not complete, line between church and state. The Democrat Party is also the home of those more likely to believe that government should playing a greater role in righting social injustice, whereas Republicans today tend to emphasize individual rights over government social engineering.

If the wise muse of *History* is our guide, barring a significant loss in wealth brought on by war or a geological calamity, which would require us to fight for our next meals again, it is unlikely we will retrieve our work ethic of the 1800s or our once more conservative religious views. Nor is it likely that America could ever return to its more homogenous cultural roots given America's birthrates and the world's current and likely future immigration patterns. If that is so, we can expect that the cultural divide we are experiencing now to remain roughly the same, if not widen, and the role it plays in our divisions to remain. In other words, if you will, there is likely a *Persistent Cultural Division Dynamic* effecting America today that features contrasting societal views and a competition to control our activist governments.

To be sure, America has had activist governments before. But that is a relative assessment. Recall that Chief Justice Marshall told us of our state-centric two-party system of the late 1700s in his five-volume work, *The Life of George Washington.*

Again, according to Marshall:

> The one struggled with unabated zeal for the exact observance of public and private engagements. . . . The

distresses of individuals were, they thought, to be allevi-
ated only by industry and frugality, not by a relaxation
of the laws, or by a sacrifice of the rights of others. . . .The
other party marked out for themselves a more indulgent
course. . . . Viewing with extreme tenderness the case of
the debtor, their efforts were unceasingly directed to
his relief. To exact a faithful compliance with contracts
was, in their opinion, a harsh measure which the people
would not bear.

Even among our comparatively tiny governments of that time, recall
what great consternation was caused when governments were used to
resolve those differences. Moving on and excluding the extraordinary
nature of *Reconstruction*, which we saw did not complete it stated goal,
the height of the activism of Republican administrations was reached
during the *Gilded Age*. Even at its height it was largely limited to pro-
tectionist policies, tariffs and land grants. Federal spending was less
than ten percent of the overall economy and those policies ended over
time. Our activist governments today and their policies dwarf those
earlier activist governments. Moreover, the Republicans of the 1900s
lost much of their zeal for activist government and for a time its mantle
was left nearly unattended until FDR and the Democrats of the 1930s
picked it up again. Today that mantle resides firmly in the hands of the
Democrat Party.

It also resides in our governments that promote those views regardless of who is in office. Excluding a calamity or the insolvency concerns
we shall shortly address, given the nearly theological nature of the fight
today, and as we shall find, in the light of their economic interests in government, the participants in the existing cultural divide can be expected
to cling to their views and their government programs.

For now, suffice it to conclude that a significant cultural divide exists.
Rather than fighting it out rhetorically in texts of antiquity or in the

editorial pages of our time, we compete over it every day in the government arena and that fight has been steadily growing over the last fifty years. We are so very divided today and we are in the *Divided Era* because those differences are being fought using immense government power.

If we narrow our scope, and look at the physical start of the *Divided Era*, keep in mind that less than a decade before the *Divided Era* started, President Reagan built a large coalition that included Reagan Democrats—a rare political feat. In Reagan's 1984 reelection, he won every state except Walter Mondale's home state of Minnesota en route to an Electoral College landslide of 525 to 13. The popular vote spread was 58.8 percent to 40.6 percent. In no election since has a winner come close to that margin, although some would say Reagan's third term was achieved with the victory of his Vice President George H. W. Bush in 1988—the first sitting vice president to get elected president since 1836. The Reagan coalition, however, did not last. Just five years later, in the early 1990s, politics had become decidedly different. The presidential election of 1992 featured a split decision. In the years leading up to that election, Bush 41 (Bush, Sr.) lit a short fuse of division. He divided the country, and the Republican Party in particular, by breaking his "no new taxes" pledge. Many Republicans saw Bush's deal with Democrats to raise taxes and purportedly cut spending as unacceptable backroom dealing in addition to a broken promise and bad economics. Remember, it is always the strongest marker of political division when a president's own party is divided over his actions—such as Lincoln's policies on *Reconstruction*, Grant's policies on currency, and President Johnson's policies on civil rights and Vietnam in the 1960s.

The Bush 1990 tax increase, along with the existing monetary policy, hurt the economy. Intended to reduce the deficit, the deficit instead climbed from $221 billion in 1990, the year of the Bush budget deal, to $290 billion in 1992. Bush's broken promise and leadership style engendered a fairly strong Republican primary challenge, a rarity against a sitting incumbent, from conservative stalwart Pat Buchanan. That challenge weakened Bush and further divided Republicans. Although Bush won the nomination, the existing economic and budget deficit problems resulted in Bush being challenged in his effort to be reelected not only by a Democrat, Bill Clinton, but also by an independent/third party challenge from Ross Perot. Perot's candidacy was catalyzed by those deficits—a negative manifestation of growing government and demonstration of its power to divide. Bush received just 37 percent of the popular vote—a total reminiscent of incumbent Republican Benjamin Harrison's poor showing during *Our Gilded Age of Division*, in the election of 1892, which also included a third party challenge. Ross Perot finished with an astonishing 18.9 percent of the popular vote even if he won no electoral votes. With just 43 percent of the popular vote, just 4 percent better than Lincoln's 1860 total, Bill Clinton became our forty-second president—a victory that hardly represented a consensus election. Indeed, the 1992 election was only the eleventh time a president had been elected with less than 50 percent of the popular vote and the first time since Richard Nixon in 1968—a year the Democrat Party was divided over the Vietnam War.

Just after he took office, despite his divided victory, Bill Clinton embarked on a series of acts that divided the electorate further. While those acts included Clinton's "Don't Ask, Don't Tell" policy, it was the combination of a tax hike and his Health Security Act, which partisans predictably dubbed "Hillarycare," that proved to be the Stamp Act of the *Divided Era*.

With regard to taxes, Clinton had campaigned on tax cuts—a promise he made not long after the country had been divided by Bush 41's divisive, broken-promised tax increase. Clinton, like Bush before him, failed to keep his promise—the combined effect of which jaded voters' views of government and politicians. In his first year in office, Clinton also divided Congress by pushing through that tax increase without a single Republican vote and *with over forty Democrats voting against it.*

Clinton's budget "passed by a narrow margin, 219–213 in the House and 50–49 in the Senate."[934] With that one act, Clinton almost completely repaired Republican disunity across the country and in Congress. The tax increase also provided substantial impetus for the Republican takeover of the House two years later after a forty-year hiatus. The tax increase alone, however, was not the whole catalyst of that takeover or the *Divided Era*.

In addition to the political effect of the tax increase, beginning with a task force just after his inauguration in January of 1993, Clinton pushed for what he hoped would be his signature presidential achievement—universal health care paid by employers. Like Obamacare fifteen years after it, Clinton's efforts in that regard were viewed as a significant expansion of government power. From the start, partisanship, controversy, and a lawsuit dogged the initiative. Some of that related to the secret doings of the task force that was headed by Clinton's wife, Hillary Clinton, which ran afoul of open government rules. Opposition to the proposed program ran wide and deep. Predictably, Republicans and conservatives in unison opposed the plan. Libertarians objected to the expansion of government. Even the media was skeptical that there was a crisis worthy of a one thousand–page bill (rather unheard of at the time) and such an unwieldy expansion of government.

Perhaps most significant for our purposes, Hillarycare divided the Democratic Party again. Senator Daniel Patrick Moynihan, a very well-respected Democrat Party elder, stated that "anyone who thinks [the Clinton health care plan] can work in the real world as presently written isn't living in it." Summing up the divisive nature of large government expansion and its potential to be a catalyst for partisanship,

> just ten weeks before the 1994 elections, Martha Derthick of the University of Virginia wrote ... of the plan produced by Hillary Clinton's 500-person task force: 'In my many years of studying American social

policy, I have never read an official document that seemed so suffused with coercion and political naiveté . . . with its drastic prescriptions for controlling the conduct of state governments, employers, drug manufacturers, doctors, hospitals and you and me.'[935]

In the end, and not long before the 1994 midterm elections, Clinton's health care legislation failed in the Democrat-controlled Senate—a huge defeat from his own party for the ambitious young president and his wife—and with that, the foundation of the *Divided Era* was laid.

The results of the 1994 election just weeks later, which cost the Democrats the House, were in large part due to Clinton's failure to understand the tenuous nature of his victory two years before. Rather than undertake consensus-building acts at the outset, as other presidents have done in similar divided circumstances, Clinton's aggressive agenda actually increased the divide that existed at the time of his election. *History* knows that, in the wake of the 1994 election, Clinton switched tactics with the help of Dick Morris. As a result, Clinton won reelection but once again with less than 50 percent of the vote—one of only two presidents who have won election twice with less than 50 percent of the vote, Woodrow Wilson being the other. Despite Clinton's reelection, or perhaps as part of it, the *Divided Era* continued to build. From that point on, America was treated to divided government, a presidential scandal and a Republican-led impeachment, which drew the intense ire of Democrats and the media, significantly increased the partisanship of the age, and very much deepened our divisions—perhaps irretrievably so during the Clinton presidency.

If we pause for a moment, it is important to note that it was not the actions of Clinton alone nor the Republicans alone that resulted in the *Divided Era* we have today. Nor was a long period of division worthy of the name the *Divided Era*, a certainty in 1994. To be sure, the actions of the leaders of the time using government had sown division.

It was the actions over the twenty years that followed, however, inclusive of the dynamics we have studied, which in fits and starts turned the Clinton-era divisions into the *Divided Era*.

Recall that, in the past, our high-stakes conflicts were more or less resolved. We adopted a constitution. We fought a civil war. We came up with a single currency. Tariffs gave way to income taxes. With resolution, the partisanship related to those issues receded. The federal government was less than 10 percent of the overall economy for our first hundred years. Federal regulations barely existed and touched very few industries and the average citizens almost not at all. If you lived in the countryside, it was almost possible to imagine Harlow Giles Unger's description of the colonies we read earlier where "settlers isolated in the hamlets and woods of New England had lived free of almost all government authority for more than 150 years."[936] In short, government was simply not overbearingly prevalent outside those major clashes. Under those circumstances, division during any one era, once a decision was made, could recede and people could go back to their lives.

In the last twenty years, however, government is nearly everywhere, and seemingly everywhere there are political clashes over what government is doing. At this point, it is difficult not to be affected by government. Previously, we listed some of the most contentious issues of our day. The economy. Immigration. Taxes. Obamacare. Medicare. Jobs. Welfare. Energy. Deficits. Regulations. Voter fraud. Voter ID. The Middle East. Global warming. Common Core. Public pensions. Property rights. Gay rights. Pro-choice versus Pro-life. Regulations. Government contracts. The Second Amendment. Race. Gender. Class warfare: the 1 percent versus the 99 percent. Church versus State. Big business versus Labor. NeoCons, Hawks, and Doves. Red States versus Blue States. Rural Americans versus the cities. Taxpayers versus tax users. Government unions versus taxpayers. States versus the federal government. The Executive branch versus Congress. The EPA and Justice Department versus free enterprise. The IRS versus Conservatives. The NSA versus Americans. Government pensioners versus government operations.

What do all of them have in common? The exercise of governmental power is at the center of each of them. That is why the halls of Congress and the hearing rooms of our legislatures are among our most important forums. Today and every day, governments are picking countless winners and losers and imposing taxes on someone to pay for the process. All the while, they are fostering a competition among those prospective winners, losers, and taxpayers. That competition, combined with the mix of difficult issues we face today that add to our traditional philosophical battles, is the key to the *Divided Era*. Before we discuss that competition and those growing battles, let us first look at the signposts of our division.

Signs of Division in the Divided Era

Like our previous divisive periods, the United States of 2015 is experiencing the historical dynamics we have discussed throughout the book. First, in response to countless government actions, citizens are reacting in partisan terms (the *Partisan Catalyst Dynamic*) as evidenced by the Tea Party, the proliferation of political action committees and special interest groups, increased lobbying, and the amount of money pouring into elections around the country. Some citizens react by staging rallies or protests—for example, the Tea Party and Occupy—and even states use the legislative and referendum process or our courts to override federal government action. Second, in escalating fashion, government acts, citizens, political parties, and states react and government acts again (the *Escalating Partisanship Dynamic*)—such as the passage of Obamacare, the votes to repeal it, the multiple lawsuits challenging it, and the President's use of executive orders and court appeals in response. Third, despite the passage of certain laws, Obamacare is one example, there is lasting division on many issues—again, think of those many repeal votes undertaken by the House Republicans and the continuing opposition to Obamacare by a majority of voters along with litigation hoping to curb or end it (i.e., a *Lasting Division Dynamic*). Amidst that division, partisanship at times appears to be extreme and the political rhetoric coarsens. There are also those seeking compromise and those seeking to elevate those conciliatory efforts over the passions of the partisans (the *Olive Branch Dynamic*). The one question that remains for *History* to answer (here again referring to the wisdom of time) is whether someone will successfully apply the *Refusal to Compromise Dynamic* to bring the country to a new historical plateau. Before we get to that latter point, let us draw more comparisons between *Our Gilded Age of Division* and today, in order to bring home the nature of the *Divided Era*.

If we recall our discussion of *Our Gilded Age of Division*, we saw many signs of division. They included closely divided electorates, close presidential elections, third party activity, huge sums spent on elections, a high degree of partisan activity, not to mention hyperbole and a competition for government spoils. All of those elements are present in America today.

Starting with a divided electorate, recall from chapter 1 that just before the 2012 presidential election, a Rasmussen Reports poll found the very different Democrat Joe Biden and Republican Paul Ryan tied at 44 percent. If we broaden our perspective, according to the venerable polling company Gallup, we find that every year between 1988 and 2010, those self-identifying as Republicans, Democrats, and Independents each finished within percentage points of each other and all within the narrow thirty-percentile range. Returning to Rasmussen, its Generic Congressional Ballot poll tells a remarkable story. Between April 21, 2013, and August 10, 2014 (a period in between elections during which partisanship theoretically cools), Rasmussen polled *likely* voters fifty-nine times asking them whether they would vote for a Republican or Democrat in their local congressional election. No candidate names were used. Of those fifty-nine times, the two parties finished within the polling margin of error, +/- 2 percent of each other, forty-five times or 76 percent of the time. Eleven times the parties were tied, and there were seventeen lead changes. At the outset, in the April 21, 2013, poll, the Democrats held a two-point advantage, 41 percent to 39 percent. At the conclusion, in the August 10, 2014, poll, the Republicans were ahead 40 percent to 39 percent. In other words, for fifteen months in between elections, likely voters were essentially split evenly between the parties.

Similarly, in July of 2014 and within the time period of the Rasmussen polling we referenced, ahead of the 2014 midterm election, and with control of the US Senate in play, Quinnipiac University asked *registered* voters which party they wanted in control of the House and the Senate. By a margin of 46 percent to 44 percent, a result within the margin of error, registered voters stated they wanted Republicans in charge of both the Senate and the House. In other words, on the question of which party voters wanted to run the Congress, a question about the future, another poll found voters were evenly divided between Republicans and Democrats.

Delving deeper into the August 10, 2014, Rasmussen poll, it questioned likely voters whether they felt the country was more or less divided over the last four years. Sixty-seven percent said the nation was more divided than four years ago—a telling statistic for the *Divided Era*. Perhaps even more telling, when asked who was to blame for that growing division, 35 percent blamed President Obama, 34 percent blamed congressional Republicans, and 23 percent blamed them both. In other words, even in our understanding of why we are divided, Americans are evenly divided.

As enlightening as polls may be, the results of elections often provide a more concrete analysis. Recall that during *Our Gilded Age of Division*, two presidents won the presidency despite losing the popular vote. In our history, that has occurred just four times, and two of them occurred within twelve years of each other during *Our Gilded Age of Division*. In 1876, Rutherford B. Hayes lost the popular vote by 250,000 votes but won the Electoral College vote by a single vote. In 1888, Grover Cleveland won the popular vote by ninety thousand votes but lost the Electoral College vote to Benjamin Harrison 233–168.

It would be 112 years between the time Benjamin Harrison lost the popular vote in 1888 while winning the presidency and the 2000 election. It was in 2000 that George W. Bush joined that very small group of presidents. Bush lost the popular vote to Al Gore by 540,000 votes yet Bush won the Electoral College vote 271–266. That election also featured a legal challenge with regard to the outcome in Florida that was decided by the US Supreme Court. Continuing our discussion of close elections, of the twenty presidents in US history that won reelection, President Obama's 2012 Electoral College margin was larger than that of only James Madison, Woodrow Wilson, Harry Truman and George Bush of 2004. In other words, our last two presidents garnered two of the five smallest Electoral College reelection margins in our history.

Beyond the presidential elections, recall that in *Our Gilded Age of Division*, control of the House of Representatives changed five different times before settling into a decade of Republican control. Moving closer in time, between 1955 and 1993, a thirty-eight-year period, the Democrats had control of the House every year. In the 1994 election, roughly the start of the *Divided Era*, Newt Gingrich and the Republicans pulled a stunning upset. In another signpost of the *Divided Era*, between 1994 and 2010, control of the House changed three times. During roughly that same period, control of the governorships was equally competitive and divided. Every year between 1970 and 1993, the Democrats had controlled the majority of the governorships. Between 1994 and 2004, however, the Republicans controlled a majority of those offices. Then, between 2006 and 2010, the Democrats retook control of the majority, which then flipped back to the Republicans in 2011. At the outset of the *Divided Era*, control of the US Senate was in the hands of the Democrats by a margin of 53–47. Control of that body was then tied when the Republican Bush 43 replaced the Democrat Clinton in the year 2000. It then went back to Republican control as a result of the 2002 and 2004 elections. After the 2006 election, it was tied again before control was taken by the Democrats after the 2008, 2010, and 2012 elections only to be regained by Republicans after the 2014 election.

The fight to control the state houses was even more competitive. From 1956 to 1992, the Democrats had controlled the majority of state legislatures every year but 1968, when each party controlled twenty state houses with the rest split. That changed starting in 1994. Between 1994 and 2014, nine times Republicans had control of more state legislatures, the Democrats six times, and one year they tied. All in all, the back and forth of those elections demonstrates that, politically, Americans have been so closely divided over the last twenty years and that in nearly every election year there was a lot up for grabs.

In addition to divided electorates, close elections, and changing control of the Senate, House of Representatives, governorships and state houses, evidence of the *Divided Era* also includes considerable third party activity. According to Gallup, three times between 2007 and 2013, as much as 58 percent or more of Americans said a major third party was needed. In 2013, that percentage stood at 60 percent while just 26 percent of Americans believed the two major parties were doing an adequate job. Not coincidentally, that dissent found a home.

We have already spoken briefly about the Tea Party Movement and the Occupy Movement. The Tea Party had its most influential political election according to many in 2010. That year it played a key role in the Republican takeover of the House of Representatives. In April of that year, Gallup declared "Tea Partiers Are Fairly Mainstream in Their Demographics." Its polling showed that 28 percent of adults were Tea Party "supporters," including 49 percent of Republicans, 43 percent of Independents, and 8 percent of Democrats. Ideologically, 70 percent of conservatives supported the Tea Party while 22 percent of moderates and even 7 percent of self-identified liberals. In 2014, a study based out of the College of William and Mary of eleven thousand *Freedom Works* members, a leading Tea Party group, found that 23 percent identified as something other than Republican.[937] In other words, the Tea Party Movement's appeal, among Americans, was not limited to conservative Republicans. In Congress, the Tea Party Caucus formed in 2010. It has always been comprised of only Republicans and rose to over sixty members of the House and Senate. While obviously they don't represent a third party, their overt affiliation with the Tea Party Movement is not insignificant.

Perhaps the most evident measure of the influence and prevalence of the Tea Party is the bite of the invective of their opponents: Democrat leaders throughout the country and many in the media. For instance, the Senate majority leader, Democrat Harry Reid of Nevada, has repeatedly blamed congressional Republicans' "strict adherence to tea party ideology" for the partisan gridlock in Washington. Reid also said the GOP's "blind adherence to tea party *extremism* is making it impossible" to reach compromises. (Italics added.) Again, from his point of view, and many in the media who cover the Tea Party, it is not government infringing upon rights that causes a reaction from the aggrieved. They believe partisanship is the problem—as if it exists independently of government action. Beyond that, many Democrat leaders, despite clear evidence that many disaffected Democrats are Tea Party members, have along with the media accused the Tea Party Movement of being racist—a charge that cannot be factually sustained, but is a clear measure of the partisanship and division of the times.

The Occupy Movement reached its height in 2011. According to Gallup polling in November of that year, American support for the Occupy Movement was falling to 24 percent with 38 percent of Democrats supporting the movement, 24 percent of Independents, and 9 percent of Republicans. Unlike the Tea Party, however, the Occupy Movement does not have a congressional caucus and its influence has waned since 2011.

Beyond the Tea Party and the Occupy Movement, there are traditional third parties as well. Perhaps chief among them in influence today is the Libertarian Party. It is currently on the rise because of voter concern over big government overreach, changing social views, a growing isolationist sentiment, and the Pauls—Ron and Rand. Ron Paul, a former Libertarian Party member, ran for president in the Republican Party in 2012 and ignited a wildfire in the form of the Liberty Movement. That same year, "Libertarian presidential candidate Gary Johnson received about 1.3 million votes—more than any other third-party candidate. Johnson's tally, amounting to about 1 percent, is the largest for a non-major-party candidate since Ralph Nader's Green race in 2000, said J. David Gillespie, author of a book on third parties."[938] According to Rand Paul, the Liberty Movement has "been 'winning' the big policy battles on Capitol Hill and . . . their message could grow even stronger in the coming years if former Secretary of State Hillary Rodham Clinton becomes the next Democratic nominee for president."[939] Paul's latter reference is to Clinton's support for taking certain military action in Syria, which runs afoul of the movement's growing isolationist sentiments.

While the Liberty Movement, not unlike the Tea Party, is not a third party per se, the combined effect on both is changing Republican Party politics in several ways. First, they have fielded candidates in Republican primaries that have won, notwithstanding "establishment" support for other candidates. Ted Cruz's 2012 Senate victory and the 2014 defeat of the number-two Republican House leader, Eric Cantor, in a primary are among those high-profile, significant victories. Beyond that, Rand Paul is correct in noting that the Tea Party/Liberty Movement is causing Republicans in Congress to take notice of Tea Party/Liberty Movement positions and to bend their politics to take Tea Party/Liberty Movement—and Libertarian Party—voters into account. Recall that during *Our Gilded Age of Division*, although parties like the Greenback Party did not have large numbers in elected positions, the closely divided makeup of the electorate required the major parties to compete for Greenback Party supporters, which they did by co-opting its issues to attract their voters. The Tea Party/Liberty Movement is having the same effect on the Republican Party today.

★   ★   ★

At this point, we need to pause to place the Tea Party/Liberty Movement in greater perspective. We have seen the emergence of third party movements during prior divided periods. If we return to the example of the Greenback Party, it will help us in our analysis of the *Divided Era*. During *Our Gilded Age of Division*, a very prominent issue (one larger than almost any issue we face today) was the issue of what type of currency we should have: gold, silver, paper, or a mix of those species. That issue had had huge economic implications for debtors, creditors, and the economy as a whole. It also had been deeply dividing the major parties for decades, and in that leadership void, the Greenback Party emerged, focused keenly on that issue—hence the name of the party. Greenback Party members were elected to Congress and state houses— all representing their position for easy money to help farmers and other debtors. The major parties, amid a closely divided electorate, bent their policies (or promised to do so) and election efforts where they could to attract Greenback Party voters.

At this point, the critical dynamic to understand is that the Greenback Party arose to deal with a major issue of the day, which was unresolved in the hands of the major parties. That marker represents a pure, historical validation of (a) the political and economic importance of the currency issue and (b) the persistent division that existed over that issue across the nation and within the major parties. Again, according to Kevin Phillips, in his biography of William McKinley, from 1873 to 1900, "no American issue throbbed more deeply."[940] During *Our Gilded Age of Division*, the politics of it represented a major *Persistent Division Dynamic*.

It is, of course, one of the core premises of this book that a primary catalyst of our division today is the divisive nature of big government. Pure evidence of that is the rise of Tea Party/Liberty movements. They exist primarily as a reaction to growing government. That is their catalyst and they firmly believe that the major parties support a system of government too large for their liking. They are demanding that the issue be addressed to a far greater degree than either party, especially the Republican Party, is doing. In short, at the core of the *Divided Era* is division over the size of government and, much like during *Our Gilded Age of Division*, we have a third party movement focused on an issue at the core of our division.

★ ★ ★

The Tea Party/Liberty and Occupy movements do not represent all we need to understand of third party movements in the *Divided Era*. As I stated earlier, third party movements are an expression of discontent with the major parties. The rise of the "independent" or "decline to state" voter is a clear sign of that discontent as well. A McClatchy-Marist poll taken in December of 2013 "found 41 percent of registered voters called themselves independent, a much higher percentage than either political party can claim. Gallup found the independent total last year at 42 percent, the highest since it began asking 25 years ago."[941] Not coincidentally, the Pew Research Center also found that just ahead of the 2012 election, "both parties [had] become smaller and more ideologically homogeneous."[942] In fact, according to Pew, the "overall share of Americans who express consistently conservative or consistently liberal opinions has doubled over the past two decades from 10 percent to 21 percent . . . and ideological thinking is now much more closely aligned with partisanship than in the past. As a result, ideological overlap between the two parties has diminished."[943] Those findings and others caused Pew to entitle their 2012 report "Partisan Polarization Surges in Bush, Obama Years."

Meanwhile, at the writing of this book, those who self-identify as independents number more than ever and continue to outnumber either major party. Obviously, they do so because they are not sufficiently pleased with the stances and actions of the major parties. So why hasn't a separate third party arisen during the *Divided Era*? In my view, that is far more a measure of the high hurdles competitive third parties face, not a lack of desire. The monetary costs of running national elections, and competing in Top 2 primary systems, which allow only the two highest vote-getters on the general election ballot and therefore effectively limit November races to the two major parties, are prohibitive hurdles. Put another way, no third party candidate likely will be able to raise and spend $1 billion to run for president as the major party candidates did in 2012—let alone field candidates around the country. Even so, the number of non-major-party voters requires the major parties of today to compete fiercely for that independent vote.

Three more very important dynamics of the *Divided Era* are emerging, which are reminiscent of *Our Gilded Age of Division* and even our Civil War period. First, recall that during the mid-to-late 1880s, the electoral votes of states were fairly predictable. Lincoln was elected without the support of a single Southern state and wasn't even on the ballot in some Deep South states. The Mason-Dixon Line became a predictor of political outcomes for decades. Today a similar dynamic is on the rise and deepening. The South, once solid for Democrats, has been solid for Republicans for decades. Indeed, after the 2014 elections, every Southern senator and governor was a Republican, and Republicans controlled every Southern state house. Beyond that is the Red State/Blue State divide and within those states a divide between the major cities and suburbs and countryside. Studies have shown that in presidential years, the vast, vast majority of votes for the Democrat candidate come from the major cities of the US, while the Republican candidate's votes come from what has become known as "fly-over country," everywhere but those cities. Indeed, as Josh Kron points out in his article "Red State, Blue City: How the Urban-Rural Divide Is Splitting America," since 1984 "more and more of America's major cities have voted blue each year, culminating in 2012, when 27 out of the nation's 30 most populous cities voted Democratic."[944] As I have stated, obviously we are not as divided as during our prior civil wars—but the trend of the Blue state versus Red state divide is deepening. As Bill Bird states in his book, *The Big Sort*, one hundred million Americans have moved in the last decade and "over the past three decades, they have clustered in communities of sameness, among people with similar ways of life, beliefs, and, in the end, politics."[945] How dramatic has that sorting been? According to Bird, in 1976, "less than a quarter of Americans lived in places where the presidential election was a landslide. By 2004, nearly half of all voters lived in landslide counties."[946] In other words, Blue is becoming more Blue and Red more Red—a dynamic that, while resulting in more homogenous states, necessarily results in more divisive national elections.

That growing dynamic also raises the importance of the swing states. Recall that during the chapter "Our Gilded Age of Division," we discussed how New York and Indiana were of such great importance in that regard. In the *Divided Era* the swing states have become Florida, Ohio, Colorado, and Virginia, and as Bush v. Gore made clear in 2000, an entire election could turn on the outcome of just one state. With that, we should turn to consider the business of politics in the *Divided Era*. In the America of 2015, party politics is big business and the major parties, their supporters, and fundraisers are at the center of it. Recall that during *Our Gilded Age of Division*, it was the golden age of the two-party system. Most voters got their information through the trusted source of their party and its sympathetic newspapers. It was during this age that get-out-the-vote ("GOTV") efforts leaped forward in importance and in sophistication. At the same time big money was making its way into American politics to pay for the campaigns that were growing in competitiveness. Today we are still dominated by the two-party system. The use of talking points and sophisticated GOTV data and targeting of voters supplied to party regulars by their parties is on the rise again. Further, Republicans and Democrats also tend to obtain their news from media outlets largely favorable to their views, and money is pouring into elections.

If we consider money and politics first, it was during *Our Gilded Age of Division* that McKinley's presidential candidacy, and fear for his populist opponent William Jennings Bryan, "opened the purses of Carnegie, Frick, Morgan, and Rockefeller in amounts of $250,000"[947]—a completely unheard-of sum previously that rivals the mega-donors of today. Given that there was no one to rival them at the time, the effect of their spending was lopsided. It is no secret today that the amount of money spent on elections is exploding—on both sides. The media is rather transfixed on the political spending of the conservative billionaire Koch brothers, Charles and David Koch, while others rightfully note that the liberal billionaires George Soros and Tom Steyer likely have spent more than the Kochs. Regardless, both have spent tens of millions, either personally or through their related organizations. Dwarfing them, however, is how much labor unions spend, almost exclusively for the benefit of Democrats, which was estimated to be as much as $1.7 billion in the 2012 election cycle alone.[948] In addition to that, there is the rise of Super PACs—political action committees that aggregate money and spend it on elections. The amount of money raised and spent by the Super PACs is quite significant even if it is not as much as the labor unions. In the 2014 cycle, nearly a half billion dollars was raised and spent by those PACs. Overall, according to OpenSecrets.org, the "Total Cost of US Elections" rose from less than $2 billion in the 1998 midterms, to over $2 billion in the 2002 midterms, just under $3 billion for the 2006 midterms, then over $3.5 billion in 2010 and $3.67 billion in 2014. In presidential years, the money spent was over $3 billion in 2000, over $4 billion in 2004, over $5 billion in 2008, and over $6 billion in 2012.

Where does all that money go? Well, between 1986 and 2012, the average amount spent by the winning candidate for the House rose, in constant 2012 dollars, from $753,274 to $1,596,953—a 100 percent increase. As for the winning US Senate candidates, the average amount they spent rose from $6,426,200 to $10,351,556.[949] In 2014, the average amount spent became a seemingly meaningless figure. With control of the US Senate in play, again according to OpenSecrets.org, more than $80 million was spent just by outside groups and parties for the North Carolina Senate race alone—with the campaigns spending over $32 million. In the otherwise Red, non-swing state of Georgia, the campaigns spent nearly $40 million and over $85 million was spent by all sides for the Iowa seat.

When it comes to presidential elections, "President Obama had slightly more than $1.1 billion spent on him by his campaign, the Democratic National Committee and the top super PAC devoted to his reelection, Priorities USA Action. Mitt Romney, meanwhile, had right between $1 billion and $1.1 billion spent on him by his campaign, the Republican National Committee and his super PAC, Restore Our Future."[950] In 2008, Barack Obama's winning campaign spent $801.5 million and John McCain spent $376.3 million (in 2012 dollars). In 2004, the winner George W. Bush spent $449.8 million and John Kerry spent $402.4 million (in 2012 dollars). In 2000, George W. Bush spent $231.3 million and defeated Al Gore (in the Electoral College) after Gore spent $170.9 million (again in 2012 dollars).[951] If you take a closer look at those numbers, you see that the amount spent by the winning presidential campaign doubled from 2000 to 2004, and then doubled again from 2004 to 2008.

As for the major parties, the cost and scope of their political activities are expanding as well. As with any other age, the job of the parties is to get voters to the polls on Election Day. During *Our Gilded Age of Division*, that meant getting voters to the polls and handing them pre-filled-out ballots to ensure party loyalty. Obviously, pre-filled-out ballots are a thing of the past. Nevertheless, the competition between the Republican Party and the Democratic Party to get their voters to the polls is reaching new heights. According to the RNC Party Chairman, Reince Priebus, the party efforts going into the 2014 midterms were "two-tiered: restructure the party on a tactical level to match the sophisticated and data-driven efforts of the Obama campaign, and create a communications plan to sell the GOP's message to voters it failed to connect with in 2012."[952] The RNC was responding to the fact that, in 2008 and 2012, by all accounts the Democrats and the campaign of Barack Obama outpaced their Republican counterparts in using technology, social networking, and the like, to get people to the polls. In her article "RNC Plays Catch-Up On Data, Ground Game," Shushannah Walshe reported that "after the Obama campaign won widespread praise for a sophisticated data operation that helped to pinpoint the issues voters cared about and turn those voters out on Election Day,"[953] the Republican National Committee hired a "dedicated staff" for their catch-up effort. According to Fox News, the Republican National Committee "hired former Facebook engineer Andy Barkett to fill the newly created post of chief technology officer." Barkett told FoxNews.com he was working to close the "digital divide."[954] After the 2014 midterm elections, it was generally believed Republicans did just that.

Today the major parties "micro-target" voters by keeping track of their voting and even spending habits to determine how to motivate them to vote cycle after cycle. The parties also keep a record of their discussions with individual voters and donors to strengthen their relationship with them for the long term. How far we have come since the days of Lincoln wanting each Whig volunteer to keep in contact with a handful of Whig voters and to make sure they got to the polls—how far technologically, but not in basic purpose or philosophy.

Beyond its technological efforts, the RNC is pouring significant resources into efforts to reach minority voters around the country. To accomplish all of that, in the 2014 cycle, the RNC raised and spent more than $200 million, part of which paid for the deployment of RNC staff across the country, in a hierarchical structure, to implement the RNC's GOTV effort nationwide. At the state and local level, that structure is nearly replicated by state, county, and precinct operations. For their part, the Democrats had more than just a technological advantage in their competition with Republicans for GOTV. They too spend hundreds of millions of dollars per cycle to entice voters to the polls and have organizational structures throughout the United States. They have an important added asset Republicans do not have, however—namely, labor unions. In addition to the billions of dollars labor unions spend during election cycles, they also provide hundreds of thousands of campaign workers, often paid, to ensure Democratic success. Republicans have no similar group that helps them, but instead rely largely on volunteers. Either way, over the last twenty years, the number of people involved in the major party GOTV efforts is growing, right along with money in politics, not to mention the consultant class that makes its living off all of them.

Summing it all up, the business of politics is indeed a big and growing business. Shortly, we will discuss why that has become so important. For now, suffice it to say that the amount of money being spent in general, on GOTV efforts in particular, is rising along with the sophistication of operations—yet another parallel between the *Divided Era* and *Our Gilded Age of Division*.

As you can imagine, with so much at stake, the *Divided Era* and *Our Gilded Age of Division* share other characteristics as well. Four more comparisons will suffice for our analysis. The first relates to voter fraud. During *Our Gilded Age of Division*, we saw voter intimidation in the South, ballot stuffing (which resulted in more votes than voters in some places), and considerable efforts to undermine the democratic process. Today, cries of voter fraud are becoming commonplace. Predictably, the partisans of our age are divided on whether voter fraud is a serious issue. One of the nation's foremost authorities on the issue, John Fund, has written two books on the subject: *Stealing Elections: How Voter Fraud Threatens Our Democracy*, and *How Fraudsters and Bureaucrats Put Your Vote at Risk*—the latter of which he coauthored with Hans von Spakovsky. Predictably, Fund's books have been met with partisan rebuttals including this rebuke from Media Matters, a Left-leaning group, which declared in 2004: "John Fund's book on voter fraud is a fraud." A decade later, in 2004, in his article for the *National Review*, "Dems' Voter-Fraud Denial—How do you address a problem they insist doesn't exist?" Fund highlighted the issue of potential voter fraud in North Carolina, where 35,750 voters were found to have the exact same first name, last name, and date of birth as people who voted in other states. To highlight the importance of the issue, Fund points out that in 2008, "Barack Obama only carried North Carolina by 14,177 votes out of 2.3 million cast."[955]

Supporting John Fund's view is a study published in 2014 that found that "6.4 percent of non-citizens voted in 2008 and 2.2 percent of non-citizens voted in 2010. . . . Because non-citizens tended to favor Democrats (Obama won more than 80 percent of the votes of non-citizens in the 2008 CCES sample), we find that this participation was large enough to plausibly account for Democratic victories in a few close elections. Non-citizen votes could have given Senate Democrats the pivotal 60th vote needed to overcome filibusters in order to pass health-care reform and other Obama administration priorities in the 111th Congress."[956]

Of course, we cannot forget this headline from an op-ed by Peter Roff published in 2010 in *U.S. News & World Report*: "Al Franken May Have Won His Senate Seat Through Voter Fraud." In it, Roff notes that Franken's margin of victory, 312 votes, was less than the number of felons who illegally voted in just one Minnesota county. How important was Franken's victory? He was the necessary sixtieth procedural vote for the passage of Obamacare out of the US Senate. In other words, even a small amount of voter fraud among over one hundred million votes can have far-reaching implications.

Let us now briefly consider the role of the media during the *Divided Era*. Recall that for the first hundred years of our country, our press was rather overtly partisan. There were newspapers and pamphleteers that supported the Federalists and those that supported the Anti-Federalist cause. During the Civil War and *Our Gilded Age of Division*, there were "party" newspapers as well, newspapers that were tied to the parties and expected spoils if their favorite party was in power. While that is not the case today, what is important about that history is that the source of information for party members—that is, voters—was the parties themselves and their supportive newspapers. As such, they received a partisan view of the events of the day—a dynamic that undoubtedly reinforced partisan views and activities.

That same dynamic is gaining prevalence today. According to Pew Research, the viewers of Fox News tend to be more Republican than the electorate at large. By the same token, those that watch CNN and MSNBC tend to be more Democratic than the population at large. A Pew study revealed that "between 1998 and 2008, the share of Republicans saying they regularly watch Fox News rose 22 points, from 14% to 36%. Meanwhile, the share who regularly watch network evening news fell 15 points and the share who regularly watch CNN declined by eight points."[957] The data indicated a similar movement by Democrats toward CNN and MSNBC. Again, such a dynamic likely reinforces existing views of partisans, broadens the foundation of divisions in the *Divided Era*, and is reminiscent of our prior divided eras.

Further, and just as important, we know that the rhetoric of Sam Adams and other pamphleteers fueled the partisanship of *Our Revolutionary Thoughts*. During the Civil War, the partisan newspapers more than egged on their partisan readers. So much so that Donald E. Reynolds wrote a book called: *Editors Make War: Southern Newspapers in the Secession Crisis*. Today, the Left regular decries Fox News for its effect on Republicans and with the same regularity, if not more, the Right believes the likes of MSNBC and CNN have the same effect on the Left. Again, what is new is really rather old.

We also need to make a comparison to other divisive periods in our history as they relate to the escalating political rhetoric of today. It is probably true that each generation believes the politeness of its age is less than the age before. We have seen, however, just how ferocious the rhetoric of past leaders has been. Washington wrote that if the Constitution was not adopted, the next would be "drawn in blood." Angry over the acts of James Madison, Patrick Henry threatened "rivulets of blood." In the years before his presidential run, future President James Garfield generalized with this diatribe while campaigning for Republicans: "Every Rebel guerilla and jayhawker, every man who ran to Canada to avoid the draft, every bounty-jumper, every deserter, every villain, of whatever name or crime, who loves power more than justice, slavery more than freedom, is a Democrat." If our presidents and leaders of the past could speak in such terms, perhaps we should be more philosophical and less concerned about the rhetoric of today.

Even if we are more philosophical about our rhetorical fighting, it is likely that the rhetoric of today is more coarse than that of twenty years ago. Among the Democrats, former Congressman George Miller of California said the Republicans were using "jihad" against Obamacare. Similarly, Senior White House advisor Dan Pfeiffer said of White House differences with Republicans: "What we're not for is negotiating with people with a bomb strapped to their chest." White House Press Secretary Jay Carney once referred to a budget passed by the Republican House as "blatant extortion." DNC Chair Debby Wasserman-Schultz said of continuing Republican opposition to Obamacare (a position held by a majority of Americans since it was passed):

> You have Republicans on the other side who are irra-
> tional and not playing with a full deck. Would you—if

you didn't like the redesign of your kitchen, would you burn the whole house down or would you try to make modifications to the kitchen? These people have come unhinged.

Not to be outdone, House Minority Leader Nancy Pelosi said: "But for many of them, I call them legislative arsonists. They're there to burn down what we should be building up in terms of investments and education and scientific research and all that it is that makes our country great and competitive." Pelosi went one step further as the 2014 midterm elections approached when she said on a Left-leaning TV show: "Civilization as we know it today would be in jeopardy if the Republicans win the Senate." As for President Obama, of Republicans he stated:

We've got one party in Congress right now that has been captured by ideologues whose core premise is "no" . . . and whose principal focus at any given point in the day is trying to figure out how can they make people sufficiently cynical, sufficiently angry, sufficiently suspicious that they can win the next election. I hate to be blunt about it, but that's the play. And, by the way, when I say a party has been captured, it's because I actually want an effective, serious, patriotic, capable, sober-minded Republican Party.

Early in his term, when the Democrats were pushing the Stimulus Bill and then Obamacare without any Republican support, the president, Nancy Pelosi, and Senate leader Harry Reid used similar rhetoric.

The Republicans and the Tea Party are not without their response or divisive rhetoric as you might imagine in the *Divided Era*. Congressman Joe Wilson famously and in unprecedented fashion yelled out "You lie!" to President Obama during a nationally televised speech on health care in front of a joint session of Congress—a tactic that immediately resulted in a gush of donations for Wilson from partisan supporters old and many new. Republican Congressman Steve King was accused of "slapping" or "wiping" a picture of Nancy Pelosi at a rally when she was speaker of the House. Minnesota Congresswoman Michelle Bachmann told a radio audience, "I want people in Minnesota armed and dangerous on this issue of the energy tax because we need to fight back. Thomas Jefferson told us 'having a revolution every now and then is a good thing,' and the people—we the people—are going to have to fight back hard if we're not going to lose our country."

Meanwhile headlines such as "Negative Campaign Rhetoric Reaches New Level of Ugly," from NPR about the 2012 election, are not uncommon in any cycle. Perhaps the most important, if not the most strident, sign of the times was a recent statement that came from an unlikely source. In 2013, Supreme Court Justice Antonin Scalia, known for his blunt talk, during a speech suggested that if the income tax "reaches a certain point, perhaps you should revolt." Apparently, the power to tax has the power to drive even Supreme Court justices to intense rhetoric. In the final analysis, it does appear that the rhetoric of today is heightened.

One last comparison must be made. Recall that during *Our Gilded Age of Division* the party that won the presidency was the party that was able to hand out spoils in the forms of hundreds of thousands of federal jobs. It wasn't until the Pendleton Act that that practice was ended. Thereafter, a more permanent federal bureaucracy was created where jobholders' tenure was not ended with each change in power. America today has a similar dynamic that fuels competitive elections around the country. Broadly speaking, the Democrat parties of all of the states as well as the national party pursue policies that result in the expansion of the number of government workers. Many Democrat leaders simply support greater government employment.

Republicans and their parties, by contrast, most often support a reduction in the number of government workers—and nearly always support less government employment than the Democrats. That difference in the parties plays out in our competitive elections and is a significant reason public employee unions are such big financial players and nearly exclusive supporters of Democrats. Public employee unions know very well that they are competing for jobs and pensions at the same time as they are competing to elect officeholders. In other words, the spoils of government jobs are a major factor in our divisions once again.

It is important to note, at this juncture, how asymmetric the motivations are with regard to elections based on the above dynamic. The Democrat Party and its supportive unions each election are competing for income, jobs, and compulsory union dues. Winning, therefore, is not just ideological for them—it is economic. That is not to say winning Republican presidents don't pick winners and losers. They do. But on this issue of employment, it is important to understand that many Democrats and their public employee unions have far greater personal motivation to compete for spoils. That is one reason they compete for the attention of voters to a far greater degree than Republicans. Democrats and the public employee unions message, organize, and evangelize every day of the year. To a very real extent, it is their livelihood. Republicans, on the other hand, believe in limited government and therefore see the election process as a seasonal undertaking. The massive growth in public employee unions since the 1970s and the corresponding growth in government is clear testament as to who is winning that competition on a very broad level.

The Causes of Our Enduring Division

At this point, it is inarguable that we have entered the *Divided Era* in American politics. America today exhibits all the symptoms of our previously divided eras: a closely divided electorate, close elections, third party movements focused on a critical issue of the day, elections that are big business, sharp partisan rhetoric, polarizing media, and the partisan dynamics we have discussed. We have discussed the catalysts of the start of the *Divided Era*. The remaining question is, Why did it continue after 1996? There are essentially three broad reasons beyond the dynamics we have already discussed and the symptoms we have chronicled.

First, like virtually any period in our history, and especially our periods of division, significant issues are facing the American electorate today. However, there are two differences from prior periods. They comprise the second and third reasons we are in the *Divided Era*. The second reason is that—as a result of the significant growth in our governments—those governments have and are using more power. So empowered, they are tackling a greater number of significant issues than in the past, even if no one of those issues rises to the level of a major issue of the past. As a result, the overall number of partisan catalysts today (e.g., the amount of decisions our governments make, the number of winners and losers they pick, and taxes associated with that) dwarfs prior periods. Further, with ever-larger government there is the ever-larger competition for government spoils and also for a way to avoid paying for those spoils—paying taxes. As a result, the political and economic stakes have been raised substantially and it really matters today who is elected president as well as who controls Congress and the state houses. That second dynamic, the unavoidable result of growing government, combined with significant policy differences, is significantly enlarging the third reason we are in the *Divided Era*: our rapidly growing philosophical divide.

Let us first consider the significant political issues facing America today. They are numerous. We begin with immigration. In the 2014 cycle, the issue of immigration, legal and otherwise, surged to the forefront of American political differences. Differences over immigration have been growing in political intensity for decades. For a time in 2014, it eclipsed the troubled economy, unemployment, people's disappointment with government, and difficult foreign affairs. It provided high drama in the 2012 Republican presidential debates over the fate of twelve million people thought to be here illegally. In the 2014 cycle, the surge of Central American immigrants and the response of the president and the Congress certainly proved to be a partisan flash point as did the President's Executive Order, after the midterm elections, that granted certain rights to such immigrants. For many years, the politics of immigration, the associated gridlock, and intense rhetoric favored the Democrats, by attracting Latino voters, and gave Democrats little reason to resolve the issue. Meanwhile, Republicans have been unable to rise above their own division on the issue. There is little doubt that there is a *Persistent Division* with regard to that issue—among Americans at large, between the parties and even within them—much like the currency issue of *Our Gilded Age of Division*. However, as a matter of historical reference, the issue simply does not compare to the magnitude of the hundred-year tariff fights, slavery, the Constitution, or the decision to make or wage war. It is indeed a major issue and the divisions related to it are understandable—but it is only a piece of the *Divided Era* puzzle, not the core reason it has emerged.

Obamacare has represented a significant and rather divisive issue since 2009. It is a comparatively younger issue than illegal immigration. Even so, health care has for decades been at the top of voter concerns, and, as we saw, Hillarycare was a catalyst of our division in the early 1990s. For its part, it is worth remembering that Obamacare was passed along strictly partisan lines and a majority of Americans have never supported it. Obviously, Obamacare is a significant catalyst of partisanship and the fact that it continues to be the subject of legal and political challenges, as well as negative polling, is a strong indication that Obamacare is and will be subject to a *Persistent Division Dynamic* as well. However, Obamacare as well is only a piece of the *Divided Era* puzzle, not the core reason it has endured.

If we turn to the economy, we know that in the 2014 cycle, the state of the economy, like any other bad economy, played a role in election politics and the rhetoric of the parties and their supporters. The economy was not helpful to the Democrats in the years between 2010 and 2014. The Republicans suffered even worse politically in 2008 because of the state of the economy. It too postdates the start of the *Divided Era* and so cannot be the core reason it began or has endured. It does not rise to the level of the issues that fostered *Our Gilded Age of Division*, although in that age economic downturns exacerbated our divisions.

Of the remaining issues I highlighted at the start of the chapter, none of them individually rises to the level of the major factors in prior divided eras. For instance, the tussle between big labor and business has been going on for decades, including during the period when the Democrats had the upper hand in American politics. That issue is likely no more divisive now than in years past.

We did see, in 2014, race relations take center stage after the midterm elections. The divisions over that issue garnered considerable media attention, in large part, because of the deaths of two Black men in connection with crimes, which did not result in indictments of the police involved in their death, and the execution murders of two New York City policemen, along with protests across the nation. In the wake of those events, a significant number of Americans were of the belief that race relations had worsened under the presidency of Barack Obama. Whether that is correct or not, the fact remains that to a considerable degree, racial politics has, throughout our history, tended to reinforce voting patterns. After the Civil War, Black voters supported the Republican Party. Today, it means increased voter loyalty of Blacks to the Democrat Party. It too represents a *Persistent Division Dynamic* even though it is not the driving feature of the *Divided Era*.

In fact, none of the issues we face today rival the hundred years of disproportionate taxation suffered by the American South, let alone slavery, the Civil War, or the Revolution. None approach the issue of replacing one governing system, the Articles of Confederation, with another, the Constitution. At this point, none of the issues today would

have been among the top three issues of *Our Gilded Age of Division*—
the period most like our own—namely, the currency issue, the Southern Question, and tariffs. Instead, the changing nature of our divisions
today includes the ubiquitous nature of government; the many issues it
decides, catalyzing reactions; its cost and the associated competition for
its spoils; and the growing divide over taxes and income.

Our Larger Governments

The hands of American government are nearly everywhere and not
invisible. In our $17 trillion economy, our local, state, and federal gov-
ernments spend more than one in every three dollars. Calvin Coolidge's
last budget, in 1928, was $3 billion—the modern day equivalent of just
$42 billion; in other words, the federal government today spends almost
8,000 percent more. During Coolidge's time, there were no expenditures
by our governments, at any level, to pay for the retirement or health care
of government employees or private citizens. By the end of the 1930s,
however, and the start of the *New Deal Era* of government programs,
federal spending alone tripled and Social Security began. Eighty years
later, inclusive of the Great Society programs and the War on Poverty,
everything had changed.

According to the Congressional Budget Office (CBO), federal expenditures were over $3.4 trillion in 2013. Taking inflation into account,
that is well over 300 percent more than when, in January of 1981, newly
inaugurated President Ronald Reagan said "Government is not the solution to our problem; Government is the problem." During the *Divided
Era*, federal spending has doubled again and the CBO expects that
spending to rise to an astonishing $5.8 trillion in 2024 largely because of
entitlements.[958] The growth in federal spending, however, does not tell
the whole story of the growth in our governments. Increases in state and
local spending have followed a similar path as federal spending. In 1980,
the year Reagan was first elected, when the federal government was

spending $590 billion, state and local governments were spending $430 billion. In 2014, state and local governments spent nearly $3 trillion—or just a half trillion less than the federal government. Overall, local, state, and federal spending exceeded $6.2 trillion in 2014.[959]

Prior to 1930, federal expenditures on what we understand as welfare today were nonexistent. Instead, funding programs for the poor were the purview of the state and local governments. At the time, they spent $300 million or the equivalent of $4.2 billion today on assistance to the poor. In 2014, state and federal welfare spending exceeded $500 billion—an increase of more than 11,800 percent even though the US population increased less than 300 percent. Many now consider such programs a federal "right" or an "entitlement"—even though those programs didn't exist at the federal level our first 140 years. How many think that way? One possible indicator is that, in 2014, one-third of all Americans were receiving some form of means-tested federal welfare benefits, over $400 billion a year—and that one-third does not include people receiving Social Security or Medicare, the two programs that nearly exceed 40 percent of the federal budget or nearly $2 trillion per year.

Government has grown in other ways as well. Beyond huge budgets, welfare, Social Security, and Medicare, recall that the first federal regulations were not imposed until *Our Gilded Age of Division* and started with the railroads in the late 1870s. The federal government didn't even publish federal regulations until 1935. In 1949, there were fewer than twenty thousand pages of regulations. Sixty years later, as with spending, everything has changed. The regulations related to Obamacare alone exceed twenty-three thousand pages—with the Dodd-Frank financial regulations adding over fourteen thousand. In 2013, Americans spent 10.38 billion hours on regulatory-related paperwork, an increase of nearly 158 million hours from 2012.[960] In 2014, the *yearly* cost to comply with federal regulations was said to top $1.86 trillion, or just less than one-eighth of the overall economy.[961] That equates to $15,000 per family per year.[962] Worse yet, a study covering the period between 1949 and 2011 indicated that regulations

> reduced real output growth by about two percentage points on average [annually] over the period 1949–2005. That reduction in the growth rate has led to an accumulated reduction in GDP of about $38.8 trillion as of the end of 2011. That is, GDP at the end of 2011 would have been $53.9 trillion instead of $15.1 trillion if regulation had remained at its 1949 level.[963]

While I am not advocating the elimination of every regulation since 1949, the point remains clear: the power to regulate is significant and extremely consequential—and therefore divisive.

★   ★   ★

So, overall, just how big is our federal government? You might ask the federal government. They are likely to boast about it. According to the Small Business Administration (SBA), which trains private citizens and businesses on how to compete for government contracts, "U.S. Government is the world's largest buyer of products and services. Purchases by military and civilian installations amount to nearly $600 billion a year, and include everything from complex space vehicles to janitorial services." The SBA was not and is not wrong. The United States government, from our Founders' humble plans, to Coolidge's limited budgets, has now become the biggest single entity in the history of the world. It spends more than any entity on the globe and gives away more than any entity in the world—and Americans, state governments, state agencies, American businesses, foreign governments, and even foreign business, to name a few, all compete for it.

The size of government and the growth of its budgets have plainly accelerated during the *Divided Era*. However, that still does not tell the whole story of why we are in the *Divided Era* of American politics. With great size comes great power—and today our governments are exercising just that.

The Growing Power of Government

During the *Divided Era*, the growth in power of our governments has accelerated right along with their spending. Especially at the federal level, executive power has grown substantially in the last twenty years. Beyond that, the growth in the power of the bureaucracy has been explosive. That growth in power, by definition, comes at the expense of individual freedoms. In turn, that by definition is a *Partisan Catalyst Dynamic* and it is a core factor in the *Divided Era*. It would be impossible in a book of this size to capture the extent of the growth of government power in the last twenty years. Nevertheless, some broad examples can be given.

First, it is not unimportant to our analysis that, during the *Divided Era*, America has been at war. International wars tend to be unifying at their outset and divisive if they are carried on too long or are prosecuted without a definitive relation to security at home. The wars in Afghanistan and Iraq certainly followed that paradigm in the last twenty years—Vietnam did to an even greater extent in the 1960s. In fact, much of the division at the end of the presidency of Bush 43 (Bush, Jr.) is owed to our extended foreign wars. In the past, division over past wars receded. As of 2015, that has yet to happen—in part as a result of the continuing nature of the War on Terror. Fought on uncommon grounds and in uncommon ways, the War on Terror is a continuing process, which is bound to lead to divisions regardless of who is the president. It also has placed a premium on military intelligence. That intelligence need, born amid an explosive technological age, has resulted in an unprecedented ability of government to extend its power. Under Bush 43, the creation of the Homeland Security Department was a classic example of how governments over time tend to centralize power especially in reaction to external dangers. Recall that Lincoln was accused of the same during the Civil War. Under Bush 43 and Obama, beyond the Homeland Department, the reach of the NSA has grown significantly as well. In no small part, it has played a role in deepening our divisions in the *Divided Era* as well as fostering the Liberty Movement—not to mention making strange bedfellows of the likes of Ralph Nader and the Tea Party Movement.

The executive power of the presidency has grown substantially as well. That has occurred in two major respects. First, there has been considerable growth in the power of the executive branch and, second, with respect to the use of Executive Orders. If we start with the latter, keep in mind that prior presidents have used Executive Orders in much greater numbers than today. The first to explode the practice was Teddy Roosevelt who made use of 1,081 Executive Orders, whereas his four predecessors used fewer than 200. Woodrow Wilson set a new record with 1,803 before his output was dwarfed by FDR's use of 3,552—or more than 290 per year during his prolonged presidency. Most recently, President Clinton used only 364 in eight years and Bush 41 used 291 in four. President Obama's numerical pace has been roughly the same as Bush 43; however, Obama's use of "Presidential Memorandums," according to *USA Today*, puts Obama on par with Harry Truman for issuing the most such directives.[964] Further, few can seriously argue that the nature of some of Obama's orders has represented anything but unprecedented change in the nature of executive orders. For instance, more than forty times President Obama used executive orders to change written language of his health-care law, Obamacare. Obama's use of such orders has engendered the most partisan reaction to such orders in the last half-century and even an unprecedented lawsuit by the Republican Speaker of the House John Boehner. Unless those orders are undone, they will have represented a substantial centralization of power in the executive branch of the federal government—in essence, the ability to change laws passed by Congress.

The growth in the power of federal agencies has been explosive as well. According to Constitutional Law Professor Jonathan Turley and one-time supporter of President Obama, in his *Washington Post* piece "The Rise of the Fourth Branch of Government," that "exponential growth has led to increasing power and independence for agencies. The shift of authority has been staggering. The fourth branch now has a larger practical impact on the lives of citizens than all the other branches combined."[965] Turley, of course, has been an impassioned critic not only of the growth of the bureaucratic state, but also of President Obama's use of Executive Orders—even though Turley had previously supported President Obama. Returning to the growth in the "fourth branch," according to Richard W. Rahn, in his 2011 article "Democracy versus Bureaucracy,"

> The rise of the bureaucratic state, at least in the U.S., is only about 80 years old. The number of federal employees grew slowly over the first hundred years of the American Republic so by the time of the first Grover Cleveland administration in the 1880s, there were still fewer than 100,000 federal civilian employees. By 1925, the number had grown to about a half a million, and now there are almost 3 million civilian federal government employees, plus another 17 million state and local government employees.[966]

The growth in the bureaucratic state has meant that the power of those agencies has grown immensely during the *Divided Era* and especially since 2009. Some of that growth, as we have already discussed, relates to the War on Terror. That growth progressed under both Bush 43 and Obama. Some of that growth relates to the response to the financial crisis of 2008, which was caused in significant part by the use of government power to inflate the housing market over many years. The response was the passage of Dodd-Frank, a law that regulated financial institutions and added more than fourteen thousand pages of regulations. According to Wayne Abernathy, an executive vice president at the American Bankers Association, "The United States has never had a piece of legislation that's required so many new [banking] regulations. . . . That is no exaggeration."[967] The implementation of that law has placed enormous power in the hands of federal regulators and had a significant economic impact. For instance, "more than a dozen Washington area banks and credit unions have merged with one another in recent years, citing heightened regulation as a factor. Others have done away with mortgage divisions and clamped down on consumer loans. At least one local bank has expanded its compliance team seven-fold to 35 full-time employees in four years."[968] That economic effect is hardly limited to Washington, DC.

Overall, according to Douglas Holtz-Eakin, a former director of the nonpartisan Congressional Budget Office, "it would be difficult for anyone to pretend that this isn't a high-water mark in terms of regulation."[969] As Ben Goad and Julian Hattem point out in their article "Regulation Nation: Obama oversees expansion of the regulatory state,"

> More "major rules," those with an annual economic impact exceeding $100 million, were enacted in 2010 than in any year dating back to at least 1997, according to the CRS. And over Obama's first three years in office, the *Code of Federal Regulations* increased by 7.4 percent, according to data compiled by the Chamber of Commerce. In comparison, the regulatory code grew by 4.4 percent during Bush's first term.

Many believe that the Environmental Protection Agency (EPA) represents the most dramatic example of the growing power of the bureaucracy. If you simply browse the website of the EPA, and its page

"Milestones in U.S. EPA and Environmental History," the site reads like a history of expanding governmental power. Keep in mind that in the preamble of the Clean Air Act, it states that "air pollution prevention . . . at its source *is the primary responsibility of States and local governments.*" (Emphasis added.) The same holds true for the Clean Water Act. In that law it states, "It is the policy of the Congress to recognize, preserve, and protect *the primary responsibilities and rights of States* to prevent, reduce, and eliminate pollution." (Emphasis added.) Such language, let alone the Tenth Amendment, has hardly deterred the EPA from expanding its own power at the expense of state power.

For instance, under the Clean Air Act and the Clean Water Act, the EPA has the authority to "disapprove" a state action to meet national environmental goals.[970] When the EPA does that, it can effectively invalidate state efforts and expenditures. Under President Clinton, that occurred forty-four times in his second term. Under President Bush, the EPA did that forty-two times in his first term and just twelve times in his second. Under President Obama, that occurred ninety-five times in his first term.[971] Incredibly, in 2014, California was still putting together the details of two tunnels in the Sacramento Delta region and a bond to pay for it when the EPA rendered its opinion that the unfinished proposal would violate federal law. Apparently, the EPA couldn't even wait for the plans to be finished before it decided to override the potential will of California and its voters.

Beyond the disapproval process, the EPA also exercises the power to substitute "federal implementation plans" (FIPs) for state action. According to the American Legislative Exchange Council, in its 2013 report *The U.S. Environmental Protection Agency's Assault on State Sovereignty*, a FIP is the "EPA's most provocative action in its relationship with states. A FIP entails the complete usurpation of a state's regulatory authority."[972] Under President Clinton's second term, the EPA did that just once. It occurred just once during President Bush's eight years in office. Under President Obama's first term, it occurred nineteen times.

In 2014, the United States Supreme Court validated the EPA's expansive definition of its regulating powers of the Clean Air Act even though the EPA "acknowledged that certain provisions in the Clean Air Act do not easily lend themselves to regulating greenhouse gases such as carbon dioxide, which is ubiquitous in the environment."[973] Not satisfied with its growing power, in 2014 the EPA announced plans to regulate streams and wetlands. That brought an immediate partisan response. Indeed, at the outset of the announcement, "more than a dozen Republican lawmakers [were] pushing the Environmental Protection Agency to reconsider asserting regulatory authority over streams and wetlands amid intense backlash from farm groups over the agency's proposed water rule."[974] If we turn to the EPA and coal, Mike Grunwald of *Time* wrote in June of 2014, in an article called "New Carbon Rules the Next Step in Obama's War on Coal":

> For five years, the coal industry and its fossil-fueled allies in the Republican Party have accused the Obama Administration of waging a war on coal. They claim the administration's new plan to limit carbon emissions at existing power plants is really about carbon emissions at existing coal plants. They see the carbon rules that the president announced Monday, like his previous rules limiting mercury, smog, and coal ash, as a thinly disguised effort to make coal power uneconomical. . . .They're right, of course.[975]

Obviously, the EPA is demonstrating that the power to regulate is enormous and has real consequences. Its aggressive actions under President Obama, many of which were taken after 2009 when the president was not able to get a bill out of Congress because of political division, unquestionably represented an accumulation and use of power by the federal government. So much so that even the liberal legal lion, Harvard Professor Laurence Tribe, wrote an article in late 2014, despite his support of EPA goals, entitled "The Clean Power Plan Is Unconstitutional," noting that "the EPA acts as though it has the legislative authority to re-engineer the nation's electric generating system and power grid. It does not."[976]

Beyond the EPA, there are many more examples of growing federal power. Often states succumb to that power in exchange for federal funds. Highways have often come with strings attached—the uniformity of the legal drinking age owes much to that dynamic. During the last five years, the emergence of federal education dictates known as Common Core, which followed federal standards adopted during the Bush 43 years, used a similar dynamic. The federal government also rendered a national lunch menu for schools and tied funds to that as well. In 2014, there were states that pulled back from both of those Obama-era programs.

For its part, the imposition of the requirements of Obamacare led to much litigation in the years that followed its passage. It led to an unprecedented fight between the Catholic Church and the Democrat Party—not to mention lawsuits—over the requirement that Church institutions provide contraceptives. One of the most divisive Supreme Court cases of the *Divided Era*—which engendered one of the biggest partisan responses of 2014—was the private company Hobby Lobby's lawsuit over the requirement to provide certain contraceptives. Health and Human Services was not satisfied with the approximately twenty types of contraception Hobby Lobby was providing pursuant to federal regulations—HHS wanted Hobby Lobby to provide all of the twenty-four required. Keep in mind those twenty-four were *not* in the Obamacare law. They were federal mandates created by federal bureaucrats after the law was passed.

Of course, the growing power of government is not limited to the federal government. The growth in state expenditures to nearly $3 trillion is a similar storyline as the growth in federal power—although the states encroach more upon local governments than does the federal government. When it comes to encroachment of power, governments tend to pick on governments not their own size—only those of smaller size. For our purposes, California can provide yet another regulatory example. *Sacramento Bee* columnist Dan Walters, in his September 7, 2014, article entitled "Unelected Bureaucrats and Boards Continue to Acquire More Power," quoted Democrat Assemblyman Mike Gatto from Los Angeles on the issue. Walter quotes Gatto as follows:

> Now it is the executive branch that makes most "laws." They are called regulations but they have the same effect as law, and are just as binding. Yet these bureaucrats were never elected and do not answer to the people. By appointing people to these executive agencies, and by telling them what to do, a governor or president can broadly dictate the day-to-day affairs of millions of Americans with almost no outward signs of wielding power. And if the legislature dares to try to override some regulation, the governor or president can simply veto the bill. This is a serious imbalance of power.

Of course, Gatto is understandably writing about the imbalance in power between legislatures and the executive. Notice that the plight of the average American is left out of his complaint. We are in the *Divided Era*, however, in part because of the increasing competition for that growing power along with the partisan reaction of an increasingly helpless electorate to that growing power.

Competing for Spoils and Avoiding the Bad

A government that spends so very much, taxes so very much, and regulates so very much surely has moved beyond the Founders' ideals of limited government. As we have seen throughout the book, even before our federal government was created, the proper role of government was debated—and has been ever since. The intensity of that argument today is a key to the *Divided Era*. As the Pew Research Center study of 2012 demonstrates when it found "the largest divides between committed supporters of Barack Obama and Mitt Romney are over *the scope and role of government in the economic realm*," (Emphasis added.) Americans are still fighting the same fight that Federalists and Anti-Federalists fought and that Hamilton and Madison fought—nearly two hundred and thirty years later. The difference now is that there is so much more in spoils at stake—and each year that the stakes grow, by definition, our elections become more important.

Indeed, rather than Americans eeking out a living on the frontier and defending themselves against its vagaries, well over half of all Americans are either (1) receiving welfare, Social Security, Medicaid, or Medicare; (2) employed by our governments or receiving pension or health-care benefits related to those government jobs; or (3) directly or indirectly dependent on government purchasing or contracts with private industry—that $600 billion the SBA boasts about. All of that dependence on government is 100 percent dependent on someone obtaining the funding for the program, pension, or contract in question—and what a competition it has become to get that funding.

Evidence of that growing competition is all around America today.

Money Spent on Elections

The competition for government spoils and the process of obtaining funding for programs starts with elections. It is our most obvious form of political competition. We have already seen the growth in the amount of money spent on candidates and elections. The doubling of the amount spent on the presidential elections by the winning presidential candidates in 2004 and 2008 is stark evidence of the growth in the competition for spoils. It is important to note how broad-based that competition growth has been. Contrary to certain perceptions, presidential campaigns don't just rely on large donors. For instance, in June of 2012, incredibly, the losing presidential candidate Mitt Romney received donations from more than 563,000 people en route to raising over $100 million in that month alone.[977] Note that in 2000, the winner, George Bush, raised "only" $200 million. Beyond the growth in the amount and source of campaign donations, the rise of PACs is a very visible part of the competition as well. According to the Center for Responsive Politics, in 1998, just after the *Divided Era* began, spending by outside groups on elections amounted to just over $10 million. In 2012, that number topped $1 billion. Regardless of which side of the aisle you are on, or if you consider yourself in the middle, the explosive and recent growth in the amount of money raised and spent on American elections is a clear sign that the competition to control American governments, and therefore a good deal of their spoils, is heating up.

Money Spent on Lobbying

It has nearly become a national pastime to lobby politicians after we elect them. Lobbying is by definition a competition for government spoils and preferences. Not surprisingly, the amount of money spent on lobbying has grown right along with the growth in government—if not exceeded it. According to Lee Drutman, PhD, in his work *The Business of America is Lobbying*, between 1999 and 2009 (a period within the *Divided Era*), direct lobbying expenses spent just on government in Washington rose 87 percent and, since 1981, the number of lobbying organizations listed in the *Washington Representatives* directory has risen to fourteen thousand—a doubling of the number of lobbying organizations. The growth in lobbying expenditures, according to Drutman, over roughly the same period, *rose twice as fast* as the federal budget. One example of that is the US Chamber of Commerce. According to OpenSecrets.org and the Center for Responsive Politics, the US

Chamber of Commerce increased its lobbying expenditures by 60 percent *just between 2008 and 2010*. Finally, Drutman points out that, at
one time, business lobbying was largely reactive to Washington (e.g., in
the 1970s). Now, the amount business spends to proactively lobby with
the intent to shape government decisions is nearly equal to that which
it spends to ward off detrimental Washington action. As for warding off
the actions of government, and a clear example of a *Partisan Catalyst
Dynamic*, according to *Bloomberg News*,

> the U.S. auto industry is stepping up its lobbying and
> spending on political donations as the White House
> moves to boost fuel economy standards. . . . GM spent
> $5.5 million during the first six months of 2011 to try to
> influence Congress and federal agencies, up from $4.1
> million in the same period a year earlier, according to
> lobbying disclosures released this week. Chrysler, con-
> trolled by Fiat, more than doubled its lobbying spending
> to $2.4 million from $1.1 million.

According to Henry Payne in his 2011 article "The Obamaconomy's
Growth Industry: Lobbying," "Bigger government means bigger lobbying budgets to influence its decisions—and more money for pols to bro-
ker disputes."[978] Does all that lobbying work? Well, the Wall Street firm
Strategas Research Partners LLC established an index of those S&P 500
firms that "exhibited the greatest lobbying intensity." Turns out that for
the ten years before Strategas started the Index and for the five years
since, the companies in the Index outperformed the S&P 500. Is that
pure coincidence or smart competitive politics? You decide.

Of course, the growth in lobbying is not limited to Washington, DC.
In Wisconsin, for example, public and private unions spent more than
$5 million for all of 2009 when the governor was a Democrat. In their
battles with Wisconsin Republican Scott Walker, however, they spent

more than $7 million in just the first six months of 2011. In California, lobby expenditures total nearly $300 million per year. Incredibly,

> government-on-government lobbying is the single larg-est segment of lobbying of California's state Legislature. Water districts, city councils and school districts spend more than bankers, pharmaceutical companies, health care or any other category, according to the California Secretary of State's Office. In all, local governments spend about $45 million annually to influence the 120 elected state lawmakers and a host of other bureaucrats and political appointees who influence state politics.[979]

In other words, local municipalities tax residents and then spend some of those tax dollars to lobby the state government, in part to get back tax dollars paid to the state government by local residents to fund local programs for residents. In light of that, can there be any doubt that the increased lobbying is a clear indicator of our increasing competition over government spoils in the *Divided Era*?

Corporate Welfare Wars

Who lobbies the most? American business spends over two-thirds of all lobbying dollars directly in Washington, DC.[980] Why? Proactive lob-bying can often result in obtaining corporate welfare. We have already mentioned the success of companies that lobby. As for specific examples of corporate welfare competition, consider the 2014 Export/Import Bank furor. According to the Export/Import Bank, "The Export-Im-port Bank of the United States is the official export credit agency of the United States. Our mission is to ensure that U.S. companies—large and small—have access to the financing they need to turn export opportuni-ties into sales." In other words, the federal government taxes Americans and uses some of that tax money to get loans in the hands of selected businesses—their political winners. It is pure corporate welfare in the minds of many. One example of how the rise of the Tea Party/Liberty Movement has affected the Republican Party was the sudden lack of Republican support in 2014 for the reauthorization of the bank—a program which used to have bipartisan support. In the face of rising Republican opposition, Minority Leader Nancy Pelosi pushed for the reauthorization of the bank, believing that could result in a government shutdown that would hurt Republicans in the 2014 elections—an example of how politicians use government spoils for purposes other than helping intended recipients.

As to why government programs matter economically, according to a Reuters story, the "Export-Import Bank backed $37.4 billion in exports in 2013. Scrapping the Bank would be a blow to Boeing, Caterpillar, General Electric and other U.S. companies that rely on Ex-Im financing to make sales in export markets where commercial lending is scarce."[981] That represents a win for those companies and a loss for the likes of Delta Airlines, which argued that "one of Delta's most significant international competitors can save over $20 million using Ex-Im financing. This subsidy amounts to our foreign competitor getting a free additional wide body plane for every eight new planes it buys."[982] Obviously, government subsidies are big business and the competition for them is as well.

The story, however, does not end there. In the era of tighter budgets, the battle over corporate welfare has been extended to forums beyond the halls of Congress. According to *Bloomberg News*, in its January 2014 article "Federal Spending Cuts Slice Contract Awards 11% in 2013," "Contractors face 'years of increased competition as the pie shrinks,' [quoting] Rob Nichols, co-chairman of the government contracts group at law firm Covington & Burling LLP. 'They're looking to preserve as much of the pie as possible through congressional outreach, bid protests and other competitive tools.'"[983] According to Jaime Garcia, president of Seville Government Consulting, a company that helps companies win government contracts, quoted in the *Washington Post* article "With budget tightening, disputes over federal contracts increase," "Budgets are going down, which means competition for what contracts remain has increased tremendously. . . . [Companies] are making strategic decisions about protesting because they have to. A lot of companies can't afford to lose that contract."[984] The *Post* notes that the "number of losing companies' protests to the Government Accountability Office, which handles the vast majority of bid protests, has increased from 1,352 in 2003 to 2,429" in 2013.[985]

States also are big players in the corporate welfare competition. For instance, in 2014, California and Nevada competed in rather public fashion for the placement of a battery factory for the electric car manufacturer Tesla. Nevada's overall package, which included $1.25 billion in tax breaks, proved better for Tesla despite the passage of tax breaks for Tesla to use by the California legislature if Tesla brought the factory to California. In 2014, California passed similar legislation for the space flight industry and Hollywood—breaks signed by California Democrat Governor Jerry Brown. Staying with Hollywood for a moment, "the number of states offering film production incentives grew from just a handful in the early 2000s to a majority of states by 2010. . . . Thirty-nine states and Puerto Rico have film production incentives on their books for 2014."[986]

For its part, in 2013, New York started its own "Start-Up NY" project that offers a ten-year tax break to companies that start a business in certain tax-free zones. In-between states, like Kentucky, boast seven different programs offering businesses incentives to locate in Kentucky. At a more basic level, states like Florida and Texas lure individuals and business to their states by touting their lack of a personal income tax. During his term as governor of Texas, Republican Rick Perry made numerous trips to California to coax businesses to California—and successfully so.

Beyond the competition between businesses to get government

spoils, we cannot forget the ire such programs have long engendered. After the Great Society programs President Johnson started, there was the argument about whether to fund "guns or butter"—war or welfare. Today, you often hear the same said of corporate welfare versus welfare and entitlement spending.

Entitlement Competition

There may be no greater example of the competition over spoils than the elevation of programs above the reach of everyday political competition. Long ago, Social Security and Medicare were politically given "entitlement" status that placed their funding beyond political dispute. It is true that periodically the programs have been subject to reforms so that they remain "viable," but compared to all other funding, each year theirs is on automatic pilot, as opposed to discretionary funding. Of course, that means that over 40 percent of the federal budget is beyond yearly appropriation and immune from political competition. They have such relative immunity even though no one sanely believes those programs can go into the future untouched. In fact, polls show that half of millennials don't believe that Social Security will even exist by the time they retire. Nevertheless, Social Security has long been called the "third rail" of politics—implying the death of any politician that dares consider its significant reform—and for good reason.

For instance, in 2005, the newly reelected President George W. Bush's effort to "privatize" a small portion of Social Security (a concept not far from FDR's original plan for Social Security and a similar concept to that which flourishes in Singapore today) was proof of the danger of Social Security politics. His proposal was met with a ferocious partisan response. Long before Bush's proposal, an entire industry had grown around the issue of defending Social Security. AARP, formerly known as the American Association of Retired Persons, regularly joins forces with the National Committee to Preserve Social Security

& Medicare and the Alliance for Retired Americans, among others, to lobby for Social Security. In response to Bush's 2005 proposal, those groups competed against Bush by spending more than $50 million lobbying to defeat Bush's proposal.

Interestingly enough, in 2011, amidst a trillion-dollar deficit, AARP signaled an openness to reducing Social Security benefits. What did it get for testing that moderate water? A small wildfire was set and partisan reactions followed, such as an op-ed in the *Huffington Post* entitled "It's Time to Burn My AARP Card."[987]

Politically fighting over Medicare funding is nearly as cutthroat as that of Social Security. During the political fight over Obamacare, which began in 2009, a significant political fight arose over President Obama's plan to reduce the amount of money appropriated for Medicare, and shift that money to pay for Obamacare. The amount in question was said to be $700 billion. Previous to that, the Democrats were staunch defenders of Medicare and cast Republicans as the party that wanted to reduce Medicare benefits. Their support of Obamacare (a new entitlement in competition with an old entitlement), however, caused a political upheaval on the issue and now Republicans have become the party defending Medicare and seeking to restore its funding.

Such upside-down competitions are not limited to Washington, DC. In California a similar dynamic took hold in the early part of this decade with respect to education. The competition for government spoils in California reached its height with respect to education in 1988. That year Californians amended their state constitution by passing Prop 98. The effect of that law today is a mandate that education receive 40 percent of the total California yearly budget. In recent years balancing the budget has been quite difficult. As a result, the competition for program funding became heightened. The education establishment in California asserted that the Democrats, who had a legislative supermajority, were shorting the education budget. Republicans in the state legislature used that political circumstance to demand that other programs be cut in favor of the full funding of education.

The Growing Competition Over Public Employee Pensions

Perhaps the single greatest competition today is over public employee union pensions and health care along with the growth of public employee unions. In chapter 1, I described the epic political battle between Wisconsin Governor Scott Walker and the public employee unions and Democrats who opposed him. That larger fight was over proposed reforms that could have diminished the membership and power of public employee unions. In the *Divided Era*, there seems to be a story related to public employee union pensions nearly every week.

In 2014, among many, many headlines on the subject, you could read the following:

- "Educators fight back against pension attacks across the country"
- "Democrats fighting over ruinous public employee benefits"
- "Chicago unions organize to fight potential pension cuts"
- "Christie's new pension reform push could lead to new surge in N.J. retirements"
- "Bankrupt city fighting to open a crack in California's Pension Agency"
- "Phoenix leaders fighting over pension-reform ballot language"
- "Corbett plunges into public fight for pension bill"
- "California public employee pension reform: The war begins"

In 2014, California was said to have $1.1 trillion in government debt at the state, county, local, and municipal government levels. Over half of that was said to be related to public pension and health-care debt. Two years earlier, in California, public unions believed their unions and pensions were jeopardized by a union reform measure known as Prop 32,

which would have disallowed automatic deductions from union paychecks. It also would have banned corporate and union donations to
state and local candidates. The partisan implications of such a bill were
not hard to understand, and they led to more than $130 million being
spent for and against the measure, which ultimately failed. The California Teachers Association alone spent more than $21 million of the
$73 million spent in opposition to the measure. Keep in mind that all
of that Teachers Association money was derived from automatic deductions from paychecks—paychecks funded by taxpayer money. In 2014,
also in California, a local judge rocked union and education politics by
declaring that teacher tenure, a system that makes it nearly impossible
as a practical matter to fire a teacher, was unconstitutional because stu-
dents were not being sufficiently educated, in part due to bad teachers.
Not surprisingly, Democrat Governor Jerry Brown appealed that judicial decision. Another judge, this time in bankruptcy court, ruled that
San Bernardino could reduce pension obligations through bankruptcy.
If that holds up, that could produce a sea change in American politics.

Of course, we cannot forget that unions spent over $1.7 billion in
the 2012 election cycle. That is not just a recent phenomenon. Between
1989 and 2014, roughly the period of the *Divided Era*, according to
OpenSecrets.org, ten of the top fourteen political donors were unions.
Of them, four are public employee unions, including overall #2—the
American Federation of State, County & Municipal Employees, #3—
the National Education Association, #10—the Service Employees
International Union, and #12—American Federation of Teachers. On
average, only 3 percent of the overall union donations were given to
Republicans and over 79 percent were given to Democrats. Much of
their spending efforts, of course, relate to preserving hard-fought union
member rights.

In the coming years, the battle over pensions will likely intensify, this
time between proponents of the operating budgets of governments that
are being squeezed by pension and health-care liabilities. According to

the Democratic Mayor of San Jose, pension-minded Chuck Reed, in his July 2014 article entitled "Pension costs draining California school budgets," "Cutting services to pay for pensions is inevitable." He noted that in California, "the additional cost of fully funding teachers' retirement will exceed $5 billion per year, an amount that may be more than 5 percent of total K–12 spending."[988] Overall, in 2014, the California teachers pension was said to have a "$167 billion net pension liability."[989] Despite those numbers, or perhaps because of them, the competition for education funding remains fierce in California.

California is hardly alone. In Rhode Island in 2014, the *Daily Surge* noted in an August 2014 article entitled "Rhode Island Dem Fights Unions Over Pensions" that "many liberal Democrats have been willing to contemplate pension reforms because the high costs of paying out benefits to retirees is starting to compete with other budget priorities." However, that willingness arrived too late in many instances. The municipal bankruptcy of Detroit was brought on in large part because of pension liabilities. A major legal issue in that bankruptcy is whether pension liabilities can be reduced in bankruptcy. Returning to California, a 2012 headline of the *Sun News* read: "Rising pension costs hurt San Bernardino, other Southern California cities." Indeed, several cities have declared bankruptcy at least in part hoping to reduce pension liabilities. In the years to come, in the competition for government funding, the potential for more such bankruptcies will be on the rise.

The Proliferation of Interest Groups

We have already seen that the amount of money spent on elections by outside groups has ballooned from $10 million in 1998 to over $1 billion in 2012. We have also seen the growth in lobbying. Part of those increases is owed to the proliferation of those outside groups. Prior to 1970, interest groups were generally lumped into three categories: business, labor, and agriculture.[990] After 1970 and the expansion of government and its power under Johnson and Nixon, the number of public interest groups began to grow right along with the growth in government. The emergence of interest groups, away from the prior focuses referenced above, to social issues, trade associations issues, and public interest issues is an important dynamic in the *Divided Era*.

Interest groups are generally focused on a narrow set of issues as compared with political parties as a whole. Indeed, according to Thomas T. Holyoke in his book *Interest Groups and Lobbying: Pursuing Political Interests in America*, the "upside of interest groups is that they can and do provide focused representation for small groups of people organized around narrow, well-defined interests that could probably not ever be priorities for political parties."[991] In that way, they act very much like a single-issue third party, absent electoral activity. Instead of forming their own party, they seek to influence government, candidates, and the parties through donations, lobbying, public comment, and endorsements, to name a few methods. These range from the famous, national, and large groups like the National Rifle Association, the American Medical Association, and the National Organization for Women, to the not-so-famous, nor national, nor large groups such as East Contra Costa County Habitat Conservancy in the East Bay region of Northern California.

By 2011, the growth in the number of interest groups had already grown to over eighteen thousand.[992] One example of that growth, according to Pew Research, is the "number of organizations engaged in religious lobbying or religion-related advocacy in Washington, D.C., [which] has increased roughly fivefold in the past four decades, from fewer than 40 in 1970 to more than 200" by 2012.[993] According to Holyoke, "Special-interest lobbying in the nation's capital always appears to be booming, just as it has always been associated with political corruption, the buying and selling of influence, and flagrant disregard for the public interest."[994] To be sure, all those special interest groups compete for the ear and funding of voters, politicians, and our governments.

Of course, it is often the claim of voters and politicians that a politician of the other party is the tool of "special interests" or that special interests are ruining our country. The most important points to make, however, regarding special interests and their growth is that historically the larger government gets, the more groups come into being—and therefore the larger the competition between those groups for government funding.

⋆   ⋆   ⋆

Ever more money in politics, increased lobbying, the proliferation of special interest groups, expanded fights over corporate welfare, entitlements, and public employee union pensions are some of the major examples of our growing political competition in the *Divided Era*. In plain terms, the larger the government pie, the greater the number of spoils and preferences and therefore the more intense the competition for government spoils. It simply is no coincidence that at the same time as the growth in government has accelerated, the growth in money in politics also has occurred, along with the growth in special interests and the overall competition for government funding. Larger government, by definition, means greater political competition. Greater political competition, by definition, leads to greater partisanship and ultimately political division. Further, as we have now seen, once government becomes large, and people or businesses become dependent on it, even the shrinking of government leads to greater partisanship and ultimately political division. It is within that *Persistent Division Dynamic* that we find ourselves today.

How Big Government Suppresses Voting

We have one last consideration before we can take up possible ways to reduce our political tensions; we need to consider one last aspect of the

Divided Era. If we take one last look at *Our Gilded Age of Division*, we recall that it featured exceedingly high voter turnout rates for presidential elections—reaching nearly 82 percent in 1876, and consistently in the 70th percentile. Of course, that was only among men. During the *Divided Era, despite everything at stake*, the voting rates have been as low as 49 percent in 1996, but generally in the mid-50s, to a high of only 57.5 percent in 2012—an upward trend but still well below the levels of the 1800s.

Although the *Divided Era* shares many characteristics of *Our Gilded Age of Division*, high voting rates are not among them. So why are our voting rates so much lower than in *Our Gilded Age of Division*? Taking a slightly broader viewpoint, we find that voting rates were higher throughout the 1800s than they were in the 1900s and since then. In fact, our presidential voting rates essentially have been stuck in the mid-50s for the last century—although at times they have dipped into the high 40s and into the low 60s. The question of *why* persists, and many have posited theories.

It is my view that voting rates were higher in the 1800s for four reasons. First, our Republic was rather new by historical comparison. The novelty of the experiment and the passion it took to create it likely resulted in a populace that cherished voting rights to a greater degree than we have today. A cherished right is a more exercised right. Second, elections often could produce real results in the 1800s such as during the Civil War period and in *Our Gilded Age of Division—and voters and the parties knew that*. Voting led to obvious, immediate, and consequential results. Just ask the South after Lincoln's election. Certainly, the importance and effects of patronage alone meant that election results mattered, especially during *Our Gilded Age of Division*. Voting led directly to jobs during that period of time. As George Plunkitt said during *Our Gilded Age of Division*, "You can't keep an organization together without patronage. Men ain't in politics for nothin'. They want to get somethin' out of it."[995] The extinguishment of the patronage system, over time, changed the imperative of elections, parties, and therefore turnout. In my view, those reduced incentives in turn reduced the value of voting.

Third, once the high-stakes 1800s ended, especially after the consequential last fifty years of that century, America went through a five-decade period where governments were not nearly as consequential—and generally left us alone. Yes, we entered two world wars, the income tax code came into being, and government was growing. The income tax code, however, directly affected only a small percentage of Americans at the outset. It would be decades before the income tax code would literally become a divisive political issue that could rival the effects of the tariff system in the 1800s. Both world wars were rather short in duration and therefore did not result in long-term divisions (a clear contrast from the wars of the *Divided Era*). Indeed, to a large degree, those wars wound up being far more unifying experiences (the parties were more unified on the subject) than the wars of the second half of the 1900s. As for the growth in government, it was held in comparative check for the better part of the first three decades (a long time in politics), before we reached the *New Deal Era*. Americans by and large did not petition government for help and the federal government was not in that business like it is today. Even after 1935, when FDR pushed through the second and more significant round of New Deal legislation and government growth started in earnest, government still was not ubiquitous for most Americans. To be sure, there was opposition to FDR's actions and presidencies. On the other hand, FDR was president for twelve years—the only president to serve that long—and it would have been longer but for his death. Without question, consensus in the country at that time was on his side.

In short, significantly more was politically at stake during the last fifty years of the 1800s than the first fifty years of the 1900s. Therefore, the first fifty years of the 1900s were less divisive. In my view, that is the most significant reason voting rates for those years were lower than the prior fifty years. Recall from chapter 5 that few people came to James

Monroe's reelection nomination convention because nothing was at stake and there was no national campaign that year. It should be obvious that when less is at stake, that would tend to diminish interest in voting. Since the 1950s, the lower turnout rate pattern continued under the relatively stable politics of the time, at least as demonstrated by the control of Congress and state legislatures, until the Reagan years when politics began to change and the issue of the size of government moved to the center of politics.

The fourth reason, in my view, is that I believe that even though the stakes are rising as a result of big government, for several reasons I believe that that same big government is also discouraging even higher voting rates. Foremost among those reasons is that voters are rather unenthusiastic about government today. For instance, according to a September 2014 *Washington Post*–ABC News survey, only 1 percent (that is not a typo) are "enthusiastic" about how government works. Part of that relates to their distaste for Congress—the approval ratings of which have hit record lows in the *Divided Era*. Part of that relates to comparatively weak approval ratings for presidents during the *Divided Era*. Part of that relates to voters' approval ratings for the parties, which have slipped below the 50 percent mark since 2009, according to Gallup. We also cannot forget the rise in the number of those Americans who identify as Independents.

We also should consider this remarkable indicia of the *Divided Era*. Nearly one quarter of Americans, in a Reuters survey, "were strongly or provisionally inclined to leave the United States, and take their states with them." In each region of the country at least 19 percent were of that view (demonstrating a remarkably broad-based sentiment) and the Southwest harbors 34 percent with that view. Not surprisingly, those who claim Tea Party affiliation responded favorably to that notion at the highest rate.[996] Whether those who expressed a desire to have their state secede would seriously act upon that tomorrow if given the chance is open to question. Nevertheless, it is an expression of considerable discontent with government and the possibility of reforming it.

Further, we need to keep in mind that many Americans don't believe that there is a sufficient difference between the parties. Recall the high voting rates during the *Gilded Age*. Previously I quoted historian Charles W. Calhoun who attributes those rates, in large part, because "Republicans and Democrats differed sharply over matters of public policy and offered voters real choices at the polls."[997] Today, many feel the parties are not offering them a real choice. Certainly the rise of the Tea Party and Liberty Movement is evidence of that—and for many Americans, that is a disincentive to vote. There also are others that plain just don't vote because "nothing ever gets done"—at least that is what 60 percent of the voters of a 2012 "unlikely" voter poll conducted by a nationwide *USA Today*/Suffolk University poll thought.

That last belief, along with the nature of our governments that grant direct access to politicians and bureaucrats, both of whom have power and hand out spoils, encourages special-interest activity and special-interest or single-issue voting. In America today, few voters think government is going to undergo a makeover. It has become too monolithic to do so—so many say: Why bother? You can add to them the many voters who are less ideological and more issue oriented. Through special-interest activity, on the other hand, nearly anyone can influence government directly in ways their votes simply cannot. All in all, absent a higher need to vote, such as in the second half of the 1800s, voting overall is depressed.

So why are things not getting done to voters' satisfaction? Of course, for many Americans, the answer to that question is that our parties and politicians fight too much. That, of course, is why I wrote this book and why I called it *The Divided Era*.

CHAPTER 10

Bridging the Gap
in the Divided Era

The health of a democratic society may be measured by the quality
of functions performed by private citizens.
—Alexis de Tocqueville

We have finally arrived at the time to consider possible strategies, if not solutions, for bridging our partisan divide. While it is easier to consider the past than to fashion the solutions of the future, organizing the past can never be more than half the task. So it is time to put our new understandings to the test. As we do, on the one hand, our task is made harder because we know that the map of the future will offer a different terrain and therefore different challenges. On the other hand, we also know societal motivations change at the same leisurely pace as does the DNA within us and therefore nearly represent a constant in our political equations. So, even though the details and circumstances will change, we will likely seek advantages much like we have before, take stands when our perceived rights are abridged, and cling to the comforts and assurances of our beliefs when challenged. In other words, the future may change but we will be largely the same. Even amidst movement, there is some stability.

In offering the following suggestions, I start with the assumption that partisan gridlock is now more than just a predictable outcome. We have reached a different juncture than we have in the past. Unlike our prior challenges, the story of the *Divided Era* is of a gridlock more permanent. We may take some comfort in knowing that our Founders wanted checks and balances—a measure of institutional gridlock, if you will—for a reason. They wanted a federal government that moved slowly and was dependent on consensus as the gateway to significant change. Recall that they designed our federal government not only in reaction to the centralized and therefore all-too-efficient monarchy of King George, but also as a reaction against the post-Revolution runaway democracies of our state governments. Their philosophical acceptance of divided government was a deliberate effort to keep the federal government from becoming too nimble, too large, and too intrusive. They really did want to slow the activities of government. If they could keep government from operating too quickly, they hoped, they could slow its growth and thereby preserve freedom. It has certainly worked to a greater degree than any prior republics or democracies. Though we have reached this difficult political moment, historical success is not just defined by the present but also defined by the details of the journey.

The problem now is that the same dynamic of slowly moving government also inhibits the course correction of problems now entrenched. If it took more than two hundred years to amass $18 trillion in federal debt, it is likely our form of government will make it difficult, in a measured way, to unwind the problems that led to that debt as well. Even so, some agreement must be reached on such issues as the national debt. That and other problems cannot simply go on—even if *History* is not optimistic on the prospects of how to solve such problems.

As we begin divining such solutions, it is worth quickly mentioning once more the cause of our divisions. Simply stated, the political partisan is the natural offspring of government action. When government acts, it changes the rights and privileges of someone, or perhaps many. It usually asks some, often those different from the beneficiaries of its initial act, to pay for that government action. It also sets off a competition for its spoils. Thus, we have seen through the centuries that opposition and partisanship are inevitable consequences to governmental impositions. Recall that it was the British Stamp Act that fostered Patrick Henry's cry for *Liberty or Death*. He did not shout that in a vacuum but, instead, in a legislative hall in an effort to undo the imposition of the tax. The more our collection of municipal, state, and federal governments do, as a simple function of mathematics—and yes it is that simple—the more likely they are to engender divisions, competition for spoils—and therefore partisans.

We should also know by now that our fifth president, James Monroe, ran unopposed for reelection and not by accident. It was in significant part because of the combination of his leadership, Anti-Federalist design, and the effects of government overreach in the hands of the more activist Federalists. Today, by contrast, we have seen how our governments and their $6 trillion aggregate budgets have Americans gripped in a competition for public benefits that likely rivals the "empowered envy" of democratic Greece in the third century BC.[998] Faced with claims of inequality of wealth, Athenians legally set upon each other with excessive democratic measures of redistribution meant to "correct" such problems of history. Athens's internal legislative wars, and the dissension of its former subjugated allies, weakened its external resolve to the point where those divisions eased Athens's conquering by Philip of Macedon.[999] It is a history not sufficiently unlike America today as we fight among ourselves and avert our attention from world affairs spinning out of control. We also must remember, we engaged once before in that same rush of government action to correct perceived private wrongs just after our Revolution. In doing so, we set off forces which caused Alexander Hamilton to ponder the possibility of war among the newly freed colonies.

Of course, it is usually the conceit of the people of any age to largely ignore the warnings of the past and instead march ahead unheeded under the assumption that they are smarter than those that walked before them. Obviously, America has not been immune to such tendencies, and as we change from James Monroe to Barack Obama, our political competition increases with each passing government appropriation.

If we are to rise above the current partisan divide, we must be more understanding than to blame the partisans for their largely reactionary, if not self-interested, participation. It is human nature for them to want a say about their world that is being involuntarily changed around them at an ever-faster pace. Indeed, there is no historical standard for an acceptable level of partisanship. If there was, what is the acceptable level of partisanship for the American coal industry today? The federal government has let it be known that it wants to end the coal industry. Should the industry compromise or just walk away from its way of life? Did Patrick Henry walk away over a tax that likely would have less than a penny for most transactions?

Rather than ask such questions, we must do as our Founders once did and accept human nature. We also accept that humans often prefer excessive democracy, a political form of instant gratification. Knowing all of that, we must fashion solutions that take all that into account, as opposed to simply blaming partisans and igniting even more fires.

So how can we take a step back from our most recent partisan heights?

First, it is important to recognize that providing a laundry list of government reforms and then concluding the book will not be a satisfactory answer for anyone, let alone be realistic. Yes, we must stop demanding that our governments do ever more or every little thing. Yes, we need government to do less and to tax less. Yes, we must stop spending more than we take in. We understand that our current tax and spend levels already lead to an endless and—I hope you'll agree after reading this book—unacceptable level of competition that pits Americans and their political parties against each other. Further, we accept that further taxing and spending will only increase our political battles. Simply providing a list of preferable laws, however, doesn't answer the question of how to pass all of those proposals amidst this gridlock of the *Divided Era*. A fair conclusion of this book requires more than a facile list over which we would undoubtedly fight absent a less partisan path.

Second, since we know it took more than two hundred years to go from governments that spent 3 percent of the overall economy to governments that now spend 33 percent, we must also recognize that the problem will not simply unwind itself. Indeed, one entrenched feature of the *Divided Era* is that we cannot simply vote to spend a lesser amount. There will be no up or down vote or series of votes like there was to adopt the Constitution and end the partisan argument. Nor are we likely to rise up and elect a Congress and a president that will agree to honor our demand to limit government spending to 25 percent or 10 percent of the economy—even if they promise beforehand to do so. To the contrary, we will need to consider more far-reaching ideas and demonstrate resolve and patience in the process—and in the *Divided Era*, those two items are not in abundant supply.

Third, we must understand that it is also our reality that government policies have resulted in a huge number of people who are dependent on government either through social welfare programs, corporate welfare, or government contracts, or those whose employment is dependent on the business of government. None of those people, and they number more than half of all Americans, will easily, if at all, vote to reduce their slice of the pie. Their partisanship is now personal and they will look at change with more than a skeptical eye. For that reason, they will be against change—a reverse form of conservatism, if you will. They are also beyond the reach of simple partisan appeals—theirs has become a practical concern of dollars and cents. That will remain especially true when politicians count on and promote such dependency as part of their electoral strategy. They too are unmotivated to change the existing dynamic upon which they cynically profit in the short term, all to our long-term detriment. Yes, it is true that a Reagan can come along and for a time alter the trajectory in the growth of a government. But the federal government is now at least three times the size it was when Reagan said that "government is not the solution to our problems. Government is the problem." Similarly,

the success of bipartisan welfare reform that took place under Bill
Clinton has all but been reversed. So transitory can success be amidst
a larger movement.

Fourth, we must understand that throughout all of history, voters
of democracies, and even the subjects of dictators, on balance always
want more from their government. Under the Roman Republic, they
were now and then appeased by spectacles in the Coliseum and by the
distribution of free grain (an ancient form of welfare). In America today,
seemingly every news story of woe begets a politician's promise of a government response. That is why we have nearly 2,300 federal programs
that provide subsidies. Taking a broader look, the history of the world
is that government starts out smaller than it finishes and it is a distinct
minority in history that has voted for less. Any solution, therefore, will
have to somehow provide both more and less at the same time.

With all those caveats, it may seem an impossible task to expect even
a reduction in our partisan animus—but change is possible. It can happen, on the margins, if we have a strong leader capable of building consensus such as a John F. Kennedy or Ronald Reagan. It could change
significantly if, by a lack of leadership, we are overrun by events.

Keep in mind that it is nearly a maxim of history that events play a
larger role than individuals in driving the course of history. It is those
events, more often than not, that call forth leaders who may otherwise
be unheard. As Will and Ariel Durant described it, the "great man . . .
grows out of his time and land, and is the product and symbol of events
as well as their agent and voice; without some situation requiring a new
response his new ideas would be untimely and impracticable."[1000] We
have understood that when we recognized that Patrick Henry rose to
his occasion in reaction to an event—the imposition of the Stamp Act.
Without that direct tax, he would not have offered his resolutions in
that time and space. If he had, he would have found a scant audience
for his "treasonous" resolutions, let alone his cry for liberty. Similarly,
Thomas Paine's uncommon *Common Sense* would have gone largely

unread during James Monroe's presidency of limited government. As it relates to today, the leader of tomorrow who advocates the solutions I propose may well find a greater audience under the difficult circumstances of a government insolvency than under less urgent fiscal circumstances. Time, of course, will disclose all, but only with its leisurely permission.

What Leadership Should Do
Before a Serious Crisis

There are a number of strategies that should be undertaken prior to the United States reaching a serious crisis. At this point, we should define a serious crisis as being a government's insolvency to the point of being unable to pay bills, as Detroit faced in 2013, California in 2009 when it issued IOUs to creditors, and the California cities that have declared bankruptcy. Beyond them, there are at least two dozen major cities in the United States in danger of bankruptcy as of this writing. California was said to be $1.1 trillion in debt in 2014 among its cities, counties, other government entities, and the state—much of it tied to pensions and medical retirement benefits "owed" to state employees. Seven states are said to have less than 30 percent of their future pension needs funded, with Illinois and Connecticut leading the way at just 24 percent and 25 percent respectively. Such fiscal moments, unless sanity prevails, could lead to involuntary government shutdowns, partial or otherwise, which always feature high-stakes partisan fights over what to do. The list of potential crises should also include the danger of becoming such a divided country that we become so obsessed with internal fighting, like Athens of the third century BC, that we weaken our ability to defend others and ourselves from external threats.

Of course, just because we haven't reached the definition of a serious crisis we are discussing above, doesn't mean that we aren't facing crises in government. The Veterans Administration scandal that came to light in

2014 is a crisis of government as well. Very clearly, the Veterans Administration runs a huge government health-care program that has more than failed our veterans. Given the magnitude of the problems, critics can rightfully ask whether government can effectively administer such a huge program. Given that, as a political matter, nearly everyone cares for veterans, the bipartisan nature of the criticism and even support for certain reforms may well guide us as we look ahead.

★　★　★

So let us consider possible solutions, preferably before we reach any such dangerous insolvency. To bridge our partisan divide, I suggest the following:

1. We should use the wisdom found in the governing examples of Washington, JFK, and Reagan and elect a president committed to setting and achieving unifying national goals;

2. We should adopt a real government reform agenda to make the government we have work and from which all reforms can benefit;

3. We simply must replace the current income tax system with a less divisive system of collecting taxes, either with a true flat tax or, even better, by replacing it with a tax system not based on class differences, such as a consumption tax; and

4. We must rely far more on the character of Americans, which was so well recognized by Alexis de Tocqueville, to undertake private acts for the welfare of their cities, states, and country.

The Examples:
Washington, Kennedy, and Reagan

As we consider the governing examples of George Washington, John F. Kennedy, and Ronald Reagan, let us first consider a few points. First, their successes, as we shall see, have very much in common. Second, the trio also represents a Republican in Reagan, a Democrat in Kennedy, and the man many perceive to be the least partisan of any president we have ever had, George Washington. In other words, potential success is not limited to a leader of one party or another. Third, there is a reason they are considered in such high regard, so they are worth emulating.

If we start with Washington, and any lesson in leadership likely should, recall that in chapter 4 we discussed *Washington's Unifying Moment*. Washington obviously became president under incredibly difficult circumstances. In the fourteen years that preceded his presidency, the country passed through a gauntlet that included the Stamp Act, Patrick Henry's "Give me liberty or give me death" moment, British troops being stationed in people's homes and elsewhere to quell dissent, Patriot resistance, a Boston Massacre, a "shot heard round the world," a Declaration of Independence, a revolution, restless state governments, Articles of Confederation, and a constitutional battle. That is a lot for any fourteen-year period and sure enough, it was contentious all the way. When Washington was sworn in, there were no precedents for his acts to come. The rhetorical battles of Federalists and Anti-Federalists were not merely memories but thoughts among his advisors. We know Washington succeeded in making the American experiment real. He did so because he had a unifying vision. That vision, of a united set of states, was Washington's single-minded goal for the country. By his will, and by nearly every act he took, he forged a country by getting disagreeing factions to agree on that one goal and undertake the required acts to make sure the goal was reached. His success was due in no small part to Washington keeping not only government focused on his goal of a united set of states, but the country as well. Washington was so well respected that nearly everyone wanted to be on his moving train of leadership. We need a leader who can foster that kind of momentum again.

The election of 1960, which elevated John F. Kennedy to the presidency, featured diverse candidates and was an exceptionally close election. Nixon hailed from California and Kennedy from Massachusetts. Kennedy received 49.7 percent of the sixty-eight million votes cast to Richard Nixon's 49.5 percent. Nixon won more states but Kennedy won more electoral votes, and with that Kennedy became the first president to have lost more states than he won. The South, in some respects still unreconciled to Civil Rights, saw unpledged electors vote for a segregationist Democrat, Senator Harry F. Byrd, for president. Kennedy's candidacy stirred religious emotions because he was the first Catholic nominee. In the background lurked the memories of prior wars, the Cold War, and a listless economy that suffered three recessions during Eisenhower's eight years in office. Kennedy won, but in the aftermath of the election, questions lingered over whether the election, the closest since 1916, had been stolen. In the final analysis, although there certainly have been more divisive elections in our history, the fact remains that Kennedy took office with a split electorate.

The election of 1980, which was won by Ronald Reagan, took place in a time of great uncertainty, economic difficulty, national shame, and a divided and angry electorate. In the years before the election, because of the series of bad economic policies put into place by Lyndon B. Johnson, Richard Nixon, Gerald Ford, and Jimmy Carter, the economy was declining, and inflation and unemployment had reached double digits along with interest rates above 23 percent. To a significant degree America, not to mention the fifty-two people, had been held hostage by Iran for well over a year. Events had progressed into such despair that it was discussed openly whether one man could fulfill the office of the presidency. When the presidential campaign for the 1980 election started, conservatives were angry with the path of government and also with moderate Republicans. Democrat voters were discouraged and there was a burgeoning Independent Party movement, of which John Anderson would take the helm. The Independent Anderson came out of the gate with the support of 19 percent in the polls, a figure not seen on an Election Day since Theodore Roosevelt bolted from the Republican Party nearly seventy years earlier in the 1912 election. The 1980 election was rather pointed with the Democrats asserting that Reagan threatened the safety of the nuclear world with his policies. In order to win, Reagan had to appeal to conservatives on the Right and Independents in the middle. Reagan did just that by adopting an agenda of economic growth that united conservatives, moderate Republicans, and Independents. Importantly, Reagan did not win by vilifying a part of the electorate within his party or without. His agenda was so successful that John Anderson did not win a single precinct in America—not even his own. So in the end, Reagan won, but much like Kennedy before him, Reagan took the oath of office amidst much division and uncertainty.

The presidency of John F. Kennedy was as eventful as it was short. Kennedy faced enormous challenges that included the Bay of Pigs, the Cuban Missile Crisis, a Nuclear Test Ban Treaty, the continuing Civil Rights issue, trouble in the Middle East, and, of course, Vietnam. Kennedy also faced an economy that was declining because of the policy choices of FDR, Truman, and Eisenhower. Despite those difficulties, many of which arrived early in Kennedy's two-and-a-half-year presidency, Kennedy was determined that America should move forward and beyond those problems. Kennedy set goals for America and Americans to achieve. Kennedy wanted America to take on what he described as the *New Frontier*. In making that request, Kennedy was not seeking to accomplish his goals for the country—which included a reviving economy, peace for all time, starting the Peace Corps, and putting a man on the moon by the end of the decade—by relying on

government action alone. To the contrary, Kennedy famously said at
the Democratic convention in 1960:

> For the problems are not all solved and the battles are
> not all won—and we stand today on the edge of a New
> Frontier. . . . But the New Frontier of which I speak is
> not a set of promises—it is a set of challenges. It sums
> up not what I intend to offer the American people, but
> what I intend to ask of them.

In his inaugural address Kennedy would follow up on that sentiment
and put another challenge to Americans when he stated: "Ask not what
your country can do for you; ask what you can do for your country."

In time, Kennedy would ask the American people to partner with him
when it came to the economy. Rather than socially engineering Americans
with a program requiring them to change their ways and then sending an
invoice in the form of new taxes to pay for it, Kennedy wanted Americans
to do what they do best: earn money, save, and invest—thereby aligning
his political goals with their personal, economic goals. At the time Kennedy took office, the top marginal tax rate was 90 percent. That meant
that if someone earned enough to fall in that bracket, the federal government would take 90 percent of their applicable income. Those rates
above 90 percent had prevailed since the Roosevelt years. Three presidents
claimed they were necessary to balance the budget. However, that prevailing thought and policy discouraged savings, capital formation, and invest-
ment, and therefore reduced the growth of the economy over time and the
tax revenues that could have been realized. In his January 24, 1963, message to Congress, advocating a large cut in tax rates, Kennedy completed a
revolution in thought by stating:

> I repeat: our practical choice is not between a tax-cut
> deficit and budgetary surplus. It is between two kinds

of deficits: a chronic deficit of inertia, as the unwanted result of inadequate revenues and a restricted economy; or a temporary deficit of transition, resulting from a tax cut designed to boost the economy, increase tax revenues, and achieve—and I believe this can be done—a budget surplus.

Kennedy's tax policies were the center of his proposed economic program. His desire to revive the economy and solve the decades-long problem of deficits would be based largely on the actions of private individuals—not government programs or spending. Kennedy did not select which individuals would be part of his efforts. In no way did Kennedy seek to pit some Americans against others. He did not vilify one sector of society like Theodore Roosevelt or FDR did to justify their actions. To the contrary, Kennedy's program was open to all and he sought to inspire all of America to partner with him in this important effort. Sadly, of course, Kennedy's life was cut short. His tax-cut policies were enacted by Congress, however, which lowered the top rate to 70 percent in the wake of Kennedy's assassination. President Johnson, who was not otherwise an advocate for tax reduction policies, signed the tax reduction legislation largely in deference to Kennedy. Once enacted, the tax-rate reductions inspired Americans to revive the American economy through their own personal efforts. Record economic growth followed for three straight years.

The Kennedy tax-rate cuts were an unqualified success. If Kennedy had not been killed, and he had signed into law those rate cuts, American politics could be quite different today. Despite the success of those cuts, which spurred the economy and resulted in a 62 percent increase in federal revenues, President Johnson reversed some of their benefits and raised capital gains tax rates before the end of his presidency. While no one can say for sure, it is likely Kennedy would not have reversed his own policy choice in the face of its overwhelming success. A successful

JFK, utilizing what is considered a conservative policy today (i.e., tax rate cuts), could have redefined presidential politics for generations. Even without obtaining that credit, we can recognize that Kennedy's policy was not politically divisive in nature. It was a unifying vision that worked and is part of his enduring legacy.

Ronald Reagan also took office at a time when the economy was declining. The top individual income tax rate was still at the 70 percent rate that President Johnson had signed into law. In the twelve years in between, however, not only had Johnson signed into law an anti-growth tax rate increase on capital gains, but also presidents Nixon, Ford, and Carter grew the federal government and its regulatory reach. At the same time, taxes were on the rise in our states, counties, and cities. Overall, the economy was shrinking and racked with inflation. Picking up where Kennedy left off, Reagan once again partnered with the American people and asked them to revive the American economy. Once again he made his political goal their economic goal. Strangely enough, the Reagan tax-rate cuts were enacted after he, too, endured an assassin's bullet. Reagan survived, of course, and signed his rate cuts into law. Combined with his other policies and a Federal Reserve committed to wringing inflation out of the economy, primarily Americans—not federal spending—revived the economy and set it on a path to ninety-two straight months of economic growth. That growth did not end until Reagan's successor George H. W. Bush signed into law tax legislation that hurt the economy and divided us politically. Once the economy adjusted to that bad bill, it resumed its growth until the full effect of Clinton's tax increase worked its way through the economy—a tax increase that politically divided the nation and left America with its highest tax burden in history.

Reagan is now regularly regarded in polling as the greatest president since World War II. His crossover appeal reached new heights when Reagan Democrats became an identifiable group that supported his policies and, in time, his reelection. Reagan's reelection was assured in part because although some of his policies, especially in foreign affairs, caused division, Reagan governed by and large as he campaigned. He did not vilify his opponents or pit any significant sector of Americans against another. Like Kennedy's economic agenda, Reagan's economic agenda was open to everyone. In short, he unified Americans like few prior presidents in our history. He did that by partnering with the majority of the American people. So successful was Reagan, that the far less charismatic George H. W. Bush became one of only four sitting vice presidents to be elected president and the first in almost a century and a half.

We can contrast the unifying goals of Washington, Kennedy, and Reagan with less unifying and therefore less successful presidents. Early on in our discussion, we saw that John Adams's presidency became mired in division in significant part because he signed the Alien and Sedition Act. Outlawing opposition speech, of course, is likely one of the most divisive acts a president can take. Adams's inability to rise above partisanship played a key role in his divisive loss to Jefferson, and for that, Adams became the first one-term president. His son, John Quincy Adams, suffered a similar fate. He too took office after a divisive election, which featured the infamous "Corrupt Bargain" that allowed Adams to take the presidency over Andrew Jackson. Jackson had received the most electoral votes, but not a majority in the 1824 election. That lack of a majority threw the election into the House of Representatives. John Quincy Adams had placed second. The fourth place finisher, Henry Clay, was no fan of Jackson and threw his support to Adams, assuring his selection by the House of Representatives. Jackson's supporters referred to the Clay/Adams deal as a "corrupt bargain" because Adams named Clay his secretary of state. John Quincy Adams's aggressive domestic agenda rooted in an active federal government (which was a departure from Monroe's policies and angered state-centric politicos) and his inability, if not refusal, to build political bridges left him unable to rise above the partisanship of his age and made him the second president to serve just one term.

If we move far forward, to 2008, we find that Barack Obama also took office amid a divided electorate. Poorly paired with partisans House Majority Leader Nancy Pelosi and Senate Majority Leader Harry Reid, after a Bush presidency that ended amid great partisanship, Obama chose not to follow Bush's early model of bipartisanship. Bush, of course, the loser of the popular vote, faced his own divided electorate. Rather than start with a divisive agenda, in 2001, the first year of his presidency, Bush worked with Democrat partisan icon Ted Kennedy on a large education bill known as the No Child Left Behind Act. Later Bush again found bipartisan support, including eleven Democrat senators and even Independent/Socialist Bernie Sanders, for his Medicare Part D proposal. Beyond that, Bush's approach to the faltering economy sought unity—not division. As a result of the recession at the end of the Clinton presidency (brought on because of the highest US tax and regulatory burden in history), and then 9/11, the economy sharply declined. In response, Bush lowered tax rates for all Americans. Like JFK and Reagan before him, Bush did not pick a targeted group to help nor another to blame. The economy recovered smartly and Bush achieved Republican congressional gains not only in his first midterm election, but also for his reelection. By making rare gains in three consecutive elections, if we include his initial presidential election, Bush also tempered the Divided Era for a short period.

By contrast, the tenor and programs of President Obama were never unifying. Like FDR and Teddy Roosevelt, he campaigned against large parts of the electorate in his campaign and literally vilified some Americans en route to getting legislation passed along strictly party lines. Barack Obama's first legislative act, passed just months after he took office, the so-called Stimulus Bill, did not garner a single Republican vote. Based largely on the political spending wish list of House Majority Leader Nancy Pelosi and Senate Majority Leader Harry Reid, the bill provided no crossover appeal, such as tax or regulatory reform, for Republicans. The next year, Obama's signature piece of legislation, Obamacare, despite significant public opposition in addition to Republican opposition, also passed without a single Republican vote. Obamacare, of course, required significant change in the habits and rights of Americans. Indeed, the rights of millions of people and businesses were affected—a key reason for the opposition to the legislation. Rather than court crossover support for the bill, Obama, Pelosi, and Reid demeaned significant portions of the opposition. When it came to tax policy, as we have seen, Obama has taken a page from FDR's playbook and used the tax code as a political rallying point instead of a method to achieve a unifying economic recovery like JFK and Reagan. Obama also has pushed income inequality as an issue from the time he started campaigning through his reelection and passage of a tax bill that raised tax rates on some Americans. Of course, by political definition, pitting one class of Americans against another is divisive and encourages resentment between the classes, as we saw in chapter 8.

All in all, rather than partnering with the American public on the economy, Obama sent them a tax bill for his expensive and extensive programs—programs for which they had no personal stake in their success because an insufficient number of Americans were his partner in the endeavor. To the contrary, a majority of voters have never supported Obamacare and, among them, many knew an expensive tax bill had to be paid. If we confine our review of a presidency to whether the country was more unified or less unified, and nothing more, the fact that by mid-2014, 67 percent of Americans believed the country was more divided than it was four years earlier, clearly the Obama presidency cannot be considered successful.

If a greater sense of unity is to be recovered, we shall have to lean on the examples of Washington, JFK, and Reagan to the exclusion of the Adamses, father and son, and Obama. We shall need a new leader who will engage *all* Americans in a purpose instead of pitting some against others. What follows are potential policies for such a president.

Bridging the American Divide
Through Reform Policies

If the basic premise of this book is correct, that we are in a *Divided Era*, then we must assume that many of the next presidents will take office among a divided electorate. If they wish to be successful in the long term, those presidents will be required to sustain the momentum their elections or any short-term mandates may provide. As the complexity of our government and likely the disappointment of its programs grow, the first such step for that president should be a significant, unifying government reform strategy.

A sensible reform program should be comprised of the following:

1. The new president and his or her party should choose a significant government program that is not working. Obviously, that should not be too difficult in this day and age. The first such choice should be capable of some resolution so that the art of the possible can actually be achieved.

2. A material reform of that program should be designed.

3. Our enterprising leader, and/or his or her party, should then quietly build support among leaders in the public and private sector for the proposed reform. Once the foregoing is achieved,

4. That leader, and/or his or her party, should then hold a press conference wherein he or she explains:

   a. The original purpose of the nonworking program;

   b. Who was originally supposed to have benefitted from the nonworking program;

   c. The reformed program;

d. Why the reformed program will benefit the intended beneficiaries more than the current failed program; and

e. How much money the reformed program will save taxpayers.

The importance of the latter two elements cannot be underestimated. The current beneficiaries of any program will not want to see
their benefits reduced willingly. As such, the reform will have to be real.
It must include an improvement in services to offset the hue and cry
of perceived losses. Given the modern age of technology and the gifted
minds of our private sector leaders, this is an enterprise that can't be
beyond our abilities. The reform must also save taxpayers money. The
savings can then be used to sustain other existing programs and assure
others that money will not run out for all.

The next step is beyond critical.

The next step will be to build consensus for the proposed reform
among the electorate. To do so, our enterprising leader should bypass
the American media and aggressively use the bully pulpit to build support for the program throughout the country. The new president should
not rest until not only a legislative majority supports the reform but also
a significant majority of Americans understand and support the reform.
Once that is achieved, and it may take some time, the vote for the reform
should be held—*but not before*. Building public consensus on an issue
will be key and likely more important than building congressional consensus or the details of the reform for our purposes.

It is tempting, of course, for any president to want to strike while
the iron is hot and rush to get approval of his or her program. Nor-
mally, that is smart, first-hundred-days politics. In the *Divided Era*,
however, that will ill serve the remainder of his or her presidency. Such
a rush job risks escalating existing partisanship rather than building
the consensus the next president will need to break our persistent divisions. Instead, the new president should be nearly single-minded in

this effort—at least to the partial exclusion of others. Once the reform is achieved, the president can move on to another reform effort fresh off his or her victory and with the added momentum a carefully chosen reform could provide.

Obviously, events such as natural disasters or war may and have sidetracked a president's agenda. Some will argue that a president cannot limit a presidency to such a plodding course. Of the first concern, there is little that can be done to the timing and nature of such an event except to handle it well. Often, such events can be unifying if undertaken in the right manner. As for the second concern, of which there can be more control, we would do well to understand that most successful presidencies know but a few significant and lasting successes during their term—two, perhaps three, rarely four. Carter could claim the peace process between Egypt and Israel and nothing more—hence his one-term presidency. Reagan could claim his tax/regulatory reform and resultant economic success, the victory of the Cold War, and the reinvigoration of America. In time, his altering of military focus to Strategic Defense Initiative–type strategies may join those other significant accomplishments—witness the success of that focus in the Israeli/Hamas War of 2014. Of course, those successes led to a national unity not seen since.

If the successful Reagan presidency can be limited to just three or four major items, it should be apparent to future presidents that if they chase too many rabbits at once, they likely will not catch any one of them—especially in the *Divided Era*. Understanding the limits of the modern presidency, a more focused agenda that carefully builds unity can certainly build on a single success and perhaps lead to the two or three successes. Obviously, that initial reform effort should begin shortly after his or her inauguration so as to capitalize on the honeymoon period during which, even in the *Divided Era*, goodwill comparatively abounds. The prize to be won, however, if the president wants to be successful during the remainder of his or her term, will be unity.

Ending the Divisive Practice of the Income Tax

We have seen throughout this book, and especially in chapter 8, how taxes have been divisive throughout all of history. Our income tax system, under which roughly half of Americans pay income tax and half do not, is by definition divisive. It is matched in time and place with the fact that more than half of all Americans are dependent on some form of government assistance—leading to the resentful argument by some that they are working to pay for the other half. Closely tied to those problems is the issue of inequality in assets and income, an issue pushed so very prominently by President Obama and the Democrats during Obama's second term. The convergence of those issues is more than a politically toxic and divisive brew. Quite frankly, few, if any, civilizations have avoided serious and destructive social discord, if not rebellion, when their leaders have fanned the flames of inequality and simultaneously adopted policies that stagnate an economy and increase inequality. America simply cannot continue down that divided path.

Consider about the fate of third-century Athens and wonder how different it was from our own divided time. "The change from landed to movable wealth produced a feverish struggle for money, and the Greek language had to invent a word, *pleonexia*, to denote this appetite for 'more and more.'... Fortunes were made and unmade with a new rapidity.... The nouveaux riches... built gaudy houses, decked their women with costly robes and jewels, spoiled them with a dozen servants, and made it a principle to feed their guests with none but expensive drinks and foods."[1001]

Meanwhile, and not unlike our own time, the "middle classes... had lost much of their wealth, and could no longer mediate between the rich and the poor, between unyielding conservativism and utopian radicalism."[1002] Of the times, Plato described "two cities... one the city of the poor, the other of the rich, the one at war with the other." In our times, recall the 2004 campaign speeches of John Edwards wherein he spoke of "two Americas."

According to Will Durant, the "poor schemed to despoil the rich by legislation and revolution [and] the rich organized for protection against the poor."[1003] So bitter were the times, that Isocrates wrote: "The rich have become so unsocial that those who own property had rather throw their possessions into the sea than lend aid to the needy, while those in poorer circumstances would less gladly find a treasure than seize the possessions of the rich." What followed in the bitter class warfare of the time included not only government efforts at redistribution and a distrust of "democracy as empowered envy," but also murderous class violence that left Greece and its allied states badly divided—so divided in fact, that with their energy sapped, they all but ignored the outside world until they were conquered by Philip of Macedon in 338 BC.[1004]

Certainly America has not reached that point in its own history, but was there not violence and destruction of property in connection with the Occupy Movement? In Oakland, every year downtown banks spend tens of thousands of dollars replacing windows broken by protestors. The Left regularly assures us that poverty is a predictor of crime and writes of the same with such titles as "Want to Fight Crime? Address Income Inequality."[1005] Meanwhile, Harvard economist Kenneth Rogoff, coauthor of a best-selling book on financial crises, *This Time It's Different*, believes "that the high unemployment rate and high levels of debt in the U.S. will sooner or later trigger serious 'social unrest from the income disparities in the U.S.'"[1006] According to David Cay Johnston, the "puzzle for the Davos set is why the declining fortunes of the vast majority have not touched off social upheaval in America."[1007] In the same article, Johnston noted that "Plutarch wrote two millennia ago" that "an imbalance between rich and poor is the oldest and most fatal ailment of all republics," and that "not much more than two centuries ago the falling fortunes of most Frenchmen brought the monarchy to a sharp-edged end." Perhaps the editorial board of *USA Today* sums up that viewpoint by writing that the "impact of America's growing income inequality can be seen in protests, ranging from Occupy Wall Street in 2011 to the fast-food worker strikes" and that if "the trend were to continue indefinitely—with nearly all benefits of a growing economy going to a select few and the American Dream dashed for the rest—*extreme* social tensions would be inevitable."[1008]

Amid such dire warnings, past and present, it should be incumbent on strong leaders to steer America away from such an abyss. To avoid the fate of France, whose rebellion was finally quelled by the armor of Napoleon, not by the *Enlightenment* of its elites, and to avoid the similar fate of Greece more than two thousand years before, American policy must restore economic growth and end the politics of class warfare. Remember that in the late 1800s and early 1900s, the issue of income inequality was prevalent as well. There were the likes of Rockefeller, Carnegie, and Vanderbilt standing in stark contrast to the plight of the newly urbanized worker, amid the inequities of early capitalism. The plight of the poor of the 1800s, in nearly every way, far, far exceeded the plight of the vast majority of the poor today, who have access to emergency rooms, technology, public schools, and other assistance unimagined by the poor of the late 1880s. Only the extended growth of the economy ameliorated the tension of the late 1800s and began to create the middle class out of those same poor workers—long before the existence of widespread welfare. Today, however, our income tax system is an impediment to sustained economic growth and fuels the politics of class warfare instead of ending it.

It will be and is, of course, the cry of the Left that the rich should pay a greater share of income taxes. However, as we have seen, IRS figures show that for the last two decades the top 1 percent have paid in excess of 35 percent of income taxes and the top 5 percent have paid more than half of all income taxes. Also according to the IRS, the top 1 percent already pays more in income taxes than the bottom 90 percent. We know the percentage the top has been paying has been increasing for decades. So, if rising tax rates and tax burdens could cure income and asset inequality, wouldn't it have worked already? If not, and "more" is required, at what higher income tax rate or tax burden would it work? I ask for no answer to the question given the absurdity of asking whether it is even possible that such a small percentage could pay all income taxes without doing what they have done throughout all of history: shelter income, avoid income, underreport earnings, retire, or move. We saw that after the top tax rate rose to 77 percent under Woodrow Wilson, and we see it today with more than a trillion dollars sheltered overseas. That is because, as we have seen, there is a point at which higher rates produce less revenue than lower rates.

Frankly, there simply is no example in history where high income tax rates or lopsided tax burdens "corrected" income inequality or substantially improved the lot of the poor. Not a single one. Yes, history has many examples of higher rates imposed for social ends. For a time, they suppress economic growth and reduce incomes—creating the illusion of equality. They do not, as America saw during the Great Depression with marginal tax rates as high as 94 percent, build incomes for the poor or the middle class over substantial periods—a dynamic wholly dependent on jobs growth. That is because sustained economic and job growth and high tax rates/burdens are sworn enemies. High tax rates and lopsided tax burdens stagnate incomes across the board and fall more onerously on the poor, who often are trapped in a cycle of government dependence—a dynamic which prevents the "have nots" from acquiring jobs and wealth. That is, in part, the story of America from 2010 to 2015. Only sustained economic growth can lift the middle class and the poor.

Ultimately we must ask: When and where in history have the policies and politics of class warfare led to meaningful and lasting beneficial societal change? The answer is nowhere. After all, there is a reason it is called class warfare and not class unification.

At best, those policies lead to economic stagnation and political division. Keep in mind a stagnant economy means, more or less, a fixed economic pie to be divided by politicians—in essence, a competition for spoils. That is, as we have learned, divisive by definition.

At worst, in the hands of cynical politicians, many times the policies and politics of class warfare have led to revolution, which Will Durant would tell us results in the destruction of property and the "redistribution of poverty," *not* wealth. Durant also would tell us that the idealist who advocates socialist policies (often the political outcome of class warfare), and attempts to seduce others to his socialist ways, forgets the relative poverty of the equality he seeks amidst his nostalgia for simpler and "fairer" times.

As for the politics of it all, it is a maxim of history that sustained economic stagnation leads to political discontent—virtually everywhere and in every time. In the final analysis, the only thing persistently high tax rates have done is serve as a politically divisive tool for the expedient politician.

The answer for America today cannot be to fall deeper into the trap of divisive class warfare. If the existing lopsided tax burden has not quelled income inequality by now, it never will. It will, however, result in ever-greater social discord and class warfare. In order to end that vicious downward economic and political cycle, the existing income tax code must be replaced. Either it must be replaced altogether by a system that raises revenue not based on class, for example, a national sales tax or a consumption tax; or it must be so flattened and the myriad of exemptions removed so that the code once again becomes about raising tax revenue and not about politics or class warfare. It is no small historical irony that former Soviet-bloc countries, which America helped free, make use of flat taxes while tax burdens in America are becoming more lopsided.

Of course, in taking this position, I am certainly not so naïve as to think that the political process it would take to make such a change wouldn't involve political competition and acrimony. Certainly, it is a given that one of the most competitive government spoils Americans and their businesses seek is favorable tax treatments. A recent Reason-Rupe poll, however, "asked Americans if they would support or oppose changing the federal tax system to a flat tax, where everyone pays the same percentage of his or her income, finding that 62 percent favor the flat tax and 33 percent are opposed. When asked where they would set the flat tax, the average response was 15 percent."[1009] In other words, there may be more consensus than we think on the subject and Americans as a whole may have more sense than the social engineers they elect of late. In sum, it is time to steer America away from tax-driven divisions, and responsible leadership can no longer court the alternative. If we do not, we are headed for one of the worst cycles of escalating partisanship and persistent division in our history, not to mention a lower standard of living.

Quality Functions and Private Citizens

The United States, of course, didn't always have a large government. In fact, Calvin Coolidge's last federal budget was just $3 billion (approximately $42 billion in today's dollars), not the $4 trillion likely to be spent in 2015. In other words, our government today is more than 8,000 percent larger today than it was under Coolidge. America survived its history of smaller government prior to 1928. Indeed, America helped win a world war, settled a continent, and was poised to dominate the twentieth century. How did our country cope without big government? Alexis de Tocqueville, a French historian of aristocratic heritage, toured America nearly a century before and published his observations in a two-volume set called *Democracy in America*; he provided us with an important hint. Tocqueville came from the perspective of a French civilization that endured a revolution not long after ours, endured Napoleon and his wars, and then became a constitutional monarchy just before he arrived in America. According to Tocqueville,

The citizen of the United States is taught from his earliest infancy to rely upon his own exertions in order to resist the evils and the difficulties of life; he looks upon social authority with an eye of mistrust and anxiety, and he only claims its assistance when he is quite unable to shift without it. This habit may even be traced in the schools of the rising generation, where the children in their games are wont to submit to rules which they have themselves established, and to punish misdemeanors which they have themselves defined. The same spirit pervades every act of social life. If a stoppage occurs in a thoroughfare, and the circulation of the public is hindered, the neighbors immediately constitute a deliberative body; and this extemporaneous assembly gives rise to an executive power which remedies the inconvenience before anybody has thought of recurring to an authority superior to that of the persons immediately concerned. If the public pleasures are concerned, an association is formed to provide for the splendor and the regularity of the entertainment. Societies are formed to resist enemies which are exclusively of a moral nature, and to diminish the vice of intemperance; in the United States associations are established to promote public order, commerce, industry, morality, and religion; for there is no end which the human will, seconded by the collective exertions of individuals, despairs of attaining.

In other words, in the absence of government, Americans relied on the actions of private individuals to perform functions that many likely see as exclusive the realm of government today. In 1840, Tocqueville continued his thoughts by stating:

Americans group together to hold fêtes, found semi-
naries, build inns, construct churches, distribute books,
dispatch missionaries to the antipodes. They establish
hospitals, prisons, schools by the same method. Finally,
if they wish to highlight a truth or develop an opinion
by the encouragement of a great example, they form an
association.

In rather simple terms, either by necessity or choice, as Tocqueville
would say, America must return to an era with public "functions performed by private citizens."

Is that possible in the *Divided Era*?

Sadly or otherwise, we do not have to use imagination to answer that
question. We need merely to think of Detroit. The once great city of
Detroit peaked at a population of nearly two million in 1950. It was once
the fourth largest city in America and likely even more rich. Today it is the
eighteenth largest. In the last decade alone it has shrunk by 25 percent to
a population of just seven hundred thousand people. Along with that lost
population or because of it, Detroit has lost half a million automotive-
related jobs—so troubled is the Motor City. What wasn't being reduced
during that period of time was Detroit's public sector costs. Indeed,
from just "2008 to 2011, health insurance costs for Detroit employees
and retirees . . . jumped 62% to $186 million a year, the *Detroit Free Press*
reported. Pension contributions in that period jumped 140 percent, from
$50 million to $120 million."[1010] It doesn't take a math major to understand that a reduced number of jobs and a declining population mean
lower tax revenues, notwithstanding Detroit having some of the highest
tax rates in the nation. Indeed, the higher tax rates exacerbated Detroit's
problems, especially when matched with the higher public debt, which
always and everywhere implies higher taxes to come. That combination
has driven residents and businesses out of the city limits.

What happens to a city under such circumstances? The answer was that the city simply ran out of money. Lacking money, the city chose, not illogically, to stop funding certain city operations. With that, let us consider the role of the Mower Gang in the *Divided Era*. You see, one of the functions the city of Detroit chose not to fund was the care of certain city parks. It was in February of 2013 when the mayor of Detroit, former basketball star Dave Bing, announced that Detroit would be closing more than four dozen city parks. In reality, closing a city park meant not much more than the city would no longer pay for park maintenance. Residents affected by such closings inquired about them and were told as much. Faced with the prospect of growing grass and unsightly parks, bereft of a need for their own pensions as a price of action, local citizens did the thinkable—they formed their own association, the Mower Gang, and started taking care of the parks themselves. Using their own resources, and among themselves, there is little partisanship, just action. It is a picture of the simpler time that Tocqueville described and praised; and, as Ronald Reagan would say, "It can be done."

Of course, we do not have to wait for cities or states to announce bankruptcy to achieve such a goal. Sticking with parks, New York City's Central Park Conservancy is also in keeping with Tocqueville's vision. For decades, the Central Park Conservancy has been managing New York's Central Park under a contract with the city of New York. Of course, Central Park is one of New York's, if not America's, greatest landmarks. According to the Conservancy's own website, "The era of decline in the 1960s and 1970s led to Central Park Conservancy's formation. Central Park Conservancy is uniquely qualified to prevent future declines and ensure the Park's care for current and future generations." In other words, the Conservancy was born of an era of prior budget shortages. The Conservancy is "responsible for all aspects of the park maintenance, as well as capital improvements and restorations" and funds 75 percent of the operating budget for the park through private donations. Clearly, the Conservancy represents "quality of functions performed by private citizens." Quite frankly, there is no reason why every park in America couldn't be run in similar fashion if one of America's greatest parks, Central Park, can thrive under such cost-effective management.

The Conservancy is a form of a public-private partnership. The United States actually lags in the use of such partnerships as compared to Canada and other countries with regard to infrastructure and health-care construction.[1011] With respect to Canada, not only have public-private partnerships saved taxpayers money:

> Officials in British Columbia have encountered a unique problem in recent years that most jurisdictions would be thrilled to have: Infrastructure projects are being completed not just on time, but early. Way too early. Builders have been finishing hospitals, for example, so far ahead of schedule that they haven't even been allocated operating funds. "We had to limit how early they could be built," says Sarah Clark, president and CEO of Partnerships British Columbia.[1012]

We need not limit our discussion to construction activity. Returning to the problems of the Veterans Administration (VA) that were so prominent in 2014, while there was no doubt Congress threw billions of dollars at the problem in somewhat less-than-scrupulous fashion, part of the bill "voucherized" medical care for veterans. The VA, of course, provides medical care to American veterans. The 2014 VA scandal, however, exposed the fact that the very large government medical provider was severely backlogged in providing care and therefore not providing care efficiently to veterans—sometimes with fatal results. In order to address that backlog, Congress authorized a public-private partnership of sorts by permitting American veterans to seek care at private hospitals to obtain the care instead of being limited to government facilities.

There was remarkably little partisanship over the issue. Both parties moved relatively quickly to respond to the problems that were exposed—so much so that it could be said they appropriated before they analyzed. The key to the lack of partisanship over the issue was that there was unanimity on the importance of the goal. It was widely believed that the public, let alone veterans, were not going to stand for a failure by Congress to address the problem. In other words, the public was already sold on the need for action in the minds of the politicians who feared political backlashes. In the case of the VA, the issue sold itself and action was therefore swift and teaches us one last critical lesson about the *Divided Era*.

Final Thoughts

We have reached the end of our journey through the divided eras of American history. We have come to understand that government is more than a question of social good and compromise. A country as large as the United States is today, or as idealistic as it was at the time of our founding, or as divided as it was during the Civil War and its aftermath, has many diverse interests. When we pass from voluntary association to government mandate, those separate interests, along with our natural competitiveness, come to the forefront.

Invariably, we find that one man's public good infringes on another man's freedom, or beliefs, or income. It is that moment, that self-interest, a core trait of the human species since the dawn of time, that often awakens our competitive nature, turns self-interest into partisanship. As *Our Revolutionary Thoughts*, *Our Constitutional Divide*, the Civil War, *Reconstruction* and *Our Gilded Age of Division* showed us, if the issues are large enough, sustained partisanship can, and often does, lead to persistent division.

In the past, our limited government allowed the peaks of our differences to recede. Like every great civilization before us, however, in the drive to protect ourselves and in the attempt to wish away the inequities of life, we have grown government to the point of it being omnipresent.

In doing so, we have invited government to exert its say in almost every aspect of our lives. The trouble with that, as Thomas Jefferson once said, is that "here are so many wants. So many affections and passions engaged, so varying in their interests and objects, that no one can be conciliated without revolting others."

As we face the future, and those varying interests and objects, conciliation and revolt, we need to be philosophical enough to accept the nature of man. Our Founders, mindful of the people about them and their nature, understood that government was by definition as much a compromise as a source of division. They knew that each use of power was a limitation of others' rights—and so they attempted to limit government, in part to limit the importance of our elections, reduce our divisions and keep America as one.

While it may not seem so now, the *Divided Era* can end. The key to stepping away from our partisan edge will be for us to finally understand that ever larger government fosters division. We must find leaders capable of building consensus even whilst our budgets tighten. We must raise up leaders who understand that they should partner with the American people, not seek to change them. We must have leaders who understand the value of a unifying vision and have the character and resolve to maintain it—and that leadership starts with our own understanding.

If we can recapture that understanding, we can begin again, and recapture *Washington's Unifying Moment*.

Notes

Chapter 1: A Glimpse at Our Divided Present

1. Harlow Giles Unger, *Lion of Liberty: Patrick Henry and the Call to a New Nation* (Cambridge, MA: Da Capo Press, 2010), 32–33.

Chapter 2: The Storm Before the Calm

2. Justice John Marshall, *The Life of George Washington* (Philadelphia: C. P. Wayne, 1804–1807), Vol. 5.
3. Ron Chernow, *Washington: A Life* (New York: Penguin, 2010), 281.
4. Ibid., 458.
5. Ibid., 812.
6. Henry Cabot Lodge, *George Washington* (Boston: Houghton Mifflin Co., 1889), Vol. 1.1.
7. Richard Brookhiser, *Gentleman Revolutionary: Gouverneur Morris, the Rake Who Wrote the Constitution* (New York: Free Press, 2003), 79.
8. David McCullough, *1776* (New York: Simon & Schuster, 2005), 226.
9. Lodge, *George Washington*, Vol. 2.
10. Ibid.
11. Jefferson in a letter to the Rev. Charles Clay, referenced in Willard Sterne Randall, *George Washington: A Life* (New York: Henry Holt & Company, 1997), 463.
12. Jon Meacham, *Thomas Jefferson: The Art of Power* (New York: Random House, 2012), 270.
13. Lodge, *George Washington*, Vol. 2. Lodge wrote that Washington had "High and splendid character, great moral qualities for after-ages to admire, he had beyond any man of modern times." In his work, Lodge rhetorically asked: "Has any man ever lived who served the American people more faithfully, or with higher and truer conception of the destiny and possibilities of the country?"
14. Unger, *Lion of Liberty*, 32.
15. Gordon S. Wood, *The Idea of America, Reflections on the Birth of the United States* (New York: Penguin, 2011), 27. David Leonard was a well-known loyalist and pamphleteer at the time.
16. Unger, *Lion of Liberty*, 31.
17. Ibid. According to Unger, "Although England had won the Seven Years' War, her victory left the government nearly bankrupt, with a national debt of £130 million (nearly $8 billion today) £300,000 in annual costs of military garrison to protect American colonists against Indian attacks."
18. Ibid.
19. Ibid.

20. Ibid.

21. John Ferling, *Independence: The Struggle to Set America Free* (New York: Bloomsbury, 2011), 151–52.

22. James Henry Stark, *The Loyalists of Massachusetts and The Other Side of the American Revolution* (Boston: John Stark, 1910), 35.

23. Dorothy Denneen Volo and James M. Volo, *Daily Life During the American Revolution* (Westport, CT: Greenwood Press, 2003), 49.

24. Ferling, *Independence*, viii.

25. Ibid.

26. Kevin Phillips, *1775: A Good Year for Revolution* (New York: Penguin, 2012), 197.

27. Ferling, *Independence*, viii.

28. Phillips, *1775: A Good Year*, 96.

29. Gary B. Nash, *Revolutionary Founders, Philadelphia's Radical Caucus That Propelled Pennsylvania to Independence and Democracy*, in *Revolutionary Founders: Rebels, Radicals and Reformers in the Making of the Nation*, Alfred F. Young, Gary Nash, and Ray Raphael, Editors (New York: Alfred A. Knopf, 2011), 67.

30. Unger, *American Tempest, How the Boston Tea Party Sparked a Revolution* (Cambridge, MA: Da Capo Press, 2011, 112.

31. Ibid.

32. Ferling, *Independence*, 255.

33. Unger, *American Tempest*, 183.

34. Kevin Phillips, *The Cousins' Wars: Religion, Politics, Civil Warfare, and the Triumph of Anglo-America* (New York: Basic Books, 1999), 133–134.

35. Nash, *Revolutionary Founders*, 67.

36. Phillips, *1775: A Good Year*, 85–86.

37. Phillips, *The Cousins' Wars*, 135.

38. McCullough, *1776*, 10.

39. Ferling, *Independence*, 354.

40. Alfred E. Young, *Revolutionary Founders, Ebenezer Mackintosh, Captain General of the Liberty Tree* (New York: Knopf, 2011), 15–16.

41. Ibid.

42. John C. Miller, *Sam Adams: Pioneer in Propaganda* (Stanford, CA: Stanford University Press, 1936), 53.

43. Ferling, *Independence*, 56, 77.

44. Unger, *American Tempest*, 81.

45. Paul Johnson, *A History of the American People* (New York: HarperCollins, 1997), 140.

46. Lodge, *George Washington*, Vol. 2.

47. Johnson, *A History of the American People*, 140.

48. Jill Lepore, *Revolutionary Founders: A World of Paine*, in Young and Nash, *Revolutionary Founders: Rebels, Radicals and Reformers in the Making of the Nation,* 87.

49. Ferling, *Independence*, 218.

50. Frank Smith, *Thomas Paine: Liberator* (New York: Frederick A. Stokes, 1938), 5.

51. Johnson, *A History of the American People*, 153.

52. Ibid.

53. Ibid.

54. Ibid., 155, citing Alexander Young, *Chronicles of the First Planters* (Boston: Little & Brown, 1846), 254.

55. Smith, *Thomas Paine: Liberator*, 5.

56. Lepore, *World of Paine*, 89.

57. Volo and Volo, *Daily Life During the American Revolution*, 211. Citing Claude Halstead van Tyne, *Loyalists in the American Revolution* (Ganesvoort, NY: Corner House Historical Publications, 1999), 2.

58. Sydney George Fisher, *The Struggle for American Independence*, Vol. 1 (Philadelphia & London: J. B. Lippincott company, 1908) 17. The English believed that by quelling the French ambitions in America, and thereby freeing Americans of that danger, the Americans then felt so secure they would press for their own freedom. By contrast, the argument went, that if the French had remained a threat, Americans would still be reliant on the British and would not have pressed for their own freedom.

59. John Nerone, *Violence Against the Press: Policing the Public Sphere in US History* (New York: Oxford University Press, 1994), 34.

60. Johnson, *A History of the American People*, 153.

61. Ferling, *Independence*, 67.

62. John R. McGeehan, M.A, *First Continental Congress*. http://www.netplaces.com/american-history/foundations-of-freedom/first-continental-congress.htm.

63. McCullough, *1776*, 116.

64. Phillip Papas, *That Ever Loyal Island: Staten Island and the American Revolution* (New York: New York University Press, 2007), 59.

65. According to John Ferling in his book *A Leap in the Dark: The Struggle to Create the American Republic*, " . . . the labyrinthian political struggles that accompanied the war and persisted in its aftermath have been long forgotten, save by a few scholars." We shall try to avoid that fate. (New York: Oxford University Press, 2003), xiii.

66. Carol Sue Humphrey, *The Revolutionary Era: Primary Documents on Events from 1776 to 1800* (Westport, CT: Greenwood Press, 2003), 33. "The colonies seemed to be facing an impossible situation. Great Britain had a population four times the size of the United States. It had one of the best armies in the world, and it was supplemented by hundreds of Hessians, hired mercenaries from central Europe. And Britain had the best navy in the world, which should have enabled it to blockade American ports and shut the United States off from contact with the rest of the world. In the eyes of many people, the chances for the colonials to win their independence seemed very slim."

67. McCullough, *1776*, 50.

68. Lois Clinton Hatch, *The Administration of the American Revolutionary Army* (New York: Longmans, Green and Co., 1904), 4.

69. Humphrey, *Primary Documents from 1776 to 1800*, 33.

70. Johnson, *A History of the American People*, 159. Although, as the war moved into its fifth year the King of England believed that the loss of their American Colonies would lead to the loss of other British Colonies in a domino effect.

71. Phillips, *The Cousins' Wars*, 157.

72. Stuart D. Brandes, *Warhogs: A History of War Profits in America* (New York: Longmans, Green and Co., 1904), 32.

73. Ferling, *Leap in the Dark*, 167.

74. McCullough, *1776*, 49–50.

75. McCullough, *1776*, 24.

76. Neil Longley York, *Turning the World Upside Down: The War of American Independence and the Problem of Empire* (Westport, CT: Praeger, 2003), 94.

77. Ibid., 97.

78. Chernow, *Washington*, 391.

79. William Graham Sumner, *The Financier and the Finances of the American Revolution* (New York: Dodd, Mead & Co., 1891); see also Chernow, *Washington*, 391.

80. Kevin Phillips, *1775*, 106.

81. Max M. Edling, *A Revolution in Favor of Government: Origins of the U.S. Constitution and the Making of an American State*, (New York: Oxford University Press, 2008), 151.

82. William M. Fowler, Jr., *American Crisis: George Washington and the Dangerous Two Years After Yorktown, 1781 – 1783* (New York: Walker & Co., 2011), 24.

83. Ibid.

84. Ibid., 25.

85. Ibid., 27.

86. Ferling, *Leap in the Dark*, 182.

87. Paul Johnson, *George Washington: The Founding Father* (New York: Harper Perennial, 2009), pg. 158 (ebook edition),"By the end of 1779, $241.6 million had been issued and this was only part of the borrowing, which included foreign loans, state loans, U.S. Loan Certificates, and other paper and produced the worst inflation in U.S. history. By 1780 the Continentals were in practice valueless." See also Fowler, *American Crisis*, 23–27.

88. Marshall, *Life Of George Washington*, Vol. 4.

89. Ferling, *Leap in the Dark*, 182.

90. Unites States National Science Foundation, *Climate Played a Role in the American Revolution* "Compared with mean temperatures for the entire century, southern New England was cool during the period of 1740 to 1776. In the 1750s and 1760s, the temperatures were so cold that Indian corn did not mature. The years also alternated between wet and dry, and had fluctuating growing seasons. In growing seasons from 1740 to 1776, eastern Massachusetts farmers were stopped 17 times by late spring or early fall frosts. With all of these climate fluctuations, the resulting harvests were often below expectations." http://www.nsf.gov/news/

frontiers_archive/12-97/12amrev.jsp.http://www.nsf.gov/news/frontiers_archive/12-97/12amrev.jsp.

91. Lois Clinton Hatch, *The Administration of the American Revolutionary Army*, 92.

92. Lodge, *George Washington*, Vol. 1; Lois Clinton Hatch, *The Administration of the American Revolutionary Army*, 93. According to the Marquis de Lafayette: "The unfortunate soldiers were in want of everything; they had neither coats, nor hats, nor shirts, nor shoes; their feet and legs froze till they grew black, and it was often necessary to amputate them....On December 23 [1977] there were 2898 men unfit for duty on account of lack of shoes and clothing; on February 5 the number had risen to 3989, an increase of more than a thousand in less than two month. Washington wrote in disgust: 'Perhaps by mid-summer, he [the soldier] may receive thick stockings, shoes, and blankets, which he will contrive to get rid of in the most expeditious manner. In this way, by an eternal round of the most stupid management, the public treasure is expended to no kind of purpose, while the men have been left to perish by inches with cold and nakedness!'" See also Chernow, *Washington*, 324.

93. Johnson, *A History of the American People*, 160.

94. Ferling, *Leap in the Dark*, 175.

95. Ibid., 204.

96. Johnson, *A History of the American People*, 160.

97. Washington letter to John Parke Custis, January 22, 1776.

98. Lois Clinton Hatch, *The Administration of the American Revolutionary Army*, 137.

99. Randall, *George Washington*, 383.

100. Chernow, *Washington*, 285.

101. Harlow Giles Unger, *John Hancock, Merchant King and American Patriot*, (New York: John Wiley & Sons, Inc., 2000), 50, 56.

102. Randall, *George Washington*, 204.

103. Brandes, *Warhogs: War Profits*, 44.

104. Ibid., 10. Also Chernow, *Washington*, 328.

105. Ibid.

106. Ferling, *Leap in the Dark*, 219–220.

107. Ferling, *Leap in the Dark*, 219–220.

108. Ferling, *Leap in the Dark*, 219–220.

109. Brandes, *Warhogs: War Profits*, 42.

110. Ibid. "When the British occupied Philadelphia in 1777, dozens of new stores opened, some of which were specialized firms catering specifically to the needs of British officers. Washington found it necessary to dismantle some flour mills near Wilmington, Delaware, in order to keep them from supplying enemy troops in Philadelphia."

111. Ibid.

112. Phillips, *Cousins' Wars*, 162.

113. Ibid., 134.

114. Jeffrey J. Crow, Larry E. Tise, *The Southern Experience in the American Revolution* (Chapel Hill: University of North Carolina Press, 1978), 174–75.

115. John Ferling, *Setting the World Ablaze: Washington, Adams, Jefferson, and the American Revolution* (New York: Oxford University Press, 2000), 166.

116. Phillips, *Cousins' Wars*, 162.

117. Winston S. Churchill, *The Age of Revolution*, 1951 cited in Phillips, *Cousins' Wars*, 161.

118. Stephen G. Kurtz and James H. Hutson, *Essays on the American Revolution* (Chapel Hill: University of North Carolina Press, 2011), 142.

119. Ibid., 143. Citing Colonel Robert Gray's *Observations on the War in Carolina*, South Carolina *Historical and Genealogical Magazine,* XI (1910), 153.

120. Phillips, *Cousins' Wars*, 128.

121. Ibid., 168–89.

122. Ibid., 162.

123. John B. Frantz, William Pencak, *Beyond Philadelphia: The American Revolution in the Pennsylvania Hinterland* (University Park: Pennsylvania State University Press, 1998), xxv.

124. James S. Leamon, *Revolution Downeast: The War for American Independence in Maine* (Amherst: University of Massachusetts Press, 1993), 104.

125. Charlemagne Tower, Jr., *The Marquis de la Fayette in the American Revolution: With Some Account of the Attitude of France toward the War of Independence*, Vol. 1, (Philadelphia: J. B. Lippincott Company, 1895) 68.

126. Lois Clinton Hatch, *The Administration of the American Revolutionary Army,* 5.

127. Chernow, *Washington*, 202, 207, 235, 294.

128. George Washington Letter to Robert Morris, cited in Lodge, *George Washington*, Vol. 1.

129. Chernow, *Washington, 288.*

130. Lois Clinton Hatch, *The Administration of the American Revolutionary Army,* 24.

131. Ferling, *Leap in the Dark*, viii.

132. Journals of The Continental Congress, 1774–1789, Volume 18, p. 906.

133. Charles Francis Adams, *Letters of John Adams, Addressed To His Wife*, (Boston: Charles C. Little and James Brown, 1841) p 15.

134. Fowler, *American Crisis*, 135.

135. Ibid.

136. Ibid.

137. Ibid.

138. Ibid.

139. William Edward Hartpole Lecky, James Albert Woodburn, *The American Revolution, 1763–1783* (New York: D. Appelton, 1898), 434.

140. Ibid, 434–436.

141. Ibid.

142. Ibid.

143. Fowler, *American Crisis*, 211.

144. Ferling, *Setting the World Ablaze*, 305.

145. Harlow Giles Unger, *The Life and Times of Noah Webster* (New York: John Wiley & Sons, Inc., 1998), 64.

146. Ibid.

147. Fowler, *American Crisis*, 110.

148. Chernow, *Washington*, 428.

149. Fowler, *American Crisis*, 211.

150. Ibid.

151. Ibid., 110.

152. Merrill Jensen, *The New Nation: A History of the United States during the Confederation, 1781–1789* (New York, Vintage Books, 1950) 57–58.

153. Ibid.

154. Unger, *Life and Times of Noah Webster*, 64.

155. Fowler, *American Crisis*, 134.

156. Unger, *Life and Times of Noah Webster*, 64.

157. Ibid.

158. Ibid., 65.

159. Chernow, *Washington*, 327.

160. Fowler, *American Crisis*, 133.

161. Chernow, *Washington*, 328.

162. Fowler, *American Crisis*, 211.

163. Chernow, *Washington*, 256.

164. Ibid., 373.

165. Allan Nevins, *The American States During and after the Revolution* (New York: Macmillan, 1927), 544.

166. Andrew Burstein and Nancy Isenberg, *Madison and Jefferson* (New York: Random House, 2010), 58.

167. Ferling, *Leap in the Dark*, 191.

168. Nevins, *American States during and after the Revolution*, 117.

169. Ibid.

170. Burstein and Isenberg, *Madison and Jefferson*, 60.

171. Brookhiser, *Gentleman Revolutionary*, 48.

172. Ferling, *Leap in the Dark*, 179.

173. Burstein and Isenberg, *Madison and Jefferson*, 60.

174. Ibid.

175. Chris DeRose, *Founding Rivals: Madison vs. Monroe* (Washington, D.C.: Regnery History, 2011), 55.

176. Burstein and Isenberg, *Madison and Jefferson*, 60.

177. Ibid., 86. "Once the Articles of Confederation were ratified, [Madison] immediately perceived the need for an amendment calculated to 'cement & invigorate the federal Union.'"

178. Thomas Jefferson's February 15, 1783, letter to Edmund Randolph.

179. Nevins, *American States during and after the Revolution*, 544.

Chapter 3: Our Constitutional Divide

180. Forest McDonald, *The Intellectual Origins of the Constitution* (Lawrence, Kansas: University Press of Kansas, 1985).

181. Anti-Federalist Brutus, assumed to be the New York lawyer Robert Yates, from his first article published in the *New York Journal*, October 18, 1787.

182. Wood, *The Idea of America*, 253.

183. Woody Holton, *Unruly Americans and the Origins of the Constitution* (New York: Hill & Wang, 2007), 26.

184. Holton, *Unruly Americans*, 27.

185. Ibid., 27–28.

186. Edling, *Revolution in Favor of Government*, 151.

187. Ibid., 153.

188. Ibid.

189. Ibid., 152.

190. Melvyn R. Durchslag, *State Sovereign Immunity: A Reference Guide to the United States Constitution* (Westport, CT: Praeger, 2002), 5.

191. Nevins, *American States during and after the Revolution*, 500;

192. Holton, *Unruly Americans*, 29. Nevins, *The American States during and after the Revolution*, 492. Italics in the original. "When the States in 1777–78 first abandoned or reduced their reckless paper issues, they had to turn, however reluctantly, to such direct levies as the people had never felt."

193. Ibid., 168.

194. David P. Szatmary, *Shays' Rebellion: The Making of an Agrarian Insurrection* (Amherst: University of Massachusetts Press,1980), 38–41.

195. Holton, *Unruly Americans*, 127.

196. James Madison letter to Thomas Jefferson dated October 24, 1787.

197. Holton, *Unruly Americans*, 5.

198. Unger, *Life and Times of Noah Webster*, 63.

199. Ibid.

200. Ibid.

201. DeRose, *Founding Rivals,* 93.

202. Publius, The Federalist VIII, published in the New York Packet, November 10, 1787. In Federalist XVI, published December 4, 1787, in the New York Packet, Hamilton raised the prospects of "civil war" in the absence of the Constitution.

203. Szatmary, *Shays' Rebellion*, 38.

204. Robert J. Taylor, *Western Massachusetts in the Revolution* (Providence, RI: Brown University Press, 1954), 128.

205. Ibid., 143.

206. Ibid., 146.

207. Ibid.

208. Ibid., 160.

209. George F. Smith, *Shays Fought the Revolution's Final Battle, and We Lost*, Oct. 16, 2005, citing Richards, Leonard L., *Shays's Rebellion: The American Revolution's Final Battle* (Philadelphia: University of Pennsylvania Press, 2002) "In a letter of October 23, 1786, Knox told Washington the rebels 'see the weakness of government' and thus feel free to pay little if any taxes. According to Knox, the rebels believed that since the joint exertions of all protected the property of the United States from Great Britain, it rightfully belongs to all. The rebels, Knox explained, believe that anyone who 'attempts opposition to this creed is an enemy to equity and justice, and ought to be swept [from] the face of the earth . . .' On November 8, 1786, James Madison wrote to Washington saying he and other officials had taken the liberty of nominating him to lead the Virginia delegation at a May convention in Philadelphia. The upcoming convention, as Alexander Hamilton had stated, would discuss how 'to render the constitution of the Federal Government adequate to the exigencies of the Union . . .' On March 19, 1787 Knox wrote Washington hinting that (1) he would be given the president's chair at the upcoming convention, and (2) he would not be presiding over some middling conference of officials tinkering with the 'present defective confederation,' but instead would lead a prestigious body of men as they created an 'energetic and judicious system,' one which would 'doubly' entitle him to be called The Father of His Country."

210. Will and Ariel Durant, *The Lessons of History* (New York: Simon & Schuster, 1968), 68.

211. Unger, *Life and Times of Noah Webster*, 79.

212. Pauline Maier, *Ratification: The People Debate the Constitution, 1787–1788* (New York: Simon & Schuster, 2010), 11.

213. Edling, *Revolution in Favor of Government*, 154.

214. Maier, *Ratification*, 11.

215. DeRose, *Founding Rivals*, 61.

216. Edling, *Revolution in Favor of Government*, 154.

217. Ibid., 154–55.

218. Maier, *Ratification*, 14.

219. Ibid.

220. Szatmary, *Shays' Rebellion: The Making of an Agrarian Insurrection*, 82.

221. Noah Webster, Sketches of American Policy, 1785.

222. Maier, *Ratification*, 14–18.

223. Lodge, *George Washington*, Vol. 2, 23.

224. Douglas Southall Freeman, *George Washington, A Biography*, 7 Vols. (New York: Charles Scribner's Sons), 537, cited in Chernow, *Washington*, 523.

225. From a Letter from George Washington to Charles Carter, December 27, 1787 printed in the *Virginia Herald*.

226. Maier, *Ratification*, 14.

227. Washington Letter to Henry Knox, February 3, 1787.

228. Wood, *The Idea of America*, 129.

229. Burstein and Isenberg, *Madison and Jefferson*, 182.

230. Maier, *Ratification*, 18.

231. Ibid., 19.

232. DeRose, *Founding Rivals*, 125.

233. Unger, *Lion of Liberty*, 185.

234. Unger, *Life and Times of Noah Webster*, 88.

235. Noah Webster, Sketches of American Policy, 1785.

236. Unger, *Last Founding Father, James Monroe*, 58–59.

237. Ibid., 68.

238. Burstein and Isenberg, *Madison and Jefferson*, 168.

239. Wood, *The Idea of America*, 129.

240. Ibid., 131.

241. Holton, *Unruly Americans,* 168.

242. Alfred Young, Gary B. Nash, and Ray Raphael, *Revolutionary Founders*, 218–219.

243. "A Fellow Citizen," "Willing to Learn," The True Policy of New jersey Defined; Or Our Strength Led to Exertion, in the Improvement of Agriculture & Manufacturing, By Altering the Mode of Taxation, and by the Emission of Money on Loan . . ." 9Elizabeth-Town, N.J., 1786) 33-34. Cited in Holton, *Unruly Americans,* 163.

244. "Impartiality," *New Hampshire Mercury*, September 6, 1786, cited in Holton, *Unruly Americans*, 167.

245. Unger, *John Hancock, Merchant King and American Patriot*, 311.

246. Ibid.

247. Ibid.

248. Holton, *Unruly Americans,* 163.

249. Marshall, *Life of George Washington.*

250. Unger, *Last Founding Father, James Monroe*, 77. (Italics mine).

251. Brookhiser, *Gentleman Revolutionary* (New York: Simon & Schuster, 2003), 87–92.

252. Maier, *Ratification*, 37.

253. Ibid.

254. Ibid., 36.

255. From James Madison's September 30, 1787 letter to George Washington. (Italics mine).

256. From James Madison's October 24, 1787 letter to Thomas Jefferson. (Italics mine).

257. Burstein and Isenberg, *Madison and Jefferson*, 165, 171.

258. Maier, *Ratification*, 37.

259. Ibid.

260. Ibid., 41.

261. Unger, *Last Founding Father, James Monroe*, 77.

262. Ibid.

263. Unger, *Lion of Liberty*, 207.

264. Ibid., 211.

265. Ibid., 199.

266. Maier, *Ratification*, 42.

267. The statement was printed on November 6, 1787, in the *Independent Gazetteer* and is attributed to William Findley who served in the Revolutionary War and the State legislature of Pennsylvania.

268. Although there is no certainty as to the identity of Cato, it is widely speculated that it was former New York Governor George Clinton. Historically, Cato was a Roman figure that defended Roman Republicanism against Julius Caesar's dictatorial ways.

269. Centinel I, Oct 5, 1787, *Independent Gazetteer*, Philadelphia.

270. Additional complaints focusing on the theme of the loss of *Liberty* include the following among many others: "If you adopt it in toto, you will lose every thing dear to freemen, and receive nothing in return but misery and disgrace." *Philadelphiensis* IV, Benjamin Workman (December 12, 1787); "This enormous innovation, and daring encroachment, on the liberties of the citizens." A Democrat Federalist, Pennsylvania Herald, Philadelphia, October 17, 1787; "What compensation then are you to receive in return for the liberties and privileges belonging to yourselves and posterity, that you are now about to sacrifice at the altar of this monster, this Colossus of despotism." Philadelphiensis [Benjamin Workman] IV (December 12, 1787); "A general Government, however guarded by declarations of rights or cautionary provisions, must unavoidably, in a short time, be productive of the destructive of liberty." Robert Yates and John Lansing, Jr. to Governor George Clinton, *Daily Advertiser*, New York, January 14, 1788.

271. Thorton Anderson, *Creating the Constitution: The Convention of 1787 and the First Congress* (University Park, PA: Pennsylvania State University Press, 1993), 174–75.

272. Unger, *Lion of Liberty*, 205 (emphasis added).

273. Ibid. (emphasis added).

274. Ibid. (emphasis added).

275. Maier, *Ratification*, 60.

276. Ibid., 62.

277. Ibid., 63.

278. Lynch, *Negotiating the Constitution: The Earliest Debates over Original Intent* (Ithaca, NY: Cornell University Press, 1999), 38–39. "Proponents of the Constitution pushed to obtain the requisite number as quickly as possible, using Washington's support to secure speedy approval."

279. Lynch, *Negotiating the Constitution,* 39.

280. Lynch, *Negotiating the Constitution,* 49.

281. Maier, *Ratification*, 61.

282. Anderson, *Creating the Constitution*, 175.

283. Unger, *Last Founding Father*, 82.

284. Unger, *Lion of Liberty*, 205 (emphasis added). Maier, *Ratification*, 64.

285. Unger, *Lion of Liberty*, 205 (emphasis added).

286. Unger, *Last Founding Father*, 205.

287. Ibid., 82.

288. Ibid., 83–84 (emphasis added).

289. Lynch, *Negotiating the Constitution*, 32.

290. Maier, *Ratification*, 74.

291. Ibid., 70.

292. Unger, *Lion of Liberty*, 204.

293. Ibid., 202.

294. Ibid., 208.

295. Maier, *Ratification*, 93.

Chapter 4: Washington's Unifying Moment

296. Burstein and Isenberg, *Madison and Jefferson*, 162.

297. Ethan Fishman, William D. Pederson, Mark J. Rozell, *George Washington, Foundation of Presidential Leadership and Character* (Westport, CT: Praeger, 2001), 4.

298. Mark J. Rozell, William D. Pederson, Frank J. Williams, *George Washington and the Origins of the American Presidency* (Westport, CT: Praeger, 2000), 177.

299. Lodge, *George Washington*, Vol. 1, 81.

300. Ibid., 86.

301. Chernow, *Washington*, 61.

302. Ibid., 168.

303. Ibid.

304. Ibid.

305. Unger, *Last Founding Father*, 19. "On June 15, 1775, the Continental Congress named George Washington commander in Chief of the Continental Army. After pledging to serve without pay, Washington rode off to Cambridge, Massachusetts."

306. Randall, *George Washington*, 282.

307. Chernow, *Washington*, 191–192.

308. *Phillis Wheatley, The Poet That Challenged the Revolutionaries*, in Young, Nash, and Raphael, *Revolutionary Founders*, 109.

309. Joseph Dillaway Sawyer, *Washington,* Vol. 1 (New York: Macmillan, 1927), 509.

310. Chernow, *Washington*, 219.

311. Ibid.

312. Lodge, *George Washington*, Vol. 2, 388.

313. Chernow, *Washington*, 467.

314. Randall, *George Washington*, 412.

315. Chernow, *Washington*, 467.

316. Randall, *George Washington*, 433.

317. Burstein and Isenberg, *Madison and Jefferson,* 675, "Pierce Butler of South Carolina wrote in 1788 that the reason the delegates were willing to extend such power to the president was because they 'cast their eyes towards General Washington as President.'" Citing Rossiter, 1787: Grand Convention, 222. Brookhiser, *Gentleman Revolutionary*, 86. ("Brooding over the entire

discussion was the silent presence of Washington, who had in effect been the nation's executive as commander in chief, and had set a very high bar (too high?) for trustworthiness."

318. Burstein and Isenberg, *Madison and Jefferson,* 162.

319. Brookhiser, *Gentleman Revolutionary*, 91–92.

320. Maier, *Ratification*, 436.

321. Meacham, *Thomas Jefferson, The Art of Power*, 220.

322. Maier, *Ratification*, 186.

323. Unger, *John Hancock, Merchant King and American Patriot*, 320

324. Burstein and Isenberg, *Madison and Jefferson*, 186.

325. Maier, *Ratification*, 436.

326. Ibid.

327. Ibid.

328. Burstein and Isenberg, *Madison and Jefferson*, 186.

329. Harlow Giles Unger, "Mr. President," George Washington and the Making of the Nation's Highest Office (Boston: Da Capo Press, 2013), 107.

330. Ibid., 108.

331. Chernow, *Washington*, 609.

332. Wood, *The Idea of America*, 239.

333. Unger, *John Hancock, Merchant King and American Patriot*, 203.

334. Chernow, *Washington*, 638.

335. McCullough, *1776*, 226

336. Chernow, *Washington*, 227.

337. Ibid., 247.

338. Lodge, *George Washington*, Vol. 1, 388, 330–31.

339. Sawyer, *Washington*, 143.

340. Chernow, *Washington*, 209.

341. United States George Washington Bicentennial Commission, *History of the George Washington Bicentennial Celebration*, (Washington, D.C.: United States George Washington Bicentennial Commission, 1932), 243.

342. Chernow, *Washington*, 227.

343. Ibid., 290.

344. Burstein and Isenberg, *Madison and Jefferson*, 144.

345. Wood, *The Idea of America*, 148.

346. Unger, *Last Founding Father*, 17.

347. Unger, *John Hancock, Merchant King and American Patriot*, 204.

348. Wood, *The Idea of America*, 148.

349. Chernow, *Washington*, 502.

350. Wood, *The Idea of America*, 149.

351. Randall, *George Washington*, 450.

352. Ibid., 449.

353. Ibid., 256.

354. Ibid., 405–06.

355. "On May 28, 1781, a powerless Governor Jefferson appealed to Washington to lead the bulk of his army to Virginia. The reappearance of their long-absent native son would, he said, "restore full confidence of salvation" . . . Two weeks later, when Jefferson was no longer governor, Richard Henry Lee would propose in no uncertain terms that Washington return to his state as a military dictator . . . "let Congress send him immediately to Virginia, and as the head of the Federal Union let them possess the General with Dictatorial power until the General Assembly can be convened." Burstein and Isenberg, *Madison and Jefferson*, 81.

356. Randall, *George Washington*, 405–06.

357. Ibid., 408.

358. Unger, *Last Founding Father*, 51.

359. Randall, *George Washington*, 408.

360. Ibid., 409.

361. Unger, *Last Founding Father*, 51.

362. Meacham, *Thomas Jefferson, The Art of Power*, 156.

363. Burstein and Isenberg, *Madison and Jefferson*, 675, "Pierce Butler of South Carolina wrote in 1788 that the reason the delegates were willing to extend such power to the president was because they 'cast their eyes towards General Washington as President.'" Citing Rossiter, 1787: Grand Convention, 222.

364. Fishman, Pederson, and Rozell, *George Washington, Foundation of Presidential Leadership and Character*, 131.

365. Chernow, *Washington*, 195.

366. Richard Brookhiser, *Gentleman Revolutionary*, 28.

367. Paul Johnson, *George Washington: The Founding Father* (New York: Harper Perennial, 2009); Sawyer, *Washington*, 143–149. ("Washington's frontier experience is seen to have been of inestimable value, both to his country and to himself." Washington's detailed "Journal" of his expedition West was published in 1764 by his superior. He protested such publicity – something he would do throughout his career. The details he kept of French military positions/ actions in Ohio were used by the British Army.)

368. Johnson, *George Washington: The Founding Father*, 138 (ebook edition).

369. Chernow, *Washington*, 93.

370. Johnson, *George Washington: The Founding Father*, 140 (ebook edition).

371. Chernow, *Washington*, 151.

372. Ibid.

373. Randall, *George Washington*, 422.

374. Chernow, *Washington*, 150–151.

375. Johnson, *George Washington: The Founding Father*, 140 (ebook edition).

376. Randall, *George Washington*, 425.

377. Ibid., 428.

378. Ibid.

379. Cited in Paul Johnson, *George Washington: The Founding Father*, 141–2 (ebook edition).

380. Unger, *Last Founding Father*, 71.

381. Unger, *Lion of Liberty*, 191.

382. Randall, *George Washington*, 434.

383. Johnson, *George Washington: The Founding Father*, 149 (ebook edition).

384. Randall, *George Washington*, 436.

385. Chernow, *Washington*, 543.

386. Ibid., 542.

387. Randall, *George Washington*, 436.

388. Johnson, *George Washington: The Founding Father*, chapter 5.

389. Amy H. Sturgis, Ed., *Presidents from Washington through Monroe, 1789–1825: Debating the Issues in Pro and Con Primary Documents* (Westport, CT: Greenwood Press, 2002), 82, 15. (Washington "did everything he could during his time in office to make his vision for the nation reality." "If Washington held one goal above others for his administration, he wanted to encourage citizens from the disparate states to see themselves as members of one united nation. In the Farewell Address, he reminded the people that they were "Children of one common Country.")

390. Randall, *George Washington: A Life*, 452.

391. Rozell, Pederson, and Williams, *George Washington and the Origins of the American Presidency*, 28.

392. Chernow, *Washington*, 595.

393. Maier, *Ratification*, 436.

394. Chernow, *Washington*, 595.

395. Ibid.

396. Unger, *Last Founding Father*, 94–95.

397. Randall, *George Washington*, 469.

398. Chernow, *Washington*, 608.

399. Rozell, Pederson, and Williams, *George Washington and the Origins of the American Presidency*, 6. "The president made four official tours. On October 15, 1789, Washington began his month long visit to New England, traveling to each of the states except Rhode Island and Vermont, which were not yet in the federal system. He visited Long Island on April 20, 1790, and Rhode Island in August of that same year. The next year George Washington left on April 7, 1791, for a three-month tour of the South that covered 1,816 miles, spending most of his time in North and South Carolina and Georgia."

400. Johnson, *George Washington: The Founding Father*, Chapter 6.

401. Chernow, *Washington*, 608.

402. Unger, *John Hancock, Merchant King and American Patriot*, 322.

403. *The Cousins' Wars: Religion, Politics, Civil Warfare, and the Triumph of Anglo-America*, 131.

404. Lodge, *George Washington*, Vol. 2.

405. Rozell, Pederson, and Williams, *George Washington and the Origins of the American Presidency*, 28.

406. Lodge, *George Washington*, Vol. 2.

407. Richard Brookhiser, *Gentleman Revolutionary*, 158.

408. Rozell, Pederson, and Williams, *George Washington and the Origins of the American Presidency*, x.

409. Chernow, *Washington*, 458.

410. Ibid., 812.

Chapter 5: The Secret Behind the Era of Good Feelings

411. The Miller Center, James Monroe, The Campaign of 1820, http://millercenter.org/academic/americanpresident/monroe/essays/biography/3.

412. John C. Miller, *Alexander Hamilton: Portrait in Paradox* (New York: Harper & Brothers, 1959), 221.

413. Ibid., 225.

414. George Rogers Taylor, *Hamilton and the National Debt* (Boston: Heath, 1950), 1.

415. Ibid.

416. Joseph A. Murray, *Alexander Hamilton: America's Forgotten Founder* (New York:.., Heathe]this is 2 pages: 9 and 252?]]s? I can' Algora, 2007), 132.

417. Ibid., 131.

418. Ibid., 135.

419. Ibid., 135–136.

420. Ibid., 136.

421. David F. Burg, *A World History of Tax Rebellions: An Encyclopedia of Tax Rebels, Revolts, and Riots from Antiquity to the Present* (New York: Routledge, 2004), 312.

422. Thomas P. Slaughter, *The Whiskey Rebellion: Frontier Epilogue to the American Revolution* (New York: Oxford University Press, 1988), 3.

423. Ibid.

424. Burg, *Tax Rebellions*, 314.

425. Stephen G. Kurtz, *The Presidency of John Adams: The Collapse of Federalism* (Philadelphia: University of Pennsylvania Press, 1957), 242.

426. Kurtz, *The Presidency of John Adams*, 239.

427. A. J. Langguth, *Union 1812* (New York: Simon & Schuster, 2006), 76.

428. Ibid.

429. Ibid.

430. Ibid.

431. Kurtz, *The Presidency of John Adams*, 242.

432. Ibid., 274.

433. Langguth, *Union 1812*, 77.

434. Kurtz, *The Presidency of John Adams*, 269.

435. Ibid., 268.

436. Langguth, *Union 1812*, 78.

437. Ibid.

438. Ibid., 77.

439. Ibid.

440. Meacham, *Thomas Jefferson, The Art of Power,* 312; See also Kurtz, *The Presidency of John Adams,* 298.

441. Langguth, *Union 1812,* 79. , Simon & Schuster, New York, 2006.

442. Ibid.

443. Ibid.

444. Ibid.

445. Kurtz, *The Presidency of John Adams,* 301.

446. Meacham, *Thomas Jefferson, The Art of Power,* 312.

447. Ibid.

448. Ibid., 312–317.

449. Ibid., 317.

450. Lance Banning, *The Sacred Fire of Liberty: James Madison and the Founding of the Federal Republic* (Ithaca, NY: Cornell University Press, 1995), 387.

451. Ron Chernow, *Alexander Hamilton* (New York: Penguin, 2004), 587.

452. Burstein and Isenberg, *Madison and Jefferson,* 358.

453. Burstein and Isenberg, *Madison and Jefferson,* 364.

454. Burstein and Isenberg, *Madison and Jefferson,* 349.

455. Meacham, *Thomas Jefferson, The Art of Power,* 372.

456. Ibid., 364.

457. Burstein and Isenberg, *Madison and Jefferson,* 359.

458. Meacham, *Thomas Jefferson, The Art of Power,* 357.

459. Ibid., 377.

460. Ibid., 368–69.

461. Ibid., 252.

462. Jefferson, First Annual Message to Congress, December 8, 1801.

463. Ibid.

464. Ibid.

465. Jefferson, Second Annual Message to Congress, December 15, 1802.

466. Ibid.

467. Burstein and Isenberg, *Madison and Jefferson,* 392.

468. Meacham, *Thomas Jefferson, The Art of Power,* 392.

469. Thomas Fleming, *The Louisiana Purchase* (New York: Wiley, 2003), 149–150.

470. Burstein and Isenberg, *Madison and Jefferson,* 403–404.

471. Meacham, *Thomas Jefferson, The Art of Power,* xix.

472. Edward Payson Powell, *Nullification and Secession in the United States* (New York: G.P. Putnam's Sons, 1897), 201.

473. Ibid., 202.

474. Ibid., 203.

475. Ibid., 219.

476. Sturgis, *Presidents from Washington through Monroe*, 121.

477. Burstein and Isenberg, *Madison and Jefferson*, 480–81.

478. James H. Ellis, *A Ruinous and Unhappy War: New England and the War of 1812* (New York: Algora, 2009), 72.

479. Burstein and Isenberg, *Madison and Jefferson*, 481.

480. Ellis, *A Ruinous and Unhappy War*, 74.

481. David S. and Jeanne T. Heidler, *The War of 1812* (Westport, CT: Greenwood Press, 2002), 43.

482. Ibid.

483. Ibid.

484. Ibid., 51.

485. Glenn Tucker, *Poltroons and Patriots: A Popular Account of the War of 1812*, Vol. 2 (Indianapolis, IN: Bobbs-Merrill, 1954), 651.

486. Heidler and Heidler, *The War of 1812*, 53.

487. Tucker, *Poltroons and Patriots*, 664.

488. Miriam Greenblatt, *The War of 1812: America at War* (New York: Chelsea House, 1994), 113.

489. Patrick C. T. White, *A Nation on Trial: America and the War of 1812* (New York: John Wiley & Sons, 1965), 166.

490. Greenblatt, *The War of 1812: America at War*, 114.

491. Heidler and Heidler, *The War of 1812*, 52.

492. John Quincy Adams, *The Lives of James Madison and James Monroe: Fourth and Fifth Presidents of the United States* (Boston: Phillips-Samson, 1850), 210.

493. Ibid.

494. Ibid., 211.

495. Unger, *Last Founding Father*, 1.

496. Unger, *Last Founding Father*, 1–2.

497. Unger, *Last Founding Father*, 261.

498. James Lucier, *The Political Writings of James Monroe* (Washington, D.C.: Regnery Publishing, Inc, 2001), 485. That is not to say there was no competition for Monroe or complete unanimity for his nomination. Some opposed the manner in which nominations were made, i.e. by the congressional Caucus, and "a sizable faction contemplated nominating Secretary of War William Crawford," who eventually withdrew. David S. and Jeanne T. Heidler, *Henry Clay, The Essential American* (New York: Random House, 2010), 126.

499. Lucier, *The Political Writings of James Monroe*, xxiv–xxv.

500. Unger, *Last Founding Father*, 261.

501. Lucier, *The Political Writings of James Monroe*, 484.

502. Adams, *The Lives of James Madison and James Monroe: Fourth and Fifth Presidents of the United States*, 314.

503. Sturgis, *Presidents from Washington through Monroe*, 155.

504. Unger, *Last Founding Father*, 269.

505. Ibid., 271.

506. Ibid.

507. Ibid.

508. Sturgis, *Presidents from Washington through Monroe*, 156.

509. Adams, *The Lives of James Madison and James Monroe: Fourth and Fifth Presidents of the United States,* 322.

510. Ibid., 324.

511. Unger, *Last Founding Father*, 296.

512. Ibid.

513. Ibid.

514. Unger, *Last Founding Father*, 296–297. According to John Quincy Adams: "Pecuniary embarrassments, at one time assuming a most grave and threatening appearance, had been felt throughout the union during this year, but the condition of the country being really prosperous, the derangement, which had been caused by excessive speculation, and the over issues of the banks, was of temporary duration." Adams, *The Lives of James Madison and James Monroe: Fourth and Fifth Presidents of the United States,* 333.

515. "President Monroe could not be indifferent to this state of things, and he was disposed to go as far in affording relief as was consistent with his, in the main, strict construction doctrines with respect to the constitution. He again recommended therefore, the subject of giving further encouragement to domestic manufactures, paying due regard to the other great interests of the nation, to the attention of Congress." John Quincy Adams, *The Lives of James Madison and James Monroe: Fourth and Fifth Presidents of the United States,* 334.

516. Unger, *John Quincy Adams* (Boston: De Capo Press, 2012), 215.

517. Adams, *The Lives of James Madison and James Monroe: Fourth and Fifth Presidents of the United States,* 340.

518. Unger, *John Quincy Adams*, 215.

519. Ibid.

520. Heidler and Heidler, *Henry Clay: The Essential American*, 146.

521. According to John Quincy Adams, "The war between the rival parties—for they were parties living in opposite quarters of the union and divided on sectional issues—now opened. The debates in both houses were exceedingly warm, and at times ominous of the dissolution of the confederacy." *The Lives of James Madison and James Monroe: Fourth and Fifth Presidents of the United States,* 336, Phillips-Samson, 1850.

522. Heidler and Heidler, *Henry Clay, The Essential American*, 133.

523. Robert V. Remini, *Martin Van Buren and the Making of the Democratic Party* (New York: Columbia University Press, 1959), 35.

524. Ibid.

525. Ibid.

526. Ibid. (emphasis added).

527. Sturgis, *Presidents from Washington* through Monroe, 158–159.

528. Unger, *Last Founding Father*, 318.

529. Ibid.

530. Sturgis, *Presidents from Washington through Monroe*, 158–159.

531. Lucier, *The Political Writings of James Monroe*, 605.

532. Unger, *Last Founding Father*, 315–16.

533. Sturgis, *Presidents from Washington through Monroe*, 178.

534. Unger, *Last Founding Father*, 317.

Chapter 6: Our Partisan Heights: the Civil War

535. William J. Cooper, *We Have The War Upon Us* (New York: Knopf, 2012), xiii.

536. Ibid., xiv.

537. Richard Striner, *Lincoln's Way, How Six Great Presidents Created American Power* (Lanham: Rowman & Littlefield Publishers, Inc., 2010), 32.

538. Russell McClintock, *Lincoln and the Decision for War* (Chapel Hill: University of North Carolina Press, 2008), 1.

539. Bruce Levine, *The Fall of the House of Dixie* (New York: Random House, 2013), xvii.

540. James A. Rawley, *The Politics of Union: Northern Politics during the Civil War* (Lincoln: University of Nebraska Press, 1980), 7.

541. John Solomon Otto, *Southern Agriculture during the Civil War Era, 1860–1880* (Westport, CT: Greenwood Press, 1994), 17.

542. Bruce Collins, *The Origins of America's Civil War* (New York: Holmes & Meier, 1981), 29.

543. Eric Foner, *Free Soil, Free Labor, Free Men: The Ideology of the Republican Party before the Civil War* (New York: Oxford University Press, 1995), 31.

544. Johnson, *A History of the American People*, 435.

545. *Strengths and Weaknesses: North vs. South*, USHistory.org.

546. Otto, *Southern Agriculture*, 17.

547. Levine, *Fall of Dixie*, 4.

548. Ibid.

549. Ibid.

550. Ibid., 3–4.

551. Ibid., 8.

552. Ibid.

553. McClintock, *Lincoln and the Decision for War*, 14.

554. Levine, *Fall of Dixie*, 17.

555. Ibid.

556. Arnold Whitridge, *No Compromise! The Story of the Fanatics Who Paved the Way to the Civil War* (New York: Farrar, Straus, Cudahay, 1960), 29.

557. Collins, *Origins of America's Civil War*, 42.

558. Ibid.

559. Doris Kearns Goodwin, *Team of Rivals* (New York: Simon & Schuster, 2005), 142.

560. Collins, *Origins of America's Civil War*, 30.

561. Foner, *Free Soil, Free Labor, Free Men*, 42.

562. James W. Finck, *Divided Loyalties: Kentucky's Struggle for Armed Neutrality* (El Dorado Hills:, Savas Beatie, 2012), 51.

563. Foner, *Free Soil, Free Labor, Free Men*, 43.

564. Ibid., 40.

565. Joseph Eldridge, *Does the Bible Sanction Slavery?: A Discourse Delivered at Norfolk, Conn.,* February 24, 1861 (Litchfield, CT: Enquirer Office Print, 1861), 27.

566. Johnson, *A History of the American People*, 424.

567. Foner, *Free Soil, Free Labor, Free Men*, 38.

568. Johnson, *A History of the American People*, 424.

569. Cooper, *We Have The War Upon Us*, 4.

570. Ibid., 5.

571. Johnson, *A History of the American People*, 434.

572. Eric H. Walther, *William Lowndes Yancey and the Coming of the Civil War* (Chapel Hill: University of North Carolina Press, 2006), 27.

573. Walter E. Williams, "Abraham Lincoln," http://archive.lewrockwell.com/williams-w/ w-williams157.html.

574. Walter E. Williams, "Why The Civil War," http://econfaculty.gmu.edu/wew/articles/98/ civil-war.htm.

575. Johnson, *A History of the American People*, 434.

576. McClintock, *Lincoln and the Decision for War*, 1.

577. Cooper, *We Have The War Upon Us*, 5.

578. Harold Holzer, *Lincoln President-Elect: Abraham Lincoln and the Great Secession Winter 1860–1861*, Simon & Schuster, 2008), 129.

579. McClintock, *Lincoln and the Decision for War*, 1.

580. McClintock, *Lincoln and the Decision for War*, 5.

581. James B. McPherson, *Tried By War, Abraham Lincoln as Commander In Chief* (New York: Penguin, 2008), 9.

582. Levine, *Fall of Dixie*, 42.

583. Ibid.

584. Ibid., 43.

585. Ibid., 44.

586. Cooper, *We Have The War Upon Us*, 50.

587. Holzer, *Lincoln President-Elect*, 222.

588. Ibid.

589. Cooper, *We Have The War Upon Us*, 50.

590. Lincoln, President Elect, 129.

591. McClintock, *Lincoln and the Decision for War*, 9.

592. Cooper, *We Have The War Upon Us*, 49.

593. McClintock, *Lincoln and the Decision for War*, 9.

594. Cooper, *We Have The War Upon Us*, xiv.

595. McClintock, *Lincoln and the Decision for War*, 2.

596. Ibid.

597. Ibid., 8.

598. Ibid., 2.

599. Cooper, *We Have The War Upon Us*, 43.

600. Ibid.

601. Ibid., 19.

602. Ibid.

603. Ibid.

604. Ibid., xv.

605. Levine, *Fall of Dixie*, 44.

606. Ibid.

607. Finck, *Divided Loyalties*, 31.

608. Ibid., 37.

609. Ibid., 39.

610. Ibid., 34.

611. Ibid., 43.

612. Ibid., 52.

613. Ibid., 53.

614. Ibid., 56.

615. Ibid.

616. Cooper, *We Have The War Upon Us*, 41.

617. Ibid., 41–42.

618. Ibid., 55.

619. McClintock, *Lincoln and the Decision for War*, 76.

620. Cooper, *We Have The War Upon Us*, 55.

621. Donald E. Reynolds, *Editors Make War: Southern Newspapers in the Secession Crisis* (Nashville, TN: Vanderbilt University Press, 1970), 10.

622. Paul A. Cimbala and Randall M. Miller, *An Uncommon Time: The Civil War and the Northern Home Front* (New York: Fordham University Press, 2002), 55.

623. Reynolds, *Editors Make War.*, 6.

624. Ibid., 5–6.

625. Holzer, *Lincoln President-Elect*, p. 54; Reynolds, *Editors Make War*, 146, 153.

626. Reynolds, *Editors Make War*, 139.

627. Fayetteville North Carolinian, November 17, 1860 (italics in the original).

628. Charlotte Daily Bulletin, November 27, 1860.

629. Holzer, *Lincoln President-Elect*, 55.

630. Foner, *Free Soil, Free Labor, Free Men*, 325.

631. Reynolds, *Editors Make War*, 6.

632. Holzer, *Lincoln President-Elect*, 54.

633. Ibid., 52.

634. Cooper, *We Have The War Upon Us*, 56.

635. Ibid.

636. Ibid., 57.

637. McClintock, *Lincoln and the Decision for War*, 2.

638. Elizabeth R. Varon, *Disunion! The Coming of the American Civil War, 1789–1859* (Chapel Hill: University of North Carolina Press, 2008), 292.

639. Ibid., 294.

640. Ibid., 291.

641. Holzer, *Lincoln President-Elect*, 243.

642. Ibid., 240–241.

643. Ibid., 231.

644. Edward Steers Jr., *Blood of the Moon, The Assassination of Abraham Lincoln*, (Lexington, KY: University Press of Kentucky, 2001), 16.

645. McClintock, *Lincoln and the Decision for War*, 1.

646. Ibid.

647. Cooper, *We Have The War Upon Us*, 6.

648. Anrold Whitridge, No Compromise! The Story of the Fanatics Who Paved the Way to the Civil War, (New York: Farrar, Straus and Cudahy, 1960) 161.

649. Ibid., 159.

650. Ibid., 160–61.

651. Cooper, *We Have The War Upon Us*, 51.

652. Ibid, 51–52.

653. Cooper, *We Have The War Upon Us*, 6.

654. Ibid.

655. Ibid., xv

656. McClintock, *Lincoln and the Decision for War*, 8.

657. Ibid.

658. McClintock, *Lincoln and the Decision for War*, 5.

659. Lincoln's January 11, 1861 letter to J.T. Hale. (first italics added). In full, Lincoln wrote: *Confidential.* Hon. J. T. Hale Springfield, Ill. Jan'y. 11th 1861. "My dear Sir—Yours of the 6th is received. I answer it only because I fear you would misconstrue my silence. What is our present condition? We have just carried an election on principles fairly stated to the people. Now we are told in advance, the government shall be broken up, unless we surrender to those we have beaten, before we take the offices. In this they are either attempting to play upon us, or they are in dead earnest. Either way, if we surrender, it is the end of us, and of the government. They will repeat the experiment upon us *ad libitum.* A year will not pass, till we shall have to take Cuba as a condition upon which they will stay in the Union. They now have the Constitution, under which we have lived over seventy years, and acts of Congress of their own framing, with no prospect of their being changed; and they can never have a more shallow pretext for breaking up the government, or extorting a compromise, than now. There is, in my judgment, but one compromise which would really settle the slavery question, and that would be a prohibition against acquiring any more territory. Yours very truly, A. LINCOLN."

660. McClintock, *Lincoln and the Decision for War*, 1.

661. Ibid., 3.

Chapter 7: Our Gilded Age of Division

662. During the war, in an 1862 letter to the *New York Daily Tribune* editor Horace Greeley, Lincoln said, "My paramount object in this struggle is to save the Union, and it is not either to save or destroy slavery." Williams, "Why The Civil War."

663. William Archibald Dunning, *Reconstruction: Political & Economic, 1865–1877* (New York: Harper & Row, 1962), 16.

664. Robert W. Cherny, *American Politics in the Gilded Age, 1868–1900* (Wheeling: Harlan Davidson, 1997), 45.

665. Ibid., 46.

666. Paul A. Cimbala and Randall M. Miller, *The Great Task Remaining before Us: Reconstruction as America's Continuing Civil War* (New York: Fordham University Press, 2010), 1.

667. Candice Millard, *Destiny of the Republic: A Tale of Madness and the Murder of a President* (New York: Doubleday, 2011), 9.

668. Cimbala and Miller, *The Great Task Remaining before Us*, 193; Victoria E. Bynum, *The Long Shadow of the Civil War: Southern Dissent and Its Legacies* (Chapel Hill: University of North Carolina Press, 2010), 59. ["White people, wrote Colonel Samuel Thomas in September 1865, "still have the ingrained feeling that the black people at large belong to the whites at large, [and] … will cheat a negro without feeling a single twinge of their honor. To kill a negro they do not deem murder, to debauch a negro woman they do not think fornication, to take property away from a negro they do not consider robbery." With those words, Colonel Thomas, assistant commissioner of the Freedmen's Bureau for Mississippi, captured the essence of why the decade of Reconstruction to follow would be one of the nation's bloodiest and most divisive."]

669. *New Orleans Times*, March 17, 1867.

670. Cimbala and Miller, *The Great Task Remaining before Us*, 3.

671. Ibid. "As an example of this continuing violence and division between Unionists and former Confederates, Storey mentions the Reverend Arad S. Lakin. In the mid-1860s, the national churches reestablished themselves in the former slave states. In Alabama the work of the Methodist Episcopal Church was led by the Reverend Lakin. While his family taught freedpeople in Huntsville, Lakin worked to establish biracial congregations throughout the state. He carried a Navy revolver, especially after he was hunted down by the Klan and threatened with lynching in the most famous political cartoon to emerge from Reconstruction."

672. Ibid., 7.

673. William B. Hesseltine, *The Tragic Conflict: The Civil War and Reconstruction* (New York: George Braziller, 1962), 464.

674. Dunning, *Reconstruction: Political & Economic,* 6; Cimbala and Miller, *An Uncommon Time,*

107, describes the success of the effort to raise funds in the North in part due to a "flourishing economy."

675. Dunning, *Reconstruction: Political & Economic*, 10, 62.

676. Ibid.

677. Douglas R. Egerton, *The Wars of Reconstruction, The Brief, Violent History of America's Most Progressive History* (New York: Bloomsbury Press, 2014), 1.

678. Cimbala and Miller, *The Great Task Remaining before Us*, 173.

679. Charles W. Calhoun, *From Bloody Shirt to Full Dinner Pail: The Transformation of Politics and Governance in the Gilded* Age (New York: Hill and Wang, 2010, 9.

680. Edward Boykin, *Congress and the Civil War* (New York: McBride Co., 1955), 308.

681. Cimbala and Miller, *The Great Task Remaining before Us*, 185.

682. Hesseltine, *The Tragic Conflict: The Civil War and Reconstruction*, 439.

683. Melvin I. Urofsky and Paul Finkelman, *A March of Liberty: A Constitutional History of the United States*, Vol. 1 (New York: Oxford University Press, 2002), 434.

684. Cimbala and Miller, *The Great Task Remaining before Us*, 185.

685. Craig L. Symonds, *Lincoln and His Admirals: Abraham Lincoln, the U.S. Navy, and the Civil War* (New York: Oxford University Press, 2008), 273.

686. Boykin, *Congress and the Civil War*, 308.

687. Michael Vorenberg, *Final Freedom: The Civil War, the Abolition of Slavery, and the Thirteenth Amendment* (Cambridge, UK: Cambridge University Press, 2001), 143–144.

688. William B. Hesseltine, *Lincoln's Plan of Reconstruction* (Gloucester, MA: Peter Smith, 1963), 95.

689. Hesseltine, *Lincoln's Plan of Reconstruction*, 96. Dunning, *Reconstruction: Political & Economic*, 13. President Lincoln had taken up the subject of restoring civil government in the seceded states with his characteristic conservatism and caution. The basis of his policy was the belief that there existed in every one of those states an element among the people which was still loyal in feeling to the Union. This element, he expected, would rise to the surface as the military power of the Confederacy was overcome, and might then be utilized to organize a civil government which the government at Washington could properly recognize."

690. Hesseltine, *Lincoln's Plan of Reconstruction*, 97.

691. Martin E. Mantell, *Johnson, Grant, and the Politics of Reconstruction* (New York: Columbia University Press, 1973), 11–12.

692. Urofsky and Finkelman, *A March of Liberty: A Constitutional History of the United States*, 434.

693. Hesseltine, *Lincoln's Plan of Reconstruction*, 114.

694. Vorenberg, *Final Freedom: The Civil War, the Abolition of Slavery, and the Thirteenth Amendment*, 143–144.

695. Hesseltine, *Lincoln's Plan of Reconstruction*, 114.

696. Andrew L. Slap, *The Doom of Reconstruction: The Liberal Republicans in the Civil War Era* (New York: Fordham University Press, 2006), xii.

697. Egerton, *The Wars of Reconstruction,* 11.

698. Vorenberg, *Final Freedom: The Civil War, the Abolition of Slavery, and the Thirteenth Amendment*, 141.

699. Michael Les Benedict, *The Impeachment and Trial of Andrew Johnson* (New York: Norton, 1973), 4.

700. Cimbala and Miller, *The Great Task Remaining before Us*, 185.

701. Benedict, *The Impeachment and Trial of Andrew Johnson*, 4; Bruce Ackerman, *We The People, Transformations* (Cambridge, MA: Harvard University Press, 1998), 100–101.

702. Egerton, *The Wars of Reconstruction*, 18.

703. Ibid.

704. Mantell, *Johnson, Grant, and the Politics of Reconstruction*, 9–10.

705. Ibid., 10.

706. Ackerman, *We The People, Transformations*, 101.

707. Egerton, *The Wars of Reconstruction*, 230–234.

708. Cimbala and Miller, *The Great Task Remaining Before Us*, 196, 221.

709. Ibid., 196.

710. Egerton, *The Wars of Reconstruction*, 11.

711. Stephen P. Halbrook, *Freedmen, the Fourteenth Amendment, and the Right to Bear Arms, 1866–1876* (Westport, CT: Praeger Publishers, 1998), 1.

712. Faye E. Dudden, *Fighting Chance: The Struggle over Woman Suffrage and Black Suffrage in Reconstruction America* (New York: Oxford University Press, 2011), 65.

713. Egerton, *The Wars of Reconstruction*, 178.

714. Ibid., 12.

715. Ibid., 42.

716. Jeremy Black, *America as a Military Power: From the American Revolution to the Civil War* (Westport, CT: Praeger Publishing, 2002), 171. Mark Elliot, *Color-Blind Justice: Albion Tourgee and the Quest for Racial Equality from the Civil War to Plessy v. Ferguson* (New York: Oxford University Press, 2006), 125.

717.

718. Egerton, *The Wars of Reconstruction*, 114.

719. Sharon D. Wright, *Race, Power, and Political Emergence in Memphis* (New York: Garland, 2000), 14–15.

720. United States Congress, House Select Committee on the Memphis Riots, Memphis Riots and Massacres, 25 July 1866, Washington, DC: Government Printing Office (reprinted by Arno Press, Inc., 1969).

721. John Kendall, *The Riot of 1866, History of New Orleans* (Chicago: Lewis Publishing Company, 1922).

722. New Orleans Riot of 1866, http://chnm.gmu.edu/courses/122/carr/riottext.html, Claudine L. Ferrell, *Reconstruction* (Westport, CT: Praeger Publishing, 2003), 150; John S. Kendall, *The Golden Age of the New Orleans Theater* (Baton Rouge: Louisiana State University Press, 1952), 207, 514.

723. Egerton, *The Wars of Reconstruction*, 287.

724. Halbrook, *Freedmen, the Fourteenth Amendment, and the Right to Bear Arms,*), 51.

725. Donna L. Dickerson, *The Reconstruction Era: Primary Documents on Events from 1865 To 1877* (Westport, CT: Greenwood Press, 2003), 151.

726. Calhoun, *From Bloody Shirt to Full Dinner Pail*, 13.

727. Ibid.

728. Charles C. Calhoun, *Benjamin Harrison* (New York: Times Books, 2005), 31.

729. Cherny, *American Politics in the Gilded Age*, 5.

730. Calhoun, *From Bloody Shirt to Full Dinner Pail*, 9.

731. Calhoun, *Benjamin Harrison*, 3; Cherny, *American Politics in the Gilded Age*, 24.

732. Calhoun, *From Bloody Shirt to Full Dinner Pail*, 9.

733. Calhoun, *Benjamin Harrison*, 2–3.

734. Calhoun, *From Bloody Shirt to Full Dinner Pail*, XX. [[page number TK]]

735. Ibid., 9.

736. Paul Kleppner, *The Third Electoral System 1853–1892: Parties, Voters, and Political Cultures* (Chapel Hill: University of North Carolina Press, 1979), 5.

737. Jack Tager and John W. Ifkovic, *Massachusetts in the Gilded Age: Selected Essays* (Amherst: University of Massachusetts Press, 1985) 4.

738. Quentin R. Skrabec, Jr., *William McKinley, Apostle of Protectionism* (New York: Algora, 2008), 195–196. "In general, the period from 1880 to 1910 saw one of the greatest growth rates for American industry ever." "The U.S. gross national product grew from an estimated $11 billion in 1880 to $18.7 billion in 1890 to $35.3 billion in 1910." See also Kevin Phillips, *William McKinley* (New York: Henry Holt and Co., 2003), 115.

739. Christopher Levenick, "Seven Myths about the Great Philanthropists, *Philanthropy Magazine*, Winter 2011.

740. Skrabec, *William McKinley, Apostle of Protectionism*, 196, *citing Historical Statistics of the United States, 1789–1945* (Washington DC: U.S. Department of Commerce.

741. David O. and Bessie E. Whitten, *The Birth of Big Business in the United States, 1860–1914: Commercial, Extractive, and Industrial Enterprise* (Westport, CT: Praeger, 2006), xi.

742. Ibid., xi, 39.

743. Levenick, "Seven Myths."

744. Ibid.

745. H. W. Brands, *American Colossus: The Triumph of Capitalism, 1865–1900* (New York: Doubleday, 2010), 555–556.

746. Edward C. Kirkland, *A History of American Economic Life*, 36- et, seq. (New York: Appleton-Century-Crofts, 1951), 447.

747. Walter E. Williams, "Was the Civil War About Tariff Revenue?" *Washington Times*, February 19, 2013.

748. Sidney Fine and Gerald S. Brown, *The American Past: Conflicting Interpretations of the Great Issues*, Vol. 1 (New York: Macmillan, 1961), 460.

749. Williams, *Why The Civil War.*

750. Calhoun, *From Bloody Shirt to Full Dinner Pail*, 3–4; Brands, *American Colossus*, 483.

751. Calhoun, *From Bloody Shirt to Full Dinner Pail*, 23.

752. Calhoun, *Benjamin Harrison*, 2–3.

753. Calhoun, *From Bloody Shirt to Full Dinner Pail*, 84.

754. Henry F. Graff, *Grover Cleveland* (New York: Henry Holt & Co., 2002) 93.

755. Phillips, *William McKinley*, 45.

756. Skrabec, *William McKinley, Apostle of Protectionism*, 196.

757. Ibid.

758. Phillips, *William McKinley*, 48.

759. Ibid., 63.

760. Ibid., 43.

761. Lars Magnusson, *The Tradition of Free Trade* (New York: Routledge, 2004), 117, citing Tom E. Terrill, *Tariff,* Politics (Westport, CT: Greenwood Press, 1973), 7.

762. Graff, *Grover Cleveland*, 86.

763. Ibid.

764. Phillips, *William McKinley*, 42.

765. Skrabec, *William McKinley, Apostle of Protectionism*, 142.

766. Phillips, *William McKinley*, 49.

767. Calhoun, *From Bloody Shirt to Full Dinner Pail*, 13.

768. Brands, *American Colossus*, 13.

769. Calhoun, *Benjamin Harrison*, 30; Phillips, *William McKinley*, 51–52.

770. Phillips, *William McKinley*, 42.

771. Phillips, *William McKinley*, 49.

772. Calhoun, *Benjamin Harrison*, 30, 95.

773. Brands, *American Colossus*, 430.

774. Graff, *Grover Cleveland*, 86; Calhoun, *From Bloody Shirt to Full Dinner Pail*, 126.

775. Graff, *Grover Cleveland*, 102.

776. Phillips, *William McKinley*, 49.

777. Ibid., 50–51.

778. Calhoun, *Benjamin Harrison*, 94.

779. Ibid., 30; Calhoun, *From Bloody Shirt to Full Dinner Pail*, 6.

780. Republican Party Platform, 1868.

781. Calhoun, *From Bloody Shirt to Full Dinner Pail*, 21.

782. Ibid., 22–23.

783. Graff, *Grover Cleveland*, 100–101.

784. Calhoun, *From Bloody Shirt to Full Dinner Pail*, 170; Phillips, *William McKinley*, 114.

785. Calhoun, *From Bloody Shirt to Full Dinner Pail*, 46.

786. Ibid., 149.

787. Ibid., 72.

788. Ibid., 38.

789. Calhoun, *Benjamin Harrison*, 100.

790. Calhoun, *From Bloody Shirt to Full Dinner Pail*, 126–27.

791. Cherny, *American Politics in the Gilded Age*, 128.

792. Phillips, *William McKinley*, 73.

793. Ibid., 74.

794. Brands, *American Colossus*, 490–91.

795. Phillips, *William McKinley*, 74. (emphasis added).

796. Ibid.

797. H. Wayne Morgan, *From Hayes to McKinley: National Party Politics, 1877–1896* (Syracuse, NY: Syracuse University Press, 1969), 18.

798. Ibid.

799. Ibid.

800. Ibid.

801. Stanley P. Hirshson, *Farewell to the Bloody Shirt: Northern Republicans & the Southern Negro, 1877–1893* (Bloomington: Indiana University Press, 1962), 14. (emphasis added).

802. Cherny, *American Politics in the Gilded Age*, 23.

803. Ibid.

804. Calhoun, *From Bloody Shirt to Full Dinner Pail*, 94.

805. Ibid., 5.

806. Egerton, *The Wars of Reconstruction*, 241.

807. Robert J. Kaczorowski, *The Politics of Judicial Interpretation: The Federal Courts, Department of Justice, and Civil Rights, 1866–1876* (New York: Fordham University Press, 2005), xiv.

808. Calhoun, *From Bloody Shirt to Full Dinner Pail*, 76.

809. Egerton, *The Wars of Reconstruction*, 67.

810. Calhoun, *From Bloody Shirt to Full Dinner Pail*, 115. (emphasis added).

811. Morgan, *From Hayes to McKinley*, 339.

812. Calhoun, *From Bloody Shirt to Full Dinner Pail*, 129.

813. Ibid., 130.

814. Ibid., 7.

815. Cherny, *American Politics in the Gilded Age*, 14.

816. Ibid.

817. Mark Wahlgren Summers, *Party Games: Getting, Keeping, and Using Power in Gilded Age Politics* (Chapel Hill: University of North Carolina Press, 2004), 235.

818. Morgan, *From Hayes to McKinley*, 454.

819. Calhoun, *From Bloody Shirt to Full Dinner Pail*, 53.

820. Ibid., 76.

821. Ibid.

822. Cherny, *American Politics in the Gilded Age*, 13.

823. Morgan, *From Hayes to McKinley*, 31–32.

824. Ibid., 31.

825. Calhoun, *From Bloody Shirt to Full Dinner Pail*, 79.

826. Ibid.

827. Summers, *Party Games*, 4.

828. Cherny, *American Politics in the Gilded Age*, 12.

829. Summers, *Party Games*, 20.

830. Cherny, *American Politics in the Gilded Age*, 11.

831. Ibid.

832. Calhoun, *From Bloody Shirt to Full Dinner Pail*, 8.

833. Cherny, *American Politics in the Gilded Age*, 11.

834. Ibid, 12.

835. Ibid.

836. Ibid., 44.

837. Calhoun, *From Bloody Shirt to Full Dinner Pail*, x.

838. Ibid., 7.

839. Ibid.

840. Ibid., 8.

841. Cherny, *American Politics in the Gilded Age*, 47.

842. Ibid.

843. Summers, *Party Games*, 195.

844. Cimbala and Miller, *The Great Task Remaining before Us*, 192.

845. Cherny, *American Politics in the Gilded Age*, 96.

846. Graff, *Grover Cleveland*, 106.

847. Cherny, *American Politics in the Gilded Age*, 96.

848. Calhoun, *Benjamin Harrison*, 146–147; Calhoun, *From Bloody Shirt to Full Dinner Pail*, 140; Graff, *Grover Cleveland*, 106–107.

849. Graff, *Grover Cleveland*, 109.

850. Ibid., 110.

851. Brands, *American Colossus*, 432–33.

852. Phillips, *William McKinley*, 49.

853. Cherny, *American Politics in the Gilded Age*, 32.

854. Ibid., 70.

855. Calhoun, *From Bloody Shirt to Full Dinner Pail*, 89.

856. Ibid.

857. Millard, *Destiny of the Republic*, 84.

858. Summers, *Party Games*, 106.

859. Ibid.

860. Ibid., 12.

861. Ibid., 16.

862. Ibid., 5.

863. Ibid.

864. Ibid.

865. Ibid., 75.

866. Ibid., 25.

867. Ibid., 3.

868. Ibid.

869. Ibid., 23.

870. Calhoun, *From Bloody Shirt to Full Dinner Pail*, ix–x.

Chapter 8: The Power to Tax Involves the Power to Divide

871. Woodrow Wilson, *The Earliest Forms of Government*, 1898.

872. Burg, *Tax Rebellions*, xi.

873. Ibid.

874. Ibid., xv.

875. Ibid.

876. Edith Mary Wightman, *Gallia Belgica* (Oakland: University of California Press, 1985), cited by David Burg, *Tax Rebellions*, 49.

877. Noel Lenski, *Failure of Empire: Valens and the Roman State in the Fourth Century A.D.* (Oakland: University of California Press, 2002), 284.

878. David J. Geary, *Before France and Germany* (New York: Oxford University Press, 1988), cited in Burg, *Tax Rebellions*, 37–38.

879. A. D. Lee, *From Rome to Byzantium AD 363 to 565: The Transformation of Ancient Rome* (Edinburgh: Edinburgh University Press, 2013), 223.

880. Burg, *Tax Rebellions*, 51, citing Naphtali Lewis, *Life in Egypt Under Roman Rule* (Oxford, UK: Clarendon Press, 1983).

881. Durant and Durant, *Lessons of History*, 60–61.

882. Burg, *Tax Rebellions*, 51.

883. Thomas Sowell, *"Trickle Down" Theory and "Tax Cuts For The Rich,"* Hoover Institution Press, 2012.

884. Ibid.

885. "New Luxury Tax Trimming Boat Sales," *New York Times*, July 21, 1991, http://www.nytimes.com/1991/07/21/nyregion/new-luxury-tax-trimming-boat-sales.html.

886. A. S. Turberville, *Johnson's England: An Account of the Life & Manners of His Age* Vol. 1 (Oxford, UK: Clarendon Press, 1933), 312.

887. Burg, *Tax Rebellions*, 240.

888. Ibid. 25, 34, 36, 46, 47, 49.

889. Ibid., 31–32.

890. *Power in Colonial Peru: The 1779 Tax Rebellion of the Negro Militia of Lambayeque* (Atlanta: Phylon, 1972), 33.

891. Judith M. Brown and William Roger Louis, *The Oxford History of the British Empire*, Vol. 4 (Princeton, NJ: Princeton University Press, 2006), 559.

892. Wu Xiao An, *Chinese Business in the Making of a Malay State, 1882–1941: Kedah and Penang* (New York: Routledge-Curzon, 2003), 108.

893. William Roger Louis, Alaine M. Low, Andrew Porter, *The Oxford History of the British Empire*, Vol. 3 (New York: Oxford University Press, 1999), 196.

894. Samuel K. Cohn Jr., *Lust for Liberty: The Politics of Social Revolt in Medieval Europe, 1200–1425: Italy, France, and Flanders* (Cambridge, MA: Harvard University Press, 2006), 194.

895. Peter Davies, *The Extreme Right in France, 1789 to the Present: From de Maistre to le Pen* (New York: Routledge, 2002), 312.

896. Michael Adas, *Prophets of Rebellion: Millenarian Protest Movements against the European Colonial Order* (Chapel Hill: University of North Carolina Press, 1979), 68.

897. *CBC News*, "Separatists form new party in Alberta," January 2001, http://www.cbc.ca/news/ canada/separatists-form-new-party-in-alberta-1.269437.

898. Burg, *Tax Rebellions*, xv.

899. Ibid., 175–177, citing Henry Kamen, *The Iron Century* (London: Weidenfeld and Nicolson, 1971); Emmanuel Le Roy Ladurie, Trans. Mary Feeney, *Carnival in Romans* (New York: George Braziller, 1979).

900. Christopher Shepard, *The Civil War Income Tax and the Republican Party, 1861–1872* (New York: Algora, New York, 2010), 34.

901. Ibid., 36.

902. Ibid., 49.

903. Ibid., 41.

904. Ibid., 36–37.

905. Ibid., 50.

906. Richard J. Joseph, *The Origins of the American Income Tax, The Revenue Act of 1894 and Its Aftermath* (Syracuse, NY: Syracuse University Press, 2004), 179; Festus P. Summer, *William L. Wilson and Tariff Reform, a Biography* (Rutgers, NJ: Rutgers University Press, 1953), 176.

907. https://archive.org/stream/speechofhondavid00hilliala - page/6/mode/2up. (emphasis added).

908. Summer, *William L. Wilson and Tariff Reform*, 172–173. (emphasis added).

909. Phillips, *William McKinley*, 124.

910. Ibid.

911. Edmund Morris, *The Rise of Theodore Roosevelt* (New York: Coward, McCann & Geoghegan, 1979), 712; Phillips, *William McKinley*, 1119.

912. Morris, *The Rise of Theodore Roosevelt*, 712.

913. Brands, *American Colossus*, 430.

914. The Tax History Project 1900 to 1932, The Income Tax Archives, http://www.taxhistory.org/ www/website.nsf/Web/THM1901?OpenDocument

915. Ibid.

916. Burton Folsom Jr. and Anita Folsom, "FDR's Class Warfare: A Tutorial for Obama," December 2011, http://spectator.org/articles/36533/fdrs-class-warfare-tutorial-obama (emphasis added).

917. Will Durant, *Heroes of History* (New York: Simon & Schuster, 2002), 95.

918. Folsom and Folsom, "FDR's Class Warfare: A Tutorial for Obama."

919. Ibid. (emphasis added).

920. Ibid. (emphasis added).

921. Tax Foundation, *Tax Equity and the Growth in Nonpayers*, http://taxfoundation.org/article/tax-equity-and-growth-nonpayers

922. Ibid.

923. Ibid.

924. Ibid.

925. Chart courtesy of the National Taxpayers Union http://www.ntu.org/tax-basics/who-pays-income-taxes.html

926. Michael Tanner, "The American Welfare State How We Spend Nearly $1 Trillion a Year Fighting Poverty—and Fail," CATO 2012.

927. Folsom and Folsom, "FDR's Class Warfare: A Tutorial for Obama."

928. Arthur Laffer, Stephen Moore, Rex A. Sinquefield, Travis H. Brown, *An Inquiry into The Nature and Causes of the Wealth of States: How Taxes, Energy, and Worker Freedom Change Everything* (New York: Wiley, 2014), xvii.

929. Ibid., xxi.

930. Ibid., 56.

931. Ibid.

932. Ibid., xii.

933. Ibid., 43.

Chapter 9: Our House Divided

934. Regional Oral History Office, *1993 Omnibus Budget Reconciliation Act*.

935. George Will, "Inoculated For Exuberance?" *Washington Post*, November 10, 2006.

936. Unger, *Lion of Liberty*, 32–33.

937. Abby Rappaport, "Three New Facts about the Tea Party," *The American Prospect*, April 2013.

938. PolitiFact Florida, "Libertarians say they're the third largest political party," September 9, 2013.

939. Seth McLaughlin, *Paul: Liberty movement is winning and could help GOP win too*, *Washington Times*, September. 19, 2013.

940. Phillips, *William McKinley*, 49.

941. David Lighman, "As Independent Voters' Numbers Rise, GOP Hurt Most," *McClatchy Washington Bureau*, January 21, 2014, http://www.mcclatchydc.com/2014/01/21/215122/as-independent-voters-numbers.html#storylink=cpy.

942. Pew Research Center, "Partisan Polarization Surges in Bush, Obama Years, Trends in American Values: 1987–2012."

943. Eric Pianin, "How Growing Partisanship Is Splitting the U.S. in Two," *Fiscal Times*, June 12, 2014.

944. Josh Kron, "Red State, Blue City: How the Urban-Rural Divide Is Splitting America," *The Atlantic*, November 20, 2012.

945. Bill Bishop with Robert G. Cushing, *The Big Sort* (New York: Houghton Mifflin, 2008), 5.

946. Ibid., 6.

947. Skrabec, *William McKinley, Apostle of Protectionism*, 142.

948. Paul Blumenthal and Dave Jamieson, "Koch Brothers Are Outspent By A Labor Force Millions Of Times Their Size, But . . . ," *Huffington Post*, March 15, 2014.

949. Source: Campaign Finance Institute analysis of Federal Election Commission data.

950. Aaron Blake, "Both Romney and Obama ran $1 billion campaigns," *Washington Post*, December 7, 2012; see also Nicholas Confessore and Jo Craven McGinty, "Obama, Romney and Their Parties on Track to Raise $2 Billion," *New York Times*, October 25, 2012.

951. Brent Cox, "How Much More Money Do Presidential Candidates Raise Today?" *The Awl*, November 6th, 2012. http://www.theawl.com/2012/11/presidential-fundraising-adjusted-for-inflation

952. Mark Preston, "GOP chief plans major overhaul to party," CNN.com, January 24, 2013.

953. Shushannah Walshe, "RNC Plays Catch-Up On Data, Ground Game," ABC News, May 7, 2014.

954. Jeremy A. Kaplan, Michael Roppolo, "GOP 2.0: RNC pushing tech to hit back in 2014," *Fox News*, August 23, 2013.

955. John Fund, "Dems' Voter-Fraud Denial - How do you address a problem they insist doesn't exist?" *National Review*, April 3, 2014.

956. Jesse Richman and David Earnest, "Could non-citizens decide the November election?" *Washington Post*, October 24, 2014.

957. Pew Research Center, "Partisanship and Cable News Audiences," October 2009. http://www.pewresearch.org/2009/10/30/partisanship-and-cable-news-audiences/

958. Congressional Budget Office, *An Update to the Budget and Economic Outlook: 2014 to 2024*, August 27, 2014.

959. Figures courtesy of USgovernmentspending.com.

960. Breanna Deutsch, "Regulation blizzard: Government adds 1,516 pages to the Federal Register," *The Daily Caller*, February 17, 2014.

961. Based on a study by the Competitive Enterprise Institute.

962. Wayne Crews & Ryan Young, "Regulations Cost Your Family $15,000 a Year," RealClearpolitics.com, June 2, 2014.

963. Mark J. Perry, "Federal regulations have lowered real GDP growth by 2% per year since 1949 and made America 72% poorer," *American Enterprise Institute*, June 26, 2013.

964. Gregory Korte, *Obama issues 'executive orders by another name'*, USA Today, December 14,23014.

965. Jonathan Turley, "The Rise of the Fourth Branch of Government," *Washington Post*, May 24, 2013.

966. Richard W. Rahn, "Democracy versus Bureaucracy," *Washington Times*, December 6, 2011.

967. Abha Bhattarai and Catherine Ho, "Four years into Dodd-Frank, local banks say this is the year they'll feel the most impact," *Washington Post*, February 7, 2014.

968. Ibid.

969. Ben Goad and Julian Hattem, "Regulation Nation: Obama oversees expansion of the regulatory state," *The Hill*, August 19, 2013.

970. Alec.org, "The U.S. Environmental Protection Agency's Assault on State Sovereignty," 2013.

971. Ibid.

972. Ibid.

973. Robert Barnes, "Supreme Court: EPA can regulate greenhouse gas emissions, with some limits," *Washington Post*, June 23, 2014.

974. "GOP lawmakers push EPA to ax proposed water rule amid outcry from farmers," Foxnews.com, April 4, 2014.

975. Mike Grunwald, "New Carbon Rules the Next Step in Obama's War on Coal," *Time*, June 1, 2014.

976. Laurence H. Tribe, The Clean Power Plan Is Unconstitutional, Wall Street Journal, December 22, 2014.

977. Romney fundraising totals courtesy of Polipundit.com.

978. Henry Payne, "The Obamaconomy's Growth Industry: Lobbying," *National Review Online*, July 27, 2011.

979. Ben Baeder, "Who pays the most for California government lobbying in Sacramento? Government," *Whittier Daily News*, July, 6, 2014.

980. Lee Drutman, PhD, in his work, *The Business of America is Lobbying.*

981. "Delta Air CEO to back U.S. Export Import Bank support to Boeing: WSJ," Reuters, June 24, 2014.

982. Delta Airlines Newsroom, June 25, 2014.

983. Jonathan D. Salant and Kathleen Miller, "Federal Spending Cuts Slice Contract Awards 11% in 2013," Bloomberg, January 15, 2014.

984. Christian Davenport, "With budget tightening, disputes over federal contracts increase," *Washington Post*, April 4, 2014.

985. Ibid.

986. National Conference of State Legislatures Report, "State Film Production Incentives and Programs," March 28, 2014.

987. Eric Kingson, "It's Time to Burn My AARP Card," Huffintonpost.com, June 17, 2011.

988. Chuck Reed, "Pension costs draining California school budgets," *San Diego Union Tribune*, July 25, 2014.

989. Calpensions.com, "CalSTRS debt report drops from $167B to $59.5B," 2104 report.

990. R. Alan Hays, "The Role of Interest Groups," *The Democracy Papers.*

991. Thomas T. Holyoke in *Interest Groups and Lobbying: Pursuing Political Interests in America* (Boulder: Westview Press, 2014), 4.

992. Ibid., 270.

993. Pew Research, "Religion & Public Life Project," May 15, 2012.

994. Holyoke in *Interest Groups and Lobbying*, 23.

995. Cherny, *American Politics in the Gilded Age*, 15.

Chapter 10: Bridging the Gap in the Divided Era

996. Jim Gaines, "One in four Americans want their state to secede from the U.S., but why?" Rueters.com, September 14, 2014.

997. Calhoun, *Benjamin Harrison*, 2–3.

998. Durant and Durant, *Lessons of History*, 75.

999. Ibid.

1000. Ibid., 34.

1001. Will Durant, *The Life of Greece*, (New York: Simon and Schuster, 1939) p. 464–65.

1002. Ibid, 465.

1003. Ibid.

1004. Ibid 466–67

1005. Mark Buchanan, "Want To Fight Crime? Address Economic Inequality," *Bloomberg*, January 6, 2013.

1006. Robert Lenzner, "Harvard's Rogoff Expects Serious Social Unrest Due To Income Disparities In The U.S.," *Forbes*, February 10, 2011.

1007. David Cay Johnston, "Inequality may spark unrest, Davos elites worry," *Al Jazeera America*, January 22, 2014.

1008. "Growing wealth gap opens gate to unrest: Our view," *USA Today*, October 7, 2013. (Emphasis added).

1009. Emily Ekins, "62 Percent of Americans Say They Favor a Flat Tax," Reason.com, April 15, 2014.

1010. Kyle Smith, "Detroit Gave Unions Keys to the City, and Now Nothing Is Left," Forbes.com, 2013.

1011. Ryan Honeywell, "Why Isn't the U.S. Better at Public-Private Partnerships?" Governing.com, February, 2013, http://www.governing.com/topics/finance/gov-public-private-partnerships-in-america.html.

1012. Ibid.